# Dedication

This book is dedicated to Mothers
and Grandmothers everywhere who
passed on the art of cooking.

It is dedicated to the cooks
of today who are busy in their
kitchens now.

And it is dedicated to our children,
the cooks of tomorrow.

# Introduction and Acknowledgments

One evening back in March of 1987, as I sat copying recipes into a three-ring binder, I had a sudden inspiration to compile a cookbook. I called my sister Virginia, who is just a year older than I, and asked if she would be interested in helping me put a cookbook together. She agreed to help, so the two of us sent out letters to friends and relatives asking if they wanted to share recipes. The response was overwhelming. Approximately 170 contributors sent around 1500 recipes.

The company planning to print our cookbook, G&R Publishing from Waverly, Iowa, said we should stay close to 1000 recipes. We combined recipes that we could, often putting several names with similar or duplicate recipes. After the first printing we filled in the empty spots with 100 more recipes, and brought our total to over 1100 recipes.

Sometime during the early nineties, a friend of ours said he would be interested in printing our cookbook. We were happy to let him do so. The business has since changed ownership, but we still get our cookbooks printed at Little Mountain Printing in Richland, Pennsylvania.

In 1999 Virginia and her husband LaVerne felt their lives were busy enough without shipping out cookbooks and all that goes with it, so they sold their half. The Basics and More is now owned by Ray and I and some of our children.

This 2005 revision is the first major change since the Basics and More Cookbook hit the market in May of 1988. Along with approximately 200 new recipes we added more subcategories as well as a more thorough index.

The Basics and More Cookbook was the first of our three cookbooks. In 1997 our family compiled the Practical Produce Cookbook to complement our produce business. Then in 2002 we put together a cookbook from our Grandmothers' recipe collections using recipes from the 1920's, 30's and 40's.

Our family has grown since we first made the Basics. Back then we had only three children. We now have six: Scott, Katrina, William, Kerra, Kelsie, and Kristie. Our children are a tremendous blessing to us and Ray and I would like to acknowledge their help and support. They have been, for the most part, very longsuffering when the table was cluttered, the computer in use, and the meals late.

Ray and I would like to thank LaVerne and Virginia Hoover. Without their support the Basics and More Cookbook may never have become a reality.

We would also like to thank all who contributed recipes 18 years ago, as well as those who more recently contributed recipes for the revised version of the Basics and More Cookbook.

Above all we want to thank God for His blessings to us. We thank Him especially that He made the way possible so we, through Jesus, can someday join Him in Heaven - where we will no longer hunger or thirst.

Until then, I hope you will enjoy using the revised Basics and More Cookbook. God bless you!

Elsie Hoover
2005

# Weights and Measures

| | |
|---|---|
| 3 teaspoons | 1 tablespoon |
| 4 tablespoons | 1/4 cup |
| 8 tablespoons | 1/2 cup |
| 16 tablespoons | 1 cup |
| 4 cups | 1 quart |
| 4 quarts | 1 gallon |
| 1 ounce | 28.35 grams |
| 1 quart | .95 liter |
| 1 liter | 1.06 quarts |
| 1 gallon | 3.8 liters |
| 16 ounces | 1 pound |
| 1 ounce liquid | 2 tablespoons |
| 8 ounces liquid | 1 cup |

# Food equivalents

| | |
|---|---|
| 3 1/2 to 4 cups powdered sugar | 1 pound |
| 2 1/4 cups brown sugar, packed | 1 pound |
| 2 cups granulated sugar | 1 pound |
| 4 cups sifted flour | 1 pound |
| 1 to 1 1/4 cups uncooked macaroni | 2 1/4 cups cooked |
| 1 cup dry white rice | 3 cups cooked |
| 28 soda crackers | 1 cup crumbs |
| 14 squares graham crackers | 1 cup crumbs |
| 22 vanilla wafers | 1 cup crumbs |
| 16 large marshmallows | 4 ounces |
| 4 ounces cheese | 1 cup shredded |
| 1 cup heavy cream | 2 cups whipped |
| 1 cup well-chilled evaporated milk | 3 cups whipped |
| 1 medium lemon | 3 tablespoons juice |
| 1 orange | 1/3 cup juice |

# Abbreviations
## Used in this cookbook

| | |
|---|---|
| tsp. | teaspoon or teaspoons |
| T. | tablespoon or tablespoons |
| oz. | ounce or ounces |
| lb. | pound or pounds |
| pkg. | package or packages |

# Substitutions

| FOR... | YOU CAN USE... |
|---|---|
| 1 Tablespoon cornstarch ........ | 2 T. flour or 1 1/2 T. minute tapioca |
| 1 cup cake flour ...................... | 1 cup less 2 T. all-purpose flour |
| 1 cup sugar ........................... | 1 cup honey; reduce other liquid 1/4 cup. Reduce baking temperature 25° |
| 1 teaspoon baking powder ..... | 1/4 teaspoon soda and 1 teaspoon cream of tartar. |
| 1 cup whole milk..................... | 1/2 cup evaporated milk and 1/2 cup water. |
| 1 cup sour milk or buttermilk | 1 T. lemon juice or vinegar plus milk to make 1 cup. Let stand 5 minutes. |
| 1 cup sour cream ................... | 3 T. butter plus buttermilk or yogurt to make 1 cup. |
| 1 cup heavy cream ................. | 2/3 cup milk and 1/3 cup butter |
| 1 cup light cream ................... | 1 T. melted butter plus milk to make 1 cup |
| 1 cup whipping cream, whipped | 2/3 cup well-chilled evaporated milk, whipped |
| 1 cup miniature marshmallows | About 10 large marshmallows, cut-up |
| 1 square baking chocolate ..... | Three T. cocoa and 1 T. shortening |
| 1 teaspoon dry mustard ......... | 1 T. prepared mustard |
| 1 garlic clove ......................... | 1/8 teaspoon garlic powder OR 1/4 teaspoon garlic salt; reduce salt 1/8 teaspoon. |
| 1 T. fresh herbs | 1 teaspoon dried herbs OR 1/4 teaspoon powdered herbs |
| 1 small onion ......................... | 1 T. dry onion flakes, rehydrated |
| 1 cup bread crumbs ............... | 3/4 cup cracker crumbs |
| 2 cups tomato sauce | 3/4 cup tomato paste and 1 cup water |

# Table of Contents

# BREAK—
# FAST

# EGG DISHES

## FLUFFY CHEESE OMELET

*For a more elaborate omelet, sprinkle with browned sausage or top with cheese sauce.*

4 eggs, separated
1/4 tsp. salt
1/8 tsp pepper
1 T. flour

1 T. water
1 T. butter, softened
3 T. butter
1/2 cup grated cheese

Separate eggs carefully so you don't mix egg yolks with egg whites. Add salt to whites and beat on highest speed until whites form peaks. Add pepper, flour, water and softened butter to egg yolks; beat until thick and lemon colored, about 3 minutes. Gently fold yolk mixture into whites. Melt 3 tablespoons butter in skillet. Add omelet and cover tightly. Simmer 4 minutes until bottom is golden brown and top is dry. Sprinkle cheese on half of the omelet. Crease down the middle; fold omelet in half. Serve immediately.

*Mrs. LaVerne (Virginia) Hoover, Goshen, IN       Mrs. Larry Zimmerman, Elkhart, IN*

## INDIVIDUAL GREEN PEPPER OMELET

2 tsp. butter
2 T. minced green pepper
2 tsp. minced onion

2 eggs, beaten
Salt and red pepper
1 slice Velveeta cheese

Melt butter in a small skillet. Sauté pepper and onion. Add eggs and sprinkle with salt and red pepper. Top with cheese when eggs are set.

*Mary Ann Martin, Sauk Centre, MN*

## OVEN OMELET I

8 eggs
1 cup milk
1 tsp. salt
1/4 tsp. salt
1/4 tsp. dry mustard
1/8 tsp. paprika

1/8 tsp. onion powder
1/8 tsp. pepper
3 T. chopped onion
3 oz. shaved ham
1 cup shredded mozzarella, Swiss
   or Cheddar cheese

Beat eggs and milk together. Add next 6 ingredients and beat. Stir in remaining items. Pour into a greased 9-inch square pan. Cook, uncovered, at 325° for 45 minutes.

*Mrs. Luke Hoover, Goshen, IN*

***We cannot direct the wind, but we can adjust the sails.***

1

# OVEN OMELET II

*Turkey ham or smoked sausage links can be used instead of ham.*

1/4 cup butter or margarine
18 eggs, beaten
1 cup sour cream
1 cup milk
2 tsp. salt
1/4 cup chopped green pepper

1/4 cup chopped onion
2 cups shredded cheese
1 1/2 to 2 cups cubed cooked ham
4 oz. can mushrooms, opt.

Heat oven to 325°. Melt butter in a 13x9 pan, coating bottom and sides. Mix remaining ingredients and pour into pan. Bake approximately 1 hour and 15 minutes.

# OMELET SANDWICHES

*No cornflakes on hand?  Bake plain or sprinkle with cheese.*

16 slices bread, buttered
8 slices cheese
1 lb. shaved ham
6 eggs
3 cups milk

1/2 tsp. dry mustard
1/2 tsp. salt
1/2 cup butter or margarine
1 cup crushed cornflakes

Make eight sandwiches using cheese and ham. Put in a greased 13x9 pan. Mix eggs, milk, mustard and salt; pour over sandwiches. Refrigerate overnight. In the morning melt butter, mix with cornflakes; put on top. Bake at 350° for 1 hour.

*Renetta Brovont, New Era, MI*

# SCRAMBLED EGGS

1 T. butter
4 eggs

1/2 tsp. salt

Melt butter in a skillet. Combine eggs and salt; pour into skillet and stir until done.

# EGG DUTCH

5 eggs
1 tsp. salt
Pepper

1 heaping T. flour
1 cup milk

Put in a bowl in order given; beat well. Pour into a hot, buttered skillet; cover. Cook over medium-low heat. Cut and turn when about half done, stir like scrambled eggs, or fold in half for an omelet. We like to eat them with syrup.

*Mrs. Carlton Zimmerman, Brooten, MN*

## TOMATO AND EGG SCRAMBLE

| | |
|---|---|
| 1 small onion, chopped | 1/2 tsp. salt |
| 2 T. butter | 1/8 tsp. pepper |
| 1 T. flour | 6 eggs |
| 1 cup tomatoes | 1/2 cup milk |
| 1 tsp. Worcestershire sauce | 1 T. butter |

Brown onion in butter. Blend in flour; stir in tomatoes, Worcestershire sauce, salt and pepper. Simmer till thickened, 5 to 10 minutes. Beat eggs and milk. Melt butter in another skillet; add eggs; stir until done. Fold in tomato mixture.

*Edna Miller, Snover, MI*

## EGG MUFFIN

| | |
|---|---|
| 2 eggs | 1 thin slice cooked ham |
| 1 slice of cheese | 1 English muffin or bread |

Scramble and season eggs; fry lightly. Top with cheese. Put ham on muffin and place eggs on top. Cover until ready to eat so cheese melts.

*Mrs. Marvin (Lydia) Sensenig, Penn Yan, NY*

## COUNTRY BREAKFAST SKILLET

| | |
|---|---|
| 2 T. butter or margarine | 8 eggs |
| 1 1/2 cups diced cooked potatoes | 1/2 tsp. salt |
| 1/2 cup chopped green pepper | 1/8 tsp. pepper |
| 1/2 cup chopped onion | Cheese slices or shredded |
| 1/2 tsp. salt | cheese |

Melt butter; add next 4 ingredients. Cover and cook 5 minutes or until tender. Beat eggs with salt and pepper. Pour eggs over vegetables and cook till set. Top with cheese.

## BREAKFAST BURRITOS

*Chopped tomatoes or olives can be added before salsa*

| | |
|---|---|
| 1 lb. sausage | 1/2 tsp. salt |
| 1 onion | 8 flour tortillas, warmed |
| 1/2 green pepper | 1 cup shredded cheese |
| 6 eggs | Salsa |

Fry sausage, onion and green pepper. Remove excess grease. Mix eggs and salt; pour into skillet. Cook until set. Equally divide sausage/egg mixture into warmed tortillas. Sprinkle with cheese; top with salsa. Roll up tortillas and serve immediately.

3

# HAM AND EGG CUPS

1 1/2 cups biscuit mix
1/4 cup plus 2 T. cold water
1 tsp. instant minced onion
12 thin slices cooked ham

6 eggs
Salt and pepper
Parsley flakes

Mix biscuit mix, water and onion. Press in bottom and side of six greased custard cups. Line each with 2 slices of ham. Break an egg into each cup. Sprinkle with salt, pepper and parsley. Bake on lowest rack at 400° for 15 to 20 minutes, or until eggs are set.

# BACON AND EGG PIZZA

8 oz. can biscuits (or make your
    own dough)
3 eggs, beaten
1 T. milk

1/8 tsp. salt
5 slices fried bacon, crumbled
1 T. chopped onion
1 cup shredded Cheddar cheese

Flatten biscuits on pizza pan. Combine eggs, milk and salt. Pour onto biscuit dough. Sprinkle with bacon, onion and cheese. Bake at 350° for 20 minutes.

# CHEESY EGG BAKE

1 cup biscuit mix
1 1/2 cups cottage cheese
2 cups (8 oz.) grated cheese
1 tsp. dried onion or 1 T. fresh
    onion

1 tsp. dried parsley
1/4 tsp. salt
6 eggs, lightly beaten
1 cup milk
3/4 cup butter

Mix ingredients in order given, except butter. Melt butter in a 13x9 pan. Pour in cheese and egg mixture, spreading evenly. Bake at 350° for 40 minutes or till set.
*Elaine Martin, Nappanee, IN*

# BREAKFAST BAKE

5 eggs
2 T. cream
1/4 tsp. salt
1/8 tsp. pepper

1/8 tsp. seasoned salt
2 slices buttered bread, cubed
Shredded or sliced cheese

Put first five ingredients in blender. Put bread cubes into a square, greased baking dish. Pour egg mixture over bread. Bake at 350° for 15 minutes or until firm. Top with cheese and return to oven until cheese is melted.
*Vera Fox, Memphis, MO*

# BREAKFAST CASSEROLE I

*Try substituting ham or chicken for bacon, or serve with mushroom sauce.*

2 cups bread cubes
1/2 lb. bacon, diced and fried
8 eggs

2 cups milk
1 tsp. salt
Paprika

Spread bread cubes evenly in a 13x9 pan; sprinkle bacon on top. Beat eggs and milk; add seasoning and pour over bread. Bake at 350° for 45 minutes or until set.

*Mrs. Mervin (Lucille) Martin, Wallenstein, Ontario, Canada*

# BREAKFAST CASSEROLE II

6 eggs, beaten
2 cups milk
6 slices bread, cubed
1 tsp. salt

1 tsp. dry mustard
1 lb. sausage, bacon, ham or hot
 dogs
1 cup cheddar cheese, shredded

If using sausage or bacon fry and drain. Mix everything together and let stand overnight. Bake in an uncovered 13x9 pan at 350° for 45 to 60 minutes or until set. This can also be made by putting bread in first and pouring combined remaining ingredients over it. Velveeta cheese slices can be used instead of shredded cheddar cheese.

*Sarah Imhoff, Sheridan, MI        Mrs. Cyrus Kulp, Auburn, NY        Esther Martin, Decker, MI*
*Velma Martin, Nappanee, IN        Mrs. Phillip Zimmerman, Versailles, MO*

   **Because eggs contain all the essential amino acids they provide complete protein. Eggs are also an excellent source of vitamin B12. A large two ounce egg provides 6 grams of protein and has around 80 calories.**

# BREAKFAST CASSEROLE III

1 lb. sausage
12 eggs, well beaten
10 3/4 oz. can mushroom soup

1/2 cup milk
1 cup grated Cheddar cheese

Brown sausage, stirring until crumbly. Drain and remove from skillet. Scramble eggs in a small amount of pan drippings until partially set. Mix together soup and milk in a separate bowl. Layer sausage and eggs in a 1 1/2 quart rectangular casserole. Top with soup mixture and cheese. Bake at 350° until cheese is melted.

*Connie Rodes, Milford, IN*

5

# SPRING BREAKFAST STRATA

8 eggs
3 cups milk
1 T. Dijon mustard
1 tsp. basil
1 tsp. salt
2 T. melted butter

2 T. flour
10 bread cubes
2 cups cubed cooked ham
2 cups cooked asparagus
2 cups shredded cheese
2 cups sliced fresh mushrooms

Beat eggs, milk, mustard, basil and salt. Gently stir in remaining ingredients until mixed. Pour into a greased 13x9 pan. Cover and refrigerate 8 hours or overnight. Bake at 350° for 1 hour or until a knife inserted in the center comes out clean. Let stand 5 minutes before cutting.

# BREAKFAST QUICHE

1/2 lb. bacon, diced
1/4 cup chopped onion
2 cups shredded Swiss or other
    cheese
2 T. flour

9-inch unbaked pie shell
3 large or 4 medium eggs
1 cup milk
1/4 tsp. salt
1/4 tsp. dry mustard

Fry bacon. Remove bacon; save 1 tablespoon bacon drippings. Sauté onion in drippings 5 minutes. Toss together bacon, onions, cheese and flour. Spread in pie shell. Whisk together remaining ingredients and pour over cheese mixture. Bake, uncovered, at 350° for 35 to 40 minutes, or until a knife inserted in the center comes out clean. Let stand 5 to 10 minutes before serving.

# CREAMED EGGS

6 hard-cooked eggs
2 T. butter
2 T. flour
1 tsp. salt

1/8 tsp. pepper
2 cups milk
6 to 8 slices toast

Peel and chop eggs. Melt butter in saucepan. Add flour and seasoning. Stir until well blended. Add milk, stirring constantly. Cook until smooth. Add eggs to hot sauce. Serve on toast.

*Mrs. James Kulp, Unity, WI*

***Just think how happy you would be if you lost everything you have right now – and then got it all back.***

# CREAMED BACON AND EGGS

6 slices bacon
2 onions, sliced
10 3/4 oz. can mushroom soup
1/4 cup milk
5 hard-cooked eggs, sliced

2 cups (8 oz.) shredded Cheddar
  cheese
Dash of salt and pepper
English muffins, split and toasted

Fry bacon until crisp; remove from skillet. Drain fat, reserving 2 tablespoons. Sauté onion in bacon fat. Stir in soup, milk, eggs, cheese and seasonings. Pour into 10x6 baking dish. Top with crumbled bacon. Bake at 350° for 20 minutes. Serve over muffin halves.

*Mrs. John (Twila) Kulp, Mosinee, WI*

# WESTERN EGGS AU GRATIN

1/2 lb. Velveeta cheese
1/2 cup salad dressing
1/3 cup milk
1 cup cooked chicken or ham

1/4 cup sliced olives
2 T. finely chopped onion
4 hard-cooked eggs, sliced

Combine cheese, salad dressing and milk. Stir over low heat until smooth. Add remaining ingredients; heat. Serve on toast, biscuits or English muffins.

# POTATO EGG CASSEROLE

4 strips bacon, fried
4 cups cooked diced potatoes
3 hard-cooked eggs, chopped
10 3/4 oz. can cream of chicken
  soup

1 cup milk
Salt and pepper
Minced onion
1/2 cup shredded cheese

Crumble fried bacon. Layer potatoes, bacon and eggs in casserole. Blend soup, milk, salt, pepper and onion. Pour over top. Sprinkle with cheese. Bake at 350° for 30 minutes.

*Anna Mae Hoover, Reinholds, PA*

*The little worries that we meet each day*
*May lie as stumbling-blocks across our way;*
*Or we may make them stepping-stones to be*
*Nearer each day, O Lord, our God, to Thee!*

# PANCAKES, ETC.

Stir pancake batter only until dry ingredients are moistened. Do not overbeat; lumps are fine. Cook on a hot griddle or skillet. If pancake batter has sufficient shortening, little or no shortening is needed. Turn pancakes when bubbles appear and edges look dry. Keep in mind the second side doesn't take as long as the first. Add a half cup to a cup of peanut butter or fruit to pancake batter for a different taste.

## DELICIOUS PANCAKES

*To make buttermilk pancakes use buttermilk instead of milk. Decrease baking powder to 2 teaspoons and add 1 teaspoon of soda.*

2 eggs
1 1/4 cups flour
1 T. baking powder
1 tsp. sugar

3/4 tsp. salt
1/3 cup melted butter
1 1/4 cups milk

Beat eggs slightly; sift dry ingredients. Add butter and milk to eggs. Stir in dry ingredients. Cook on a hot griddle or skillet.

*Charlotte Martin, Goshen, IN*

## AMERICAN NORWEGIAN PANCAKES

1 1/2 cups buttermilk
3 egg yolks
1/4 cup melted shortening
1 1/2 cups flour

1 T. baking powder
1/2 tsp. soda
1/4 tsp. salt
3 egg whites, stiffly beaten

Combine buttermilk, yolks and shortening. Combine dry ingredients and add first mixture. Fold in egg whites. Makes 18 pancakes using two tablespoons batter for each. For wheat pancakes use part wheat flour.

*Mrs. Norman Burkholder, Mertztown, PA     Mrs. Ernest Newswanger, Kutztown, PA*

## LIGHT WHEAT PANCAKES

1 cup flour
1/2 cup wheat flour
1/2 tsp. salt, scant

2 tsp. soda, scant
2 cups thick sour milk, more if
   needed

Combine flours, salt and soda. Add milk and mix. Fry in lots of butter or margarine. A little wheat germ or bran can be added.

*Rachel Newswanger, Barnett, MO*

## WHOLE WHEAT PANCAKES

2 cups whole wheat flour
3 T. sugar
1 tsp. salt
3 to 4 tsp. baking powder

2 eggs
1 1/2 cups milk
5 T. cooking oil

Mix dry ingredients. Beat eggs well; add milk and oil. Add to dry ingredients; mix.

*Irene Peachey, East Flat Rock, NC*

## GOLDEN WHOLE WHEAT PANCAKES

*This recipe uses flour made from Golden 86 white wheat.*

2 eggs
2 3/4 cups milk
1/2 cup cooking oil
3 cups white whole wheat flour

1/4 cup sugar
1 tsp. salt
4 tsp. baking powder

Beat first three ingredients. Combine and mix in remaining ingredients.

*Mrs. Ray (Elsie) Hoover, Stratford, WI*

## CORNMEAL PANCAKES

2 eggs
1 3/4 cups milk
3 T. cooking oil
1 cup flour

1 cup corn meal
1 T. baking powder
1 tsp. salt

Beat eggs; add milk and oil. Combine and mix in remaining ingredients.

*Mrs. Ray (Elsie) Hoover, Stratford, WI*

## OATMEAL PANCAKES

*These moist pancakes taste almost like fried oatmeal.*

1 egg
1 1/2 cups cooked oatmeal
3/4 cup milk
2 T. melted butter

1/2 cup flour
1 tsp. baking powder
1/4 tsp. salt

Beat first four ingredients. Combine and mix in remaining ingredients. Use a little more salt if not using leftover oatmeal.

*Kelsie LaRaye Hoover, Stratford, WI*

**Life is measured by depth, not length.**

In a hurry? The pancake recipes on this page save time by using pancake mix. Use your imagination and create your own favorites. Remember not to beat too vigorously.

## APPLE CINNAMON PANCAKES

1 T. sugar
3/4 tsp. cinnamon

1 cup shredded apples
2 cups prepared pancake mix

Mix sugar and cinnamon and sprinkle over apples. Stir apples into batter. Cook on a hot greased griddle.

*Mrs. Ray (Elsie) Hoover, Stratford, WI*

## OATMEAL RAISIN PANCAKES

1/2 cup oatmeal
2 cups water
2 cups dry pancake mix

2 T. sugar
1/2 tsp. cinnamon
1/2 cup raisins

Combine oatmeal and water. Let stand 5 minutes. Add remaining ingredients.

*Mrs. Ray (Elsie) Hoover, Stratford, WI*

## PEACH PANCAKES

2 cups dry pancake mix
1 1/2 cups water

1/2 cup peach syrup
1/2 cups chopped peaches

Combine mix and liquids. Stir in peaches. Cook on a hot greased griddle.

## SQUASH PANCAKES

2 small fresh yellow summer
   squash
2 cups pancake mix

2 eggs
1/2 cup milk

Steam or cook squash until soft. Put all ingredients, except milk into a bowl. Beat, add milk gradually. You may need more or less milk. This batter can be made the night before and refrigerated. Cooked butternut squash may be used too.

*Mrs. Norman Burkholder, Mertztown, PA*

***The seed of wrongdoing may be sown in secret, but the harvest cannot be concealed.***

# PANCAKE MIX

12 cups flour, whole wheat flour
   or buckwheat flour
3/4 cup sugar

4 cups dry milk
2 T. salt
3/4 cup baking powder

Mix well and store in a tight container. When ready to make pancakes beat together 1 egg, 1 cup water, and 2 T. cooking oil. Stir in 1 1/2 cups mix. Dry milk can be omitted if milk is used instead of water.
*Mrs. Carlton Zimmerman, Brooten, MN*     *Lizzie Hoover, Goshen, IN*

# WHOLE GRAIN PANCAKE MIX

3 cups whole wheat flour
2 1/2 cups rye, buckwheat or soy
   flour, do not use all soy
1/2 cup oatmeal
1 cup wheat germ

1 cup cornmeal
5 T. baking powder
1 T. salt
2 T. bone meal powder, opt.

Combine ingredients; store in tight container in refrigerator. To make pancakes beat together 2 cups milk, 2 eggs, and 1/2 cup cooking oil; stir in 3 cups mix. For spicy pancakes add 1 teaspoon each of cinnamon, ginger, and cloves.
*Hannah Kulp Family, Mt. Hermon, KY*

# APPLE WAFFLES

1 1/4 cups pastry flour
1 T. sugar
1/4 tsp. salt
1/2 tsp. cinnamon
2 tsp. baking powder

2 eggs, separated
1 cup milk
1 3/4 cups finely chopped apples
6 T. melted butter or lard

Combine dry ingredients. Beat yolks. Add milk and combine with flour mixture. Beat until smooth. Add apples and butter. Fold in stiffly beaten egg whites.
*Mrs. Isaac Brubacker, Versailles, MO*

# OATMEAL WAFFLES

1 1/2 cups quick oatmeal
1/2 cup wheat flour
1 tsp. soda
1 tsp. salt

2 eggs, beaten
2 cups buttermilk
6 T. butter, melted

Combine first four ingredients. Stir together eggs, buttermilk and butter; mix with dry ingredients. Bake in a preheated waffle iron. Eat with syrup or applesauce.

11

# BLUEBERRY WAFFLES

2 eggs, separated
2 cups buttermilk or sour milk
2 cups flour
2 tsp. baking powder

1 tsp. soda
1 tsp. salt
1/2 cup melted butter
1 cup fresh or frozen blueberries

Add buttermilk to egg yolks. Beat well. Add flour, baking powder, soda and salt. Beat until smooth. Stir in melted butter and blueberries. Beat egg whites until soft peaks form. Fold into batter. Bake in a preheated waffle iron on medium heat, 5 to 8 minutes, until steaming stops and waffles are brown.

# GOLDEN BROWN WAFFLES

1 3/4 cups flour
1 T. baking powder
2 tsp. sugar
1/2 tsp. salt

4 eggs, separated
1 1/3 cups milk
1/2 cup melted butter

Combine dry ingredients. Beat egg yolks. Add milk and butter. Stir into dry ingredients. Beat egg whites until stiff; fold into batter. Bake in a waffle iron until golden brown.

*Mrs. Cyrus Kulp, Auburn, NY*

# FRIED CORNMEAL MUSH

1 cup yellow cornmeal
1 tsp. salt

1 cup cold water or milk
3 cups water

Combine cornmeal and salt with cold water. Bring three cups water to a boil. Stir in cornmeal mixture. Cover and cook 10 minutes. Pour into a wet loaf pan. Cool; refrigerate overnight. Cut into 1/4 to 1/2 inch slices, dip into flour and fry in a greased skillet until brown. Turn once. Serve with butter and syrup.

# FRENCH TOAST

*For cinnamon French toast add 1/3 teaspoon cinnamon to the egg mixture.*

2 eggs
1/2 cup milk

1/4 tsp. salt
6 slices bread

Combine eggs, milk and salt. Dip bread in egg mixture. Cook on a greased griddle approximately 3 minutes per side. Serve with syrup, honey, jelly or sugar.

## CINNAMON TOAST

1/4 cup butter, softened
2/3 cup sugar

1 T. cinnamon
Toasted bread

Combine the first three ingredients and spread on toast. Refrigerate leftover cinnamon butter.

## PANCAKE SYRUP

4 cups brown sugar
1/2 cup corn syrup or molasses

2 cups water
2 tsp. maple flavoring or vanilla

Bring sugar, syrup and water to a boil. Remove from heat and add maple flavoring. This can also be made without corn syrup.

*Mrs. Marvin (Lydia) Sensenig, Penn Yan, NY       Mrs. Aaron Weaver, Penn Yan, NY*

# BREAKFAST ROLLS AND CAKES

## BREAKFAST ROLLS

*These make-at-night-bake-in-the-morning rolls are great for special occasions.*

1 pkg. yeast
1/4 cup warm water
4 cups flour
1 tsp. salt
1 tsp. grated lemon rind
1/4 cup sugar

1 cup butter or margarine
2 eggs, beaten
1 warm cup milk
1 cup sugar
1 T. cinnamon

Dissolve yeast in water. Combine flour, salt, lemon rind and 1/4 cup sugar. Cut in butter. Combine eggs, milk and yeast; add to flour mixture. Cover tightly and refrigerate overnight. In the morning, divide dough in half; roll each piece into an 18x12 inch rectangle. Spread with soft butter if you like. Sprinkle with remaining sugar and cinnamon. Roll up tightly; cut into 1-inch slices. Place on a greased cookie sheet; flatten with palm of hand. These do not need to rise. Bake at 400° for 12 minutes. Frost or glaze if desired. Rolls can be cut thinner and not flattened, then baked at 350°.

*Mrs. Vernon Kurtz, Ewing, IL       Mrs. Elverne Martin, Nappanee, IN*

***When you throw mud at someone, you are the one losing ground.***

# MAKE-AHEAD COFFEECAKE

2/3 cup butter, softened
1 cup sugar
1/2 cup brown sugar
1 cup buttermilk
2 cups flour
1 tsp. soda

1/2 tsp. salt
1 tsp. cinnamon
1 cup chopped dates or raisins
1/2 cup brown sugar
1/2 tsp. cinnamon
1/2 cup chopped nuts

Cream butter and sugars. Add buttermilk. Combine and gradually add dry ingredients. Add dates. Spread into a13x9 pan. Combine remaining ingredients and sprinkle on top. Cover and refrigerate overnight or for a couple of days. Bake at 350° for 45 to 50 minutes. Serve warm.

*Mrs. Ray (Elsie) Hoover, Stratford, WI*

# OAT CAKES

2 cups oatmeal
1/2 tsp. baking powder
1/2 tsp. salt

1 1/4 cups oatmeal
2 T. cooking oil
6 to 8 T. hot water

Grind 2 cups of oatmeal to 1 1/2 cups of flour in the blender. Combine oat flour, baking powder, salt and 1 cup oatmeal. Stir in oil and enough hot water to make a ball of dough. Divide dough in half. Spread remaining 1/4 cup of oatmeal on work surface and roll each ball of dough around in the oats to coat. Roll each ball into a 9-inch circle. Edges will be ragged. Cut each circle into four wedges. Place on oiled and floured baking sheets. Bake at 350° for 15 minutes or at 400° for 10 minutes until firm and lightly browned. This can also be cooked in a heavy skillet; 5 to 8 minutes per side. Serve with butter and honey or jam.

*Hannah Kulp family, Mt. Hermon, KY*

# BREAKFAST CAKE I

4 cups flour
1 1/2 cups brown sugar
1 tsp. soda

4 tsp. baking powder
1/2 cup butter or margarine
1 cup water

Combine first four ingredients; cut in butter. Stir in water. Pat lightly into a 13x9 pan. Bake at 350° for 45 minutes. Eat warm or cold with cereal and milk. This is also good with hot chocolate.

*Florence Martin, Memphis, MO*

**If we had no faults, we should not take so much pleasure in noticing them in others.**

## BREAKFAST CAKE II

2 1/2 cups bran
1/4 cup flour
1/2 cup sugar (or substitute)
1 tsp. soda
1 tsp. baking powder
1 tsp. cinnamon

1 tsp. nutmeg
1/2 tsp. cloves
1/2 cup raisins
2 to 3 eggs
1 cup sour cream
1/2 cup milk

Mix dry ingredients together; add raisins. Beat in eggs (use 3 if baking in the microwave), sour cream and milk. Bake at 350° for 25 to 30 minutes. We eat this for our cereal.

*Mrs. Dan Martin, Nappanee, IN*

# CEREAL

## COOKED OATMEAL

*Stir in raisins or other dried fruit, or top with fresh, frozen or canned fruit.*

4 cups water
1 tsp. salt

2 cups oatmeal

Bring water to a boil and add salt. Use a little less oatmeal if not using quick oatmeal. Stir in oatmeal. Cook regular oatmeal 5 minutes and quick oatmeal one minute. If using quick oatmeal cook only 1 minute. Let stand several minutes before serving.

## BAKED OATMEAL

1/2 cup butter, melted
1/2 to 1 cup brown sugar
2 eggs, beaten, opt.
3 cups quick oats

2 tsp. baking powder
1 tsp. salt
1 cup milk
Raisins, opt.

Cream together first 3 ingredients. Add remaining ingredients; mix. Bake in a 10-inch square or 13x9 pan at 350° for 20 to 30 minutes. This can be mixed the night before. To make it in the microwave combine melted butter, 2/3 cup brown sugar and eggs. Add remaining ingredients, using only 1/2 cup milk. Place in a 1 1/2 quart casserole. Microwave on full power for 6 to 7 minutes. Stir several times.

*Velma Martin, Nappanee, IN*  *Charlene Ramer, Goshen, IN*  *Kathleen Ramer, New Paris, IN*
*Linda Hoover Shaum, Roann, IN*  *Sheryl Weaver, Goshen, IN*  *Anna Zimmerman, Decker, MI*
*Jolene Zimmerman, Goshen, IN*

# BUTTERSCOTCH OATMEAL

| | |
|---|---|
| 2 eggs, beaten | 1 cup brown sugar |
| 3 1/2 cups milk | 2 cups oatmeal |
| 1/2 tsp salt | 1/4 cup butter or margarine |

Mix first 4 ingredients; cook and stir until bubbly.  Stir in oatmeal; cook till bubbly. Add butter; cover and remove from heat.  Let stand 5 minutes.  Stir and serve with milk,  *Renetta Brovont, New Era, MI*

# CINNAMON APPLE GOLDEN OATMEAL

| | |
|---|---|
| 1 cup chopped apple | 1/2 cup water |
| 3 T. butter | 3 T. brown sugar |
| 1 1/2 cups quick oatmeal | 1 tsp. cinnamon |
| 1 egg, beaten | 1/4 tsp. salt |

Sauté apples in butter.  Stir in oatmeal.  Cook over medium heat, stirring constantly, 3 to 5 minutes or until oatmeal is dry and lightly browned.  Add remaining ingredients; continue cooking, stirring occasionally, 2 to 3 minutes, or until liquid evaporates.  Serve with milk or yogurt.  Increase water to 3/4 cup if using old-fashioned oatmeal.

*Janice Weaver, Unity WI*

# GRANOLA I

| | |
|---|---|
| 4 cups oatmeal | 1/2 cup cooking oil |
| 1 1/2 cups coconut | 1/2 cup water |
| 1 cup sunflower or sesame seeds | 1 T. vanilla |
| 1 tsp. cinnamon | 1 cup nuts, opt. |
| 3/4 cup sugar or 1/2 cup honey | 1/2 cup raisins, opt. |

Mix dry ingredients.  Blend next four ingredients; stir into dry mixture.  Mix well. Spread thinly on cookie sheets and toast in oven at 350° until slightly brown, stirring frequently.  Remove from oven; stir in raisins.

*Erla Horst Horning, Penn Yan, NY*      *Pauline Kulp, Stratford, WI*

# GRANOLA II

| | |
|---|---|
| 1/2 cup cooking oil | 1 lb. coconut |
| 1 cup butter or margarine | 2 cups Grape-Nuts |
| 1 cup honey | 1 cup chopped nuts |
| 2 T. molasses | 1 cup wheat germ |
| 1 T. vanilla | 1 cup sunflower seeds |
| 1/2 tsp. salt | 1/2 cup sesame seeds |
| 8 cups oatmeal | 1 cup raisins |

Preheat oven to 350°. Melt oil, butter, honey, molasses, vanilla, and salt in a large roaster. Cool slightly; stir in oatmeal, coconut, Grape-Nuts, chopped nuts, wheat germ, and seeds. Bake in shallow pans 20 to 25 minutes, stirring every 5 to 7 minutes. Add raisins after granola has cooled.

*Sarah Nolt, Fortuna, MO*

## GRANOLA III

10 cups oatmeal
4 cups whole wheat flour
2 cups flour
2 cups brown sugar
2 tsp. salt

1 3/4 cups cooking oil or melted butter
1 cup coconut
1 cup sunflower seeds or nuts

Mix ingredients together in a large bowl. Toast in oven at low to medium heat till coconut turns brown. Stir occasionally. Best when eaten with fresh strawberries or other fruit. This can also be made by using all whole wheat flour, 3 cups sugar and adding 2 teaspoons soda.

*Laura Kulp, Stratford, WI     Mrs. Ivan Zimmerman, Scottsville, KY*

## GRANOLA IV

15 cups oatmeal
3 cups brown sugar
3 cups wheat germ
3 cups sunflower seeds
3 cups chopped nuts
3 cups coconut

3/4 cup sesame seeds
1 T. salt
2 cups cooking oil
1 1/2 cups orange juice concentrate
1 T. vanilla

Mix dry ingredients together. Combine oil, concentrate, and vanilla; add to dry ingredients. Bake at 250° until crisp, stirring occasionally.

*Mrs. Lester Weaver, Manheim, PA*

## GRANOLA V

16 cups quick oatmeal
4 cups brown sugar
2 cups wheat germ
2 cups coconut
2 tsp. salt

2 tsp. cinnamon
2 cups cooking oil or melted butter or margarine
2 tsp. vanilla

Mix ingredients in a large bowl. Add vanilla to oil and add to dry ingredients. Mix well. Bake at 250° until slightly browned; stirring occasionally.

*Mary Ann Newswanger, Fortuna, MO*

# WHEAT-NUTS
*These taste like Grape-Nuts*

8 cups whole wheat flour
2 cups brown sugar
2 tsp. salt

2 tsp. soda
4 cups buttermilk
1 cup molasses

Combine dry ingredients; stir in buttermilk and molasses. Bake in cake pans until done. Cool; cut into strips and put through a food grinder. Spread crumbs onto cookie sheets and put in oven on low heat until dry.

*Mrs. Ernest Newswanger, Kutztown, PA*

# CORNMEAL-NUTS

8 cups cornmeal (3 lb.)
4 cups flour
5 cups sugar
2 T. baking powder

2 tsp. salt
1 cup butter or margarine, melted
6 cups milk

Combine dry ingredients. Add melted butter and milk; mix. Bake at 375° approximately 1 hour. Cool; crumble. Spread crumbs on cookie sheets and dry on low heat.

*Hannah Kulp family, Mt. Hermon, KY*

# BRAN-NUTS

4 cups bran
4 cups whole wheat flour
1 rounded T. soda
2 tsp. salt
4 cups buttermilk
1/2 cup honey

1/2 cup sorghum molasses
1/2 cup butter or margarine,
   melted
1 T. vanilla
1 T. vinegar
2 tsp. maple flavoring

Combine dry ingredients. Combine remaining ingredients. Add and mix well. Bake at 350° till slightly browned. When well done turn out on a cloth to cool. Rub through a wire mesh or deep fryer basket, being careful not to squeeze into dough. Keep crumbs fluffy. Spread into several pans and dry in a slow oven.

*Hannah Kulp family, Mt. Hermon, KY*

**Making excuses doesn't change the truth.**

# YEAST and QUICK
# BREADS

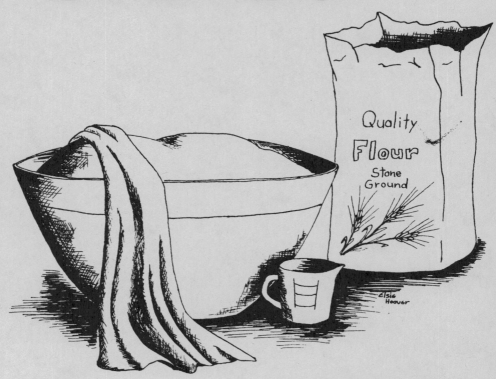

Quality
*Flour*
Stone
Ground

Elsie
Hoover

# YEAST BREADS

One package of yeast equals 2 1/2 teaspoons, or a scant tablespoon. Water or milk used to dissolve yeast should be 105° to 115°. A little sugar speeds up yeast activity, but too much sugar, as well as too much salt, will slow yeast down. Letting yeast dough rise improves texture, but rising too often or too long depletes the yeast's energy. Pasteurized milk does not need to be scalded, however scalded or warmed milk will help dissolve sugar and melt shortening.

## BREAD I

2 pkg. yeast
4 cups lukewarm water
1/2 cup sugar

1/4 cup cooking oil
1 T. salt
Approximately 10 cups flour

Dissolve yeast in water in a large bowl. Add sugar, oil and salt. Let stand undisturbed 5 minutes. Stir in flour 1 cup at a time until soft, easy to handle dough forms. Knead 10 to15 minutes, until smooth and elastic. Let rise 2 hours. Punch down. Let rise 10 minutes. Shape into four loaves. Let rise 1 hour. Bake at 350° for 30 minutes. Part wheat flour can also be used.

*Esther Horst, East Earl, PA*

## BREAD II

5 cups lukewarm water
3 pkg. yeast
1 cup sugar
2 T. salt

1 cup shortening
4 heaping cups flour
Approximately 10 cups flour

Dissolve yeast in 1 cup water (5 minutes) in a large bowl. Add remaining water, sugar, salt, and shortening. Add 4 cups flour and let stand in a warm place 45 minutes. Gradually mix in remaining flour until dough is easy to handle. Knead 5 minutes or until elastic. Let rise in a warm place until double in size, about 1 hour. Punch down. Let rise again until double in size, about an hour. Shape into six loaves and put in greased bread pans. Prick with a fork. Let loaves rise until double. Bake at 325° for 30 minutes.

*Mrs. Isaac Newswanger Jr., Carson City, MI*

*A wise man chooses his destination and accepts the way. A foolish man chooses his way and accepts the destination.*

# HONEY BREAD

1/2 cup lukewarm water
2 T. yeast
3 1/2 cups hot water
1/2 cup honey

4 cups flour
1 T. salt
1/4 cup shortening
Approximately 6 cups flour

Soften yeast in lukewarm water. Combine hot water, honey, 4 cups flour, salt, and shortening in a large bowl and beat 2 minutes. Add yeast mixture. Mix well, then let stand 12 minutes. Add remaining flour until it forms a soft dough. The last few cups may be kneaded in. Knead 10 minutes. Let rise until double in size. Punch down; let rise again until double in size. Shape into 4 loaves; place in greased bread pans. Prick with a fork. Let rise until double. Bake at 350° for 30 minutes.

*Mrs. Susan Martin, Romulus, NY*

# BREAD-MAKING TREATS

*After letting bread dough rise and punching it down again you can use it to make cinnamon rolls or other treats. Here are just two ideas – your imagination is the limit. Either white or wheat dough can be used.*

## CHEESE PUFFS

Roll bread dough approximately 1/4-inch thick; cut into 2 1/2-inch circles. Spoon a teaspoon or two of chopped onion into each circle. Top with a 1/2-inch cube of Mozzarella cheese. Stretch dough over onion and cheese; shut by pinching dough together. Place puffs on a buttered cookie sheet. Brush with melted butter and sprinkle with garlic salt. Cover and let rise for 30 minutes. Bake at 350° for 15 to 20 minutes. Do not overbake or cheese will run out. Circles can also be cut bigger and shut like a turnover if you want to add chopped green pepper, mushrooms, pepperoni or other cooked meat.

## ORANGE PULL-APARTS

Using bread dough, make 20 walnut-sized balls. Place in a greased 13x9 pan. Melt 1/4 cup butter and pour over rolls. Grate the peel of one orange and mix with 1/2 cup sugar. Sprinkle mixture over rolls. Cover; let rise until double in size. Bake at 350° for 20 to 25 minutes. Mix 1 cup powdered sugar with 1 T. butter and 2 T. fresh orange juice. Cover rolls with glaze while warm.

*Count no day lost in which you waited your turn, took only your share, and sought advantage over no one.*

# NO-KNEAD BREAD

| | |
|---|---|
| 1 pkg. yeast | 2 T. cooking oil |
| 1 1/4 cups warm water | 1 tsp. salt |
| 2 T. sugar | 3 cups flour |

Dissolve yeast in warm water in a bowl. Add sugar, oil and salt. Gradually mix in 2 1/4 cups flour, scraping bowl; mix 4 minutes on low speed. On medium speed beat 3 more minutes. Stir remaining flour in by hand, unless your mixer can handle it; mix 2 minutes more. Cover and let rise until double. Stir down with 25 vigorous strokes. Spread in a greased 9x5 bread pan. Let rise until batter reaches the top of the pan. Bake at 375° approximately 45 minutes.

# WHEAT BREAD

| | |
|---|---|
| 2 pkg. yeast | 1/4 cup cooking oil |
| 2 cups warm water | 2 tsp. salt |
| 1/4 cup brown sugar | 4 cups flour |
| 1/4 cup honey | 2 cups wheat flour |

Dissolve yeast in water. Add sugar, honey, oil, salt and flour. Let rise until double in size; punch down and let rise again. Form into 2 loaves and put into greased bread pans. Let rise again. Bake at 325° for 10 minutes then 300° for 25 minutes.

*Mrs. John (Twila) Kulp, Mosinee, WI        Verna Overholt, Due West, SC*

**Bread should be removed from bread pans as soon as it is baked. Buttering the tops of the bread makes a softer crust.**

# LIGHT WHEAT BREAD

| | |
|---|---|
| 2 cups scalded milk | 6 cups warm water |
| 1/2 cup butter or margarine | 1/4 cup yeast |
| 8 tsp. salt | 4 cups whole wheat flour |
| 3/4 cup sugar | 16 cups flour |

Dissolve butter, salt and sugar in milk. Dissolve yeast in warm water; add to first mixture. Gradually add flour and mix until elastic and not too sticky. Let rise until double in size. Punch down; let rise again. Shape into 8 loaves; let rise again. Bake at 350° until done. Butter tops when it comes out of the oven.

*Lizzie Hoover, Goshen, IN*

## 100% WHOLE WHEAT BREAD I

| | |
|---|---|
| 3 cups warm water | 1 T. yeast |
| 1/2 cup honey | 2 eggs, beaten |
| 1 T. salt | 8 to 9 cups whole wheat flour |

Mix first 4 ingredients. Let stand 5 to 10 minutes until yeast dissolves. Beat in eggs and 2 cups flour. Gradually add enough flour to make soft, workable dough. Knead 10 to 15 minutes. Let rise until double in size; punch down and let rise again. Shape into loaves and let rise again. Bake at 350° until done.

*Mrs. Phares Shirk, Liberty, KY*

## 100% WHOLE WHEAT BREAD II

*Use flour made from hard white wheat for light bread.*

| | |
|---|---|
| 5 cups warm water | 2 T. salt |
| 2/3 cup cooking oil | 1/3 cup wheat gluten |
| 2/3 cup honey | Approximately 12 cups freshly |
| 3 T. yeast | ground whole wheat flour |

Add ingredients in the order listed. Knead 10 minutes. Cover and let rise until double in size; punch down. Shape into 5 loaves and place in greased 8 1/2 x 4 1/2 bread pans. Preheat oven to 150° and *turn off* after several minutes. Place bread pans in the oven and let rise 20 to 30 minutes, until almost double in size. Bake at 350° for 35 to 40 minutes or until done. Remove from pans immediately. Brush tops with butter.

*Ray Hoover, Stratford, WI*

## HONEY WHOLE GRAIN BREAD

| | |
|---|---|
| 3 cups flour | 1/2 cup honey |
| 2 pkg. yeast | 2 eggs |
| 1 1/2 tsp. salt | 2 1/2 cups whole wheat flour |
| 1 cup water | 1/2 cup regular oatmeal |
| 1 cup cottage cheese | 2/3 cup chopped nuts |
| 1/4 cup butter | |

In a large bowl combine 2 cups flour, yeast and salt. Heat water, cottage cheese, butter and honey until very warm. Add warm liquid and eggs to flour mixture; mix well. Add wheat flour, oats and nuts. Stir in remaining flour. Knead until smooth and elastic. Let rise until double; punch down. Make 2 loaves and put into greased bread pans. Let rise again, about 1 hour. Bake at 350° for 35 to 40 minutes.

*Edith (Hoover) Martin, Sauk Centre, MN*

# RAISIN BREAD

*For a richer bread, roll into two 14x7 rectangles after the first rising. Spread each one with soft butter. Mix 2 tsp. cinnamon with 1/2 cup sugar and sprinkle over butter. Add raisins if you like. Roll up and put in bread pans.*

| | |
|---|---|
| 5 to 5 1/2 cups flour | 1/2 cup water |
| 2 pkg. yeast | 1/2 cup butter |
| 1/2 cups sugar | 2 eggs |
| 1 tsp salt | 1 cup raisins |
| 3/4 cup milk | 1 to 2 tsp. cinnamon |

In a large bowl combine 2 1/2 cups flour, yeast, sugar and salt; mix well. Heat milk, water and butter until warm, butter doesn't need to melt. Add to flour mixture. Add eggs. Blend at low speed till moistened; beat 3 minutes at medium speed. Stir in raisins and cinnamon. By hand stir in enough of remaining flour to make a firm dough. Knead 5 to 8 minutes. Place in greased bowl and turn to grease top. Cover and let rise till double in size, about 1 hour. Punch down and shape into 2 loaves. Place in greased 8x4 or 9x5 bread pans. Cover and let rise till double, 45 to 60 minutes. Bake at 350° for 40 to 45 minutes. Cover loosely with foil the last 5 to10 minutes if it gets too dark.

*Mrs. Ray (Elsie) Hoover, Stratford, WI*

**Only flour made from wheat and rye produces the necessary gluten to make raised loaves. Wheat gluten works best.**

# OATMEAL BREAD I

| | |
|---|---|
| 2 cups boiling water | 2 T. butter |
| 1 cup quick oatmeal | 1 pkg. yeast |
| 1/2 cup whole wheat flour | 1/2 cup warm water |
| 1/2 cup brown sugar | Approximately 5 cups flour |
| 1 T. salt | |

Pour boiling water over oatmeal, wheat flour, sugar, salt and butter. Cool to lukewarm. Dissolve yeast in warm water and add to batter. Add enough flour to make smooth elastic dough. Place in a greased bowl and let rise until double in size. Shape into 2 loaves; place into greased 9x5 bread pans. Let rise. Bake at 350° approximately 30 minutes. Bread is done when a dull sound is heard when lightly patted. Remove from pans; butter tops.

*Mrs. Paul Hoover, Goshen, IN*

***Listening is a way of loving.***

# OATMEAL BREAD II

2 1/2 cups boiling water
2 cups oatmeal
2 T. yeast
1 cup lukewarm water
1 cup honey

2 T. salt
3/4 cup cooking oil
4 eggs, beaten
2 cups whole wheat flour
Flour

Pour boiling water over oatmeal; cool to lukewarm. Dissolve yeast in lukewarm water. Beat together with remaining ingredients, except white flour. Work in enough flour to make dough workable, not sticky. Knead well. Grease top of dough and let rise. Punch down; let rise again. Shape into 6 loaves. Let rise. Bake at 400° for 10 minutes, then at 350° for 25 to 30 minutes more.

*Mrs. Allen Garmen, Roaring Spring, PA     Naomi Zimmerman, Goshen, IN*

# BACON AND ONION BREAD

2 T. yeast
4 2/3 cups lukewarm water
1/2 lb. bacon
1/2 cup sugar

1/2 T. salt
2 to 3 onions
Flour

Dissolve yeast in water. Fry bacon. Use the drippings for shortening in the bread. Mix all ingredients, except flour. Gradually work in enough flour to make a workable dough. Knead and let rise 30 minutes. Knead. Let rise 1 hour. Knead; let rise 1 1/2 hours. Shape into 4 to 5 loaves and put into pans. Let rise. Bake at 350° until done, approximately 35 minutes.

*Lena Martin, New Paris, IN*

# CORNMEAL YEAST BREAD

2 pkg. yeast
1/2 cup lukewarm water
1/2 cup sugar
1 1/2 tsp. salt
1/3 cup butter or margarine

3/4 cup milk, scalded
1 egg
4 to 4 1/2 cups flour
2/3 to 3/4 cup cornmeal

Dissolve yeast in water. Combine sugar, salt and butter. Pour scalded milk over mixture and cool to lukewarm. Stir in egg, 1 cup flour, cornmeal, and yeast mixture. Beat well. Stir in rest of flour to make soft dough. Knead 10 minutes. Let rise 1 hour, covered, in warm place until double in size. Punch down. Divide dough into two 8-inch bread pans. Cover; let rise until double in size. Bake at 350° for 45 minutes, or until done. Butter tops.

*Ethel Hoover, Goshen, IN*

# BIG BATCH POTATO BREAD

*Potato water gives bread a moister, if somewhat coarser, texture. Potato water, as well as milk, gives bread a little longer shelf-life.*

9 cups water, including potato
　water
3 1/2 T. yeast
1 cup sugar
1 cup lard

1/4 cup salt, scant
4 cups cooked mashed potatoes
2 1/2 lb. whole wheat flour
8 lb. flour

Dissolve yeast in 2 cups lukewarm water. In a 13-quart bowl dissolve sugar, lard, salt and potatoes in 3 cups hot water. Add 4 cups cold water; add yeast to cooled mixture. Add flour gradually till dough can be handled easily. Knead dough 10 to 15 minutes. Cover; set in warm place; let rise 1 hour. Knead several minutes; let rise another hour. Shape into 18 one pound loaves. Allow to rise till double in size. Bake at 400° for 10 minutes, then reduce to 350° for 25 minutes or till done. Brush tops with lard or butter.

*Nancy Kilmer, California, MO*

# RYE BREAD

1 pkg. yeast
1/2 cup lukewarm water
2 cups warm milk
2 T. butter

1 T. sugar or molasses
2 tsp. salt
3 1/2 cups rye flour
3 1/2 cups flour

Dissolve yeast in water. Add milk, butter, sugar and salt. Beat in rye flour. Add remaining flour and knead 5 to 10 minutes. Place dough in a greased bowl and let rise until double in size, about 2 hours. Punch down. Shape into two long loaves and place on a greased, cornmeal sprinkled cookie sheet. Cover and let rise again, about 1 1/2 hours. Bake at 350° for 35 to 40 minutes.

# FRENCH BREAD

1 pkg. yeast
1 1/4 cups warm water

2 2/3 to 3 cups flour
1 tsp. salt

Dissolve yeast in warm water; let stand 5 minutes. By hand stir in 1 1/2 cups flour and salt. Gradually stir in enough of remaining flour to make a soft dough. Knead 10 minutes. Place in a greased bowl, turning to grease top. Cover; let rise till double. Punch down. Roll or pat dough to a 12x6 rectangle. Starting with the longer side, roll up tightly. Pinch edges and ends to seal. Place on a cookie sheet. Sprinkle with cornmeal, if desired. Cover; let rise until doubled. With a very sharp knife, make 2 to 3 slashes across top of loaf. Spray or brush with cold water. Bake at 425° for 25 to 30 minutes until golden brown. For a crisper crust, spray or brush water on loaf several times during baking.

# CHEESY FRENCH BREAD

1 loaf French or Italian bread
Soft butter
Italian or pizza seasoning

1/4 cup Parmesan cheese
1 cup shredded Mozzarella
   cheese

Cut bread into 1-inch slices and place on a baking sheet. Spread with butter; sprinkle with seasoning. Top with cheeses. Bake at 350° for 20 minutes or until cheese melts.

# GARLIC BREAD

*A teaspoon of Italian seasoning can be used instead of the other spices.*

1 loaf French or Italian bread
1/2 cup butter or margarine
1/2 tsp. oregano

1/4 tsp. basil
1/4 tsp. garlic salt

Cut bread into 1-inch slices. Combine remaining ingredients and spread on one side of bread. For soft bread reassemble loaf and wrap in foil. For crusty bread place butter side up on a cookie sheet. Bake at 400° for 12 to 15 minutes.

*Mrs. Ray (Elsie) Hoover, Stratford, WI*

# GARLIC TOAST

1 loaf of bread
1/2 cup butter or margarine
1/2 tsp. Italian seasoning

1/2 tsp. onion salt
1/2 tsp. garlic powder

Slice bread to desired width. Melt butter and add remaining ingredients. Spread one or both side of bread. Cut into strips. Bake at 300° until toasted; turning once.

*Edna Miller, Snover, MI*

# ENGLISH MUFFIN BREAD

1 pkg. yeast
1 T. sugar
1/2 cup warm water
2 1/2 cups flour

1 tsp. salt
1/4 tsp soda
7/8 cup warm milk

Combine yeast, sugar and warm water; stir until dissolved. Combine flour, salt and soda and add to yeast mixture. Add warm milk. Beat well. Cover and let rise until double in size, 1 to 1 1/2 hours. Stir down and put in buttered bread pan sprinkled with cornmeal. Sprinkle top with cornmeal. Cover and let rise 40 to 45 minutes. Bake at 375° for 30 minutes, or until done. Remove from pan and cool. Cut into 1/2 inch thick slices for toast. Butter well.

# HERB BREAD STICKS

1 1/2 tsp. yeast
3/4 cup warm water
1/4 cup Parmesan cheese
3/4 tsp. salt
1/2 tsp. basil

1/2 tsp. oregano
1/4 tsp. pepper
1/8 tsp. garlic powder
1/4 cup cooking oil
2 1/4 to 2 1/2 cups flour

Dissolve yeast in water in a large bowl. Stir in everything but flour. Gradually beat in 1 1/2 cups flour; mix 2 minutes. Stir in remaining flour. Knead with a dough hook 8 minutes or by hand 10 to12 minutes. Cover and let rise until double in size. Punch down and roll into an evenly shaped 10 inch roll. Cut roll into 20 1/2 inch slices. Shape each slice into a stick and place on a greased cookie sheet 1 inch apart. Let rise 20 minutes. Bake at 350° for 20 minutes or until lightly browned.

# SOFT PRETZELS

2 pkg. yeast
1 cup lukewarm water
2 cups milk, scalded
2 T. sugar
2 tsp. salt
7 1/2 cups flour

2 quarts water
1 T. soda
1 egg, beaten
1 T. water
Coarse salt for sprinkling

Dissolve yeast in lukewarm water. Pour scalded milk over sugar and salt in a mixing bowl. Cool to lukewarm. Add yeast and 3 cups flour to milk mixture. Beat on medium for 2 minutes. Stir in remaining flour to make a soft dough. Knead 10 minutes. Place in a greased bowl; turn over and grease on top. Cover; let rise until double in size, about 1 1/2 hours. Divide dough in half. Roll into a 12x10 rectangle. Cut into ten 12-inch strips. Roll each strip into a 20 inch rope and form into pretzels. Place on lightly floured sheet. Let rise 30 minutes. Bring 2 quarts water to a boil and add soda. Add pretzels, 2 at a time. Boil 1 minute, then remove with slotted spoon. Let water drain. Place pretzels on well-greased foil covered sheets. Combine egg and water and brush onto pretzels. Sprinkle with coarse salt. Bake at 400° for 18 minutes.

*Anna Mary Evans, MO*

**Oh many a shaft at random sent, finds mark the archer little meant!
And many a word at random spoken,
May soothe, or wound, a heart that's broken.**

# QUICK BREADS

## CORNBREAD

*For something different, peel and slice about 10 apples; put them into a 13x9 pan; sprinkle with 1 1/2 cups brown sugar and a teaspoon of cinnamon. Pour 1/2 cup water into the pan and top with cornbread batter. Bake at 375° for 45 minutes, or until apples are soft. Serve with milk.*

1 cup yellow cornmeal
1 cup flour
1/4 cup sugar, opt.
4 tsp. baking powder

1/2 tsp. salt
1 cup milk
1 egg
1/4 cup cooking oil

Combine cornmeal, flour, sugar, baking powder and salt. Add milk, egg and oil. Beat until fairly smooth, approximately 1 minute. Don't overbeat. Pour into a greased 8x8 pan or put in muffin tins. Bake at 425° for 20 to 25 minutes.

*Mrs. Isaac Brubaker, Versailles, MO    Mrs. Lloyd Troyer, Stella, MO*

## BLENDER CARROT CORNBREAD

1 medium carrot, peeled and
   sliced
1 egg
1 T. cooking oil
1 cup buttermilk

1 cup yellow cornmeal
1/2 tsp. salt
1/2 tsp. baking powder
1/2 tsp. soda

Lightly grease and flour an 8x8 pan. Place carrot, egg, oil and buttermilk in blender container; cover and process until smooth. Add remaining ingredients and blend briefly to mix. Pour into prepared pan. Bake at 450° approximately 20 minutes.

*Vera Witmer, Goshen, IN*

## CRISP CORN STICKS

2 cups cornmeal
1 tsp. salt
1 1/3 cups boiling water

6 T. melted butter
1 tsp. pepper

Combine cornmeal and salt. Put boiling water in a bowl. Stir in cornmeal mixture, melted butter and pepper. Mix well. With buttered hands divide into 18 equal portions. Shape each portion in a 3 to 4 inch long by 1 inch wide stick. Bake on a greased cookie sheet at 400° for 20 minutes or until lightly browned. Serve warm.

## ONION CHEESE BREAD

| | |
|---|---|
| 1/2 cup chopped onion | 1 1/2 cups biscuit mix |
| 1 T. butter | 1 cup shredded sharp cheese |
| 1/2 cup milk | 2 T. snipped parsley |
| 1 egg, beaten | 2 T. melted butter |

Cook onion in butter until tender but not brown. Combine milk and egg. Add to biscuit mix and stir only until mix is moistened. Add onion and half of the cheese. Add parsley. Spread dough in a greased 8-inch round pan. Sprinkle with remaining cheese. Drizzle melted butter over top. Bake at 400° for 20 to 25 minutes.

*Mrs. James (Margaret) Ramer, Dallas, TX*

## UNLEAVENED BREAD

*One and a half cups half and half or evaporated milk can be used instead of cream and milk.*

| | |
|---|---|
| 5 cups flour | 1 cup butter |
| 2 T. sugar | 1/2 cup cream |
| 1/4 tsp. salt | 1 cup milk |

Mix together dry ingredients; work in butter. Add cream and milk; knead a little. Roll out 1/4 inch thick on 2 greased cookie sheets. Prick with a fork in rows an inch apart. Bake at 250° approximately 45 minutes. Break into strips when cool.

*Mrs. Eli (Dorothy) Yutzy, Sugarcreek, OH*

## APPLE BREAD

| | |
|---|---|
| 1 cup sugar | 1 tsp. baking powder |
| 1/2 cup shortening | 1/2 tsp. soda |
| 2 eggs | 1 tsp. cinnamon |
| 1 1/2 cups grated apples | 3/4 cups chopped pecans or |
| 2 cups flour | walnuts |
| 3/4 tsp. salt | |

Cream sugar and shortening. Beat in eggs. Add apples. Mix dry ingredients and add. Stir in nuts. Pour into a greased loaf pan. Bake at 350° approximately 1 hour. Do not slice until cold.

*Grasp eternal values firmly, and you will hold loosely this world's treasures.*

# APPLESAUCE BREAD

*To make applesauce raisin oatmeal bread use only 1 1/2 cups flour and add 1 cup quick oatmeal and 1 cup raisins.*

| | |
|---|---|
| 1 cup sugar | 1/2 tsp. baking powder |
| 1 cup applesauce | 1/2 tsp. salt |
| 1/3 cup cooking oil | 1 tsp. cinnamon |
| 2 eggs | 1/4 tsp. nutmeg |
| 3 T. milk | 1/4 cup sugar |
| 2 cups flour | 1/2 tsp. cinnamon |
| 1 tsp. soda | |

Beat together sugar, applesauce, oil, eggs and milk. Combine and add all but the last two dry ingredients. Stir only until well blended. Pour into a greased 9x5 loaf pan. Mix together last two ingredients and sprinkle on top. Bake at 350° approximately 1 hour.

# BANANA BREAD

| | |
|---|---|
| 1 cup brown sugar | 2 cups flour |
| 1/2 cup butter | 1 T. baking powder |
| 2 eggs | 1/2 tsp. salt |
| 1 1/2 cups mashed bananas | 1/2 cup finely chopped nuts |

Cream sugar and butter. Beat in eggs one at a time. Stir in bananas. Combine dry ingredients and add. Mix in nuts. Spoon into a greased 9x5 loaf pan. Bake at 350° approximately 1 hour, or until a pick inserted in the center comes out clean. Cool.

# BLUEBERRY PINEAPPLE BREAD

| | |
|---|---|
| 2 cups flour | 2/3 cup sugar |
| 1 tsp. baking powder | 2 eggs |
| 1/2 tsp. soda | 1/4 cup milk |
| 1/2 tsp. salt | 1/2 cup crushed pineapple |
| 1/3 cup coconut | 1 cup fresh blueberries |
| 1/3 cup butter | |

Combine dry ingredients and coconut. Cream butter and sugar until fluffy. Beat in eggs. Add milk and pineapple. Stir in dry ingredients. Fold in blueberries. Pour in a greased 9x5 loaf pan. Bake at 350° approximately 1 hour. Remove from pan to cool.

*Silence can be beautiful and impressive; don't break it unless you can improve it.*

# CRANBERRY NUT BREAD I

4 cups flour
1 1/2 cups sugar
1 T. baking powder
1 tsp. soda
1 tsp. salt
2 eggs, beaten

1 1/2 cups orange juice
1/2 cup cooking oil
2 cups cranberries, halved
1 cup chopped nuts
2 tsp. grated orange peel

Combine dry ingredients in a mixing bowl. Combine eggs, orange juice and oil; add to dry ingredients, stirring until just moistened. Stir in cranberries, nuts and orange peel. Pour into 2 greased and lightly floured 9x5 loaf pans. Bake at 375° for 55 to 60 minutes or until pick inserted in center comes out clean. Remove from pan to cool.

*Connie Rodes, Milford, IN*

# CRANBERRY NUT BREAD II

2 cups whole wheat flour
1/4 cup wheat bran or germ
2 tsp. baking powder
1/2 tsp. soda
1/2 tsp. salt
3/4 cup orange juice

1 T. grated orange rind
1/4 cup cooking oil
3/4 to 1 cup honey
2 cups coarsely chopped
  cranberries, fresh or frozen
1/2 cup chopped walnuts

Combine dry ingredients and stir in remaining ingredients. Do not beat. Divide batter into 2 greased medium loaf pans. Bake at 350° for 50 minutes or until a pick inserted in center comes out clean. Cool before cutting.

*Mrs. Jason (Mary) Martin, Mishawaka, IN*

# DATE NUT BREAD

2 cups boiling water
2 cups chopped dates
1 cup raisins
2 tsp. soda
1/2 cup butter
2 cups sugar

2 eggs
1 tsp. vanilla
4 cups flour
1 tsp. baking powder
1 tsp. salt
1 cup pecans

Mix together water, dates, raisins and soda. Cream together butter, sugar, eggs and vanilla. Stir together flour, baking powder, salt and pecans. Add flour and date mixture alternately to creamed mixture. Pour into 2 greased and floured bread pans. Bake at 350° for 1 hour. Glaze with powdered sugar and orange juice while still warm.

*Roma Jo (Martin) Miller, Goshen, IN*

# PEANUT BUTTER BREAD

1 1/2 cups flour
1 cup sugar
1 T. baking powder
1/2 tsp. salt

1/2 cup peanut butter
1 cup oatmeal
1 egg, beaten
1 cup milk

Combine dry ingredients. Cut in peanut butter. Add oatmeal, egg and milk. Stir only until blended. Pour into an 8 1/2 x 4 1/2 loaf pan. Bake at 350° approximately one hour. Remove from pan and cool.

**Mix quick breads just until dry ingredients are moistened. Fruit and nut quick breads should be removed from the pan to cool and sliced after completely cooled or refrigerated.**

# PUMPKIN BREAD

1 cup cooking oil
1 tsp. nutmeg
1 tsp. cinnamon
1 1/2 tsp. salt
4 eggs

3 cups sugar
1 cup cooked, mashed pumpkin
2/3 cup water
2 tsp. soda
3 cups flour

Beat together oil, spices, salt, eggs and sugar. Add pumpkin, water, soda and flour. Pour into 2 greased loaf pans. Bake at 350° approximately 1 hour.
*Mrs. Elverne Martin, Nappanee, IN*

# ZUCCHINI BREAD I

1 cup cooking oil
1 1/2 to 2 cups sugar
2 to 2 1/2 cups grated zucchini
3 eggs
2 tsp. vanilla
3 cups flour

1 to 3 tsp. cinnamon
1/2 tsp. baking powder
1 tsp. soda
1 tsp. salt
1/2 to 1 cup chopped nuts

Combine oil, sugar, squash, eggs and vanilla. Mix in remaining ingredients and pour into 2 greased and floured loaf pans. Bake at 325° for 1 to 1 1/2 hours. Check after the first hour.
*Rita Martin, Nappanee, IN*      *Mrs. James (Margaret) Ramer, Dallas, Texas*

**Don't worry about tomorrow – God is already there.**

# ZUCCHINI BREAD II

| | |
|---|---|
| 1 2/3 cups flour | 1 1/3 cups sugar |
| 1 tsp. soda | 1/3 cup butter or margarine |
| 3/4 tsp. salt | 1/2 tsp. vanilla |
| 1/2 tsp. cinnamon | 2 eggs |
| 1/2 tsp. nutmeg | 1 cup cooked zucchini |
| 1/2 tsp. ground cloves | 1/4 cup milk |
| 1/4 tsp. baking powder | 1/2 cup walnuts or pecans |

Combine first column. Cream sugar, butter and vanilla. Beat in eggs. Stir in coarsely mashed peeled squash. Add dry ingredients alternately with milk. Do not over beat. Add nuts. Pour into a greased 9x5 pan. Bake at 350° approximately 1 hour.

*Nancy Kilmer, California, MO*

***Look at self and you will be discouraged;***
***Look at others and you will be defeated;***
***Look at Jesus and you will be happy and victorious.***

# ADDITIONAL RECIPES

# DINNER
# ROLLS,
# DOUGHNUTS
## and   SWEET
# ROLLS

Elsie Hoover

# DINNER ROLLS

## DINNER ROLLS

1 pkg. or 1 scant T. yeast
1/4 cup warm water
3/4 cup scalded milk, cooled to
    lukewarm
1/4 cup sugar

1 tsp. salt
1 egg
1/4 cup shortening
3 1/2 cups flour

Dissolve yeast in warm water. Stir in milk, sugar, salt, egg and shortening. Add flour and knead 5 minutes. Let rise 2 hours. Punch down. Form dough into small balls and place in greased pan. Let rise 20 minutes. Bake at 400° for 15 to 20 minutes.

## 60 MINUTE DINNER ROLLS

2 pkg. dry yeast
1/4 cup sugar
1 1/2 cups warm milk

1 tsp. salt
1/4 cup melted butter
4 cups flour

Add yeast and sugar to warm milk and let stand for 15 minutes; stir in remaining ingredients. Stir well; let stand in warm place approximately 20 minutes until double in size. Form into 24 egg-sized rolls. Place on a well-greased cookie sheet. Bake at 375° for 20 minutes.

*Vera Yoder, Crawford, MS*

## REFRIGERATOR ROLLS

*This dough can be kept in the refrigerator about a week.*

2 cups boiling water
1/2 cup sugar
1 T. salt
2 T. shortening
2 eggs, beaten

2 pkg. yeast
1/4 cup warm water
1 tsp. sugar
8 cups flour

Combine first four ingredients; cool to lukewarm. Add eggs. Mix together yeast, water and sugar. Add to first mixture. Add 4 cups flour and beat well. Add rest of flour; mix well. Form into balls; let rise until double. Bake at 400° till golden brown.

*Susan Miller, Nappanee, IN*

# BUTTER ROLLS

1 cup butter or margarine
3/4 cup milk, scalded
1 pkg. yeast
1 tsp. sugar
1/4 cup warm water

2 eggs, beaten
1/2 cup sugar
1 tsp. salt
4 cups flour

Melt butter; add milk and cool until lukewarm. Combine yeast, sugar and warm water. When milk mixture is lukewarm add beaten eggs, yeast mixture, sugar, salt and flour. Mix thoroughly. Refrigerate at least 5 hours. Four hours before baking, divide dough into 3 equal parts and roll each part into a 10-inch circle. Cut each circle into 12 wedges. Roll wedges from large end to small end. Place on baking sheet and let rise 4 hours. Bake at 400° for 10 minutes.

*Charlotte Martin, Goshen, IN*

**Pasteurized milk does not need to be scalded. Scalded or warm milk will, however, help dissolve sugar and melt shortening.**

# BUTTER HORN ROLLS

*To make regular rolls shape into 1-inch balls and place an inch apart in a greased pan. Let rise before baking.*

1 pkg. yeast
1 T. sugar
1/4 cup lukewarm water
1 cup scalded milk
1/3 cup sugar

1/2 cup butter or margarine
3 eggs
1 tsp. salt
4 1/2 to 5 cups flour

Dissolve yeast and sugar in water. Combine scalded milk, 1/3 cup sugar and butter. Cool to lukewarm. After butter is melted add yeast mixture and eggs; beat well. Add salt and enough flour to make a soft, but not sticky, dough. Put in greased bowl. Let rise until double, about 3/4 hour. Knead again; let rise another 3/4 to 1 hour. Roll dough 3/8 inch thick in a 10-inch circle. Cut into pie-shaped wedges and brush with melted butter. Start rolling at the wide end and roll toward center. Place on a greased pan and let rise until light, about 1 hour. Bake at 325° for 15 to 17 minutes or until done. These rolls can be made ahead and frozen. Take out of the freezer ahead of time and warm before serving. Cover and warm up at 325° for 15 to 20 minutes or until good and hot.

*Frances Hoover, Elkhart, IN*

***If you can't change your circumstances, change your attitude.***

# WHEAT ROLLS

1 pkg. yeast
1 1/4 cups warm water
1 tsp. salt
1/4 cup soft butter

2 T. sugar
2 cups wheat flour
1 1/4 cups flour

Dissolve yeast in water. Stir in salt, butter and sugar. Add wheat flour. Gradually work in remaining flour and knead 10 minutes. Let rise in a greased, covered bowl till double in size, about 40 minutes. Punch down and shape into 16 ball and place in a greased 8x8 pan. Cover and let rise about 40 minutes. Bake at 400° approximately 25 minutes.

*Mrs. Ray (Elsie) Hoover, Stratford, WI*

To grind your own wheat, place 1 cup of wheat kernels in a blender with a glass top. With the lid securely in place blend on the highest speed approximately 3 minutes.

# OATMEAL ROLLS

3 pkg. yeast
2/3 cup warm water
3 boiling water
1/2 cup shortening
1/2 cup sugar

1 T. salt
2 cups oatmeal
1 cup flour
2 eggs, beaten
Flour

Soften yeast in warm water. Pour boiling water over shortening, sugar and salt. Stir in oatmeal and flour. Cool to lukewarm and add eggs and the yeast mixture. Beat until elastic. Let rest 20 minutes or until bubbly. Knead in enough flour to make a soft dough. Let rise; punch down. Shape into rolls or buns. Let rise again. Bake at 400° for 10 to 12 minutes.

*Thelma Martin, Osceola, IN*

# HOAGIE BUNS

2 cups lukewarm water
2 T. yeast
1/2 cup sugar
2 tsp. salt

2 eggs
1/2 cup shortening
7 to 7 1/2 cups flour

Dissolve yeast in water. Stir in sugar, salt, eggs and shortening. Gradually stir in flour. Let rise until double. Punch down and shape into buns large enough for hoagies or subs. Place on a greased cookie sheet. Let rise. Bake at 350° for 20 to 30 minutes.

*Ella Horning, Penn Yan, NY*

# DOUGHNUTS and SWEET ROLLS

## FLUFFY RAISED DOUGHNUTS

*To make apple doughnuts use only 1 1/2 cups water and add a tablespoon of yeast. Add 1 cup peeled, shredded apples with the eggs.*

| | |
|---|---|
| 2 cups lukewarm water | 2 eggs, well beaten |
| 1 T. yeast | 2 tsp. salt |
| 1/2 cup cooking oil | Approximately 6 cups flour |
| 1/2 cup sugar | |

Dissolve yeast in water. Add oil, sugar, eggs and salt. Beat in 2 cups flour. Let rise 30 minutes. Work in enough of remaining flour to make a workable dough. Knead until smooth. Let rise till double in size. Pat dough - do not roll - about 1/2-inch thick. Cut into doughnuts. Let rise. Fry in 375° fat, deep enough so doughnuts float. This recipe can also be used for sticky buns.

*Mrs. Ivan Zimmerman, Scottsville, KY*

## MASHED POTATO DOUGHNUTS

| | |
|---|---|
| 4 cups milk | 3/4 cup warm water |
| 2 cups mashed potatoes | 1 tsp. sugar |
| 1 cup shortening | 2 eggs, beaten |
| 1 cup sugar | 1 tsp. salt |
| 3 T. yeast | 9 to 11 cups flour |

Scald milk. Add potatoes, shortening and sugar. Cool. Dissolve yeast in water and one teaspoon sugar. Add to lukewarm milk mixture. Add eggs and salt. Work in flour. Let rise till double in size. Roll out 1/2 inch thick. Cut into doughnuts or 3 1/2 x 1 1/2 inch rectangles and let rise till light. Deep-fry at 375° until golden brown. Cool. Sugar, glaze, or fill.

*Mrs. James Horst, East Earl, PA*

## DOUGHNUT FILLING I

| | |
|---|---|
| 1 cup shortening | 1 cup marshmallow crème |
| 1 cup butter or margarine | Enough milk to mix |
| 4 to 5 cups powdered sugar | |

Mix well. Fill doughnuts by cutting in half; or insert a knife into the short end of the rectangle and fill with a filling filled pastry tube.

*Mrs. James Horst, East Earl, PA*

# DOUGHNUT FILLING II

3 T. flour
1 cup milk
1 cup sugar

1 cup solid shortening
1 tsp. vanilla
2 1/2 cups powdered sugar

Cook flour and milk together. Cool. Cream sugar and shortening; add flour mixture and vanilla. Cream well. Add powdered sugar.

*Lena Martin, New Paris, IN*

# CREAM STICKS

2 T. yeast
1 cup warm water
1 cup scalded milk, cooled to
    lukewarm
2/3 cup sugar

1/2 tsp. salt
1/2 cup butter or margarine
2 eggs, beaten
1 tsp. vanilla
6 cups flour

Dissolve yeast in water. Add remaining ingredients, except flour. Mix well. Stir flour in gradually. Let dough rise till double in size; punch down. Knead and form into 1 1/2 x 3 1/2-inch rectangles. Let rise. Deep-fry at 375° until golden brown. Cool and fill with one of the previous fillings. Frost with your favorite frosting or make caramel frosting by bringing 1/2 cup brown sugar, 2 T. milk, and 1/4 cup butter to a boil. Cool; add powdered sugar to the right consistency. Add 1/2 tsp vanilla.

*Lena Martin, New Paris, IN*

**Raisins, chopped pecans or other nuts, or finely chopped apples may be sprinkled on cinnamon roll dough along with sugar.**

# CINNAMON ROLLS

1/2 cup butter or margarine
1 tsp. salt
1 cup boiling water
2 pkg. yeast

1 cup lukewarm water
1/2 cup sugar
2 eggs, beaten
6 cups bread flour

Combine butter, salt, and boiling water; let stand till lukewarm. Dissolve yeast in lukewarm water. Beat eggs and sugar; add yeast and butter mixtures. Work in flour. Let rise till double in size two times. Roll out dough about 1/2-inch thick. Spread with soft butter then sprinkle with sugar and cinnamon. Nuts or raisins can be added. Roll up; cut into 1-inch slices and place in greased pans. Let rise. Bake at 375° for 15 minutes. Frost while still warm.

*Mrs. Luke Hoover, Goshen, IN*

***Life is God's gift to you. The way you live your life is your gift to God.***

## CINNAMON ROLLS with CARAMEL FROSTING

| | |
|---|---|
| 3 T. yeast | 2 tsp. salt |
| 1/2 cup warm water | 11 to 12 cups flour |
| 1 cup butter or margarine | 1 cup butter or margarine |
| 3 cups milk, scalded | 2 cups brown sugar |
| 5 eggs | 2/3 cup milk |
| 1 cup sugar | Powdered sugar |

Dissolve yeast in warm water. Put butter in milk after it is scalded. Set aside until lukewarm. Beat eggs and sugar. Add salt and yeast and milk mixtures. Work in flour. The dough will be sticky. Let rise until double in size. Punch down and roll out about 1/2 inch thick. Spread with soft butter if desired then sprinkle with sugar and cinnamon. Cut into 1-inch slices. Place into greased pans and let rise until about double in size. To make frosting, melt remaining cup of butter. Add brown sugar and milk, heating just enough to dissolve sugar. Cool without stirring; add powdered sugar.

*Mrs. James Kulp, Unity, WI*

## CINNAMON ROLLS with BROWN BUTTER FROSTING

*This big batch allows for plenty of rolls for the freezer, but the recipe can easily be cut in half if you don't want so many.*

| | |
|---|---|
| 8 pkg. or 7 T. yeast | Approximately 28 cups flour |
| 2 cups warm water | 8 eggs |
| 8 cups milk, scalded | 1/2 cup butter, browned |
| 2 cups sugar | 1/2 cup hot water |
| 2 cups shortening | 1 1/2 tsp. vanilla |
| 8 tsp. salt | Powdered sugar |

Dissolve yeast in warm water. Combine milk, sugar, shortening and salt. Cool to lukewarm. Add 10 to 12 cups flour and beat well. Add yeast and eggs. Gradually add remaining flour, (part wheat flour may be used) kneading to a soft elastic dough. Cover and let rise till double in size. Divide dough in smaller portions; press out on greased and floured surface in a rectangular shape. Spread with soft or melted butter. Sprinkle liberally with sugar and cinnamon. Roll up like a jellyroll but do not roll so tightly that centers pop up when baking. Cut into 3/4-inch slices. Place cut rolls in greased pans. Let rise until about double in size. Bake at 350° until golden brown. Remove from pans and cool. To make frosting brown the butter; remove from heat and mix in remaining ingredients, adding powdered sugar to the desired consistency.

*Alta Martin, Goshen, IN*

***Things turn out best for the people who make the best of the way things turn out.*** *Art Linkletter*

## POTATO CINNAMON ROLLS

2 cups lukewarm water
2 pkg. yeast
4 cups flour
2 cups cooked, mashed potatoes
5 eggs, beaten

1 cup lard
1 cup sugar
6 cups flour
1 T. salt

Mix water and yeast and let stand 10 minutes. Add 4 cups flour and let stand 1 hour. Add remaining ingredients. Let rise 2 hours. Roll out 1/2-inch thick and spread with soft or melted butter. Sprinkle liberally with sugar and cinnamon. Roll up and cut into 3/4 to 1-inch slices. Put in buttered pans, 1/2 inch apart. Let rise until double. Bake at 350° for 15 to 20 minutes or until done. Cool slightly then glaze or frost.

*Mrs. Aaron Weaver, Penn Yan, NY*

**A scant tablespoon of bulk yeast can be substituted for a package of yeast.**

## MAPLE ROLLS

2 T. yeast
1/4 cup warm water
3/4 cup milk
1/3 cup butter or margarine
1 tsp. salt
2 eggs, beaten
1/2 tsp. maple flavoring
1/4 cup sugar

3 1/2 to 4 cups flour
2/3 cup nuts
1/3 cup sugar
1 1/2 tsp. maple flavoring
1 tsp. cinnamon
1 1/2 cups powdered sugar
3 T. milk
Maple flavoring

Dissolve yeast in warm water. Scald milk; add butter and cool to lukewarm. Add salt, eggs, flavoring, sugar, and yeast mixture. Gradually add flour. Work dough together. Let rise to double in size, 45 to 60 minutes. Divide dough into thirds. Roll each third into a 12-inch circle. Place one third on a greased 12-inch pizza pan. Combine nuts, sugar, flavoring and cinnamon and put half onto the dough in the pan. Repeat with another circle of dough and remaining filling. Top with last circle of dough. Mark, but don't cut, a 2-inch circle in the middle, then cut from the outside edge to the circle, making 16 pie shaped wedges. Leave on the pan; twist each wedge 5 times. Let rise till double in size, about 30 to 45 minutes. Bake at 325° for 20 minutes or until done. Combine remaining ingredients and frost while warm.

*Velma Martin, Nappanee, IN*

# BUTTER PECAN KRINGLE

| | |
|---|---|
| 2 cups flour | 1/2 cup butter |
| 1 pkg. yeast | 1 egg |
| 2 T. sugar | 1/2 cup brown sugar |
| 1/2 tsp. salt | 1/4 cup butter |
| 1/2 cup milk | 1/2 tsp. cinnamon |
| 1/4 cup water | 1 cup chopped pecans |

Combine 1 cup flour, yeast, sugar and salt in a large bowl. Heat milk, water and butter until very warm. Add to flour mixture. Add egg. Beat on low speed until moistened then beat 3 minutes at medium speed. Gradually add remaining flour, stirring by hand if necessary. Refrigerate 2 to 24 hours. Punch down. Divide into two parts and roll each into an 18x6 rectangle. Combine remaining ingredients and spread a 3-inch strip down the center of each rectangle. Fold one long side of dough into center, then the other side, overlapping dough about 1 1/2 inches. Pinch edge and ends to seal. Place seam side down on a greased cookie sheet. Form into a horseshoe shape or circle if desired. Cover and let rise until light and puffy. Bake at 350° for 20 minutes or until golden brown. Cool. Sprinkle with powdered sugar, frost or eat plain.

# STICKY BUNS

*For individual buns, put a scant tablespoon of liquid into 24 muffin cups and top with a tablespoon of batter. Place muffin tins on foil or on a cookie sheets to catch any spills. Cool slightly then invert baked buns on serving platters.*

| | |
|---|---|
| 1 1/2 cups flour | 1 3/4 cups flour |
| 2 T. yeast | 3/4 cup butter |
| 3/4 cup milk | 1 cup brown sugar |
| 1/2 cup water | 1 tsp. cinnamon |
| 1/4 cup butter or margarine | 1 cup chopped nuts |
| 1/4 cup sugar | 1 T. corn syrup |
| 1 tsp. salt | 1 T. water |
| 1 egg | |

Mix 1 1/2 cups flour and yeast; set aside. Heat milk, water, butter, sugar, and salt. Add to flour and yeast. Add egg and beat 3 minutes. Add rest of flour; cover for 30 minutes. Combine remaining ingredients and heat. Pour into three 8-inch round pans. Drop 7 spoonfuls of dough into each pan. Let rise until double. Bake at 375° for 15 minutes or till light brown.

*Edna Miller, Snover, MI*

# APPLE ROLLS

2 T. butter
1/2 cup sugar
1 tsp. cinnamon
1 apple, sliced thin
Raisins
1 T. yeast

3/4 cup warm water
1/4 cup sugar
1 tsp salt
2 1/4 cups flour
1 egg
1/4 cup shortening

Melt butter in a 9x9 pan; mix 1/2 cup sugar and cinnamon and sprinkle over butter; add apple and raisins. Mix together yeast, water, 1/4 cup sugar, salt and 1 cup flour. Beat 2 minutes; add egg, shortening and 1 1/4 cups flour. Drop by spoonfuls over apples; cover pan. Let rise till double. Bake at 350° for 30 to 35 minutes. Immediately remove from pan by turning upside down.

*Edna Miller, Snover, MI*

# BUTTERSCOTCH ROLLS

1/2 cup brown sugar
1/2 cup butter, melted
36 pecan halves

Cinnamon
2 cups biscuit mix
1/2 cup cold water

Place 2 teaspoons brown sugar, 2 teaspoons butter and 3 pecan halves in each of 12 muffin cups. Sprinkle cinnamon in each. Mix biscuit mix and water; beat vigorously 20 strokes. Divide into muffin cups. Bake at 450° for 10 minutes. Invert onto platter and leave pan over rolls a few minutes.

*Mrs. LaVerne (Virginia) Hoover, Goshen, IN*

# QUICK ROLLS

2 pkg. yeast
2 1/2 cups warm water
1 box yellow cake mix

1/2 tsp. salt
2 eggs, beaten
5 to 6 cups flour

Dissolve yeast in water. Add cake mix, salt and eggs. Gradually mix in flour. Let rise 1 hour. Roll out and cut into rolls. Let rise until double in size. Bake at 350° for 15 minutes. These rolls bake fast.

*Mrs. Elvin (Mary) Hoover, Goshen, IN*

**God made you as you are in order to use you as He planned.**

## PULL-APART ROLLS

1 pkg. yeast
1 1/2 cups warm water
2 T. sugar
1 tsp. salt
1 T. shortening

4 cups flour
1 cup sugar
2 T. cinnamon
1/2 cup butter or margarine

Dissolve yeast in warm water. Add sugar, salt and shortening. Gradually add flour. Mix well. Let rise until double in size. Punch down and divide into fourths, then divide each fourth into 7 balls. Combine sugar and cinnamon. Dip balls into melted butter and roll into cinnamon mixture. Stack lightly into an angel food cake pan. Let rise till double in size again. Bake at 350° for 40 minutes.

*Ada Mae Miller, Nappanee, IN*

## QUICK PULL-APART ROLLS

4 cans (10 to a can) refrigerated
    biscuits
3/4 cup sugar
1 1/2 tsp. cinnamon

1/2 cup nuts
3/4 cup butter
1 cup sugar
1 1/4 tsp. cinnamon

Cut each biscuit in quarters. Combine 3/4 cup sugar and 1 1/2 teaspoon cinnamon. Shake biscuits in cinnamon. Stack biscuits lightly in a bundt pan or an angel food cake pan lined with wax paper on bottom. Sprinkle with nuts. In a small pan combine remaining ingredients and bring to a boil. Pour over biscuits in the pan. Bake at 350° for 40 to 50 minutes. Turn out on a plate when done.

*Mrs. Larry Zimmerman, Elkhart, IN*

***Parenting is the art of bringing children up
without putting them down.***

# BISCUITS and MUFFINS

# BISCUITS

Mix biscuits just enough to moisten dry ingredients.  Knead briefly - about 30 seconds - before cutting.  Place biscuits an inch apart for crusty biscuits and closer together for softer ones.

## BISCUITS

2 cups flour
4 tsp. baking powder
1/2 tsp salt

3 T. shortening
3/4 cup milk

Combine dry ingredients.  Cut in shortening; add milk.  Roll 1/2-inch thick and cut with a biscuit cutter or add a little more milk and make drop biscuits.  Bake at 450° for 12 minutes.  Eat with butter and jam, or gravy.

*Mrs. Phillip Zimmerman, Versailles, MO*

## STIR AND ROLL BISCUITS

2 cups flour
1 tsp. salt
1 T. baking powder

1/3 cup cooking oil
2/3 cup milk

Mix flour, salt and baking powder.  Add milk to oil, then add to dry ingredients.  Mix well with fork.  Knead slightly.  Roll out and cut into biscuits.  Bake at 400° for 10 to 15 minutes.

*Mrs. Vernon Kurtz, Ewing, IL*

## SOUTHERN RAISED BISCUITS

*To freeze these biscuits bake 5 minutes; cool.  Wrap in foil and freeze.  To serve, thaw and bake at 450° for 7 to 10 minutes.*

2 pkg. yeast
1/4 cup warm water
2 cups buttermilk
5 cups flour
1/3 cup sugar

1 T. baking powder
1 tsp. soda
2 tsp. salt
1 cup shortening

Dissolve yeast in water.  Add buttermilk and set aside.  Combine dry ingredients in a large bowl.  Cut in shortening.  Add buttermilk mixture, mixing with a fork until dry ingredients are moistened.  Knead dough lightly for a minute or two; add flour if needed.  Roll dough 1/2-inch; cut with biscuit cutter and place on lightly greased baking sheet.  Cover and let rise 1 hour.  Bake at 450° for 10 to12 minutes.

*Mrs. John (Twila) Kulp, Mosinee, WI*

# SOUTHERN BISCUITS

2 cups flour
1 T. baking powder
1 tsp. salt
2 T. sugar

1/2 cup shortening
1 egg
2/3 cup milk

Mix dry ingredients and shortening until crumbly. Beat together egg and milk; add. Drop on cookie sheet or knead and cut into squares. Bake at 400° approximately 12 minutes.

# ANGEL BISCUITS

*This biscuit dough keeps a while in the refrigerator.*

1 pkg. yeast
1/2 cup lukewarm water
5 cups flour
1 T. baking powder
1 tsp. soda

1 tsp. salt
3 T. sugar
3/4 cup shortening
2 cups buttermilk

Dissolve yeast in water. Combine dry ingredients. Cut shortening in thoroughly. Add buttermilk and yeast mixture. Mix with spoon until all flour is moistened. Cover and refrigerate. Use as needed. Roll 1/2 to 3/4 inch thick on a floured surface. Cut. Bake at 400° for 10 to 12 minutes.

*Velma Martin, Nappanee, IN*

# BUTTER DIP BISCUITS

1/3 cup butter
2 1/4 cups flour
1 T. sugar

3 1/2 tsp. baking powder
1 tsp. salt
1 cup milk

Melt butter in a 12x8 pan. Mix rest of ingredients; roll out 1/4-inch thick. Cut into squares and dip in melted butter. Bake at 450° for 15 to 20 minutes.

*Laura Kulp, Stratford, WI*

# CHEESE BISCUITS

2 cups flour
1 T. baking powder
1/2 tsp. salt

3/4 cup shredded cheese
1/3 cup shortening
3/4 cup milk

Mix dry ingredients and add cheese. Mix in shortening. Add milk. Knead dough gently 10 times. Pat or roll dough 1/2 to 3/4-inch thick. Cut with a floured biscuit cutter or cut into squares. Bake 1 inch apart for crusty biscuits and together for soft biscuits. Bake at 425° for 15 minutes.

## CORNMEAL BISCUITS

*To make oatmeal biscuits substitute oatmeal for cornmeal.*

1 1/2 cups flour
1 T. baking powder
1/2 tsp. salt

1/3 cup shortening
1/4 cup cornmeal
2/3 cup milk

Mix flour, baking powder and salt. Cut in shortening. Stir in cornmeal and milk. Knead dough a few seconds on a floured surface. Pat dough to 1/2-inch thickness. Cut into squares. Bake on an ungreased cookie sheet at 425° for 12-15 minutes.

*Thelma Martin, Osceola, IN*

## WHOLE WHEAT BISCUITS

*For a special treat, spread biscuits with apple butter before baking. Fold both sides in toward the middle. For cottage cheese biscuits reduce milk to 1/2 cup and knead 1 cup cottage cheese into dough.*

2 cups whole wheat flour
1/4 cup wheat germ
4 tsp. baking powder
1/2 tsp. salt

1/4 cup cooking oil
1 T. honey or molasses
Approximately 2/3 cup milk

Combine dry ingredients. Stir in oil until mixture is crumbly. Add honey and enough milk to make a soft dough. Roll dough 1/2-inch thick and cut into 2-inch squares or circles. Place on an oiled cookie sheet with sides touching for tender crusts; place an inch apart for crusty crusts. Bake at 425° for 15 minutes or until browned.

*Hannah Kulp Family, Mt. Hermon, KY*

## WHOLE GRAIN BISCUITS

3 cups whole grain mix (see
   following recipe)

1 cup water (or milk, if no milk in
   mix)

Combine in bowl just until moist. Drop by spoonfuls onto greased baking sheet. Bake at 425° for 10 to 12 minutes or until golden brown.

*Rhoda Schultz, West Salem, OH*

# WHOLE GRAIN BISCUIT MIX

*To use the entire mix at once, add 2 1/2 to 3 cups liquid.*

2 cups wheat flour
2 cups flour
1 cup oat bran
3/4 cup nonfat dry milk

3 T. baking powder
1 tsp. salt
1 cup shortening

Combine flours, oat bran, milk powder, baking powder and salt; mix well. Cut in shortening. Store in a tightly covered container. Keeps up to 2 weeks at room temperature or several months in the refrigerator. Milk powder can be omitted and milk added instead of water in the recipe.

*Rhoda Schultz, West Salem, OH*

# BISCUIT MIX

5 lb. flour
2 1/2 cups powdered milk
3/4 cup baking powder
2 tsp. cream of tartar

2/3 cup sugar
3 T. salt
2 lb. solid vegetable shortening

Combine all ingredients; mix well. Store in tight container. Keeps longer if refrigerated. Use with any recipe that calls for biscuit mix.

*Mrs. Norman Burkholder, Mertztown, PA*

# MUFFINS

The secret for making tender muffins is to add the beaten liquid ingredients to well-mixed dry ingredients with as few strokes as possible. Overmixing causes muffins to be tough, coarse textured and full of tunnels. Be sure, as with all our recipes, to preheat the oven. Always use baking cups or well-greased tins when making muffins. Fill muffin cups 2/3 to 3/4 full. These muffin recipes will make a dozen muffins unless stated otherwise. Muffins left in the tin a few minutes after baking will come out easier, but don't wait too long – muffins are definitely best if eaten warm.

# APPLE MUFFINS

*To make apple raisin muffins add 1/2 cup raisins with dry ingredients.*

1 cup peeled, chopped apples
1/4 cup sugar
1 3/4 cups flour
2 T. sugar
1 T. baking powder

1/2 tsp. salt
1/2 tsp. cinnamon
1 egg
1 cup milk
1/4 cup cooking oil

Mix apples and sugar; set aside. Combine dry ingredients. Beat egg; add milk and oil; add to dry ingredients. Stir in apples. Bake at 425° for 20 to 25 minutes.

*Mrs. Ray (Elsie) Hoover, Stratford, WI*

## APPLE BRAN MUFFINS

1 cup wheat bran
1 cup buttermilk
1 1/2 cups wheat flour
2 tsp. baking powder
1 unpeeled apple, grated

1/2 cup raisins
1 egg
1/3 cup cooking oil
2 T. molasses
1 1/2 tsp. vanilla

Soak bran in buttermilk 10 minutes. Combine dry ingredients, apple and raisins. Beat egg; add oil, molasses, and vanilla. Add bran mixture to dry ingredients then add egg mixture. Bake at 375° for 20 to 25 minutes.

*Vera Witmer, Goshen, IN*

## APPLESAUCE CORNMEAL MUFFINS

*For applesauce oatmeal muffins, substitute 1 1/2 cups oatmeal for cornmeal.*

1 1/4 cups flour
3/4 cup cornmeal
1/3 cup sugar
2 tsp. baking powder
1/2 tsp. soda
1 tsp. cinnamon

1/2 tsp. salt
1 egg
1 cup applesauce
1/3 cup milk
1/4 cup cooking oil

Combine dry ingredients. Beat egg; add remaining ingredients and stir into dry ingredients. Bake at 425° for 15 to 20 minutes.

*Mrs. Ray (Elsie) Hoover, Stratford, WI*

## BANANA CRUMB MUFFINS

1 1/2 cups flour
1/2 cup sugar
1 tsp. baking powder
1 tsp. soda
1/2 tsp. salt
1 egg

3/4 cup mashed banana
1/3 cup melted butter
1/3 cup brown sugar
1 T. flour
1 T. butter
1/4 tsp. cinnamon

Combine dry ingredients. Beat egg; mix in banana and butter; stir into dry ingredients. Spoon into a greased muffin tin. Combine remaining ingredients and sprinkle on top. Bake at 375° for 20 minutes or until muffins are done.

# BLUEBERRY MUFFINS

*For blueberry oatmeal muffins delete 1 cup flour and add 1 cup oatmeal.*

3 cups flour
1 cup sugar
4 tsp. baking powder
1 tsp. salt

2 eggs
1 cup milk
1/2 cup cooking oil
2 cups blueberries

Combine dry ingredients. Beat eggs; add milk and oil. Stir into dry ingredients. Fold in blueberries. Bake at 375° for 25 minutes. Makes 2 dozen.

*Mrs. James Kulp, Unity, WI*

# BRAN MUFFINS

2 cups wheat flour
1 1/2 cups unprocessed bran
1/2 tsp. salt
1 1/4 tsp. soda
1 egg

2 cups buttermilk
1/2 cup molasses
2 T. honey
2 T. melted butter

Combine dry ingredients. Beat egg; add buttermilk, molasses, honey and butter. Stir into dry ingredients. Bake at 350° for 20 to 25 minutes. Makes two dozen.

*Mrs. James Kulp, Unity, WI*

# BRAN CEREAL MUFFINS

*To make high fiber bran muffins delete bran flakes and add 2 cups 100% bran cereal.*
*Add an extra 1/4 cup of milk.*

2 1/2 cups bran flake cereal
1 cup milk
1 cup flour
1/3 cup brown sugar
2 tsp. baking powder

1/2 tsp. soda
1/2 tsp. salt
1 egg
1/3 cup cooking oil

Stir together cereal and milk and let stand 5 minutes. Combine dry ingredients. Beat egg; add oil. Stir egg mixture into cereal mixture, then into dry ingredients. Bake at 400° approximately 20 minutes.

*Laura Kulp, Stratford, WI*

*If wisdom's ways you'd wisely seek,*
*Five things observe with care,*
*Of whom you speak, to whom you speak,*
*And how, and when, and where.*

# REFRIGERATOR BRAN MUFFINS

*Six cups All-Bran can be used instead of raisin bran. Soften All-Bran with 2 cups boiling water; cool before adding. Decrease sugar to 1 1/2 cups and add a cup of raisins.*

3 cups wheat flour
2 cups flour
3 cups sugar or brown sugar
5 tsp. soda
2 tsp. salt

15 oz. box or 7 cups raisin bran
   cereal
4 eggs
4 cups buttermilk
1 cup cooking oil

Combine dry ingredients and cereal. All white flour can be used. Beat eggs; add buttermilk and cooking oil; stir into dry ingredients. This batter keeps quite a while if stored in a covered container in the refrigerator. Bake at 350° until done.

*Marian Hooley, Elkhart, IN    Mrs. LaVerne Hoover, Goshen, IN    Mrs. Luke Hoover, Goshen, IN*

# CHEESE MUFFINS

1 3/4 cups flour
1/2 cup cornmeal
2 T. sugar
1 T. baking powder
2 T. dry onion soup mix

1/2 tsp. salt
3/4 cup shredded cheese
1 egg
1 cup milk
1/4 cup melted butter

Combine dry ingredients and stir in cheese. Beat egg; add milk and melted butter. Bake at 400° approximately 20 minutes.

# CHOCOLATE CHIP MUFFINS

1 1/2 cups flour
1/2 cup sugar
1 T. baking powder
1/4 tsp. salt

1 egg
1 cup milk
1/3 cup melted butter
1 cup chocolate chips

Combine dry ingredients. Beat egg; add milk and oil. Stir into dry ingredients. Mix in chocolate chips. Bake at 375° for 20 minutes or until done.

*Doreen Zimmerman, Claypool, IN*

# CORNMEAL MUFFINS

1 1/4 cups flour
1 cup cornmeal
1/4 cup sugar
1 T. baking powder

1 tsp. salt
2 eggs
1 cup milk
1/4 cup melted butter

Combine dry ingredients. Beat eggs; add milk and butter; add to dry ingredients. Bake at 400° approximately 20 minutes. A cup of drained corn may be added.

# GINGERBREAD MUFFINS

| | |
|---|---|
| 2 cups wheat pastry flour | 1 egg |
| 1 tsp. baking powder | 1 cup water |
| 1 tsp. soda | 2/3 cup honey |
| 1 T. ground ginger | 1/3 cup blackstrap molasses |
| 1 1/2 tsp. cinnamon | 1/3 cup cooking oil |
| 1/2 tsp. ground cloves | 3/4 cup oatmeal |

Combine dry ingredients. Beat egg; add remaining liquids. Stir into dry ingredients. Stir in oatmeal. Bake at 350° for 15 or till done. Makes 16 muffins.

*Hannah Kulp Family, Mt. Hermon, KY*

# MORNING GLORY MUFFINS

| | |
|---|---|
| 1 cup wheat flour | 1/2 cup nuts |
| 1 cup flour | 1/2 cup coconut |
| 1 1/4 cups sugar | 1 apple, peeled and grated |
| 2 tsp. soda | 3 eggs |
| 1/2 tsp. salt | 1 cup cooking oil |
| 2 cups grated carrots | 2 tsp. vanilla |
| 1/2 cup raisins | |

Combine dry ingredients. Add carrots, raisins, nuts, coconut, and apple. Beat eggs; add oil and vanilla. Stir into first mixture. Bake at 350° for 20 minutes or until done. Makes 16 muffins.

*Vera Witmer, Goshen, IN*

Do not overmix muffins. Add liquids to dry ingredients and stir only until moistened. Also be sure to grease muffin tins or to use baking cups. Keep in mind too, that all baking times given, are for a preheated oven. These recipes make one dozen muffins unless otherwise noted; the amount, however, will vary according to the size of muffins.

# OATMEAL RAISIN MUFFINS

| | |
|---|---|
| 1 cup flour | 1/2 tsp. soda |
| 1 cup oatmeal | 1/2 tsp. salt |
| 1/3 cup brown sugar | 1 egg |
| 1/2 tsp. cinnamon | 3/4 cup milk |
| 1/4 tsp. nutmeg | 1/4 cup cooking oil |
| 2 tsp. baking powder | 1/2 to 1 cup raisins |

Combine dry ingredients. Beat egg; add milk, oil and raisins. Stir into dry ingredients. Bake at 400° approximately 20 minutes.

*Mrs. Ray (Elsie) Hoover, Stratford, WI     Lucy Nolt, Fortuna, MO*

# ORANGE DATE MUFFINS
*Delete dates for delicious orange muffins.*

1 whole orange
1/2 cup orange juice
1/2 cup dates or raisins
1 egg
1/4 to 1/2 cup butter

1 1/2 cups flour
3/4 cup sugar
1 tsp soda
1 tsp. baking powder
1/2 tsp. salt

Cut orange into pieces; remove seeds. Blend pieces in the blender with orange juice until finely chopped. Drop in dates, egg and butter. Blend briefly. Combine dry ingredients; mix in orange mixture. Bake at 375° for 15 to 20 minutes.
*Diane Bauman, Listowel, Ontario, Canada*

# PEACH MUFFINS

2 cups flour
2/3 cup sugar
1 T. baking powder
1/2 tsp. salt
1/4 tsp. cinnamon
1 egg

1 cup milk
1/4 shortening, melted
1 tsp. lemon juice
1/4 tsp. vanilla
1 cup diced peeled peaches

Combine dry ingredients. Beat egg; add everything but peaches. Stir into flour mixture. Fold in peaches. Bake at 400° for 15 minutes. Makes 15 muffins.
*Diane Bauman, Listowel, Ontario, Canada*

# PEANUT BUTTER BANANA MUFFINS

2 cups wheat pastry flour
1 tsp baking powder
1/3 tsp. salt
1/3 cup chopped, roasted peanuts
1/3 cup currants
1/2 cup peanut butter

1/3 cup soft butter
1/2 cup mashed banana
1/2 cup milk
1/4 cup honey
2 eggs

Combine dry ingredients, peanuts and currants. Cream peanut butter and butter; beat in remaining ingredients. Stir into dry ingredients. Bake at 375° approximately 20 minutes.
*Hannah Kulp Family, Mt. Hermon, KY*

***God has a thousand ways where I can see not one;***
***When all my means have reached their end***
***Then His have just begun.*** *E. Guyot*

53

## PINEAPPLE MUFFINS

2 cups flour
1/2 cup sugar
2 tsp. baking powder
3/4 tsp salt
1 egg

1/2 cup milk
1/2 cup butter, melted
8 oz. undrained crushed
   pineapple

Combine dry ingredients. Beat egg; add remaining ingredients. Stir into dry ingredients. Bake at 400° approximately 20 minutes.

## PINEAPPLE CARROT MUFFINS

1 1/2 cups flour
1/2 tsp. salt
1 tsp. baking powder
1 tsp. soda
2/3 cup sugar
1 tsp. cinnamon

2/3 cup cooking oil
2 eggs
1/2 cup crushed pineapple with
   juice
1 tsp. vanilla
1 cup finely grated carrots

Combine dry ingredients. Beat egg; add remaining ingredients. Stir into dry ingredients. Bake at 375° approximately 25 minutes.

## POPPY SEED MUFFINS

2 cups flour
3/4 cup sugar
1 tsp. baking powder
1 tsp. soda
1/2 tsp. salt
1 cup sour cream

1/2 cup cooking oil
2 eggs
2 T. poppy seed
3 T. milk or lemon juice
2 tsp. lemon extract

Combine dry ingredients. Combine remaining ingredients. Mix well and add to dry ingredients, stirring just until moistened. Spoon into greased muffin tins. Bake at 400° approximately 15 minutes.

## SOUR CREAM MUFFINS

1 egg
1/4 cup milk
1 cup sour cream
2 T. melted butter
2 cups flour

1/4 cup sugar
1/2 tsp. salt
1/2 tsp. soda
2 tsp. baking powder

Beat egg; add milk, sour cream and butter. Combine dry ingredients; add to other mixture. Do not over mix. Bake at 375° for 15 to 20 minutes.

*Mrs. Isaac Kulp, Millersburg, IN*

## WHEAT MUFFINS

*No buttermilk? Just use milk. Delete soda and add a tablespoon of baking powder.*

1 egg
1 cup buttermilk
1/4 cup shortening
1 1/2 cups wheat flour

1/2 cup flour
1/2 cup brown sugar
1 tsp. soda
1/2 tsp. salt

Beat egg; add buttermilk and shortening. Combine and add dry ingredients. Bake at 400° for 15 to 20 minutes. Good with fruit and milk.

*Magdalena Weaver, Goshen, IN*

## WHEAT RYE MUFFINS

1 egg
1 cup cream (or half cream and
    half shortening)
1 cup wheat flour

1 cup rye flour
1/4 cup sugar
2 tsp. baking powder
1 tsp. salt

Beat egg; add cream. Combine and add dry ingredients. Bake at 375° approximately 30 minutes. If sour cream is used add a teaspoon of soda.

*Mrs. Harvey Mazelin, Cincinnati, IA*

## ZUCCHINI OATMEAL MUFFINS

2 1/2 cups flour
1 1/2 cups sugar
1/2 cup oatmeal
1 T. baking powder
1 tsp. salt

1 tsp. cinnamon
1 cup chopped pecans
4 eggs
1 medium zucchini, shredded
3/4 cup cooking oil

Combine dry ingredients and pecans. Beat eggs; add zucchini and oil. Stir egg mixture into dry ingredients. Bake at 400° for 25 minutes.

*Charlotte Martin, Goshen, IN*

***Beware! The speck you see in your brother's eye may be the reflection of the plank in your own.***

# HONEY POPOVERS

1 cup flour
1 tsp. salt
1 T. butter, melted

3/4 cup milk
2 T. honey
2 large eggs

Combine flour and salt. Add melted butter, milk and honey. Beat in eggs. Fill greased muffin cups less than half full. Bake at 425° for 30 minutes.

*Laura Hoover Martin, Ephrata, PA*

# RYE POPOVERS

2 eggs, beaten
1 cup milk
1 T. cooking oil

1/4 tsp. salt
1 cup rye flour

Mix eggs, milk, oil and salt; beat until smooth. Beat in flour. Put in a greased popover pan. Bake at 500° for 10 minutes then at 350° for 20 minutes longer.

*Ruth Weaver, Nappanee, IN*

# SNACKS
## and
# BEVERAGES

# SNACKS

## FINGER JELLO

9 oz. flavored gelatin
1/4 cup unflavored gelatin

4 cups boiling water

Mix flavored and unflavored gelatin. Add boiling water. Stir until gelatin is completely dissolved. Pour into an oiled 13x9 pan. Fruit juice brought to a boil can be used for part or all of the water. Chill until set.

## CREAMY FINGER JELLO

12 oz. flavored gelatin
2 1/2 cups boiling water
1 cup milk

3.4 oz. pkg. instant vanilla
pudding

Dissolve gelatin in water, set aside for 30 minutes. Whisk milk and pudding about 1 minute. Add to gelatin; mix well. Pour into an oiled 13x9 pan. Chill. Cut into squares or shapes.

*Kendra Witmer, Abbotsford, WI*

## PERKY POPCORN

Cover bottom of a kettle 1/8-inch deep with cooking oil. Use enough popcorn to cover bottom of the kettle 1 grain deep. Stir or shake while popcorn is popping. Remove from heat and sprinkle with chicken flavored salt or other seasoning. Pour melted butter over popcorn if desired.

*Mrs. Marvin (Lydia) Sensenig, Penn Yan, NY*

## PEANUT BUTTER POPCORN

1/2 cup melted butter
1/3 cup sugar, rounded

1/4 cup peanut butter
6 quarts popped popcorn

Combine butter, sugar and peanut butter; mix well. Pour over popcorn; stirring to coat. Toast at 300°, stirring occasionally, until dry and crisp.

*Erla (Horst) Horning, Penn Yan, NY*

## QUICK PEANUT BUTTER POPCORN

1/2 cup sugar
1/2 cup light corn syrup or honey
1/2 cup chunky peanut butter

1/2 tsp. vanilla
4 to 6 quarts popped popcorn

Bring sugar and syrup to a rolling boil. Remove from heat and add peanut butter and vanilla. Stir well. Pour over popcorn and stir to coat.

*Rachel Weirich, Stone Lake, WI*

## CARAMEL CORN

2 cups white or brown sugar
1/2 cup sorghum or corn syrup
3/4 cup butter

1 1/2 tsp. soda
18 to 20 cups popped popcorn

Boil sugar, syrup, and butter over medium-high heat for 5 minutes. Add soda; mix well. Pour over popcorn. Put in the oven at 225° for 1 hour. Stir every 15 minutes.

*Susan Hilty Hoover, Elida, OH*

## NUTTY CARAMEL CORN

*Replace some of the popcorn with Corn Chex or other cereal for added flavor.*

2 cups brown sugar
1 cup butter or margarine
1/2 cup light corn syrup
1 tsp. salt

1 tsp. vanilla
1/2 tsp. soda
6 to 7 quarts popped popcorn
1 cup chopped peanuts

Boil sugar, butter, syrup and salt for 1 minute. Remove from heat and stir in vanilla and soda. Pour over popcorn and nuts. Put in cake pans or a big stainless steel bowl. Toast at 250° for 1 hour, stirring occasionally.

*Mrs. James Horst, East Earl, PA*

## MARSHMALLOW POPCORN BALLS

1/4 cup butter
6 cups small marshmallows

3 oz. flavored gelatin
3 quarts popped popcorn

Melt butter over low heat. Add marshmallows and stir until smooth. Remove from heat and stir in dry gelatin. Pour over popcorn. Stir quickly to coat well. Shape into balls with greased hands.

***Practice makes perfect, so be careful what you practice.***

# CRUNCHY SNACK

| | |
|---|---|
| 5 cups Cheerios | 1 cup brown sugar |
| 5 cups Rice Chex | 1 cup honey or corn syrup |
| 5 cups Corn Chex | 1/2 cup butter |
| Pretzels | |

Mix cereal and pretzels. Combine sugar, honey and butter; boil 3 minutes. Pour over cereal; mix. Spread on 2 buttered cookie sheets. Toast at 275° for 20 to 25 minutes.

*Barbara Martin, Goshen, IN*

# KNAPSACK CRUNCHES

| | |
|---|---|
| 1/2 cup peanut butter | 3 cups quick oatmeal |
| 1/2 cup honey or syrup | 1/2 cup chopped peanuts or |
| 1/2 cup brown sugar | sunflower seeds |
| 1/2 cup butter | 3/4 cup raisins |

Combine ingredients in the first column and cook over low heat until well blended. Remove from heat and add oatmeal and nuts; mix well. Spread evenly into an ungreased pan. Bake at 350° for 15 to 20 minutes, stirring occasionally until lightly browned. Stir in raisins. Cool. Break into pieces.

*Suetta Hoover, Tipton, MO*

# BUTTERED PECANS

| | |
|---|---|
| 1/2 cup butter | 3 to 4 cups pecan halves |

Melt butter in an edged cookie sheet. Stir in pecans; coat well. Bake for 30 minutes. Drain on paper towel. Cool slightly; sprinkle with salt to taste. Eat plain or with ice cream.

# TACO SNACK MIX

| | |
|---|---|
| 6 cups popped popcorn | 1 T. dry taco seasoning mix |
| 3 cups Corn Chex | 2 T. Parmesan cheese |
| 1 cup pretzels | 1 cup Cheddar cheese cubes |
| 2 T. melted butter | |

Combine popcorn, cereal and pretzels. Mix butter and taco seasoning. Drizzle over popcorn mixture. Sprinkle with Parmesan cheese; toss to coat. Add cheese cubes just before serving.

# OYSTER CRACKERS

2-12 oz. bags oyster crackers
1 cup cooking oil
1 tsp. dill weed, opt.

1 pkg. Hidden Valley Ranch
 Dressing mix
1/2 tsp. garlic powder

Mix and let stand 8 hours, stirring frequently. Keep at room temperature.

*Mrs. Isaac Kulp, Millersburg, IN      Mrs. John Kulp, Mosinee, WI*
*Mrs Dale (Margaret) Love, Goshen, IN      Ada Mae Miller, Nappanee, IN*

# HONEY MUSTARD PRETZELS

2 lb. sour dough pretzels
1 cup cooking oil
1/2 cup honey

1/2 cup prepared mustard
1/4 cup sour cream onion
 powder, opt

Break pretzels into small pieces. Combine remaining ingredients and pour over pretzels. Stir to coat. Spread on cookie sheets. Bake at 200° approximately 2 hours, stirring every 15 to 20 minutes. Any hard pretzel can be used.

*Anna Mae Hoover, Reinholds, PA*

# PARTY MIX I

6 T. butter
1 to 2 T. Worcestershire sauce
1 tsp. seasoned or garlic salt

6 to 9 cups cereal, mixed
3/4 cup salted nuts
Pretzels

Melt butter in a large pan over low heat. Stir in Worcestershire sauce and salt. Add remaining ingredients; stir to coat. Toast at 250° for 1 hour, stirring occasionally. Use a little more salt if using 9 cups of cereal.

*Anna Mary Evans, MO*

# PARTY MIX II

1/2 cup butter
1 T. soy sauce
1/2 tsp. seasoned salt
1 tsp. Worcestershire sauce
1/4 tsp. Tabasco sauce
1/4 tsp. chili powder

2 cups Chex cereal
1 1/2 cups nuts
1 cup chow mein noodles
1 cup pretzels
1 cup cheese curls or balls

Melt butter; add ingredients in first column. Combine remaining ingredients. Pour liquid over dry ingredients; mix well. Toast at 250° for an hour. Stir occasionally. Store in airtight containers.

*Sarah Imhoff, Sheridan, MI*

## SOUTHWESTERN CORN CHIPS

1/2 cup water
4 tsp. cooking oil
1 tsp. chili powder
1/2 tsp. garlic powder

1/4 tsp. ground cumin
1/8 tsp. salt
2/3 cup yellow cornmeal

Combine all ingredients but cornmeal and bring to a boil. Remove from heat and stir in cornmeal; mix well. Roll into 3/4-inch balls. Spray two cookie sheets with non-stick spray. Place balls 3 inches apart. Cover with wax paper. Flatten each ball with a glass until very thin, about 2 to 3 inches in diameter. Bake at 375° till lightly brown and crisp, 10 to 12 minutes.

*Vera Witmer, Goshen, IN*

## CHILI CORN CHIPS

2 cups sweet corn
1/4 cup chopped onion
1/4 cup chopped green peppers
1/3 cup chopped tomatoes
1 T. brewers yeast

1 tsp. salt
1/2 tsp. chili powder
1/2 tsp. garlic powder
1/4 tsp. black pepper
1/4 tsp. red pepper

Puree corn in blender; add remaining ingredients. Blend until ingredients are well blended. Spray a 13x9 pan with non-stick spray. Spread puree evenly in pan. Dry in a 90° to 100° oven overnight until dry and crinkled.

*Rosalee Kulp, Mt. Hermon, KY*

## BARBEQUED MINI FRANKS

2 lb. miniature hotdogs
1/2 cup chopped onion
1/2 cup ketchup
2 to 3 T. Worcestershire sauce

2 T. sugar
2 T. vinegar
2 tsp. mustard
1/2 tsp pepper

Place hotdogs in a single layer in a 13x9 pan. Mix remaining ingredients; pour on top. Bake at 350° for 25 minutes. Serve with toothpicks

## SAUSAGE BALLS

1 lb. bulk sausage
2 1/2 cups biscuit mix

1 cup shredded cheese

Mix everything together. Roll into small balls. Bake at 350° approximately 15 minutes or until golden brown. Serve with toothpicks.

# QUESADILLAS

3 10-inch flour tortillas
2 cups shredded Cheddar cheese

4 oz. diced green chili peppers
Salsa and sour cream

In a heavy skillet, stack tortillas with cheese and peppers in between, ending with cheese and peppers on top. Cover. Cook about 5 minutes or until cheese is melted. Cut into 6 or 8 wedges. Serve with salsa and sour cream. This can be wrapped in foil and done on a grill.

# TORTILLA PINWHEELS

8 oz. sour cream
8 oz. cream cheese
1 cup grated cheese
1/2 cup chopped green onions
4 oz. black olives, chopped

4 oz. green chili peppers, diced
Seasoned salt, to taste
Garlic powder, to taste
5 flour tortillas

Combine all but tortillas. Spread on tortillas. Roll up. Chill several hours. Cut each tortilla in 10 or more slices. Serve with salsa.

*Brenda Martin, Viola, WI*

# PIZZA BUTTER

2 cups butter
2 cups shredded mozzarella
6 oz. tomato paste or 1/2 cup
    pizza sauce

2 T. oregano
2 tsp. sugar
1 tsp. salt
1/4 tsp. garlic salt

Mix ingredients; spread on Italian or other bread. Broil until bubbly. This keeps a while in refrigerator. Less butter and more cheese can be used.

*Laura Kulp, Stratford, WI*

# PEANUT BUTTER SPREAD

1 1/4 cups light corn syrup
1 cup marshmallow crème

1/2 cup peanut butter

Combine ingredients; mix well. Spread on homemade or other bread.

# FRUITY SMORES

Spread a graham cracker square with jam; top with a softened marshmallow. Top marshmallow with sliced strawberries, bananas or whole blueberries. Cover with another graham cracker. Serve warm.

# APPLE CARTWHEELS

8 medium apples
1 cup chocolate chips
1/2 cup peanut butter

1/4 cup raisins
1 T. honey

Remove cores, leaving apples whole.  Set aside.  In blender blend chocolate chips 5 seconds.  Combine all but apples; stuff apples with mixture.  Wrap apples in plastic wrap and chill.  Slice each apple crosswise into fourths.

*Edna Miller, Snover, MI*

# CHEESEBALL

1 lb. cheese (4 c. shredded)
16 oz. cream cheese
1/3 cup minced onion

1 T. parsley flakes
3/4 tsp. garlic salt
1/8 tsp. red pepper

Combine everything, mixing by hand, until well blended.  Shape into 1 or 2 balls and roll into chopped nuts, parsley, paprika or sesame seeds.  Refrigerate until ready to serve.

# BACON ONION CHEESEBALL

10 slices bacon
16 oz. cream cheese
1/3 cup Parmesan cheese

1/4 cup salad dressing
1/4 cup chopped onion

Fry bacon; cool and crumble.  Combine all ingredients.  Garnish with nuts or parsley, if desired.

*Mrs. Luke Hoover, Goshen, IN        Mrs. Larry Zimmerman, Elkhart, IN*

# VELVEETA CHEESEBALL

2/3 box Velveeta cheese
16 oz. cream cheese
1 T. Worcestershire sauce
1 T. onion flakes or salt
1 T. parsley flakes

1 T. seasoned salt
1 T. liquid smoke (opt.)
1 cup bacon bits or other ready to
   eat meat
1/4 cup ground nuts

Have cheese at room temperature so it is easier to mix.  Mix all but nuts; form into a ball.  Roll in nuts and sprinkle with more parsley.

*Mrs. James Kulp, Unity, WI        Pauline Kulp, Stratford, WI*

**If you say nothing, nobody will repeat it.**

# HOLIDAY CHEESEBALL

16 oz. cream cheese, softened
1 can Spam, shredded
1 cup sharp cheese, shredded
1 small onion, chopped
1/2 green pepper, chopped

1 tsp. Worcestershire sauce
1/2 tsp. seasoned salt
1/8 tsp. pepper
Chopped pecans, opt.

Combine ingredients, except pecans until well blended. Shape into a ball. Roll in pecans. Refrigerate several hours before serving.

*Mrs. Clay Zimmerman, Paltinis, Romania*

# GARLIC CHEESE

1 lb. mild Cheddar cheese
1 cup pecans
2 to 4 garlic cloves

3 oz. cream cheese, softened
Chili powder

Grind cheese, pecans and garlic in good grinder or chopper. By hand, blend in cream cheese, mixing and kneading until mixture is thoroughly blended. Shape into 2 rolls, 1-inch in diameter. Roll in chili powder to cover. Wrap in plastic, then in foil. Refrigerate a day or two to ripen flavor. Serve with crackers.

*Connie Rodes, Milford, IN*

# BEVERAGES

## HOT CHOCOLATE

*To make spicy hot chocolate, add 1 teaspoon cinnamon, 1/4 teaspoon nutmeg and 1/2 teaspoon almond flavoring. For darker hot chocolate add an extra tablespoon of cocoa.*

1/3 cup sugar
3 T. cocoa
1/8 tsp. salt

1/3 cup hot water
4 cups milk
1 tsp. vanilla

Mix sugar, cocoa and salt in a medium saucepan. Add hot water; bring to a boil over medium heat, stirring constantly. Boil and stir 2 minutes. Add milk; stir and heat. Do not boil. Remove from heat and add vanilla.

*Mrs. Ray (Elsie) Hoover, Stratford, WI*

***A little leak may sink a great ship.***

# MICROWAVE HOT CHOCOLATE

2 T. sugar
1 T. cocoa

1 cup milk
1/4 tsp vanilla

Combine sugar and cocoa in a large mug. Add a little milk to make a smooth paste; stir in remaining milk. Microwave on high one minute; stir. Heat another 10 seconds or so until hot. Stir in vanilla.

# COFFEE CHOCOLATE PUNCH

6 cups water
1/2 cup instant chocolate drink
   mix
1/2 cup sugar

1/4 cup dry instant coffee
1/2 gallon vanilla ice cream
1/2 gallon chocolate ice cream

Bring water to a boil in a large saucepan. Remove from heat; add drink mix, sugar and coffee. Stir until dissolved. Cover and refrigerate 4 hours or overnight. Half an hour before serving pour into a punch bowl. Add ice cream by scoopfuls and stir until partially melted. Garnish with dollops of whipped cream or chocolate curls if desired.

*Stephanie Ramer, Nappanee, IN*

# CHILLED CAFÉ LATTE

2 T. dry instant coffee
3/4 cup warm water
1 tsp. vanilla

14 oz. can sweetened condensed
   milk
4 cups ice cubes

Dissolve coffee in water. Put warm coffee, vanilla and sweetened condensed milk in blender. Blend well. Gradually add ice cubes and blend until smooth. Serve immediately.

# BANANA CHOCOLATE DRINK

1 small banana, cut up
1/2 cup chocolate milk

1 tsp. vanilla
2 ice cubes

Put all but ice cubes in a blender; blend till smooth. Add ice cubes one at a time through hole in the lid; blend till smooth. Serve immediately.

*Ellen Newswanger, Kutztown, PA*

# HOT CHOCOLATE MIX

1 lb. instant chocolate drink mix

1 lb. dry milk
11 oz. jar dry creamer

Mix everything in a large bowl. Store in a moisture proof container. To use, fill mug half full of mix. Add hot water and stir.

*Susan Hilty Hoover, Elida, OH*

# CAPPUCCINO MIX

1 cup instant chocolate drink mix
1 cup dry coffee creamer
2/3 cup instant coffee granules

1/2 cup sugar
1/2 tsp. cinnamon

Combine ingredients and mix well. Store in an airtight container. To prepare, add 3 tablespoons mix to 1 cup hot water, or to taste.

# RUSSIAN TEA MIX

7 oz. orange drink powder
1 pkg. lemonade Kool-Aid
1 1/3 cups sugar

1/2 cup instant tea
1 tsp. cinnamon
1 tsp. ground cloves

Combine ingredients and store in a dry place. Use 2 teaspoons to one cup of hot water for an instant warm drink.

*Ellen Stoesz, Indianapolis, IN*

# HOMEMADE TEA CONCENTRATE

4 cups water
1 1/2 to 1 3/4 cups sugar

1 T. lemon juice
2 cups tea leaves

Boil water and sugar 5 minutes. Add lemon juice and tea leaves and steep for 5-6 hours. This makes 1 quart concentrate. Add 3 quarts water.

*Mrs. Elverne Martin, Nappanee, IN*     *Rita Martin, Nappanee, IN*

# BANANA SPLIT SHAKES

1 small ripe banana, sliced
1/2 cup milk
1/2 tsp. coconut flavoring

10 maraschino cherries
1 T. cocoa
3 cups vanilla ice cream

Put everything in the blender but the ice cream; blend until smooth. Add ice cream and blend until smooth. Serve immediately. Makes 4 cups.

# ROOT BEER SHAKES

1 pkg. unflavored gelatin
1/4 cup water
2 cups milk
3/4 cup sugar

1/8 tsp. salt
2 1/2 cups milk
1 tsp. root beer extract

Soak gelatin in water to soften. Scald 1 cup milk; pour over gelatin and stir to dissolve. Add sugar, salt and remaining milk. Pour into a pan and freeze. When frozen, cut into blocks and put into blender. Add the 2 1/2 cups milk and extract. Blend until smooth; serve immediately. Any flavor extract, coffee crystals or fruit may be used.

*Ella Horning, Penn Yan, NY*

# HI-VI BOOSTER

Glass of tomato juice
2 to 3 T. brewers yeast

Dash of vegetable salt
Slice of lemon

Stir brewers yeast into tomato juice; add salt and spike with slice of lemon.

*Hannah Kulp Family, Mt Hermon, KY*

# FRESH LEMONADE

*One and a half cups lemon juice can be substituted for the lemons.*

6 lemons
1 1/2 cups sugar

2 1/2 quarts cold water

Squeeze lemons or take seeds out of lemons, quarter and put in blender, peeled or unpeeled. Add sugar to pulp. Mix very well before adding water.

# ORANGE JULIUS

*Try this refreshing summertime treat using grape concentrate, or make it extra special with a scoop of ice cream in each glass.*

2 oz. or 1/3 cup frozen orange
   juice concentrate
1/2 cup milk
1/2 cup water

1/4 cup sugar
1/2 tsp. vanilla
6 ice cubes

Put everything in the blender and blend until smooth; about 1 minute. Serve immediately. For a bigger batch use 6 oz. concentrate and double remaining ingredients.

*Anna Mae Hoover, Reinholds, PA*     *Ellen Newswanger, Kutztown, PA*

# SPICY APPLE JUICE

6 cups apple juice
1/3 cup brown sugar

2 cinnamon sticks
6 whole cloves

Bring all ingredients to a boil. Simmer 15 minutes; strain. Serve warm.

# APPLE CIDER PUNCH

4 cups water
1 1/2 cups sugar
2 tsp. ginger
12 whole cloves
4 whole allspice

4 short cinnamon sticks
2 quarts apple cider
2 cups orange juice
2 cups lemon or pineapple juice

Stir sugar into water. Add spices; boil until sugar is dissolved. Simmer at least 20 minutes. Strain out spices. Combine with cider and juice. Serve hot or cold. This can also be made without the water, sugar and ginger.

*Mrs. John (Twila) Kulp, Mosinee, WI*

# CHERRY CITRUS PUNCH

7/8 cup cherry gelatin
2 cups hot water
2 cups cold water
6 lemons, squeezed or 1 T. lemon
  extract

46 oz. can pineapple juice
3 cups sugar
3 cups water
2 T. almond extract

Dissolve gelatin in hot water. Stir in 2 cups cold water; add remaining ingredients. Stir. Add a gallon of water or to taste.

*Mrs. Allen Garmen, Roaring Spring, PA*

# GREEN PUNCH

4 pints lime sherbet

3-28 oz. bottles 7-Up

Put 3 pints soft sherbet into a punch bowl. Pour in 7-Up and mix a little. (Twelve 7 ounce cans of 7-Up can be used instead of the bottles.) Add remaining pint of sherbet. Serves around 30.

*Mrs. Dale Love, Goshen, IN*

***Plan as if Christ's return were years away, but live as if it were today***

# LEMON-ORANGE PUNCH

1 cup sugar
1 cup water
12 oz. can frozen orange
    concentrate

6 oz. can frozen lemonade
    concentrate
2 quarts ginger ale
2 cups vanilla ice cream

Boil sugar and water two minutes. Remove from heat; add concentrates. Add ginger ale and ice cream. Stir occasionally till melted.

# PINEAPPLE PUNCH

4-12 oz. cans frozen orange
    concentrate
4-12 oz. cans frozen lemonade
    concentrate

46 oz. can pineapple juice
7 cups sugar
6 cups water
4-2 liter bottles ginger ale

Mix together everything but ginger ale. Add ginger ale when ready to serve. Any lemon lime soda may be used.

**To keep punch from diluting, freeze some punch in ice cube trays, or other containers, and use instead of ice cubes.**

# QUICK PUNCH

2-46 oz. cans Hawaiian Punch
1 1/2 cups lemon juice

2 liter bottle lemon-lime soda

Combine ingredients and mix well. Serve over ice.

# RASPBERRY CITRUS PUNCH

4 pkg. raspberry Kool-Aid
3 to 4 cups sugar
2 gallons water or to taste
2-46 oz. cans pineapple juice,
    chilled

2-12 oz. cans frozen orange
    concentrate
2-12 oz. cans frozen lemonade
    concentrate
2-2 liter bottles ginger ale

Mix everything except ginger ale. Add ginger ale just before serving. Makes 4 to 4 1/2 gallons.

*Mary Zook, Virginia Beach, VA*

# SLUSHY CITRUS PUNCH

2 1/2 cups sugar
3 cups water
12 oz. can frozen orange juice
   concentrate
12 oz. can frozen lemonade
   concentrate

46 oz. can pineapple juice
3 cups cold water
2-2 liter bottles lemon-lime soda
   or ginger ale, chilled
Lime slices

Bring sugar and 3 cups water to a boil. Stir until sugar dissolves; remove from heat. Stir in concentrates until melted. Combine with pineapple juice and 3 cups water; mix well. Pour into two 13x9 pans. Cover and freeze until firm. Cut each pan into 24 squares. Place squares in a 2 gallon punch bowl. Slowly pour soda over squares; stir until slushy. Garnish with lime slices. Makes about 2 gallons or 32 one-cup servings.

*Kathleen Ramer, New Paris, IN*

# STRAWBERRY PUNCH

2 tsp. grated lemon rind
8 whole cloves
1/4 cup sugar
2 cups water
1/4 cup lemon juice

12 oz. frozen orange juice
   concentrate
2-1 lb. pkg. (or two pints) frozen
   strawberries
2 liters ginger ale

Bring rind, cloves, sugar and water to a boil. Cook over low heat 5 minutes; cool. Add lemon juice and orange concentrate. Just before serving add thawed strawberries and ginger ale. Serve over ice.

*Mrs. Dale (Margaret) Love, Goshen, IN*

# WEDDING PUNCH

1 pkg. cherry Kool-Aid
1 pkg. strawberry Kool-Aid
2 cups sugar
3 quarts water

6 oz. can frozen orange juice
   concentrate
6 oz. can frozen lemonade
   concentrate
1 quart ginger ale

Mix all ingredients.

*Susan Miller, Nappanee, IN*

***Blowing out another person's candle does not light your own.***

# DIPS
## and
# SAUCES

Elsie
Hoover

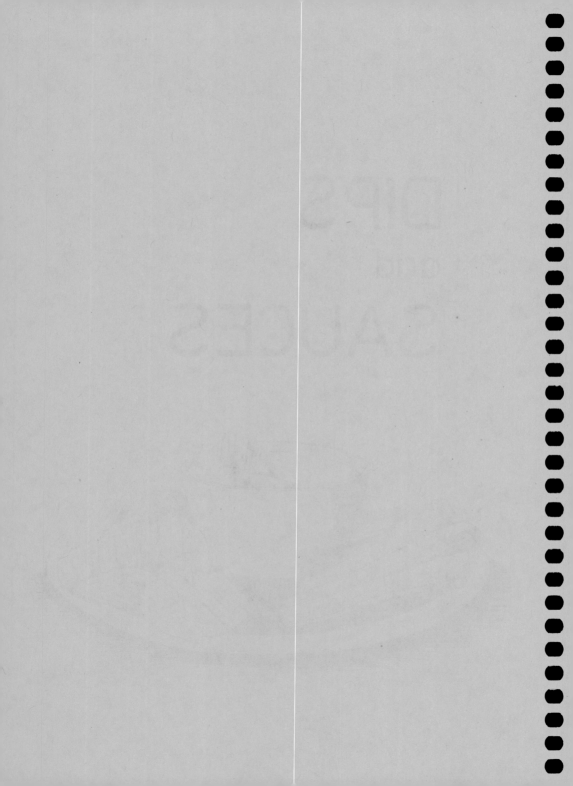

# DIPS

## APPLE DIP

*To make peanut butter dip, use 8 ounces cream cheese and add 1/2 cup peanut butter.*
*Thin with milk if necessary. Or, if you like, just add 1/4 cup peanut butter to this recipe.*

**4 oz. cream cheese, softened**
**3/4 cup brown sugar**

**1/2 cup ground nuts, opt.**
**1 tsp. vanilla**

Combine cream cheese and brown sugar. Add nuts and vanilla.
*Donnita Jones, Oregon City, OR*

## CHIP DIP

**2 cups mayonnaise**
**1 1/2 cups sour cream**
**1/2 tsp. onion salt**
**1/2 tsp. garlic salt**

**1 1/2 tsp. dill weed**
**1 1/2 tsp. parsley flakes**
**1 tsp. Accent, opt**

Combine ingredients; mix well. Refrigerate. Good with fresh vegetables, pretzels and baked potatoes as well as chips.
*Mrs. John (Twila) Kulp, Mosinee, WI*
*Ada Mae Miller, Nappanee, IN      Verna Overholt, Due West, SC*

## FRUIT DIP I

**8 oz. cream cheese, softened**
**1/2 to 1 cup marshmallow crème**

**1 to 2 cups whipped topping**
**Pineapple or lemon juice**

Combine first 3 ingredients; add enough pineapple juice to make it dipping consistency. More marshmallow crème can be used and topping deleted.
*Danette Martin, Waterloo, Ontario, Canada*

## FRUIT DIP II

**8 oz. cream cheese, softened**
**1 tsp. vanilla**
**3/4 cup brown sugar**
**1 cup sour cream**

**1 T. lemon juice**
**1 cup milk**
**3.4 oz. pkg. instant vanilla**
**    pudding**

Beat cream cheese and vanilla until smooth. Add remaining ingredients one at a time; mixing well.

# HOT BEAN DIP

*If you want a bigger batch double the recipe and put it in a 13x9 cake pan. Add cooked ground beef for an even bigger batch.*

| | |
|---|---|
| 16 oz. can refried beans | 2 T. taco seasoning |
| 8 oz. cream cheese | 2 garlic cloves, minced |
| 1 cup sour cream | 1 cup shredded cheese |

Combine all but cheese and put in a 9x9 pan. Top with cheese. Bake at 350° for 20 minutes. Top with tomatoes, onions, olives or lettuce if desired.

*Mary Faith Yoder, Unity, WI*

# HOT BEEF DIP

| | |
|---|---|
| 2.5 oz. dried beef | 8 oz. cream cheese |
| 1/4 cup chopped onion | 4 oz. can mushrooms, drained |
| 1 T. butter or margarine | 1/4 cup Parmesan cheese |
| 1 cup milk | 2 T. chopped parsley |

Rinse dried beef in hot water; drain and chop. Cook onion in butter until tender. Stir in milk and cream cheese; mix well. Slice mushrooms and add remaining ingredients. Mix well. Serve hot.

# KIDNEY BEAN DIP

| | |
|---|---|
| 16 oz. can kidney beans | 1/4 tsp. chili powder or cumin |
| 1/4 cup butter | 1 cup shredded Cheddar cheese |
| 1/4 tsp. garlic powder | |

Drain beans, reserving liquid. Mash beans to a smooth paste. Melt butter in a small pan; add beans. Cook over medium heat about 5 minutes. Stir in seasoning. Add bean liquid to reach desired consistency. Stir in cheese and heat until melted. Serve warm with corn chips.

*Mrs. LaVerne (Virginia) Hoover, Goshen, IN*

# MEATY CHEESY DIP

| | |
|---|---|
| 2 lb. ground beef or sausage | 1 lb. Velveeta cheese, cubed |
| 1 onion, chopped | 1 T. chili powder |
| 1 green pepper, chopped | 1 T. Worcestershire sauce |
| 2 cups salsa | 1 tsp. garlic salt |
| 10 3/4 oz. can mushroom soup | |

Brown beef, onion and pepper. Drain if necessary. Add remaining ingredients. Heat and stir until cheese melts.

## MICROWAVE BARBEQUE DIP

1/4 cup chopped onion
1 T. butter
1 cup ketchup

2 T. brown sugar
2 tsp. Worcestershire sauce
2 tsp. vinegar

Microwave onions and butter on high for 1 minute. Stir in remaining ingredients and cover with wax paper. Microwave 2 to 3 minutes until heated through.

## SALSA DIP

*For salsa bean dip, add a 16 oz. can of refried beans. Onions can also be added.*

1 lb. Velveeta cheese

1 1/2 cups salsa

Cook cheese and salsa over low heat until cheese melts, or microwave on high for 5 minutes, stirring twice. Serve hot with tortilla or corn chips.

## SHRIMP DIP

10 3/4 oz. cream of shrimp soup
8 oz. cream cheese, softened
1 small onion, minced
1 tsp. lemon juice

1/4 tsp. hot pepper sauce
1/2 tsp. Worcestershire sauce
1 can small shrimp

Blend soup and cream cheese. Add remaining ingredients. Serve with fresh vegetables.

*Elizabeth B. Hoover, Fort Wayne, IN*

## SOUTHWESTERN DIP

2 jalapeno peppers
2 cups sour cream

1/4 cup salsa
1/4 cup dry onion soup mix

Carefully chop peppers fine. Add remaining ingredients and mix well. Chill before serving. Serve with chips or vegetables.

*Life may not always bring us, the things we wish it would;*
*But God can take the things it brings,*
*and bless them to our good.*

73

## TUNA DIP

3/4 cup mayonnaise
8 oz. cream cheese, softened
6 oz. can tuna

1 small onion, chopped
1 tsp. Worcestershire sauce

Combine ingredients; mix thoroughly. Serve with vegetables and crackers.

**Dips, with the exception of hot dips, are best if chilled before serving. Any remaining dip should be refrigerated.**

## VEGETABLE DIP

1/2 cup sour cream
1/2 cup Cheez Whiz
1/2 cup salad dressing

1/2 tsp. Worcestershire sauce
1 T. dry onion soup mix

Combine ingredients. Keep refrigerated.

*Susan Miller, Nappanee, IN*

## FRESH VEGETABLE DIP

*No sour cream? Use mayonnaise. Good with chips, crackers or vegetables.*

8 oz. cream cheese
1 cup sour cream
3/4 tsp. garlic salt

1/4 tsp. pepper
1 1/4 cups finely chopped
   vegetables

Combine first 4 ingredients. Add any combination of chopped broccoli, carrots, cauliflower, celery, onions, peppers or vegetables of your choice.

# SAUCES

## BARBEQUE SAUCE I

1/2 cup melted butter
1 cup vinegar

2 T. salt
1/2 cup water

Combine all ingredients. Brush on steaks or chicken as they barbeque.

*Mrs. James Kulp, Unity, WI*

# BARBEQUE SAUCE II

2 cups vinegar
1 1/2 cups honey
1 cup butter or margarine
1/2 cup Worcestershire sauce
1/2 cup minced onion

3 T. chili powder
2 T. salt
2 tsp. pepper
2 tsp. paprika
1/2 tsp. red pepper

Combine ingredients and bring to a boil. Use on the grill or in the oven.

*Mrs. William (Lena) Kilmer, California, MO*

# BARBEQUE SAUCE III

1 cup ketchup
1 cup beef broth or water
1/3 cup Worcestershire sauce
1 tsp. chili powder
1 tsp. garlic powder

1 tsp. salt
1/2 tsp. pepper
1/8 tsp. red pepper
1 tsp. liquid smoke, opt.

Combine everything and simmer for 30 minutes. Use on grill or in oven.

*Mrs. Mahlon D. Schrock, Abbotsford, WI*

# BARBEQUE SAUCE IV

2 cups tomato juice
1/4 cup minced onion
3 T. vinegar
2 T. Worcestershire sauce
1 tsp. salt

1 tsp. paprika
1 tsp. chili powder
1/2 tsp. pepper
1/4 tsp. cinnamon
1/8 tsp. ground cloves

Combine all ingredients and bring to a boil. Use on the grill or in the oven.

*Vera Witmer, Goshen, IN*

# HAMBURGER SAUCE

1 cup salad dressing
1/3 cup French dressing
1/4 cup pickle relish

1 T. sugar
1 T. minced onion
1/4 tsp. pepper

Mix all ingredients and serve on hamburgers.

*Mrs. Larry Zimmerman, Elkhart, IN*

*A smooth sea never made a good sailor.*

## HONEY MUSTARD SAUCE

2/3 cup honey
1/4 cup mustard

2 T. soy sauce

Combine and mix well.  Serve with chicken or egg rolls.

## HOT MUSTARD SAUCE

3 T. dry mustard
2 T. cooking oil
2 T. water
1/4 cup sugar

1 T. cornstarch
1/2 tsp. salt
2/3 cup water
1/3 cup vinegar

Mix mustard and oil; add water and stir until smooth.  Combine sugar, cornstarch and salt in a small saucepan.  Stir in water and vinegar; cook over low heat until mixture thickens.  Remove from heat; add to mustard mixture.  Good with chicken.

*Mrs. Ray (Elsie) Hoover, Stratford, WI*

## MICROWAVE CHEESE SAUCE

1 cup milk
2 T. butter

2 T. flour
1 cup grated cheese

Heat milk 2 minutes on medium heat.  Set aside.  Melt butter 1 minute on high. Stir in flour and heat another minute on high.  Briskly stir in warm milk; blend well. Cook on high 2 1/2 minutes more, or until boiling.  Stir in cheese.

*Anna Mae Hoover, Reinholds, PA*

## MUSHROOM SAUCE

1 cup mushrooms, sliced
1/4 cup butter
1/4 cup flour

2 cups milk or bouillon
1/2 tsp. salt
1/8 tsp. pepper

Sauté mushrooms in butter about 4 minutes.  Stir in flour, cooking 2 to 3 minutes to brown it.  Gradually stir in milk; add salt and pepper.  Cook until thick, about 5 minutes.  Serve with cooked green vegetables or meats.

*Mrs. Ray (Elsie) Hoover, Stratford, WI*

*People may doubt what you say, but they will always believe what you do.*

# SEAFOOD BUTTER SAUCE

1/2 cup butter, soft
2 T. lemon juice
2 tsp. chopped parsley

1/4 tsp. salt
1/8 tsp. pepper

Cream together and serve over seafood.

# SEAFOOD SAUCE

3/4 cup ketchup
2 T. prepared horseradish
1 T. lemon juice

1 tsp. Worcestershire sauce
1/2 tsp. salt
1/8 tsp. pepper

Combine all ingredients and mix well.  Refrigerate.  Stir before using.

# STEAK SAUCE

3 T. butter
3 T. lemon juice
1/2 tsp. dry mustard

1 T. Worcestershire sauce
1/8 tsp. salt
1/8 tsp. pepper

Melt butter; add remaining ingredients.

# SOY SAUCE MEAT MARINADE

1/2 cup soy sauce
1/2 cup water
2 T. lemon juice
2 T. cooking oil, opt.

1 T. brown sugar
1 clove garlic, crushed
1/4 tsp. freshly ground pepper
1/4 tsp. hot pepper sauce

Combine ingredients.  Use to marinate beef, pork or chicken before grilling or broiling.  Baste occasionally with marinade.

*Connie Rodes, Milford, IN*

# SWEET-SOUR SAUCE

1 cup brown sugar
3/4 cup vinegar
1/2 cup ketchup

1/2 cup pineapple juice
2 T. cornstarch
1 tsp. soy sauce

Combine ingredients and bring to a boil.  Stir constantly until mixture thickens.

# TARTAR SAUCE

3/4 cup mayonnaise
1/4 cup pickle relish

2 T. chopped onion
1 tsp. dried parsley

Combine ingredients and mix well.  Serve with fish.

# MEDUIM WHITE SAUCE

*For thin white sauce use 2 tablespoons butter and 2 tablespoons flour.  For thick white sauce use 6 tablespoons butter and 6 tablespoons flour.*

1/4 cup butter
1/4 cup flour
1/2 tsp. salt

1/8 tsp. pepper
2 cups milk

Melt butter; add flour and seasoning.  Stir until well blended.  Add milk gradually, stirring constantly.  Bring to a boil and boil 2 minutes.

# SWEET SAUCES AND TOPPINGS

## BLUEBERRY SAUCE

2/3 cup sugar
2 T. corn starch
1/8 tsp. salt

1/2 cup water
4 cups fresh or frozen blueberries
2 T. lemon juice

Combine dry ingredients in a saucepan; stir in water.  Cook until thickened stirring constantly.  Add berries.  Heat if desired.  Add lemon juice.  Eat hot or cold on ice cream, cake, pancakes or French toast.

## BUTTER PECAN SAUCE

1/2 cup butter
1 cup pecan pieces
1 cup brown sugar

1/3 cup cream or evaporated milk
1/4 cup corn syrup

In heavy saucepan melt butter.  Add pecans and heat till lightly toasted and butter lightly browned.  Stir in remaining ingredients.  Cook gently until sugar is dissolved.  Do not overcook.  Serve warm or cold.

*Ray Hoover, Stratford, WI*

## BUTTERSCOTCH TOPPING I

1 1/2 cups brown sugar
1/2 cup light corn syrup
1/3 cup butter

1/4 tsp. salt
2/3 cup light cream or evaporated
   milk

Cook sugar, corn syrup, butter and salt over medium heat to 230°. Don't overcook. Cool 5 minutes; stir in cream. Serve hot or cold.

## BUTTERSCOTCH TOPPING II

1 cup light corn syrup
1 cup brown sugar
1/2 cup milk

1 T. butter
1/2 tsp. salt
1 tsp. vanilla

Cook all but vanilla for 5 minutes, stirring constantly. Remove from heat and stir in vanilla. Serve hot or cold.

*Edna Miller, Snover, MI*

## CHOCOLATE SYRUP

1 cup cocoa
2 to 2 1/2 cups sugar
1 1/2 cups hot water

1/4 tsp. salt
1 tsp. vanilla

Bring all but vanilla to a boil in a large saucepan; boil approximately 4 minutes. Remove from heat and add vanilla. Use for chocolate milk or on ice cream. Keep in refrigerator in a squeeze bottle, if you have one.

*Mrs. Clarence Martin, Snover, MI    Ellen Newswanger, Kutztown, PA*
*Mrs. Lloyd E. Troyer, Stella, MO*

## CHOCOLATE TOPPING I

1 1/2 cups sugar
2 T. cornstarch
1/4 to 1/2 cup cocoa
1/4 tsp. salt

1 1/2 cups milk
3 T. butter
1 tsp. vanilla

Combine dry ingredients; add milk and butter. Cook until thickened. Remove from heat and add vanilla. Serve hot or cold. Makes 2 cups.

*Susan Hilty Hoover, Elida, OH*

## CHOCOLATE TOPPING II

1 cup chocolate drink mix
1/4 cup milk
1/4 cup corn syrup

3 T. butter
1 tsp. vanilla
Nuts, opt.

Bring first 3 ingredients to a full boil over medium heat, stirring constantly. Remove from heat; stir in butter, vanilla and nuts. Serve warm or cold.

*Mary Ann Martin, Sauk Centre, MN*

## MICROWAVE CHOCOLATE TOPPING

2/3 cup corn syrup
1/2 cup evaporated milk

1 cup semisweet chocolate chips

Combine syrup and cream; microwave on high 1 1/2 minutes or until boiling. Add chocolate chips and stir until completely melted.

## LEMON TOPPING

1/2 cup sugar
1 T. cornstarch
1/8 tsp. salt

1 cup cold water
2 T. lemon juice
1 T. butter

Combine dry ingredients. Stir in water and lemon juice and bring to a full boil. Remove from heat; add butter. Serve with pineapple upside-down cake or white cake.

*Mrs. Luke Hoover, Goshen, IN*

*Don't be afraid to take a big step if it is required. You can't cross a chasm in two small jumps.*

# SALADS
## and
# DRESSINGS

Ehle Hoover

# VEGETABLE SALADS

## BEAN SALAD

2 cups canned green beans
2 cups canned yellow beans
2 cups canned kidney beans
1 cup chopped onions
1/2 cup chopped green pepper
1 clove garlic, minced

2/3 cup vinegar
1/3 cup sugar
1/4 cup olive or other oil
1 tsp. Worcestershire sauce
1 tsp. salt
1/8 tsp pepper

Combine cooled beans, onions, peppers and garlic.   Shake remaining ingredients in a jar; toss with bean mixture.

## KIDNEY BEAN SALAD

2 1/2 cups canned or cooked
    kidney beans
1 onion, chopped
1/4 cup chopped celery
2 hard-cooked eggs, chopped

1/4 cup salad dressing
2 T. vinegar
2 T. sugar
2 T. cream or milk
1/2 tsp. salt

Drain beans; add onion, celery and eggs.   Combine and add remaining ingredients. Chill before serving.

## NAVY BEAN SALAD

1 lb. dry navy beans
6 cups hot water
1/2 tsp. butter
2 tsp. salt
1/2 tsp. pepper
1/2 tsp. dry mustard
1/2 cup ketchup
1/2 cup cooking oil
1 tsp. paprika

1/2 cup sugar
2 T. minced onion
1/2 cup vinegar
1/2 tsp. salt
1 cup chopped ham
1 medium pepper, chopped
1 cup chopped celery
Small jar olives, chopped

Soak beans in water 1 hour.  Cook over low heat with butter, about 1 hour.  Add salt, pepper and mustard; simmer 5 minutes. Remove from heat; drain.  Combine ketchup, oil, paprika, sugar, onion, vinegar and salt and stir into hot beans. Refrigerate overnight.   Fold in remaining ingredients.

*Connie Rodes, Milford, IN*

81

## BROCCOLI SALAD I

| | |
|---|---|
| 1 bunch broccoli | 1/2 cup mayonnaise |
| 2 hard-cooked eggs, chopped | 1/4 cup sugar |
| 1 cup cubed Cheddar cheese | 1 T. vinegar |
| 1/2 small onion | 1/8 tsp. salt |
| Bacon bits | |

Cut broccoli in small flowerets; peel and chop stem. Add eggs, cheese, onion and bacon. Combine dressing ingredients; toss together lightly just before serving.

*Mary Zook, Virginia Beach, VA*

## BROCCOLI SALAD II

*For a different dressing delete vinegar and sugar, and combine half a package of Hidden Valley Ranch dip mix with 3/4 cup mayonnaise.*

| | |
|---|---|
| 1 bunch broccoli | 1 small onion, chopped |
| 10 strips bacon, fried | 3/4 to 1 cup mayonnaise |
| 1 cup salted sunflower seeds or | 2 T. vinegar |
| salted peanuts | 1/4 cup sugar |

Chop broccoli and crumble bacon; add sunflower seeds and onion. Combine dressing ingredients and toss.

*Mrs. Isaac Kulp, Millersburg, IN*      *Connie Rodes, Milford, IN*
*Mrs. Marvin Sensenig, Penn Yan, NY*

## BROCCOLI CAULIFLOWER SALAD

*Dressing can also be made using 1 1/4 cups mayonnaise mixed with 1/2 cup sugar and 2 tablespoons vinegar.*

| | |
|---|---|
| 1 head cauliflower | 2 hard-cooked eggs, opt. |
| 1 head broccoli | 1 cup mayonnaise |
| 1/2 lb. bacon, fried crisp | 1/4 cup sugar |
| 1 cup shredded cheese | 1 tsp. vinegar |
| 1 onion, chopped fine | |

Cut cauliflower and broccoli into bite-sized pieces. Add crumbled bacon, cheese and onion. Chop and add hard-cooked eggs, if desired. Combine dressing ingredients and toss just before serving.

*Karen Meador, Rossville, IN*      *Beverly Stauffer, New Paris, IN*

***Worrying does not empty tomorrow of its troubles, it empties today of its strength.***

## HOT CABBAGE SALAD

| | |
|---|---|
| 1/2 medium head cabbage | Vinegar |
| 8 strips bacon, fried crisp | 2 T. sugar |
| Bacon drippings | 1/2 tsp. salt |

Shred cabbage; crumble bacon over cabbage. Combine equal amount of vinegar with bacon drippings. Add sugar and salt, bring to a boil and pour over cabbage. Serve warm.

## CREAMY CARROT SALAD

*For a different taste, delete celery and onion and add 1/4 cup raisins.*

| | |
|---|---|
| 4 medium carrots, shredded | 2 T. sugar |
| 1/4 cup chopped celery | 2 T. vinegar |
| 1 T. minced onion | 1/4 tsp. salt |
| 2 T. mayonnaise | |

Toss carrots, celery and onion. Mix dressing ingredients and pour over vegetables. This is best made 12 hours before serving. Several tablespoons of milk can be added for creamier salad.

*Esther Brubaker, Memphis, MO      Brenda Zimmerman, Ephrata, PA*

## CAULIFLOWER SALAD

| | |
|---|---|
| 1 head cauliflower, chopped | 1/4 cup sugar, opt. |
| 1 large head lettuce, chopped | 1/3 cup Parmesan cheese |
| 1 onion, chopped | 1 lb. bacon, fried and crumbled |
| 2 cups mayonnaise | |

Combine cauliflower, lettuce and onion. Combine mayonnaise and sugar; spread over vegetables. Top with cheese and bacon. Refrigerate. Toss 30 minutes before serving. Add a little cream for thinner dressing.

*Donna Herr, Nappanee, IN      Anna Mae Hoover, Reinholds, PA      Mrs. James Kulp, Unity, WI*
*Velma Martin, Nappanee, IN*

## CAULIFLOWER PEA SALAD

| | |
|---|---|
| 3 cups chopped cauliflower | 2 T. cream or milk |
| 2 cups cooked peas, cooled | 1 tsp. seasoned salt |
| 1 cup salad dressing | |

Combine cauliflower and peas. Combine and add dressing ingredients.

# COLESLAW

| | |
|---|---|
| 6 to 8 cups shredded cabbage | 2/3 cup sugar |
| 2 carrots, shredded | 2/3 cup vinegar |
| 1 green pepper, chopped, opt. | 2 tsp. celery seed |
| 1/4 cup minced onion | 1 1/2 tsp. salt |
| 1/2 cup cold water | 1/4 tsp. pepper |
| 1 pkg. unflavored gelatin | 2/3 cup cooking oil |
| 1/4 cup cold water | |

Toss first 4 ingredients. Sprinkle with 1/2 cup water. Chill. Soften gelatin in 1/4 cup water. Mix next 5 ingredients and bring to a boil. Stir in softened gelatin. Cool until slightly thickened. Beat well; gradually beat in oil. Pour over vegetables.

*Esther Brubaker, Memphis, MO     Mrs. Clarence Martin, Snover, MI*

# CREAMY COLESLAW

| | |
|---|---|
| 1/2 head cabbage | 4 tsp. sugar |
| 1 carrot, shredded | 1 T. lemon juice or vinegar |
| 1 T. onion | 1/4 tsp of salt |
| 1/2 cup salad dressing | |

Combine vegetables. Mix remaining ingredients; stir into vegetables.

*Mrs. LaVerne (Virginia) Hoover, Goshen, IN*

# CUCUMBER SALAD

| | |
|---|---|
| 4 cups sliced cucumbers | 1/4 cup sugar |
| 1/4 cup chopped onion | 1/4 cup vinegar |
| 1 cup mayonnaise | 1/4 tsp. salt |

Combine cucumbers and onion. Mix together dressing ingredients and add. Cover and refrigerate for 2 hours.

# TOMATO CUCUMBER SALAD

| | |
|---|---|
| 2 to 3 tomatoes, peeled | 2 T. vinegar or lemon juice |
| 1 cucumber, peeled | 1/4 tsp. salt |
| 1/2 cup salad dressing | 1/4 tsp. oregano |

Dice tomatoes and cucumbers. Mix and add remaining ingredients.

# LETTUCE SALAD

1/2 head lettuce, chopped
1 cup cubed ham
1 cup cubed cheese

1/2 cup shredded carrots
1/2 cup chopped celery

Toss; serve with your favorite dressing. Onions, radishes, tomatoes, broccoli, cauliflower, or cucumbers may be added as well.

*Mrs. Marvin (Lydia) Sensenig, Penn Yan, NY*

# LAYERED LETTUCE SALAD

1 head lettuce, shredded
1 cup celery, diced
1 cup carrots, shredded
4 hard-cooked eggs, chopped
2 cups slightly cooked peas

1 medium onion, chopped
8 slices bacon, fried, crumbled
2 cups mayonnaise
2 T. sugar
1 cup shredded cheese

Layer the first 7 ingredients in the order given in a 13x9 pan. Make sure the lettuce is not wet. Mix mayonnaise and sugar; spread on top. Top with cheese. Refrigerate 8 hours or over night. Serve layered or toss. Toss in tomatoes if desired.

*Erla (Horst) Horning, Penn Yan, NY     Mrs. James Kulp, Unity, WI     Mrs. Susan Martin, Romulus,NY*

# CROUTONS

1 loaf frozen bread
1 1/4 cups butter or margarine
1 tsp. pepper

1 tsp. garlic salt
1/2 tsp. celery salt
1 heaping T. bacon bits

Cut frozen bread into 3/8-inch cubes. Melt butter and add remaining ingredients. Pour over bread cubes. Toast at 275° until crisp.

*Vera Witmer, Goshen, IN*

# CARROT-LETTUCE SALAD

Lettuce
Carrots
Cheese
2 cups sugar

1 cup vinegar
1 T. mayonnaise
1/2 cup cream
1/8 tsp. salt

Layer lettuce and carrots in a 13x9 pan; top with cheese. Combine dressing ingredients; pour on salad when ready to serve. Toss if desired.

*Janet Fox, Memphis, MO*

# GREEN LETTUCE SALAD

| | |
|---|---|
| 1 clove garlic | 2 T. snipped parsley |
| 4 cups romaine lettuce | 2 green onions, chopped |
| 2 cups head lettuce | 1 T. tarragon vinegar |
| 2 cups fresh spinach | 1 T. lemon juice |
| 1/2 cup mayonnaise | 1/4 tsp. salt |
| 1/4 cup sour cream | 1/8 tsp. pepper |

Rub the salad bowl with cut garlic clove. Save half to put in the dressing. Tear greens into bite-sized pieces. Combine remaining ingredients for dressing; mix well. Pour over greens just before serving. Toss lightly.

# TACO SALAD

*If you don't have Western dressing on hand make your own dressing by mixing 1 1/2 cups of salsa, 1/2 cup sour cream and a teaspoon or two of chili powder.*

| | |
|---|---|
| 2 lb. ground beef | Chopped tomatoes |
| 1 medium onion, chopped | Celery |
| 2 tsp. chili powder, opt. | 3 cups shredded Cheddar cheese |
| 1 1/2 tsp. salt | 1 bag taco chips |
| 2 cups kidney beans, drained | 16 oz. bottle Western dressing |
| 1 medium head lettuce, chopped | |

Brown and drain ground beef. Season with chili powder and salt. Cool. Toss with everything but chips and dressing. Stir in chips and dressing just before serving.

*Elaine Martin, Nappanee, IN*

# MEATLESS TACO SALAD

| | |
|---|---|
| 2 T. butter | 1/2 head lettuce, broken |
| 2 T. Worcestershire sauce | 2 medium tomatoes, chopped |
| 2 cups kidney beans | 1 small onion, sliced thin |
| 1 cup frozen peas, opt. | 1 cup shredded cheese |
| Chili powder | 1 bag taco chips |
| Red pepper | |

Melt butter; add Worcestershire sauce. Stir in kidney beans and peas. Sprinkle with chili powder and red pepper. Cool. Toss with vegetables, cheese and taco chips. Add your favorite dressing.

*Mary Ann Martin, Sauk Centre, MN*

# PEA SALAD

4 cups cooked peas
2 hard-cooked eggs, chopped
2 T. minced onion
1/2 to 1 cup diced cheese
1 cup cubed cooked ham, opt.

1/2 cup salad dressing
2 T. sugar
1 T. lemon juice
1 tsp. mustard

Mix together peas, eggs, onion, cheese and ham.  Combine dressing ingredients and stir into pea mixture.  Keeps well in the refrigerator.

*Mrs. LaVerne (Virginia) Hoover, Goshen, IN*

# POTATO SALAD

*If you prefer a sweeter dressing, mix 1/2 cup sugar, 1/4 cup vinegar and 1 tablespoon of mustard with a cup of mayonnaise.*

4 cups cubed, cooked potatoes (4
   medium potatoes)
1/2 to 1 cup chopped celery
1/2 cup chopped onion
1/2 cup grated carrots, opt.
1/4 cup chopped sweet pickles

4 hard-cooked eggs, chopped
2/3 cup mayonnaise
2 tsp. mustard
1 1/2 tsp. salt
3 T. chopped pimento, opt.
2 tsp. celery seed, opt

Combine potatoes, celery, onion, pickles and eggs.  Blend mayonnaise with mustard; stir in remaining ingredients.  Mix mayonnaise mixture lightly with potato mixture until well coated.  Serve on salad greens if desired.

*Sharon Fox, Baring, MO      Connie Rodes, Milford, IN*

# BIG BATCH POTATO SALAD

3 cups salad dressing
1/3 cup mustard
2 cups sugar
1 T. salt
1/2 cup milk
1/4 cup vinegar

12 cups cooked, finely diced or
   shredded potatoes
12 hard-cooked eggs, chopped
1 1/2 cups chopped celery
1/2 onion, chopped

Combine ingredients in the first column for dressing.  Combine potatoes, eggs, celery and onion; add dressing.

*Eva Schrock, Hayward, WI*

**If you don't want anyone to know it, don't do it.**

## HOT GERMAN POTATO SALAD I

| | |
|---|---|
| 2 lb. potatoes | 1 tsp. salt |
| 6 slices bacon | 1/4 tsp. pepper |
| 1 large onion, minced | 1 T. sugar |
| 1/2 cup vinegar | 2 egg yolks |
| 1/2 cup beef or chicken broth | 2 T. water |

Cook unpeeled potatoes; peel while warm; slice thin. Fry bacon till almost crisp; add onion. Cook 2 minutes; add vinegar, broth, salt, pepper and sugar. Simmer 2 minutes. Beat egg yolks and water; add. Pour over potatoes; mix gently.

*Evan Martin, Osceola, IN*

## HOT GERMAN POTATO SALAD II

| | |
|---|---|
| 5 strips bacon | 1 1/3 cups water |
| 3/4 cup chopped onion | 1/4 cup sugar |
| 2 ribs celery, chopped | 1 tsp. salt |
| 3 T. flour | 1/8 tsp. pepper |
| 2/3 cup vinegar | 8 cups sliced cooked potatoes |

Fry bacon. Drain; reserve drippings. Cook onion and celery in drippings. Stir in flour slowly; add vinegar and water. Cook till thick. Add sugar, salt and pepper; simmer 10 minutes. Add potatoes and bacon. Heat through.

*Mrs. Luke Hoover, Goshen, IN*

## BAKED POTATO SALAD

| | |
|---|---|
| 8 potatoes | Salt and pepper to taste |
| 1/2 cup chopped onion | 1/2 lb. bacon, partially fried and |
| 1 cup mayonnaise | crumbled |
| 1 lb. American cheese, diced | 1/2 cup sliced olives |

Cook potatoes; peel and dice. Mix all but olives and put into a 12x8 baking dish. Place bacon and olives on top. Bake at 325° for 1 hour.

*Connie Rodes, Milford, IN*

## PICNIC POTATO SQUARES

| | |
|---|---|
| 2 pkg. unflavored gelatin | 1/2 tsp. salt |
| 2 1/4 cups milk | 1/4 tsp. pepper |
| 1 cup salad dressing | 2 1/2 cups diced cooked potatoes |
| 1 T. mustard | 1/2 cup shredded carrots |
| 2 T. onion | 1/2 cup chopped celery |
| 2 tsp. sugar | 1/3 cup chopped pickles |

Sprinkle gelatin over 1 cup milk in saucepan. Cook over low heat until gelatin dissolves. Remove from heat; add remaining ingredients, adding potatoes, carrots, celery and pickles last. Pour into a 13x9 pan; chill. Serve in squares.

*Diane Bauman, Listowel, Ontario, Canada*

## SPAGHETTI SQUASH SALAD

3 cups cooked spaghetti squash
2 cups bite-sized cauliflower
    pieces
1 cup thinly sliced celery
1 medium onion, diced
1 green or red pepper, diced

1 tsp. dill weed, opt.
1 cup sugar
1 T. salt
1/2 cup cooking oil
1 cup vinegar
1 tsp. paprika

Combine vegetables. Put remaining ingredients in a jar with a tight lid and shake. Pour over vegetables. Chill well before serving.

*Vera Witmer, Goshen, IN*

## SPINACH SALAD I

*For an oil based dressing combine, 1/2 cup oil, 1/4 cup sugar, 2 T. vinegar, 2 T. minced onion, 1/2 tsp. salt, and 1/4 tsp. mustard.*

6 cups chopped fresh spinach
4 hard-cooked eggs chopped
6 slices fried bacon, crumbled

1 onion, chopped
1 cup alfalfa sprouts

Mix all ingredients. Serve with bleu cheese or a sour cream based dressing.

*Mary Ann Martin, Sauk Centre, MN*

## SPINACH SALAD II

1 lb. fresh spinach
2 cups fresh bean sprouts
8 oz. can water chestnuts,
    drained and sliced
4 hard-cooked eggs
1/4 cup sliced green onions
1/2 lb. bacon, fried and crumbled

1 cup sliced fresh mushrooms
3/4 cup sugar
1/4 cup vinegar
1/4 cup cooking oil
1/3 cup ketchup
1 to 2 tsp. salt
1 tsp. Worcestershire sauce

Tear washed and dried spinach into large salad bowl. Wash and drain bean sprouts (canned sprouts are okay). Toss in water chestnuts, eggs, onions, bacon, and mushrooms. Combine remaining ingredients to make dressing. Add dressing when ready to serve. Toss until spinach leaves are well coated.

*Connie Rodes, Milford, IN*

# PASTA AND EGG SALADS

## CLASSIC MACARONI SALAD

2 cups dry macaroni
1 cup diced celery
1/2 cup chopped pepper
1 small onion, chopped
1 cup mayonnaise

2 T. vinegar
1 T. mustard
1 tsp. sugar
1 tsp. salt
1/4 tsp. pepper

Cook macaroni in salt water; drain. Add celery, pepper and onion. Combine remaining ingredients; stir into first mixture. Cover and chill.

## MACARONI SALAD WITH COOKED DRESSING

6 cups cooked macaroni
4 hard-cooked eggs
2 cups chopped celery
2 small onions
2 cups carrots
2 cups sugar
1/2 cup vinegar

1/2 cup water
1 T. butter or margarine
1/2 to 1 T. mustard
Salt to taste
4 eggs
1 1/3 cups salad dressing

Mix together macaroni, eggs and vegetables. Combine sugar, vinegar, water, butter, mustard, salt and eggs; bring to a boil and boil 2 minutes. Cool. Add salad dressing; mix with first mixture. Chopped lettuce can be added.

*Mrs. Norman Burkholder, Mertztown, PA*     *Mrs. James Horst, East Earl, PA*

## BIG BATCH MACARONI SALAD

*A 6-quart kettle full of cooked and salted potatoes can be substituted for macaroni.*

1 1/4 lb. dry macaroni
24 hard-cooked eggs
1 quart sweet pickles
1 1/2 lb. cheese
1/2 large bunch celery
Carrots, radishes, and onions
3 cups salad dressing
2 cups sugar

1 1/4 cups vinegar
3 T. mustard
2 tsp. celery salt
1 tsp. black pepper
1 tsp. oregano
4 shakes seasoned salt
3 shakes paprika
2 shakes sage

Cook macaroni in salt water; drain and cool. Peel and cool eggs. Combine macaroni and diced or shredded eggs, pickles, cheese, celery, and equal parts of carrots, and radishes and onions in a 13 quart bowl. Combine dressing ingredients. Mix well. Add to first mixture and mix thoroughly.

*Mrs. William (Lena) Kilmer, California, MO*

90

## MACARONI SALAD WITH BROCCOLI

1 1/2 cups uncooked macaroni
1 1/2 tsp. salt
2 medium carrots, sliced
1 medium bunch broccoli
6 T. cooking oil
1 1/2 T. vinegar
1 1/2 T. honey

1 1/2 tsp. mustard
1/2 tsp. salt
1/8 tsp. pepper
1/3 cup sliced black olives
1/4 cup thinly sliced scallions or
　onions
1/4 cup diced red pepper

Add macaroni and salt to large pot of boiling water. Boil 7 minutes; add carrots. Boil about 2 minutes and add broccoli florets. Boil just until vegetables are crisp-tender and pasta al dente. Drain well. Whisk together oil, vinegar, honey, mustard, salt and pepper. Combine with pasta mixture and remaining vegetables. Toss gently but thoroughly. Serve warm or cold. If serving cold, rinse pasta mixture in cold water first.

*Vera Witmer, Goshen, IN*

Eight ounces of macaroni equal approximately 2 cups dry and 4 cups cooked macaroni. To cook, stir 8 ounces of macaroni into 2 quarts boiling water to which 2 to 3 teaspoons of salt have been added.

## MACARONI SALAD WITH SPINACH

3 oz. uncooked macaroni
2 cups torn spinach or lettuce
1/4 lb. ham or bologna, cubed
1/2 cup chopped celery
1/4 cup sliced radishes

1/4 cup diced cheese
2 T. minced onion
1/4 cup French dressing
1/4 cup mayonnaise
1 to 2 hard-cooked eggs

Boil macaroni in salted water. Drain and cool under running water. Combine all but last 3 ingredients. Mix together French dressing and mayonnaise. Toss. Slice eggs on top.

*Ellen Newswanger, Kutztown, PA*

## CHUNKY MACARONI SALAD

8 oz. medium shell macaroni
1 cup mayonnaise
1 small onion, chopped
1/8 tsp. pepper

2 cups cubed tomatoes
1 cup cubed ham
1 cup cubed cheese
1/2 cup stuffed olives

Cook macaroni in salted water. Drain and cool under running water. Stir in mayonnaise, onion and pepper. Carefully toss in remaining ingredients.

## TUNA MACARONI SALAD

1 cup (4 oz.) macaroni
1 cup mayonnaise
1 to 2 T. vinegar
1/2 tsp. salt
1/4 tsp pepper

6 oz. (or larger) can of tuna
1 cup chopped celery
1 small onion, chopped
1 T. dill weed, opt.

Cook macaroni. Drain and cool under running water. Combine first column. Add remaining ingredients; toss to coat.

## CHICKEN SALAD

2 cups uncooked macaroni
3/4 cup salad dressing
1/2 tsp. dill weed
1/4 tsp. pepper

2 cups diced cooked chicken
1 cup diced tomatoes
1 cup carrot slices, opt.
1 small onion, chopped

Cook macaroni in boiling salted water; drain. Cool under running water. Drain well. Combine with salad dressing, dill weed and pepper; mix lightly. Gently toss in remaining ingredients. Serve on lettuce or add chopped lettuce.

*Mrs. Ray (Elsie) Hoover, Stratford, WI*

## HOT CHICKEN SALAD

2 cups diced cooked chicken
2 cups chopped celery
3/4 cup slivered almonds
1/2 cup cheese
2 tsp. grated onion

1/2 tsp. mustard
1/2 tsp. salt
1 cup mayonnaise
1 cup crushed potato chips

Mix first 7 ingredients. Fold in mayonnaise. Put in a greased casserole and sprinkle with potato chips. Bake at 375° for 15 to 20 minutes.

*Sheryl Weaver, Goshen, IN*

## MOLDED CHICKEN SALAD

1 pkg. unflavored gelatin
2 cups chicken broth, cooled
2 cups diced cooked chicken
1/2 cup finely chopped celery
2 hard-cooked eggs, chopped

1/4 cup mayonnaise
1 T. chopped sweet pickle
1 T. lemon juice
1/4 tsp. salt

Soften gelatin in 1/2 cup broth for 10 minutes. Heat remaining broth and stir in gelatin to dissolve. Chill till it begins to set. Grind chicken; add with remaining ingredients. Pour into a loaf pan and chill.

## EGG SALAD

6 hard-cooked eggs, chopped
1/4 cup mayonnaise or salad
   dressing
2 T. finely chopped onion

2 T. pickle relish, opt.
2 tsp. mustard
1 tsp. salt
1/8 tsp. pepper

Combine all ingredients.  Mix well.  Eat plain, in sandwiches or on tomato slices.

## STUFFED EGGS

*Hard-cooked eggs are more tender if simmered for 20 to 25 minutes and not boiled.  It takes 10 minutes to hard-boil an egg.*

6 hard-cooked eggs
3 T. mayonnaise
1 tsp. mustard
1 tsp. vinegar

1/2 tsp. Worcestershire sauce
1/2 tsp. salt
1/8 tsp. pepper
Paprika

Cut shelled and cooled eggs in half lengthwise.  Remove yolks; save whites. Mash yolks and add remaining ingredients except paprika.  Mix until fluffy.  Fill egg whites with yolk mixture.  Sprinkle with paprika.  For a different taste add 2 T. chopped olives, onions, crumbled bacon or cheese.

# FRUIT SALADS

## AMBROSIA SALAD

1 cup diced oranges
1 cup seedless grapes
2 bananas, sliced
3 T. lemon juice

1 cup whipped topping
1 cup mayonnaise
1/4 cup coconut

Combine fruits; sprinkle with lemon juice.  Chill.  Fold topping into mayonnaise. Gently combine with fruit.  Top with coconut.

*Not for a single day can I discern my way,*
*But this I surely know—*
*Who gives the day will show the way,*
*So I securely go.* John Oxenham

## APPLE SALAD

3 cups chopped unpeeled apples
1 cup miniature marshmallows
1/2 cup raisins
1/2 cup coconut
1/2 cup chopped nuts or celery

1/4 cup peanut butter
1/4 cup sugar
1/2 cup mayonnaise
1/4 cup cream or milk

Combine first 5 ingredients. Mix peanut butter and sugar; stir in mayonnaise and cream. Stir into apple mixture. Chill. This can also be made using just mayonnaise for a dressing.

*Mrs. Ray (Elsie) Hoover, Stratford, WI*

## APPLE SALAD WITH COOKED DRESSING

8 apples, Delicious preferred
2 bananas
1/2 cup chopped celery
1/2 cup raisins
1/4 cup coconut
1/2 cup peanuts
1 cup sugar

1 T. cornstarch
1/4 tsp. salt
1 cup water
1/4 cup cream
1 tsp. vinegar
1 tsp. vanilla

Dice but do not pare apples. Place in a weak salt water solution or sprinkle with lemon juice so they don't get dark. Drain apples; add bananas, celery, raisins, coconut and nuts. Combine sugar, cornstarch, and salt. Stir in water, cream and vinegar; bring to a boil. Remove from heat; stir in vanilla. Cool. Add to fruit mixture.

*Arlene Hoover, Fortuna, MO*

## APPLE PINEAPPLE SALAD

*For a different dressing cook together a cup of sugar, a tablespoon of corn starch, 1/2 cup water, an egg, a tablespoon of lemon juice and a tablespoon of butter. Cool and stir into apple mixture.*

6 to 8 red apples
12 large marshmallows, cut up
20 oz. can pineapple tidbits
Nuts or grapes
1 cup pineapple juice

2 eggs
3/4 cup sugar
2 T. flour
2 T. butter
1 cup whipping cream

Leave half of the apples unpeeled for color. Dice apples and quarter marshmallows, or use 2 cups small marshmallows. Mix with drained pineapple and nuts. Cook juice, eggs, sugar, flour and butter until thick. Cool; pour over apple mixture, stirring to coat. Can be refrigerated overnight before cream is added and it stays crisp. Whip cream and add just before serving.

*Mrs. LaVerne (Virginia) Hoover, Goshen, IN     Mrs. Isaac Z. Newswanger, Kutztown, PA*

94

# APPLESAUCE SALAD WITH CREAM CHEESE FILLING

*This is also good without filling. Dissolve 1/2 cup red cinnamon candies in boiling water before adding gelatin for a tangier salad.*

6 oz. red gelatin
2 cups boiling water
3 cups applesauce
1 tsp. lemon juice

1/2 cup salad dressing
8 oz. cream cheese
1/2 cup finely chopped nuts
1/2 cup finely chopped celery

Dissolve gelatin in boiling water. Add applesauce and lemon juice. Pour half in mold or 8x8 pan and chill till set. Combine remaining ingredients and spread on top. Pour on remaining gelatin. Chill till set.

# CHERRY DUMP SALAD

8 oz. frozen whipped topping
14 oz. can sweetened condensed
  milk
21 oz. can cherry pie filling

20 oz. can crushed pineapple
1 cup chopped pecans
2 cups small marshmallows
Coconut, opt.

Combine whipped topping and sweetened condensed milk. Add remaining ingredients and chill till ready to serve.

*Mrs. James (Margaret) Ramer, Dallas, TX*

# CRANBERRY FLUFF

12 oz. fresh cranberries, chopped
20 oz. can crushed pineapple,
  drained

3/4 cup sugar
2 cups small marshmallows
8 oz. frozen whipped topping

Mix cranberries with drained pineapple and sugar. Fold in marshmallows and whipped topping. Chill. Several cups whipped cream can be used instead of frozen whipped topping.

# CRANBERRY RELISH

4 cups fresh cranberries
3 apples, cored and quartered

2 oranges, seeds taken out
2 cups sugar

Grind cranberries, unpeeled apples and unpeeled oranges in a grinder or blender. Add sugar; mix well. Chill. Best if made a day before serving.

*Mrs. Ray (Elsie) Hoover, Stratford, WI*

# FRUIT SALAD

20 oz. can pineapple chunks
2 cups seedless grapes
2 to 3 oranges
2 to 3 bananas

1 1/4 cups pineapple juice
2 T. lemon juice
1/2 cup sugar
2 T. cornstarch

Combine drained pineapple and grapes; save juice. Peel and cube oranges and bananas; add. Add enough water or orange juice to pineapple juice to make 1 1/4 cups. Combine juices, sugar and cornstarch and cook till thickened. Cool slightly; pour over fruit. Chill several hours.

# QUICK FRUIT SALAD

*Unexpected guests coming? Add a cup of miniature marshmallows.*

1 cup pineapple chunks
1 cup mandarin oranges
1 cup coconut

1 cup seedless grapes
1 cup sour cream
1/4 cup sugar, opt.

Combine fruit. Mix together sour cream and sugar; stir into fruit. Fresh orange chunks may be used.

# FRUIT SALAD WITH RICE

20 oz. can pineapple chunks
2 medium apples
1/2 cup raisins
1 cup cold cooked rice
1/2 cup pecans
2 to 3 cups small marshmallows

2 heaping T. sugar
2 T. flour
1 egg
2 T. butter or margarine
3 to 4 cups whipped topping

Drain pineapple and save juice. Mix first 6 ingredients. Mix sugar with flour; add a little pineapple juice to make a paste; mix in egg, butter and remaining juice. Cook until thick. Cool; mix with whipped topping. Combine salad and dressing.

*Connie Rodes, Milford, IN*

# FROZEN FRUIT SALAD

8 oz. cream cheese
1/2 to 3/4 cup mayonnaise or
    salad dressing
2 1/2 cups small marshmallows
16 oz. can fruit cocktail, well
    drained

15 oz. can crushed pineapple,
    well drained
1/2 cup halved maraschino
    cherries, opt.
2 cups whipped cream or topping

Blend cream cheese and mayonnaise. Stir in marshmallows and fruits; fold in cream. Pour into a 13x9 pan and freeze 6 hours or overnight. Thaw about 20 minutes before serving.

*Mrs. Ray (Elsie) Hoover, Stratford, WI*

## EASY FROZEN FRUIT SALAD

20 oz. can crushed pineapple
5 ripe mashed bananas
2 cups orange juice

1 cup water
1 cup sugar, opt.

Combine all ingredients. Freeze in a 13x9 pan or in paper cups for individual servings.

*Renetta Brovont, New Era, MI*

## MARSHMALLOW PINEAPPLE SALAD

16 oz. marshmallows
1/2 cup milk
2 cups cottage cheese
16 oz. cream cheese

20 oz. can crushed pineapple
1 cup chopped nuts
2 cups whipped cream or topping

Melt marshmallows and milk over low heat. Cream cottage cheese and cream cheese; add slightly cooled marshmallow mixture. Add well-drained pineapple and nuts after mixture is completely cool. Fold in whipped cream. Chill. Chopped maraschino cherries can be added.

*Mrs. Laureen Gerber, Fairview, MI*     *Verna Overholt, Due West, SC*

## PINEAPPLE PISTACHIO SALAD

20 oz. can crushed pineapple
1 cup small marshmallows
3.4 oz box instant pistachio
    pudding

9 oz. frozen whipped topping
Nuts and maraschino cherries,
    optional

Combine undrained pineapple, marshmallows, and pudding. Add whipped topping. Add nuts and cherries if desired. Chill.

*Doreen Zimmerman, Claypool, IN*     *Mrs. Phillip Zimmerman, Versailles, MO*

*A person is never so empty as when he is full of self.*

# GELATIN SALADS

## CARROT SALAD

3 oz. orange gelatin
1/4 tsp. salt
1 1/2 cups boiling water
8 oz. can crushed pineapple

1 T. lemon juice
1 cup grated carrots
1/3 cup chopped pecans

Dissolve gelatin and salt in boiling water. Add undrained pineapple and lemon juice. Chill till very thick; fold in carrots and pecans.

*Mrs. Ray (Elsie) Hoover, Stratford, WI*

## CHERRY CHEESE SALAD

1 quart canned cherries
15 oz. can pineapple rings
2 pkg. unflavored gelatin
2 cups cottage cheese
1/3 cups mayonnaise

2 T. lemon juice, opt.
2 T. lime juice, opt.
1/2 cup honey
1/4 cup slivered almonds

Drain juice from cherries and pineapple to make 1 1/2 cups. Soften gelatin in juice then microwave 1 minute until dissolved. Fold in cottage cheese, mayonnaise, juices and honey into gelatin mixture. Pour into a 13x9 pan. Add cherries and almonds. Arrange pineapple rings on top. Chill.

*Susanna Weaver, Nappanee, IN*

## CRANBERRY SALAD I

6 oz. pkg. raspberry gelatin
1 pkg. unflavored gelatin
2 cups boiling water
2 cups cold water
12 oz. cranberries, ground

1 cup sugar
1 cup shredded apples
1/2 cup finely chopped celery
1 lb. 8 oz. cottage cheese
3 oz. cream cheese

Combine gelatins. Dissolve in boiling water; add cold water. Add cranberries, sugar, apples and celery. Pour into mold or bowl and chill. Cream cottage cheese and cream cheese in the blender, adding cream or milk to desired consistency. Serve sauce with salad. Apple or pear sauce can be substituted for shredded apples.

*Ruth Weaver, Nappanee, IN*

## CRANBERRY SALAD II

9 oz. flavored gelatin
3 cups boiling water
2 cups cold water
20 oz. can crushed pineapple
12 oz. cranberries

3 oranges, peeled and seeded
1 orange peel
1 cup sugar
4 to 5 apples, diced small
1 cup nuts, chopped

Dissolve gelatin in boiling water. Add cold water. When partially set add undrained pineapple. Blend fresh or frozen cranberries in blender until fine. Add orange chunks and orange peel and blend until fine. Add sugar. Fold cranberry mixture into gelatin mixture; add apples and nuts. Pour into a 13x9 pan or into molds. Chill overnight. A Thanksgiving favorite.

*Frances Hoover, Elkhart, IN*

## CRANBERRY SALAD III

3 oz. pkg. raspberry gelatin
1 cup boiling water
16 oz. whole or jellied cranberry
    sauce
3 oz. pkg. lemon gelatin
1 cup boiling water

3 oz. cream cheese
1/3 cup mayonnaise
8 oz. can crushed pineapple
1 cup whipping cream
1 cup small marshmallows

Dissolve raspberry gelatin in boiling water; stir in cranberry sauce. Pour into the bottom of a 1 1/2 quart mold. Chill until partially set. Dissolve lemon gelatin in boiling water; set aside. Combine cream cheese and mayonnaise; stir in lemon gelatin and undrained pineapple. Chill until partially set. Whip cream; fold into lemon gelatin; add marshmallows. Spread lemon layer on top of cranberry mixture. Chill until set.

*Rhoda Martin, Nappanee, IN*

## SMOOTH CRANBERRY SALAD

12 oz. cranberries
2 cups water
1 cup sugar
2 cups boiling water
6 oz. red gelatin

1 pkg. unflavored gelatin
1/2 cup cold water
1 cup pineapple with juice
2 cup seedless grapes

Cook cranberries in 2 cups water; strain. Add sugar. Dissolve red gelatin in boiling water; add to cranberry mixture. Bring to a boil. Soften gelatin in cold water; stir into hot cranberry mixture. Cool until partially set. Add pineapple and grapes. Chill until firm.

*Sheryl Wenger, Marlette, MI*

## HOLIDAY SALAD

2 T. unflavored gelatin
6 T. cold water
3/4 cup sugar
3 large carrots, shredded
20 oz. can crushed pineapple, undrained

1 cup chopped celery
1 cup chopped nuts
2 to 3 cups cottage cheese
1 cup mayonnaise
16 oz. frozen whipped topping

Soften gelatin in cold water. Bring to a boil and dissolve. Stir in sugar. Cool slightly. Stir in all but whipped topping. Fold in whipped topping. Garnish with carrot curls if desired. Refrigerate. Cubes of red and green gelatin can be added. Use 1/2 cup of boiling water and 1 cup cold water for 3 ounces of gelatin. The squares need to be firm.

*Vera Fox, Memphis, MO       Mrs. Elam Hoover, Versailles. MO*

**Do not use fresh or frozen pineapple, kiwi, papaya, or guava with gelatin – it will not set.**

## HOLIDAY RIBBON RING

6 oz. strawberry gelatin
1/3 cup sour cream

6 oz. lime gelatin
1/3 cup sour cream

Dissolve strawberry gelatin in 2 1/2 cups boiling water. Pour 1 1/2 cups into a 6 cup ring mold. Chill until set, but not firm, about 20 minutes or more. Chill remaining strawberry gelatin a separate bowl; gradually add 1/3 cup sour cream. Spoon over gelatin in the mold. Chill until set, but not firm. Repeat with lime gelatin. Any flavor gelatin may be used.

*Mrs. Sam Newswanger, Goshen, IN*

## LEMON LIME PINEAPPLE SALAD

3 oz. lemon gelatin
3 oz. lime gelatin
3 cups boiling water
24 large marshmallows

6 oz. cream cheese
2 cups crushed pineapple
1 cup chopped nuts

Dissolve gelatin in boiling water; add marshmallows and cream cheese. Put in the blender and blend well. Mix in pineapple and nuts. Chill.

*Mrs. John (Twila) Kulp, Mosinee, WI*

# LIME DELIGHT SALAD

6 oz. lime gelatin
20 oz. can crushed pineapple
1 cup boiling water
1 lb. pkg. small marshmallows

1/4 cup finely chopped celery
1/4 cup chopped nuts
2 cups cream
8 oz. cream cheese, softened

Heat first 4 ingredients, including juice from pineapple, until marshmallows are melted; let congeal. Add celery and nuts; chill until firm. Whip cream and mix with cream cheese. Beat into gelatin mixture. Lemon or orange gelatin can be substituted for lime gelatin.

*Sarah Imhoff, Sheridan, MI     Mrs. Larry Zimmerman, Elkhart, IN*

# LIME PEAR SALAD

1 quart pears
8 oz. cream cheese

6 oz. lime gelatin
2 cups unwhipped cream

Drain pears; save juice. Add enough water to pear juice to make 2 cups. Heat to boiling. Add gelatin; stir to dissolve. Blend pears and cream cheese in blender; add gelatin and unwhipped cream.

*Karen Weaver, Milford, IN*

# ORANGE COTTAGE CHEESE SALAD

3 oz. orange gelatin
16 oz. cottage cheese

11 oz. can mandarin oranges
2 cups whipped topping

Mix dry gelatin with cottage cheese and drained oranges. Fold in whipped topping. Crushed pineapple or other fruit can be used instead of oranges.

*Mrs. Ray (Elsie) Hoover, Stratford, WI*

# ORANGE CREAM CHEESE SALAD LOAF

11 oz. can mandarin oranges
6 oz. orange gelatin
1 1/2 cups boiling water

1 cup cold orange juice
Ice cubes
8 oz. cream cheese, softened

Drain oranges and arrange in a 9x5 loaf pan. Dissolve gelatin in boiling water. Combine juice and ice cubes to make 2 1/2 cups. Add to gelatin and stir until slightly thickened; remove any unmelted ice. Measure 1 cup gelatin; blend into softened cream cheese. Pour remaining gelatin over orange sections in pan Top with creamy mixture. Chill at least 4 hours. To serve turn upside down lettuce leaves.

*Kathleen Ramer, New Paris, IN*

# ORANGE PEAR SALAD

*A cup of chopped celery and a cup of chopped nuts can be substituted for pears.*

1 quart pears, drained
6 oz. orange gelatin
1 1/2 cups hot water
20 oz. can crushed pineapple,
   drained, (save juice)

1/4 cup sugar
1 T. flour
1 egg, beaten
1 cup whipped topping

Put drained pears in blender and chop. Dissolve gelatin in hot water then add 1/2 cup pear juice. Add pears and pineapple. Chill until firm. Make topping by cooking pineapple juice (add water to make 1 cup), sugar, flour, and egg until it thickens. Stir constantly so it doesn't burn. Cool mixture then fold in whipped topping and spread on salad. For a thicker topping use two eggs and three tablespoons flour. Lemon gelatin can be substituted for half of orange gelatin.

*Mary Ellen Hission, Plymouth, IN*    *Mrs. Larry Zimmerman, Elkhart, IN*

# PEACH SALAD

3 oz. peach gelatin
1 cup hot water
1 cup cold water
1 pkg. unflavored gelatin
1/2 cup cold water
1 cup light cream
1 cup sugar

1/2 cup chopped walnuts
1 tsp. vanilla
8 oz. cream cheese
6 oz. peach gelatin
1 quart peaches, reserve liquid
2 cups peach liquid and water
1 cup cold water

Dissolve 3 ounces of gelatin in hot water. Stir in cold water then pour into a 13x9 pan and chill until set. Soften unflavored gelatin in 1/2 cold water; set aside. Combine cream and sugar; heat but don't boil. Stir in softened gelatin; stir to dissolve. Add nuts, vanilla, and cream cheese. Stir until smooth; pour over first layer. Chill until set. Place peach slices on top of second layer. Add enough water to peach liquid to make 2 cups. Bring to a boil; add 6 ounces of gelatin and stir to dissolve. Add cold water. Pour over peaches. Chill till set. Cut into squares to serve.

*Rhoda Martin, Nappanee, IN*

**New mercies every morning, new strength for every day,**
**New hope for every trial, new courage for the way,**
**New peace for heart and spirit,**
**New favor and new love,**
**May God bestow these blessings**
**On you from heaven above.**

## RIBBON SALAD

6 oz. cherry gelatin
2 pkgs. unflavored gelatin
1/2 cup cold water
16 oz. crushed pineapple

16 oz. cream cheese, softened
4 cups whipped cream
6 oz. lime gelatin

Dissolve cherry gelatin in 2 cups boiling water. Add 2 cups cold water. Pour into a 13x9 pan; chill till firm. Soften unflavored gelatin in cold water. Bring undrained pineapple to a boil. Remove from heat; add gelatin; stir to dissolve. Cool completely; gradually beat in cream cheese; fold in whipped cream. Pour over first layer. Dissolve lime gelatin in 2 cups boiling water; add 2 cups cold water. Pour over cream cheese mixture when it starts to congeal. Chill until firm.

*Mrs. Laureen Gerber, Fairview, MI*

## SEAFOAM SALAD

1 cup pear juice
3 oz. orange or lime gelatin
3 oz. cream cheese, softened

1 envelope Dream Whip, whipped
1 cup pears

Heat juice; add gelatin and stir to dissolve. Chill. Combine cream cheese and whipped topping and beat until smooth. Beat partially set gelatin and add to cream cheese mixture. Fold in chopped pears. Chill until set.

*Charlotte Martin, Goshen, IN*

## SEVEN LAYER GELATIN SALAD

2 pkgs. unflavored gelatin
1/2 cup cold water
2 cups milk
1 cup sugar
16 oz. sour cream

1 T. vanilla
3 oz. lime gelatin
3 oz. lemon gelatin
3 oz. cherry gelatin
3 oz. orange gelatin

Soften unflavored gelatin in cold water. Bring milk to a boil; add gelatin and stir to dissolve. Remove from heat and stir in sugar, sour cream, and vanilla. Set aside. Dissolve lime gelatin in one cup hot water. Stir in 1/2 cup cold water and pour into a 13x9 pan. Chill until set. Pour on 1 1/2 cups sour cream mixture and chill until firm. Repeat with remaining gelatin, adding sour cream between layers. When adding a new layer pour onto a spoon so it doesn't make a hole in the layer that is set. To keep moisture from forming on top do not cover while cooling.

*Elaine Martin, Nappanee, IN*     *Velma Ramer, Nappanee, IN*
*Kathleen Ramer, New Paris, IN*

## SURPRISE CABBAGE SALAD

6 oz. lemon gelatin
6 oz. lime gelatin
4 cups hot water
2 cups small marshmallows
2 cups pineapple juice

2 cups crushed pineapple
2 cups mayonnaise
3 cups shredded cabbage
2 cups nuts
2 cups whipped cream

Dissolve both gelatins in hot water; add marshmallows. Stir until dissolved. Add next four ingredients; let stand until it starts to set. Fold in nuts and whipped cream.

*Sheryl Weaver, Goshen, IN*

## UNDER THE SEA SALAD

16 oz. pkg. marshmallows
8 oz. cream cheese
3 oz. orange gelatin
1 1/2 cups very hot water
1/2 cup salad dressing

20 oz. can crushed pineapple
1 cup whipping cream, whipped
3 oz. lime gelatin
1 1/2 cups hot water

Combine and melt first 4 ingredients in a double boiler or over low heat. Cool. Add next 3 ingredients and pour into a 13x9 pan. Dissolve lime gelatin in hot water. Cool until it starts to thicken; pour over first layer.

*Mrs. Elam Hoover, Versailles, MO*

# SALAD DRESSINGS

## BACON DRESSING

1 1/2 cups mayonnaise or salad
  dressing
1/4 cup light corn syrup
1/4 cup milk

6 slices bacon, fried crisp
2 T. finely chopped onion
1 T. parsley
1/4 tsp. pepper

Combine first 3 ingredients. Crumble and add bacon; add remaining ingredients. For thinner dressing add a little more milk. Refrigerate.

*Mrs. Ray (Elsie) Hoover, Stratford, WI*

# BEAN SALAD DRESSING

2 eggs
1/2 cup sugar
1 tsp. dry mustard
1/2 tsp. salt

1/4 cup vinegar
1 cup water
1 rounded T. flour

Put all into a double boiler and cook until thickened. This can also be used for potato salad but vinegar should be increased to 1/2 cup. Refrigerate.

*Sarah Imhoff, Sheridan, MI*

# BLEU CHEESE DRESSING

1 1/2 lb. bleu cheese
2 cups mayonnaise
1 cup sour cream
2 T. cooking oil

2 T. vinegar
1 tsp. garlic salt
1 tsp. onion salt
1/2 tsp. pepper

Blend everything together in the blender. Refrigerate. Makes 1 quart.

# BUTTERMILK DRESSING

1 cup buttermilk
1 cup mayonnaise
1 tsp. garlic salt
1 tsp. parsley flakes

1 tsp. minced dried onion
1/4 tsp. Accent
1/8 tsp. pepper

Combine all ingredients. Refrigerate.

# CAESAR DRESSING

1 1/2 cups mayonnaise
1/2 cup Parmesan cheese
1/4 cup light corn syrup

2 T. vinegar
1 clove garlic, pressed
1/4 tsp. pepper

Stir all ingredients until well blended. Refrigerate. Makes 2 cups.

# CREAMY CUCUMBER DRESSING

1 1/2 cups chopped, peeled and
    seeded cucumber
1 cup mayonnaise

2 T. chopped chives or onion
1 T. milk
1 T. lemon juice

Mix all ingredients; cover and chill. For a smoother dressing blend in blender. Refrigerate.

## CREAMY GREEN DRESSING

| | |
|---|---|
| 1/2 cup mayonnaise or salad dressing | 1 T. lemon juice |
| | 1/2 garlic clove, minced |
| 1/4 cup sour cream | 1/4 tsp. salt |
| 2 T. snipped fresh parsley | 1/8 tsp. pepper |
| 1 T. chopped green onion | 1 or 2 drops green food coloring, |
| 1 T. vinegar | opt. |

Combine ingredients and mix well.  Refrigerate.

## EASY DRESSING

| | |
|---|---|
| 1/2 cup cooking oil | 2 T. minced onion |
| 1/4 cup sugar | 1/2 tsp. salt |
| 2 T. vinegar | 1/4 tsp. dry mustard |

Blend well in blender.  Good on spinach salad.

**For a very easy salad dressing, mix a half cup of mayonnaise with a half cup of salsa.**

## EMERALD DRESSING

| | |
|---|---|
| 1 cup cooking oil | 2 T. chopped green pepper |
| 1/3 cup vinegar | 2 tsp. dry mustard |
| 1/4 cup chopped onion | 1 tsp. salt |
| 1/4 cup chopped fresh parsley | 1/4 tsp. black or red pepper |

Combine ingredients in a jar; shake.  Best if let set at least an hour.  Shake vigorously before using.

## FRENCH DRESSING I

| | |
|---|---|
| 1 cup sugar | 1/4 cup vinegar |
| 1 cup ketchup | 2 T. chopped onion |
| 1 cup cooking oil | 1 T. mustard |

Put everything in the blender and blend 1 minute.  Refrigerate.

*Gladys Hoover, Sheldon, WI*

***Money is a good servant, but a cruel master***

# FRENCH DRESSING II

| | |
|---|---|
| 1 cup sugar | 1 small onion |
| 1/2 cup cooking oil | 1 T. mustard |
| 1/3 cup ketchup | 1 tsp. salt |
| 1/4 cup vinegar | 1 tsp. paprika |
| 1/4 cup water | |

Put in blender and blend until smooth.

*Mrs. Marvin (Lydia) Sensenig, Penn Yan, NY*

# SPICY FRENCH DRESSING

| | |
|---|---|
| 1 cup tomato soup | 1 tsp. Worcestershire sauce |
| 3/4 cup sugar | 3/4 tsp. pepper |
| 2/3 cup cooking oil | 3/4 tsp. paprika |
| 1/2 cup vinegar | 1/2 tsp. dry mustard |
| 1 small onion | 1/2 tsp. garlic powder |
| 1 tsp. salt | |

Blend in blender until well mixed.

*Anna Mae Hoover, Reinholds, PA*

# FRUIT SALAD DRESSING (COOKED)

| | |
|---|---|
| 1/2 cup sugar | 3 T. pineapple juice |
| 1 T. cornstarch | 2 T. lemon juice |
| 2 egg yolks, slightly beaten | 1/8 tsp. salt |
| 1/3 cup water | |

Combine cornstarch and sugar. Add egg yolks and water; stir. Cook over low heat bringing mixture to a boil; boil 1 minute stirring constantly. Remove from heat; add juices. Stir. Cool. Serve with fresh fruit.

# FRUIT SALAD DRESSING WITH CREAM CHEESE

| | |
|---|---|
| 1 cup sour cream | 1/3 cup brown sugar |
| 3 oz. cream cheese | 1/2 tsp. vanilla |

Combine ingredients; chill. At serving time layer with blueberries and peaches, or other fruit.

*Connie Rodes, Milford, IN*

## FRUIT SALAD DRESSING WITH PUDDING

3.4 oz. box instant vanilla
   pudding
1 1/2 cups milk

3 oz. frozen orange juice
   concentrate, thawed
3/4 cup sour cream

Beat pudding, milk and concentrate on low for 2 minutes. Blend in sour cream, mixing well. Serve with any fresh fruit.

*Miriam Hoover, Goshen, IN*

## EASY FRUIT SALAD DRESSING

1 cup sour cream

3 T. brown sugar

Combine and serve over fresh fruit.

## GELATIN SALAD DRESSING

2 cups whipped topping
1/2 cup sour cream

1 cup small marshmallows, opt.

Mix and spread on a gelatin salad.

## GREEN ONION DRESSING

1 1/2 cups mayonnaise
1/3 cup chopped green onion
1/4 cup light corn syrup
2 T. lemon juice

1 T. Worcestershire sauce
1 T. parsley or 1/2 cup snipped
   fresh parsley
1/4 tsp. pepper

Combine all ingredients; mix well. Cover and chill. Makes 2 cups.

*Mrs. Ray (Elsie) Hoover, Stratford, WI*

## HERB VINAIGRETTE

3/4 cup cooking oil
3 T. fresh minced herbs or 1 T.
   dried herbs
2 T. vinegar

2 T. lemon juice
1 tsp salt
Plenty of pepper

Whisk everything together.

*Vera Witmer, Goshen, IN*

## ITALIAN DRESSING

1 1/3 cups cooking oil
1/2 cup vinegar
1/4 cup Parmesan cheese
Fresh parsley
1 clove garlic
1 T. honey

1/2 tsp. celery salt
1/2 tsp. pepper
1/2 tsp. dry mustard
1/4 tsp. paprika
1/4 tsp. basil

Blend in blender until smooth. Makes 1 3/4 cups.

*Vera Witmer, Goshen, IN*

## MACARONI SALAD DRESSING (COOKED)

1 1/2 cups sugar
1/4 cup flour
1/4 tsp. salt
1 1/2 cups water

1/3 cup vinegar
1 cup mayonnaise or salad
   dressing
1/4 cup mustard

Combine sugar, flour, and salt in a saucepan. Stir in water and vinegar; cook and stir until it thickens. Cool. Add mayonnaise and mustard.

## MEXICAN DRESSING

1 cup sugar
1 cup cooking oil
1/3 cup vinegar
1/4 cup mayonnaise or salad
   dressing

1 medium onion
3 T. mustard
1 tsp. celery seed
1/2 tsp. salt

Put all ingredients into blender and blend.

*Mrs. Lloyd Troyer, Stella, MO*

## OIL DRESSING

1/2 cup olive oil
1 clove garlic, pressed

1/2 tsp. salt
Fresh lemon peel

Combine oil, garlic, and salt. Just before serving grate lemon peel over greens.

*If you want to feel rich, count all the things you have that money
can not buy.*

## THOUSAND ISLAND DRESSING I

1/2 cup mayonnaise or salad
   dressing
3 T. cream
3 T. ketchup

1 tsp. chili powder
1/2 tsp. paprika
1/4 tsp. salt
Dash of onion powder

Blend well and refrigerate. Makes 2 cups.

*Nancy Kilmer, California, MO*

## THOUSAND ISLAND DRESSING II

1/2 cup mayonnaise or salad
   dressing
1/4 cup sweet pickle relish,
   drained

3 T. chili sauce or ketchup
1 hard-cooked egg, chopped
Onion, opt.

Mix well and store in the refrigerator. Best served on crisp garden lettuce.

*Arlene Hoover, Fortuna, MO*

## LOW-CALORIE THOUSAND ISLAND DRESSING

3/4 cup vinegar
10 3/4 oz. can tomato soup
1 garlic clove, minced
2 T. chopped dill pickle
2 T. finely chopped celery

2 T. chopped fresh parsley
1 T. Worcestershire sauce
1 tsp. paprika
1 tsp. mustard
1/8 tsp. red pepper

Combine ingredients and mix well. Makes about 2 cups.

## WESTERN DRESSING

2 cups mayonnaise or salad
   dressing
1 1/2 to 2 cups sugar
1/2 cup ketchup
1/2 cup cooking oil

1/4 cup vinegar
4 tsp. water
2 tsp. mustard
1 tsp. paprika
1/2 tsp. salt

Blend all together in blender.

*Linda Hoover Shaum, Roann, IN*    *Sheryl Wenger, Marlette, MI*

***Never take on more work than you have time to pray about.***

# SOUPS
### and
# SAND
## WICHES

# SOUPS

## CREAM OF ASPARAGUS SOUP

1 1/2 cups asparagus, cut up
2 cups water
3 T. butter
1 small onion, minced

3 T. flour
3/4 tsp. salt
1/8 tsp. pepper
1 1/2 cups milk or light cream

Cook asparagus in water until tender. Sauté onion in butter; stir in flour and seasoning. Gradually add milk, stirring constantly, until thickened. Puree asparagus with cooking water in blender. Add to white sauce. Heat.

*Mary Ann Martin, Sauk Centre, MN*

## BEAN SOUP

1 1/2 cups dry navy beans
2 quarts milk
3 T. butter

Salt and pepper to taste
1/4 cup cream, opt.

Soak beans and cook until soft. Add milk and butter. Season to taste. Heat soup but do not boil. Add cream just before serving. Serve with crackers or toasted bread cubes and seasoned salt.

*Mrs. James Kulp, Unity, WI*

## CHEDDAR BEAN SOUP

2 T. butter
1/2 cup finely chopped celery
1 large carrot, chopped
1 cup chopped onion
2 cups diced potatoes
2 cups water
20 oz. can white beans

2 tsp. Worcestershire sauce
1/2 tsp. salt
1/8 tsp. red pepper
1 1/2 cups shredded Cheddar
   cheese
1 cup milk

In a large saucepan melt butter. Add celery, carrots and onions. Cook over medium heat, stirring frequently, until vegetables are tender. Add potatoes, water, beans, Worcestershire sauce, salt and pepper. Bring to a boil. Reduce heat and simmer 45 minutes. Remove from heat and stir in cheese and milk. Makes 6 cups - about 310 calories per cup.

*Laura Kulp, Stratford, WI*

## HAM AND BEAN SOUP WITH TOMATOES

2 cups dry beans
2 quarts water
2 cups diced ham
1 tsp. salt

1/4 tsp. pepper
1 large onion chopped
1 clove garlic, minced, opt.
4 cups canned tomatoes

Cover beans with water and soak overnight. Drain; add water, ham and salt. Simmer 3 hours. Add remaining ingredients; simmer 30 minutes.

## BEEF BARLEY SOUP

2 quarts beef and broth
1 quart tomatoes
1 1/2 cups barley
1 cup carrots
1 cup potatoes
1 cup celery

1/2 cup onion
1/4 cup snipped fresh parsley
1 tsp. basil
1/2 tsp. thyme
Salt and pepper to taste

Cook together till barley is soft. Stir once in awhile as barley thickens. Good for the slow cooker.

*Mrs. Elmer Sensenig, Quarryville, PA*

## BROCCOLI CHEESE SOUP

*For a different taste, substitute asparagus, cauliflower or spinach for broccoli, or add a cup of cubed cooked ham.*

2 T. finely chopped onion
2 T. butter or margarine
3 T. flour
1/2 tsp. salt
1/8 tsp. pepper
2 cups milk

1 cup shredded American cheese
2 chicken bouillon cubes
1 1/2 cups water
10 oz. pkg. frozen broccoli, or use
    fresh

In a large saucepan cook onion in butter until tender. Stir in flour, salt and pepper. Add milk all at once; cook until thickened, stirring constantly. Add cheese; stir until blended. Remove from heat. In a medium saucepan, dissolve bouillon cubes in water and bring to a boil. Add broccoli and cook until tender. Do not drain; add to cheese mixture. Stir until blended. A cup and a half of mashed potatoes can be stirred into the soup, if desired.

*Rachel Ramer, Cazenovia, WI     Beverly Stauffer, New Paris, IN*

**When you are in the wrong place, your right place is empty.**

## CHEDDAR CHEESE CHOWDER I

2 cups water
2 cups cubed potatoes
1/2 cup grated carrots
1/2 cup diced celery
1/4 cup chopped onion
1 1/2 tsp. salt
1/4 tsp. pepper

1 cup ham, bacon, tuna, sausage,
   or hamburger
2 cups grated cheese
1/4 cup butter
1/4 cup flour
2 cups milk

Cook together first column till vegetables are tender. Don't drain. Fry meat if needed; drain. Melt butter in a saucepan; stir in flour. Add milk; cook and stir until thick. Stir white sauce and meat into vegetables. Heat. Serve piping hot. If using bacon the drippings can replace part of the butter for added flavor.

*Esther Martin, Decker, MI    Lizzie Hoover, Goshen, IN*

## CHEDDAR CHEESE CHOWDER II

3 cups water
3 bouillon cubes
4 medium potatoes, peeled, diced
1 medium onion, chopped
1/2 bunch broccoli
1/2 cup diced green pepper

1/2 lb. sliced mushrooms
1/3 cup butter or margarine
1/3 cup flour
3 1/2 cups milk or light cream
4 cups (1 lb.) grated sharp
   Cheddar cheese

Combine water and bouillon in a large saucepan; bring to a boil. Add vegetables and simmer until tender. Melt butter in a saucepan; blend in flour and cook 1 minute. Gradually add milk; cook over medium heat until thickened, stirring constantly. Add cheese; stir till melted. Stir cheese sauce into vegetables. Cook until heated over low heat. Do not boil. When Lana was at the Riley Children's Hospital in Indianapolis, IN in the preschool unit – those that were able – gathered together and chopped vegetables for playtime. Later each child was served a small bowl of soup.

*Mary Ann Martin, Sauk Centre, MN*

## CHICKEN CORN CHOWDER

4 slices bacon, fried
1/2 cup onion
3 T. flour
1/4 tsp. pepper
1/4 tsp. thyme
3 cups light cream or milk

2 cups corn
1 1/2 cups cooked, diced chicken
1 medium potato
2 cups water
6 bouillon cubes

Fry onion in bacon drippings; add flour. Add everything but bacon. Simmer 30 minutes. Garnish with bacon.

## CHEESY CHICKEN SOUP

| | |
|---|---|
| 1/2 cup butter | 1 cup corn |
| 2 cups grated carrots | 4 oz. can mushrooms |
| 1 onion, chopped | 1 tsp. salt |
| 2 cups chicken broth or water | 1/4 tsp. pepper |
| 1 1/2 cups milk | 1/3 cup flour |
| 2 cups diced, cooked chicken | 1 cup grated cheese |

Cook carrots and onions in butter until tender, but not brown. Add broth and milk. If using water instead of broth add a bouillon cube or chicken soup base if you have it. Add chicken, corn, drained mushrooms, salt and pepper. Heat, but do not boil. Mix flour with 1/2 cup milk and gradually add to soup; stirring until thickened. Add cheese and stir until it melts.

## CHICKEN NOODLE SOUP

| | |
|---|---|
| 3 lb. frying chicken | 2 chicken bouillon cubes |
| 3 quarts water | 1 tsp. parsley |
| 2 1/2 tsp. salt | 1/4 tsp. pepper |
| 1 onion, chopped | 2 cups uncooked noodles |
| 3 ribs celery, chopped | |

Cook chicken in water and salt about an hour or until tender. Remove chicken. Strain broth and add all but noodles. Simmer 10 minutes then add deboned chicken and noodles. Cook until noodles are done.

*Mrs. Ray (Elsie) Hoover, Stratford, WI*

## VELVETY CHICKEN SOUP

| | |
|---|---|
| 1 cup dry rice | 1 onion, chopped |
| 3 cups water | 1/2 cup flour |
| 1 envelope dry onion/mushroom | 1 cup cream |
|    soup mix | 3 cups chicken broth |
| 1/2 cup butter or margarine | 2 cups chopped chicken |

Cook rice in water and soup mix. Melt butter and sauté onion. Blend in flour and cook until bubbly. Stirring constantly add cream and chicken broth. Cook until thickened. Add rice mixture and chicken.

*Susan Hilty Hoover, Elida, OH*

**Making excuses doesn't change the truth.**

## CHINESE SOUP

1/4 lb. lean round steak
2 T. butter
2 green onions, chopped
1 clove garlic, minced or 1/8 tsp.
   garlic powder
3 T. soy sauce

1/4 tsp. paprika
2 cups canned or fresh bean
   sprouts
4 cups chicken or beef broth
1 1/2 tsp. salt
1/8 tsp. pepper

Cut meat into thin strips. Partially frozen meat is easier to cut. Melt butter in a large skillet. Add meat, onions and garlic. Cook for 5 minutes. Add remaining ingredients and simmer 30 minutes or until meat is tender. Shredded cabbage is good with this too.

*Mrs. Ray (Elsie) Hoover, Stratford, WI*

## CHILI

1 lb. ground beef
1 onion, chopped
1 1/2 quarts tomato juice
2 cups kidney beans

2 to 2 1/2 tsp. chili powder
1 tsp. salt
1/3 to 1/2 cup brown sugar

Brown ground beef and onion. Add remaining ingredients. Simmer, uncovered, 20 to 30 minutes. If your children don't like beans in their soup, use 1 cup of the tomato juice to blend them in the blender. Sometimes I stir in a 1/2 teaspoon of soda to neutralize the acid.

*Mrs. LaVerne (Virginia) Hoover, Goshen, IN*

## THICK CHILI

*This is great topped with salsa, shredded cheese and chopped onions.*

2 lb. ground beef
1 onion, chopped
2 T. chili powder
2 tsp. salt

4 cups tomato juice
27 oz. can kidney or chili beans
   or 3 cups cooked beans

Brown beef and onions. Drain if necessary. Mix in chili powder and salt. Add tomato juice and beans. Simmer awhile if you have time, otherwise just heat through.

*Kerra Layne Hoover, Stratford, WI*

***Never be afraid to trust an unknown future to an all-knowing God.***

## CLAM CHOWDER

2 cups diced potatoes
1 medium onion, diced
1 cup diced celery
1/4 cup butter

3 T. flour
1 tsp. salt or to taste
1 or 2-8 oz. cans minced clams
3 cups whole milk or cream

Simmer potatoes, onion and celery together in a small amount of water until tender. Melt butter in a small pan. Blend in flour to make a smooth paste. Drain juice from minced clams and blend into flour mixture. Add to cooked vegetables; stir in milk and clams. Heat through; do not boil. May be frozen. Garnish with crisp bacon if desired.

*Mrs. LaVerne (Virginia) Hoover, Goshen, IN     Mrs. John (Twila) Kulp, Mosinee, WI*

## FISH CHOWDER

6 strips bacon or 2 T. butter
1/2 cup thinly sliced celery
1/2 cup chopped onion
1 lb. cod fillets
2 cups cubed potatoes
1 carrot, grated
1 1/2 cups hot water

1/2 tsp salt
1/8 tsp. pepper
1/4 tsp. thyme
1/2 cup butter
1/2 cup flour
4 cups milk
2 cups shredded cheese

Fry bacon; dry and crumble. Sauté celery and onion in drippings or butter. Add fish, potatoes, carrots, water and seasonings. Simmer till vegetables are tender. Melt butter over low heat; stir in flour. Slowly add milk, stirring constantly. Bring to a boil; add cheese and fish mixture. Garnish with bacon. Any white fish may be used. Good sprinkled with red pepper.

*Mary Ann Martin, Sauk Centre, MN*

## FISH SOUP

2 T. butter
15 oz. can jack mackerel

1 to 2 quarts of milk
Salt and pepper to taste

Brown butter. Add undrained mackerel and milk. Use as much or little milk as you like or is needed for your family. Season to taste. Serve hot with crackers. Salmon may be used but it costs more and doesn't taste much different.

*Mrs. Ivan Zimmerman, Scottsville KY*

**The trouble with trouble is that it always starts out like fun.**

# HAM STEW

4 cups cubed cooked ham
4 cups raw potatoes
2 quarts ham broth
1 quart green beans

1 quart carrot chunks, opt.
Salt and pepper to taste
Cornstarch

Combine and cook all but cornstarch until done. Add water to cornstarch and stir into soup to thicken. Excellent served with buttermilk biscuits.

*Mrs. Lloyd Troyer, Stella, MO*

# HAMBURGER STEW

1 lb. hamburger
2 cups tomato juice
1/2 cup chopped onion
1 cup potatoes
1 cup sliced carrots
1 cup lima beans, opt.

1 to 1 1/2 tsp. salt
2 T. butter
2 T. flour
1 to 2 cups milk – use 1 cup for
   thicker stew

Brown hamburger. Add tomato juice, vegetables and salt. Cover and simmer until vegetables are soft. Melt butter in a small skillet and stir in flour; add milk and simmer until thickened. Stir into hot soup and serve.

*Mrs. Allen Garman, Roaring Spring, PA     Mrs. James Kulp, Unity, WI*

# HEARTY HAMBURGER SOUP

2 T. butter
1 lb. ground beef
2 cups tomato juice
1 cup chopped onion
1 cup diced potatoes
1 cup sliced carrots

1/2 cup chopped celery
1 to 1 1/2 tsp. salt
1 tsp. seasoned salt
1/8 tsp. pepper
4 cups milk
1/3 cup flour

Melt butter in a large skillet or kettle. Brown beef and onion. Stir in all but milk and flour. Combine flour with 1 cup milk; stir into soup and bring to a boil. Add remaining milk and heat through; do not boil. Stir frequently.

*Alta Martin, Goshen, IN     Mrs. Elverne Martin, Nappanee, IN     Velma Martin, Nappanee, IN*
*Mrs. Christian Weaver, Goshen, IN*

*The splendor of the rose and the whiteness of the lily do not rob the little violet of its scent nor the daisy of its simple charm. If every tiny flower wanted to be a rose, spring would lose its loveliness.*
*Therese of Lisieux*

117

# LENTIL SOUP

1 1/2 cups lentils
6 cups water
16 oz. can whole tomatoes
2 slices bacon, diced
1 medium onion, chopped
2 carrots thinly sliced

2 ribs celery with tops, sliced
1 clove garlic, minced
2 T. lemon juice
1 1/2 tsp. salt
1/2 tsp. oregano
1/4 tsp. pepper

Rinse and drain lentils. Mix all ingredients together in a slow cooker and cook on low for 8 to 9 hours.

*Connie Rodes, Milford, IN*

# ONION CHEESE SOUP

2 T. cooking oil
4 cups diced onion
4 cups chicken broth
3 cups grated potatoes
3 cups grated sharp Cheddar
   cheese

3/4 cup evaporated milk or light
   cream
3 T. Dijon-style mustard
Salt
Pepper

In a medium saucepan heat oil and sauté onions for 5 minutes. Add broth and potatoes. Simmer 20 to 30 minutes. Let soup cool a bit then puree two thirds of it in blender. Add puree to soup; heat. Add cheese, milk, mustard. Heat on low till cheese melts. Season with salt and pepper.

*Hannah Kulp Family, Mt. Hermon, KY*

# PIZZA SOUP

1 to 2 lb. bulk sausage
1 cup sliced fresh mushrooms
1 onion, chopped
2 cups pizza sauce
2 cups water

2 cups peeled fresh or canned
   tomatoes
1/2 cup chopped pepperoni
1 tsp. Italian seasoning
1/2 tsp. salt or to taste

In a large saucepan brown sausage, mushrooms, and onion until tender. Add remaining ingredients and bring to a boil. Reduce heat and simmer 15 to 20 minutes, stirring occasionally. Canned mushrooms may be used. Serve with Parmesan cheese and olives.

*It's better to keep a friend from falling than to help him after he falls.*

## CREAMY POTATO SOUP I

3 cups potatoes, dice
1 onion, chopped
1/2 cups diced carrots
2 chicken bouillon cubes
2-10 3/4 cans cream of chicken
    soup

1 cup water
4 cups milk
1 cup corn
4 oz. Velveeta cheese
1 cup peas

Cover potatoes, onion and carrots with water and cook till tender. Add bouillon, soup, water, milk and corn; heat. When hot add cheese, stirring till melted. More or less cheese can be added. Add peas last so they stay crunchy.

*Mary Zook, Virginia Beach, VA*

## CREAMY POTATO SOUP II

3 cups chopped potatoes
1 cup water
1/2 cup chopped celery
1/2 cup chopped carrots
1/4 cup chopped onion
1 tsp. parsley

1 chicken bouillon cube
1/2 tsp. salt
1/8 tsp. pepper
1 1/2 cups milk
2 T. flour
8 oz. Velveeta cheese

Combine everything, except milk, flour and cheese. Simmer until tender. Add milk to flour to make a smooth paste. Add to vegetables while stirring and cook until thick. Add cheese; stir until melted.

*Rita Martin, Nappanee, IN*

## DUTCH POTATO SOUP

4 cups diced potatoes
3 cups water
1 1/2 tsp. salt
1/4 tsp. thyme
1/8 tsp. pepper

6 slices bacon, diced
1 medium onion, chopped
2 T. flour
1 cup milk

Bring potatoes, water, salt, thyme and pepper to a boil. Simmer till potatoes are soft. Drain, reserving broth. Mash half of the potatoes. Fry bacon; remove. Pour off all but 2 tablespoons drippings. Cook onion in drippings until tender. Stir in flour. Gradually stir in reserved broth. Stir in mashed potatoes. Add bacon and cubed potatoes. Cook, stirring constantly, until thickened. Add milk.

*Ellen Newswanger, Kutztown, PA*

119

# POLKA DOT CHOWDER

4 medium potatoes
1 2/3 cups whole milk
2 cups creamed corn

1 T. butter
1 medium onion
Sliced hot dogs

Cook diced potatoes until tender.  Add milk and corn.  Blend and cook 5 minutes over low heat.  Sauté onion in butter.  Add to soup with hot dogs. Heat through.

*Anna Mae Hoover, Reinholds, PA*

# QUICK GOLDEN STEW

4 carrots, diced
1/2 cup chopped potatoes
1 medium onion, chopped
10 oz. pkg. peas
1/2 lb. hot dogs

10 3/4 oz. can cream of celery
  soup
1 soup can of milk
8 oz. Velveeta cheese

Cook carrots, potatoes and onions until crisp-tender.  Add peas and hot dogs and cook until soft.  Stir in soup, milk and cheese.  Heat through.

*Mrs. Elmer Sensenig, Quarryville, PA*

# SPINACH SOUP

2 cups frozen spinach or 2 quarts
  fresh spinach
4 to 6 cups milk
4 hard-cooked eggs

1 tsp. salt or to taste
4 T. browned butter or bacon
  drippings
Pepper

Wash raw spinach and cook without water until tender, 3 to 5 minutes.  Chop with knife.  Add milk and chopped eggs.  Add salt, pepper and browned butter. Heat, but don't boil.  Serve hot with crackers or toast.

*Mrs. James Kulp, Unity, WI*          *Louise Shirk, Memphis, MO*

# SPLIT PEA AND HAM SOUP

2 quarts water
2 cups split peas
2 lb. ham shank
2 ribs celery, sliced
1 onion, chopped

1 carrot, chopped
1/2 tsp. salt
1/2 tsp. basil
1/4 tsp. pepper

Combine all ingredients.  Cover and simmer 2 hours or until peas are tender. Cut meat from bone and return to soup.

## TACO SOUP

1 to 2 lb. ground beef
1 onion, chopped
6 cups tomato juice

1/3 cup brown sugar, opt.
15 oz. can chili beans
1/3 cup taco seasoning

Fry ground beef and onion; drain if necessary. Simmer with remaining ingredients. Serve over crushed corn chips. Sprinkle with grated cheese and sour cream.

*Mrs. James Kulp, Unity, WI*

## CREAM OF TOMATO SOUP

1/3 cup butter
1/2 cup chopped onion
1/4 cup flour
3/4 tsp. salt

1/4 tsp. pepper
3 cups milk, scalded
1 1/2 cups hot tomato pulp,
   sieved

Sauté onion in butter. Stir in flour and seasonings. Add milk gradually, stir and cook until thickened. Gradually stir in pulp. Sugar can be added.

## OLD FASHIONED TOMATO SOUP

2 cups pulpy tomato juice
1/2 tsp. soda
4 cups whole milk

1 tsp. salt or to taste
Pepper
1 T. butter

Boil tomato juice. Add soda. Stir and quickly add milk. Add salt and pepper to taste. Heat and add butter. Serve with crackers. This can also be made using 4 cups peeled, chopped tomatoes. Brown butter in a saucepan; add tomatoes. Add salt and cook until tomatoes are soft and thin juice has evaporated. Mash tomatoes; add soda, stir milk in quickly.

*Vera Fox, Memphis, MO*

## VEGETABLE SOUP

2 to 3 meat soup bones
1 tsp salt or to taste
1/8 tsp. pepper
2 bouillon cubes
2 quarts water
2 potatoes, peeled and diced

2 ribs celery, sliced
2 carrots, sliced
2 cups fresh or canned tomatoes
1 small onion, chopped
1/4 tsp thyme or marjoram

Cover and simmer first five ingredients 2 1/2 to 3 hours. Remove bones; return meat to soup and add vegetables. Simmer another 30 minutes.

121

## BEEF VEGETABLE SOUP WITH MACARONI

1 1/2 lb. ground beef
8 cups broth or water
4 cups canned tomatoes
1 cup chopped onion

1 cup chopped celery
2 tsp. salt
1/2 tsp. pepper
1 cup uncooked macaroni

Combine all but macaroni. Bring to a boil then reduce heat and simmer 45 minutes or until beef is cooked. Add macaroni and cook, uncovered approximately 25 minutes longer. Fresh peeled tomatoes can be used. Noodles may be substituted for macaroni; simmer only 15 minutes.

Thicken soups with 2 or 3 tablespoons of oatmeal. Barley or rice also make good nourishing thickeners.

## WESTERN SUPREME SOUP

4 cups cubed potatoes
3 medium carrots, sliced
3 ribs celery, sliced
2 cups canned beef broth
1 cup canned beef
1 onion, chopped
2 tsp. salt
5 shakes oregano

5 shakes celery salt
4 shakes black pepper
4 shakes paprika
3 shakes sage
2 shakes seasoned salt
1 pinch red pepper
Parsley, opt.
Flour, water and cream

Fill a 6-quart kettle 3/4 full of water. Add vegetables, broth and beef. Start cooking; add seasonings. Cook an hour or two. Thicken like thin gravy, using flour, water, and a little cream.

*Mrs. William (Lena) Kilmer, California, MO*

## WILD RICE SOUP

1 cup uncooked wild rice
4 1/2 cups chicken broth
1/2 cup chopped onion
1/2 shredded carrot
1 bay leaf

1 tsp. basil
4 oz. can mushrooms, drained
1/4 cup snipped fresh parsley or 1
   tsp. dried parsley

Combine all but mushrooms and parsley. Bring to a boil then reduce heat and simmer 45 minutes. Remove bay leaf. Add mushrooms and parsley.

# SANDWICHES

## BEEF BAR-B-Q SANDWICHES

3 to 4 lb. trimmed boneless chuck
   roast
2 cups chopped onions
2 cups ketchup or barbeque
   sauce
1 cup celery

1 cup water
2 T. vinegar
2 T. Worcestershire sauce
2 tsp. salt
1 tsp. chili powder
1/2 tsp. pepper

Put roast in a slow cooker. Combine remaining ingredients and pour over roast. Cook on high for 6 to 7 hours or until tender. Remove roast. Shred meat when cool enough to handle. Mix with sauce. Serve on buns

## DELUXE BEEF BAR-B-Q SANDWICHES

3 lb. beef roast
3 lb. ground beef
1 1/2 cups ketchup
1 onion, chopped
1/4 c. Worcestershire sauce

1/4 cup brown sugar
2-10 1/2 oz. cans chicken gumbo
   soup
2 tsp. salt
1/8 tsp. pepper

Boil roast until tender. Drain and break into stringy bits. Brown ground beef. Drain excess grease. Combine all ingredients. Simmer 45 minutes to an hour. Serve on buns. Freeze leftovers. Remove from freezer and heat and eat when unexpected guests arrive. Everyone loves it!

*Esther Martin, Decker, MI*

## BEEF AND BEAN BURGERS

1/2 lb. ground beef
1/2 cup chopped onion
1 tsp. salt

16 oz. can pork and beans
1/2 cup ketchup or chili sauce
Dash of hot pepper sauce

Brown beef and onion. Add remaining ingredients. Stir and heat through. Spoon onto six hamburger buns.

*True faith is not just believing that God can, it is knowing that He will.*

## BROILED BEEF AND CHEESE SANDWICHES

8 slices lightly toasted bread
Mustard
8 thin slices roasted beef
12 slices cheese
Pimento, opt.

Fresh parsley sprigs, opt.
3/4 cup mayonnaise
2 tsp. horseradish
1/3 cup pickle relish
1/2 tsp. Worcestershire sauce

Cover broiler grid with foil, shiny side up. Completely spread one side of bread with mustard. Place on broiler grid, mustard side up. Put beef on bread, then cheese. Combine last four ingredients and mix well. Spread over each sandwich to within 1/2 inch of the edge. I put the cheese slice on top. Broil 3 to 4 inches from heat until dressing bubbles.

*Mrs. Mervin (Lucille) Martin, Wallenstein, Ont, CAN*

## HOT BEEF AND CHEESE SANDWICHES

*Cooked chopped ham, turkey or chicken can be used instead of beef.*

1/2 lb. chopped cooked beef
1/2 lb. chopped cheese
1/3 cup chopped onion
2 hard-cooked eggs

1/2 cup pickle relish or chopped
  olives
3 T. mayonnaise
1/2 cup chili sauce or ketchup

Mix together all ingredients and fill 12 buns. Wrap buns in foil. Bake at 350° for 10 to 12 minutes or until thoroughly heated.

*Ethel Hoover, Goshen, IN*

## BEEF FAJITAS

1/2 cup steak sauce
1/4 cup vinegar
2 T. oil
1 clove garlic, minced
1/2 tsp. hot pepper seasoning

1 lb. boneless sirloin steak
2 T. oil
1 large green pepper
1 large onion, chopped
8 flour tortillas, warmed

Combine first 5 ingredients. Cut steak into thin strips and add; coating well. Cover and refrigerate 1 to 2 hours, stirring occasionally. Remove steak from marinade; reserve marinade. Sauté steak strips in oil, 5 to 6 minutes, or until no longer pink. Remove steak and keep warm. Sauté pepper strips and onion 5 minutes. Add reserved marinade; heat to a boil. Reduce heat and simmer 5 minutes. Add steak and heat through. Spoon into warm tortillas; top with sour cream and cheese, if desired.

# CHICKEN BURRITOS
*These can be frozen after wrapping them in foil.*

3 cups shredded chicken
2 cups salsa
16 oz. can refried beans
1/2 cup water

1 envelope taco seasoning or 1/4
   cup taco seasoning
16 flour tortillas, warmed
1 lb. cheese

Simmer first 5 ingredients for 5 minutes. Put 1/3 cup of mixture on each tortilla. Cut cheese into sixteen 5 x 1/2 inch strips; put one on each tortilla. Roll and wrap in foil. Bake at 300° in a single layer until cheese melts. Serve with any or all of the following: salsa, chopped lettuce and tomatoes, jalapeno slices, guacamole, sour cream, or cheese sauce.

*Mrs. LaVerne (Virginia) Hoover, Goshen, IN*

# HOT CHICKEN SANDWICHES
*These sandwiches are also good cold.*

2 cups cooked, diced chicken or
   turkey
1/2 cup diced celery
1/2 cup diced cheddar cheese
1 tsp. pimento

2 hard-cooked eggs, chopped
2 T. chopped onion or chives
1/2 cup mayonnaise
Salt and pepper
6 hamburger buns

Combine all ingredients, except buns. Butter buns and fill with filling. Wrap in foil. Heat at 400° for 15 to 20 minutes. If you're in a hurry, heat filling in the microwave before putting it in buns.

*Rhoda Martin, Nappanee, IN*

# COD SANDWICHES

12 oz. cod, cooked, drained
1/4 cup chopped celery
1/4 cup salad dressing
2 T. minced onion

1 to 2 T. horseradish mustard
1 T. lemon juice
1/4 tsp. pepper
Dash of red pepper, opt.

Mix all ingredients. Cover and chill 1 hour. Serve on buns with lettuce.

*Lord, grant me a quiet mind, that trusting Thee, for Thou art kind, I may go on without a fear, for Thou, my Lord, art always near.* Amy Carmichael

# CONEY DOGS

8 hot dogs
16 oz. can kidney beans
1/2 cup chopped onion

1/4 cup chopped green pepper
1/4 cup ketchup
8 hot dog buns

Heat hot dogs. Drain kidney beans then mash slightly. Combine beans, onion, pepper and ketchup. Place hot dogs in buns and top with bean mixture.

# HOT DOG BURGERS

8 hot dogs, diced
1 cup diced cheese
1 T. ketchup

1 T. mustard
1 T. onion
1 T. chopped pickles

Combine all ingredients and fill 8 hot dog buns. Wrap in foil and bake at 325° for 15 minutes or until heated through.

*Edna Miller, Snover, MI*

# EGG SALAD SANDWICHES

*For a different flavor delete relish and add a tablespoon of mustard.*

3 hard-cooked eggs
2 T. mayonnaise or salad
   dressing

1 T. pickle relish
1 T. minced onion
1/2 tsp. salt

Combine all ingredients. Mix well. Makes one cup. Spread on bread.

# GRILLED HAMBURGER SANDWICHES

*If you want a cheesier burger add a slice of cheese before topping with tomato.*

1 lb. ground beef
6 oz. tomato paste
1/3 cup parmesan cheese
1/4 cup chopped onion

1/2 tsp. oregano
3/4 tsp. salt
Sliced tomatoes
English muffins

Slightly brown ground beef; drain grease. Add all but tomatoes and muffins. Chopped green pepper may be added. Place on English muffin halves; broil 15 minutes. Top with tomato slices and broil 5 minutes more.

*Charlotte Martin, Goshen, IN*

***Instead of putting others in their place, put yourself in their place.***

## BAR-B-Q HAM SANDWICHES I

1 lb. shaved or chopped ham
1/2 cup ketchup
3 T. brown sugar

1 T. vinegar
1 tsp. minced onion

Combine ingredients and bake uncovered at 300° for 1 hour. Eat on buns.

*Mrs. Luke Hoover, Goshen, IN*

## BAR-B-Q HAM SANDWICHES II

1 lb. shaved or chopped ham
1 cup ketchup
3 T. brown sugar
2 T. dark jelly

1 tsp. mustard
1/2 tsp. paprika
1/4 cup water

Combine ingredients and boil together on the stove or in a slow cooker. Eat on hamburger buns.

*Velma Martin, Nappanee, IN*

## GRILLED HAM AND CHEESE SANDWICHES

*Make a plain grilled cheese sandwich by deleting the ham.*

Put a slice of ham and slice of cheese between two slices of bread. Butter the outsides of the bread. Put in a skillet and brown lightly on both sides. For a zippier sandwich spread mustard on the inside of the bread before browning.

## HOT HAM SALAD SANDWICHES

2 rings bologna
10 medium pickles
Large chunk of cheese
1 heaping T. salad dressing

1 T. mustard
Milk
Sugar
Pickle juice

Grind first 3 ingredients together; add salad dressing and mustard. Mix with milk till smooth, not runny. Add sugar and pickle juice to taste. Put in hamburger buns; wrap in foil and warm in oven.

*Mrs. Luke Hoover, Goshen, IN*

*Yesterday is a cancelled check; tomorrow is a promissory note; today is the only cash you have – so spend it wisely.*

# HOT AND SPICY BURGERS

2 lb. ground beef
1/2 cup chopped onion
1 T. chopped, seeded jalapeno
   pepper
1 tsp. ground cumin

1 1/2 tsp. salt
1/4 tsp. pepper
1/2 cup shredded cheese
8 slices tomato
8 hamburger buns

Combine all but last three ingredients. Shape into 8 patties. Fry or grill patties then top with cheese. Place tomato slice on the bottom half of the bun. Top with burger and other bun half.

# MEXICAN SANDWICHES

1/2 cup minced onion
1/4 cup chopped celery
1 garlic clove, minced
2 T. butter
1 lb. ground beef or turkey
1 tsp. salt
1/2 tsp. pepper

1/2 cup tomato paste
1 cup water
1/2 cup cooked rice
1 T. paprika
1/2 T. chili powder
3/4 tsp. celery seed
1/4 tsp. caraway seed

Sauté onion, celery and garlic in butter. Add beef, salt and pepper. Cook till meat is browned. Stir in tomato paste and water. Add rice and remaining seasonings. Cook till thick, about 15 minutes. Spoon mixture onto split, buttered and toasted buns.

*Edna Miller, Snover, MI*

# PIEROGIES

2 cups flour
1 tsp. salt
Water to form dough
2 cups mashed potatoes

1/2 cup cheese
1 T. onion
Salt to taste
Pepper to taste

Mix flour and salt; add enough water to make dough. Roll out dough and cut into circles. Mix remaining ingredients (leftover mashed potatoes can be used) and fill half of circle. Fold dough over and press ends together firmly. Place Pierogies in boiling water till they float to the top, then take out and deep fat fry. A hot 'n chewy "go with" for chili and other soups.

*Mrs. Eugene Weaver, Fleetwood, PA*

## SLOPPY JOES I

2 1/2 lb. ground beef
1 medium onion, chopped
Salt
Pepper
2 1/2 T. Worcestershire sauce

10 oz. cream of mushroom soup
1/2 cup ketchup
1/3 cup brown sugar
1 T. mustard

Brown ground beef and onion. Sprinkle with salt and pepper. Drain. Add Worcestershire sauce, soup, ketchup, sugar and mustard. Heat and serve on warm buns.

*Elaine Weaver, Goshen, IN*

## SLOPPY JOES II

*For sloppier joes use one cup ketchup.*

2 lb. ground beef
1 onion, chopped
1/2 cup ketchup
3 T. brown sugar, opt.

1 T. vinegar
2 tsp. mustard
1 tsp. Worcestershire sauce
1 tsp. salt

Fry ground beef and onion; drain grease if necessary. Combine and add remaining ingredients. Simmer 10 to 12 minutes. Serve with buns or bread.

*Mrs. James Kulp, Unity, WI*

## SLOPPY JOES III

1 1/2 lb. ground beef
3/4 cup oatmeal
1 cup water
1 T. onion
1 tsp. salt
1/2 tsp. pepper

1 cup ketchup
1/2 cup water
6 T. chopped onion
3 T. vinegar
2 T. sugar

Combine first column in skillet and brown. Boil together remaining ingredients; add to meat mixture and simmer. Serve on buns or bread.

*Mrs. John (Twila) Kulp, Mosinee, WI*

*Each day God sends His loving aid to strengthen you and me.
We need to use this day's supply and let tomorrow be.*

# BAKED SLOPPY JOES

2 lb. ground beef
3 cups tomato juice
2 cups cracker crumbs
2 eggs, beaten

1 onion, chopped
2 tsp. salt
1/4 tsp. pepper

Mix all ingredients in a large bowl. Bake, uncovered, at 350° for 2 hours. Spoon onto buns; serve warm. Good and easy to make.

*Anna Zimmerman, Decker, MI*

# TACO BURGERS

1 lb. ground beef
16 oz. can tomatoes, cut up
1 tsp. chili powder
1 tsp. Worcestershire sauce
3/4 tsp. garlic salt
1/2 tsp. sugar

1/4 tsp. dry mustard
8 hamburger buns, split and
   toasted
2 cups shredded lettuce
1 cup (4 oz.) shredded American
   cheese

Brown beef and drain excess fat. Add undrained tomatoes, chili powder, Worcestershire sauce, garlic salt, sugar and mustard. Stir well, breaking up large pieces of tomatoes. Bring to a boil; reduce heat. Simmer, uncovered, for 15 to 20 minutes or till thickened. Spoon onto toasted buns. Sprinkle each of the burgers with shredded lettuce and cheese.

*Connie M. Rodes, Milford, IN*

# TACO FILLING

*Delete tomato sauce and add a 16 ounce can of kidney or chili beans for combination tacos.*

1 lb. ground beef
1/2 cup chopped onion
8 oz. tomato sauce

1 tsp. chili powder
1 tsp. salt
1/2 tsp. garlic powder

Brown beef and drain excess fat. Stir in remaining ingredients. Simmer, covered, for 10 minutes. Makes enough for 8 tacos.

***Everyone influences someone.***

## HOT TUNA SANDWICHES I

7 oz. can tuna
2 hard-cooked eggs, chopped
1/2 cup mayonnaise
1 cup shredded cheese
2 T. green pepper

2 T. chopped onion
2 T. chopped pickles
2 T. chopped olives

Mix everything together.  Spread on 8 hamburger buns and wrap in foil.  Bake at 250° for 30 minutes.

*Anna Mae Hoover, Reinholds, PA*

## HOT TUNA SANDWICHES II

*These sandwiches are also good cold.*

6.5 oz. can tuna, drained
3/4 cup small chunks cheese
1/2 cup chopped celery

1/4 cup chopped onion
1/2 cup mayonnaise or salad
  dressing

Combine all ingredients.  Fill 6 hamburger buns and wrap in foil.  Bake at 375° for 25 minutes or until heated through.

*The Lamplighter*

*He has taken his bright candle and is gone
Into another room I cannot find,
But anyone can tell where he has been
By all the lights he leaves behind.*

# ADDITIONAL RECIPES

*Repentance not only says, "I'm sorry", it also says, "I'm through".*

# VEGETABLES

# VEGETABLES

## CRUNCHY ALMOND ASPARAGUS

1 lb. fresh asparagus
2 cups crushed seasoned
  croutons
8 oz. (2 cups) shredded cheddar
  cheese

10.5 oz. can cream of chicken
  soup
1/2 cup chopped unblanched
  almonds
1 T. melted butter

Cut asparagus into 3/4 inch pieces. Cook in 1 cup lightly salted boiling water till tender-crisp. Drain asparagus; reserve liquid. Combine seasoned crumbs and cheese; set aside. Combine soup, reserved asparagus liquid and asparagus. Layer half of crumb mixture in a buttered 2-quart casserole. Top with half of asparagus. Repeat with remaining ingredients. Toss chopped almonds with melted butter. Sprinkle over casserole. Bake at 350° for 30 to 35 minutes.

*Elaine Martin, Nappanee, IN*

## ASPARAGUS CASSEROLE

1/4 cup butter
1/4 cup flour
1/2 tsp. salt
2 cups milk

4 cups cooked asparagus
4 hard-cooked eggs
1 cup grated cheese
Salt and pepper to taste

Melt butter; add flour and salt. Stir well. Add milk gradually, stirring constantly. Bring to a boil and boil 2 minutes. Combine with remaining ingredients. Top with buttered bread crumbs, if desired. Bake at 375° until warm and bubbly.

## BAKED BEANS I

1 lb. dry navy beans
1/2 lb. bacon
1 medium onion
2 cups tomato juice

1/2 to 3/4 cup brown sugar
1/2 cup molasses
1/2 cup ketchup
1 T. salt (scant)

Cook beans until soft. Drain beans; add remaining ingredients. Bake at 350° for 2 hours.

*Esther Horst, East Earl, PA*    *Lydia Ann Ramer, Elkhart, IN*
*Mrs. Ivan Zimmerman, Scottsville, KY*

# BAKED BEANS II

4 quarts cooked and salted beans
1 cup brown sugar
1 cup ketchup
1 T. mustard (heaping)

1/2 tsp. onion salt
2 dashes Accent
Bacon or hot dogs

Combine all but meat. Onions may be used instead of onion salt. Top with bacon or hot dogs. Bake at 350° for 2 hours or till thick.

*Sarah Imhoff, Sheridan, MI*

One pound of navy beans equals approximately 2 1/3 cups of beans. Soaking beans overnight reduces cooking time. Beans should be cooked in three times their volume of unsalted water. They will triple in volume when they are cooked. Add acidic substances like lemon juice, tomato juice or vinegar after beans are soft since acid makes beans firm.

# BOSTON BAKED BEANS

*To put in a slow cooker, follow instructions below. After adding ingredients to drained, tender beans, cook on low for 10 to 12 hours (high for 4 to 5, stirring occasionally). Uncover and turn on high the last hour for thicker beans.*

2 cups dry navy beans
6 cups water
1/4 lb. bacon, diced
1/2 cup dark molasses or maple
  syrup

1/4 cup brown sugar
1 small onion, chopped
1 1/2 tsp. salt
1 tsp. dry mustard

Boil beans in water 2 minutes. Soak 1 hour or overnight. Add bacon and simmer until beans are tender, about 11/2 hours. Drain, saving 1/2 cup liquid. Add remaining ingredients. Bake uncovered at 350° for 1 hour or until desired consistency.

*Mrs. Ray (Elsie) Hoover, Stratford, WI*

# SPEEDY BAKED BEANS

1 lb. bacon, diced
2 medium onions, chopped
7-16 oz. cans baked beans
1 cup brown sugar

1/4 cup molasses
2 T. Worcestershire sauce
1 1/2 tsp. dry mustard

Fry bacon until crisp. Add onions and fry until tender; add remaining ingredients. Heat approximately 20 minutes, stirring occasionally. Makes 22 servings.

## QUICK REFRIED BEANS

1/4 cup lard or cooking oil
1/4 cup minced onion

2-16 oz. cans kidney beans
1 tsp. garlic salt

Fry onion in lard. Mash beans and add with salt. Cook and stir until well mixed. Pinto beans may also be used.

## BEAN ENCHILADAS

1 cup chopped onion
1 clove garlic, minced
2 T. cooking oil
3 cups canned tomatoes, drained
2 tsp. chili powder
1 tsp. cumin
1/2 tsp. salt
2 T. cooking oil

1/2 cup chopped onion
1 clove garlic, minced
16 oz. can pinto beans
1 tsp. chili powder
1/4 tsp. salt
8 soft tortillas
1 cup shredded cheese

To prepare sauce, cook onion and garlic in oil until soft. Add tomatoes, chili powder, cumin, and salt. Bring to a boil and simmer 10 minutes. In another skillet heat oil and cook onion and garlic till tender. Add beans, chili powder and salt; heat through. Divide beans onto tortillas. Roll shut and place in a shallow baking dish. Top with sauce then cheese. Bake at 250° for 30 minutes.

## BEAN SAUSAGES

3 cups cooked beans, drained
1 cup soft whole wheat bread
   crumbs
1 tsp. sage
1 tsp. salt

1/4 tsp. pepper
1 large clove garlic, minced
2 eggs
2 T. water
Flour

Grind beans; add bread crumbs, seasonings and 1 egg. Form into 20 sausages about 3" long and 1/2" thick. Beat remaining egg with water. Dip each sausage into egg, then roll into flour to coat. Put enough oil in a skillet to generously cover the bottom and sauté sausages, shaking to brown all sides. Or place in a flat pan; drizzle lightly with oil and broil for about 5 minutes on each side until nicely browned. Good with fried eggs or in spaghetti sauce.

*Hannah Kulp Family, Mt. Hermon,*

**A part of kindness consists in loving people more than they deserve.**

# KIDNEY BEAN CASSEROLE

| | |
|---|---|
| 4 cups canned kidney beans | 2 T. vinegar |
| 1 medium onion, chopped | 2 tsp. mustard |
| 1/2 cup ketchup | 1 tsp. salt |
| 3 T. brown sugar | 4 strips bacon |

Combine beans and onion. Combine and add all but bacon. Pour into baking dish and lay bacon (fried or raw) on top. Bake at 375° for 45 minutes. Simple, quick and delicious!

*Mrs. Eugene Weaver, Fleetwood, PA*

# GREEN BEAN CASSEROLE

| | |
|---|---|
| 2 T. flour | 1 cup sour cream |
| 2 T. butter | 24 oz. frozen beans, cooked |
| 1 tsp. salt | 8 oz. (2 cups) grated cheese |
| 1 tsp. sugar | 1/2 cup cornflake crumbs |
| 1/4 tsp. pepper | 1 T. butter |
| 1 tsp. onion, grated | |

Combine flour and butter. Cook gently. Remove from heat. Stir in seasonings and sour cream; fold in cooked beans. Place in baking dish and cover with cheese. Top with crumbs mixed with butter. Bake at 350° about 30 minutes.

*Mrs. Cleon (Carol) Bauman, Elmira, Ont. Canada*

# EASY GREEN BEAN BAKE

*One or two cups shredded cheese can be substituted for mushroom soup.*

| | |
|---|---|
| 10.5 oz. can cream of mushroom soup | 2 tsp. soy sauce |
| 1/4 cup milk | 1/8 tsp. pepper |
| | 4 cups canned green beans |

Stir together everything but beans; add beans. Bake at 350° for 25 minutes or until hot. Good topped with French fried onions or bread crumbs.

# BAR-B-QUED GREEN BEANS

| | |
|---|---|
| 3 quarts green beans | 1 cup brown sugar |
| 1 onion, chopped | 6 slices bacon |
| 1 cup ketchup | |

Drain cooked, salted beans (or use canned) and put in a baking dish. Mix onion, ketchup, and sugar and pour over beans. Bacon slices may be placed on top or chopped and mixed in. Cover. Bake at 275° for 4 hours.

*Janet Fox, Memphis, MO*

# HARVARD BEETS

1/3 cup sugar
2 T. cornstarch
1 tsp. salt
1/4 cup vinegar

1/4 cup beet liquid or water
3 cups diced cooked beets
2 T. butter

Combine sugar, cornstarch, and salt; add vinegar and beet liquid. Simmer uncovered until thickened and clear, about 5 minutes. Add beets and heat through. Add butter before serving.

**A cup of broccoli has only 40 calories but provides almost twice the Recommended Dietary Allowance of vitamin C.**

# BAKED BROCCOLI

*For a colorful as well as tasty dish use a mixture of broccoli, cauliflower, and carrots.*

2-10 oz. pkgs. frozen chopped
    broccoli
1 large egg
2/3 cup mayonnaise
10 oz. cream of mushroom soup

1 onion, finely chopped
1 cup grated cheese
1/2 cup fine dry bread crumbs
2 T. butter, melted
Paprika

Cook broccoli and drain well. Whisk egg slightly. Add mayonnaise and soup and whisk to blend. Stir in broccoli, onion and cheese. Turn into an oblong 1_ quart baking dish. Mix bread crumbs and butter and sprinkle on top. Sprinkle with paprika. Bake at 350° approximately 35 minutes or until sides begin to bubble.

*Connie Rodes, Milford, IN*

# SCALLOPED CABBAGE

*Broccoli, cauliflower or other vegetables may be used.*

6 cups shredded cabbage
6 T. butter
6 T. flour
1 tsp. salt

1/2 tsp. pepper
3 cups milk
1 1/2 cups grated cheese
Bread crumbs

Cook cabbage 8 minutes. Melt butter; add flour and seasonings. Blend thoroughly. Stir in milk gradually. Cook till thick; add grated cheese. Stir till melted. Drain cooked cabbage; mix with cheese sauce. Put in baking dish. Top with buttered bread crumbs. Bake at 350° for 20 minutes or until crumbs are browned.

*Mrs. Isaac Kulp, Millersburg, IN*

# SWEET AND SOUR CABBAGE

6 cups shredded cabbage
1 cup water
1 tsp. salt
2 T. flour

1/4 cup sugar
1/4 cup vinegar
1 egg

Cook cabbage in water and salt. Make thickening of remaining ingredients. Stir into cabbage. Cook until thick, 1 to 2 minutes.

*Edna Miller, Snover, MI*

# CHINESE STYLE CABBAGE

1 T. shortening
1 T. butter
1 1/2 cups shredded cabbage
1/2 cup chopped celery

2 T. diced green pepper
2 T. diced onion
1 tsp. sugar
1/4 tsp. pepper

Melt fats in the skillet. Add vegetables and seasonings to skillet and stir well. Cover tightly and allow vegetables to steam 5-6 minutes over moderate heat. Shake skillet once in awhile to prevent ingredients from sticking to skillet. Two tablespoons water may be substituted for shortening and butter.

*Connie Rodes, Milford, IN*

**Carrots are an excellent source of beta carotene, an antioxidant nutrient that the body converts to vitamin A.**

# BAKED CARROTS

3 eggs, separated
2 1/2 cups cooked carrots
2 cups milk
1 cup bread crumbs

3 T. melted butter
1 T. chopped onion
1 tsp. salt
1/4 tsp. pepper

Beat egg whites. Mix remaining ingredients together. Add egg whites. Put in baking dish. Bake at 350° for 1 hour.

*Mrs. Ivan Zimmerman, Scottsville, KY*     *Mrs. Amos Horst, Ephrata, PA*

*When praying, don't give God instructions. God listens to prayer, not advice.*

# CREAMY CARROT CASSEROLE

4 cups sliced carrots
3/4 cup mayonnaise
1/4 cup chopped onion
2 T. horseradish, opt.
1/2 tsp. salt

1/4 tsp. pepper
14 soda crackers, crushed
1 T. melted butter
2 T. snipped parsley
1/2 cup shredded cheese

Cook carrots till tender. Mix mayonnaise, onion, horseradish, salt and pepper. Add to carrots. Sprinkle crackers, mixed with melted butter over carrots. Top with cheese. Bake till heated through.

*Edith Hoover Martin, Sauk Centre MN*

# CELERY CASSEROLE

6 cups 1-inch celery slices
1 1/2 cups shredded process
cheese
10.5 oz. can cream of chicken
soup, undiluted

1/3 cup slivered or sliced
almonds
1 T. butter or margarine

Cook celery in boiling water 8 minutes; drain. Alternate layers of celery, cheese and soup in greased casserole, ending with soup. Lightly brown almonds in butter and sprinkle over top of celery mixture. Bake at 350° for 20 or 30 minutes or till heated through.

*Carol Hoover, Plymouth, IN*

# BACON CORN

4 slices bacon
1 small onion

1/2 green pepper
2 cups cooked corn

Fry bacon till crisp. Remove bacon and all but 2 to 3 tablespoons of bacon drippings; sauté onion and pepper. Stir in corn and heat through. Sprinkle bacon on top before serving.

# CHEESY CREAMY CORN

6 cups fresh or frozen corn
11 oz. cream cheese, cubed
1/4 cup butter, cubed

3 T. water
3 T. milk
6 slices American cheese

Thaw corn if frozen. Combine all ingredients and put in a slow cooker. Cook on low for 4 hours. Stir once or twice and stir well before serving.

*Anna Mae Hoover, Reinholds, PA*

# CORN PIE

1 1/4 cups fine cracker crumbs
1/2 cup butter, melted
2 T. butter
1 1/4 cups milk, divided
2 cups fresh corn

1/2 tsp. salt
2 T. flour
1/2 tsp. onion salt
2 eggs, beaten

Combine crumbs and 1/2 cup butter. Reserve 1/2 cup of crumbs for topping. Line 9 "pie pan with remaining crumbs. Combine 2 T. butter, 1 cup milk, corn and salt. Bring to a boil; reduce heat and cook 3 minutes. Add flour to remaining 1/4 cup milk; mix to smooth paste. Add slowly to corn, stirring constantly. Cool 2 to 3 minutes or until thick. Cool slightly; add onion salt. Add eggs slowly, stirring constantly. Pour into crumb-lined pan. Sprinkle remaining crumbs on top. Bake at 400° for 20 minutes.

*Mrs. Jacob Oberholtzer, Liberty, KY*

Because red onions have a milder sweeter flavor than do white and yellow onions they are often used in salads. White and yellow onions are more often used in cooking. Heating onions gives them a milder, sweeter taste.
The onion family includes not only leeks, shallots, garlic and chives, but also includes tulips, hyacinths and lily-of-the-valley.

# ONION PIE *(Zwibel Kuchen)*

1 1/2 cups flour
1/2 tsp. salt
1 1/2 tsp. caraway seed
1/2 cup shortening
2 to 3 T. water
3 cups thinly sliced onion

3 T. butter
1/2 cup milk
1 1/2 cups sour cream
2 eggs, well beaten
1 tsp. salt
3 T. flour

Mix first 3 ingredients; cut in shortening. Add enough water to make dough soft but not sticky. Roll out and put in 10" pie pan. Bake at 450° for 12 to 15 minutes or till golden brown. Sauté onions in butter until light brown. Spoon into baked pie shell. Add milk, 11/4 cup sour cream, and salt, to the eggs. Blend flour with remaining 1/4 cup sour cream. Combine with egg mixture; pour over onions in shell. Bake at 325° for 30 minutes or until firm in center. Garnish with crisp bacon, if desired.

*Mrs. Jacob Oberholtzer, Liberty, KY*

# ONION RINGS I

*These can be frozen.  To reheat, place on an ungreased cookie sheet and bake at 350° for 6 or 7 minutes.*

1 large Spanish or Bermuda
   onion
2/3 cup milk

1/2 cup flour
3/4 tsp. baking powder
1/4 tsp. salt

Cut onion crosswise into 1/4 inch slices; separate into rings.  Combine remaining ingredients to make batter. Heat oil 1 inch deep in a large skillet.  Dip each ring into batter using tongs; let excess batter drip off.  Fry a few at a time until golden, about 2 minutes.  Drain on paper towel.

*Mrs. Larry Zimmerman, Elkhart, IN*

# ONION RINGS II

1 egg, beaten
1/2 cup water
2 tsp. lemon juice
1 T. cooking oil

1/2 cup corn meal
1/2 cup flour
1 1/2 tsp. baking powder
1/2 tsp. salt

Beat together egg, water, lemon juice and oil.  Mix all ingredients together.  Dip onion rings into mixture and deep fat fry at 375°.

*Rachel Weirich, Stone Lake, WI*

# ONION PATTIES

3/4 cup flour
2 tsp. baking powder
1 T. sugar
1/2 tsp. salt

1 T. corn meal
2 1/2 cups finely chopped onion
Milk

Stir all ingredients together, adding enough milk to make a thin batter.  Drop a teaspoon at a time into hot oil in skillet.  Turn once.

*Mrs. Elam Hoover, Versailles, MO*

# PEAS WITH MUSHROOMS AND ONIONS

4 oz. can mushrooms
1/4 cup chopped onion
2 T. butter

2 cups cooked and salted peas,
   drained

Sauté mushrooms and onion in butter until tender.  Add peas.

*He that will not command his thoughts soon loses command of his actions.*

# CROWDER PEA GUMBO & RICE PATTIES

3 T. cooking oil
1 large onion, chopped
1 clove garlic, chopped
1/2 cup chopped green pepper
1-inch piece chili pepper, sliced
   thin
2 1/2 to 3 cups okra, sliced into
   wheels
2 cups canned or fresh tomatoes,
   diced

4 sprigs parsley
1 bay leaf
1/2 tsp. dried basil
2 cups cooked crowder peas,
   drained
1 cup pea water, approx.
1/4 tsp. hot pepper sauce
Cooked brown rice

Heat oil and sauté onion and garlic, 3 to 5 minutes. Add peppers and okra; sauté 5 minutes longer. Add tomatoes and seasoning; cover and simmer 15 to 20 minutes over low heat until okra is tender. Add peas and enough water to make a generous amount of thick gravy. Add salt if necessary. Serve over rice patties or cooked rice. To make rice patties use 1/2 cup of cooked brown rice per person. With moist hands compress rice into patties. Dredge patties in flour. Cover skillet with oil. When hot, brown patties on each side. Press gently with a spatula to keep shape and enhance cooking. Flip several times if necessary.

*Hannah Kulp Family, Mt. Hermon, KY*

# MASHED POTATOES

8 medium potatoes
1 tsp. salt

1/4 cup butter
4 to 6 T. milk

Peel and cook potatoes; mash. Add salt and butter. Gradually add milk, beating until light and fluffy. Can be topped with additional butter and sprinkled with pepper or served with gravy.

# CREAMY POTATO PUFFS

*If you want to serve this without baking, substitute 1/4 to 1/2 cup milk for the egg and a tablespoon or two of chives for the chopped onion.*

4 cups mashed potatoes
8 oz. cream cheese
1 egg, beaten

1/3 cup chopped onion
1 tsp. salt
Dash of pepper

Combine hot mashed potatoes and cream cheese; mix well. Add remaining ingredients. Bake at 350° for 45 minutes.

*Mrs. Clay Zimmerman, Paltinis, Romania*

# REFRIGERATOR MASHED POTATOES

5 lb., 9 large, or 4 cups mashed
   potatoes
1 to 2 cups sour cream
6 to 8 oz. cream cheese

2 tsp. onion salt
1 tsp. salt, opt.
1/4 tsp. pepper
2 T. butter or margarine

Add remaining ingredients to mashed potatoes and beat until light and fluffy. If they seem stiff add a little milk. Pour into a greased 13x9 pan; cool. Keeps 2 weeks in refrigerator. Freezes well. Bake at 350° for 30 minutes or until heated through. Grated cheese can be mixed in or sprinkled on top.

*Mrs. James Horst, East Earl, PA*     *Sheryl Weaver, Goshen, IN*

# MASHED POTATO CHEESE PIE

2 to 2 1/2 cups mashed potatoes
2 T. flour
1 tsp. baking powder
Salt and pepper
1 egg

2 T. melted butter
2 eggs
1 cup cream
3/4 cup grated cheese
Salt and pepper

Combine potatoes (leftovers are fine), flour, baking powder, salt and pepper, egg, and butter; press into a 9" pie plate. Combine remaining ingredients and pour into crust. Bake at 350° for 35 to 45 minutes or until knife comes out clean.

*Mrs. Cleon Bauman, Elmira, Ont. Canada*

**Potatoes are highly digestible and are a good source of vitamin C, vitamin B6 and potassium. A medium potato eaten with the skin provides over 40% of the Recommended Daily Allowance (RDA) of vitamin C for adults and has around 75 calories. Baking, steaming, and microwaving preserve more nutrients than boiling. Using potato water helps recover some of the lost nutrients.**

# POTATO FILLING

1 cup hot mashed potatoes
1 egg, well beaten
2 cups bread cubes
1 small onion, minced
1/4 cup diced celery

1 T. minced parsley
2 T. melted butter
1 tsp. salt
1/2 tsp. poultry seasoning
1/8 tsp. pepper

Mix potatoes (leftovers are fine) with egg. Soak bread in cold water and squeeze dry. Add to potato mixture. Add remaining ingredients; mix well. Eat plain or in stuffed peppers. Parboil peppers 5 minutes before stuffing. Bake at 375° for 25 minutes.

# SCALLOPED POTATOES

| | |
|---|---|
| 1/4 cup butter | 3 cups milk |
| 1/4 cup flour | 6 cups thinly sliced or shredded |
| 1 tsp. dried parsley | potatoes |
| 1 tsp. salt | 1 onion, chopped |
| 1/4 tsp. pepper | |

Melt butter; stir in flour, parsley, salt and pepper until smooth. Gradually add milk; bring to a boil. Cook and stir for one minute. Place potatoes and onion in a 2 1/2 quart casserole. Pour sauce on top and mix. Cover and bake at 375° for 1 and 1/2 hours.

**Most of the nutrients in a potato are found near the surface.**

# EASY SCALLOPED POTATOES

| | |
|---|---|
| 8 cups shredded potatoes | 1 cup shredded cheese |
| 1 tsp. salt | 2 cups milk |
| 10.5 oz. can cream of mushroom | 1/4 cup butter or margarine |
| soup | 1/2 medium onion |

Mix all ingredients in a 13x9 pan. Sprinkle with pepper. Bake at 350° for 1 1/2 hours.

*Mrs. Luke Hoover, Goshen, IN*

# GOURMET SCALLOPED POTATOES

*Two cups grated cheese may be substituted for cheese soup - or delete cheese soup altogether.*

| | |
|---|---|
| 8 boiled potatoes | 10.5 oz. can cheddar cheese soup |
| 1/4 cup butter or margarine | 1/2 - 1 tsp. salt |
| 1/4 cup chopped onion | 1/4 tsp. pepper |
| 1 1/2 to 2 cups sour cream | 3/4 cup crushed cornflakes |
| 10.5 oz. can cream of chicken | 2 T. butter or margarine |
| soup | |

Dice or slice potatoes. Sauté onions in butter. Add next 5 ingredients. Mix with potatoes; place in casserole. Top with a mixture of butter and crumbs. A 1/2 cup of cheese may be used instead of butter in the crumbs. Bake at 350° for an hour. If using a 13x9 pan bake only 30 to 40 minutes.

*Lizzie Hoover, Goshen, IN    Mrs. James Kulp, Unity, WI    Susie St. John, Avordton, OH*

# POTATOES AU GRATIN

4 cups sliced potatoes
8 oz. Velveeta or other cheese,
   cubed

1/2 cup chopped onion
1 tsp. dry mustard
1/4 tsp. pepper

Cook potatoes 8 to 10 minutes or until fork tender; drain. Toss with remaining ingredients. Bake in a covered 2 quart casserole at 350° for 25 minutes or until cheese is melted. Stir before serving.

# GOURMET CHEESE POTATOES

*This recipe can be doubled or tripled and put in a slow cooker. Adding hot dogs or smoked sausage turns this into a main dish.*

1/4 cup butter
1/4 cup chopped onion
1/4 cup flour
1 to 1 1/2 tsp. salt
1/4 tsp. pepper

1 1/2 cups milk
2 cups grated cheese
4 cups cooked cubed potatoes
1/4 cup dry bread crumbs
1 T. butter

Sauté onion in butter until soft. Add flour, salt and pepper. Gradually add milk and cook till thickened. Add cheese and stir till melted. Mix with potatoes or arrange in layers in a 1 1/2 quart casserole. Top with buttered bread crumbs or sprinkle with paprika and butter. Bake at 350° about 25 minutes.

*Mrs. Ray (Elsie) Hoover, Stratford, WI     Mrs. Marvin Sensenig, Penn Yan, NY*

**Potatoes are the world's largest and most economically important vegetable crop.**

# TWICE BAKED POTATOES

*These can be made ahead and heated just before serving.*

2 large baking potatoes
4 strips bacon, diced
1/4 cup chopped green onion
2 T. Parmesan cheese
1/2 cup sour cream

1/2 tsp. salt
1/2 tsp. white pepper
2 T. melted butter
Paprika

Scrub potatoes; dry and prick with a fork. Bake at 400° for 1 hour. Fry bacon till crisp. Leave 2 to 3 tablespoons of drippings in skillet. Add onion and sauté till tender but not brown; remove from heat. Scoop out potato insides and add to skillet. Add cheese, sour cream and seasonings; mash and blend thoroughly. Heat through over low heat. Spoon mixture into potato shells; drizzle with melted butter and sprinkle with paprika. Bake at 350° for 15 to 20 minutes.

*Connie Rodes, Milford, IN*

145

# BAKED POTATO TOPPER

1 cup shredded cheese
1/4 cup soft butter

1/2 cup sour cream
Chopped onion to taste

Whip everything together until fluffy.  Serve on baked potatoes.

*Mrs. James Kulp, Unity, WI*

**Potatoes should be stored in a cool, dark place but should not be refrigerated.  Temperatures below 45° change the starch to sugar and give potatoes a funny taste.**

# BAKED SLICED POTATOES

*For cheesy potatoes sprinkle one cup shredded cheese on top and bake 10 to 15 minutes longer.*

4 large baking potatoes
1/4 cup melted butter
1/4 cup cooking oil

2 cloves garlic, minced
1/2 to 1 tsp. salt
1/2 tsp. dried thyme

Cut unpeeled potatoes into 1/4-inch thick slices.  Overlap slices in a buttered 13x9 pan.  Mix butter and oil.  Brush slices with mixture.  Pour the rest over potatoes.  Sprinkle with garlic, salt and thyme or delete thyme and sprinkle with Parmesan cheese and red pepper.  Bake at 400° for 25 to 30 minutes or until browned at the edges.

*Mary Ann Martin, Sauk Centre, MN*      *Kathleen Ramer, New Paris, IN*

# GOLDEN PARMESAN POTATOES

*For garlic potatoes, omit Parmesan cheese and parsley and add 1/2 teaspoon garlic salt to flour mixture.*

1/3 to 1/2 cup butter
3 lb. potatoes (6 large)
1/4 cup flour
1/4 cup Parmesan cheese

3/4 tsp. salt
1/8 tsp. pepper
Chopped parsley, opt.

Melt butter in a 13x9 pan.  Peel potatoes and cut into large chunks or slices.  Mix next 4 ingredients in a plastic bag and shake well; add potatoes and shake until well coated.  Place in a single layer in melted butter.  Bake at 375° for 60 to 90 minutes, turning once.  Sprinkle with parsley before serving.

*Ethel Hoover, Goshen IN      Mrs. William (Lena) Kilmer      Mrs. Isaac Kulp, Millersburg, IN
Karen Meador, Rossville, IN      Karen Riffey, Bernville, PA*

# CRUNCH-TOP POTATOES

| | |
|---|---|
| 1/3 cup butter | 2 tsp. salt |
| 3 or 4 large potatoes | 1 1/2 cups shredded cheese |
| 3/4 cup dry bread crumbs | 1 1/2 tsp. paprika |

Melt butter in a jellyroll pan in a 375° oven. Add single layer of potatoes cut lengthwise in 1/2-inch slices; turn once in butter. Mix remaining ingredients and sprinkle on top. Bake at 375° for 30 minutes or until done and tops are crisp.

*Thelma Martin, Osceola, IN*

# HARVEST TIME POTATOES

| | |
|---|---|
| 6 slices bacon | 1 1/2 tsp. salt |
| 4 cups raw, thin sliced potatoes | 1/2 tsp. pepper |
| 1 onion, diced | 1/2 tsp. dry mustard |
| 2 cups cooked tomatoes or 1 cup | 1 tsp. sugar |
| tomato juice | 1/4 tsp. celery salt |

Fry bacon; drain and set aside. Sauté potatoes and onion in bacon grease about 10 minutes, turning occasionally. Add remaining ingredients and simmer 20 minutes or till tender and juice is thickened. Add chopped bacon.

*Anna Mae Hoover, Reinholds, PA*

# POTATO PATCHES

| | |
|---|---|
| 6 medium potatoes | 1/4 tsp. pepper |
| 1/2 cup chopped onion | Parsley |
| 3 T. flour | Milk |
| 1 tsp. salt | |

Shred potatoes; rinse and drain. Stir in all but milk. Add enough milk to make a thin batter. Heat oil in a skillet and drop batter by tablespoon; fry on both sides.

*Vera Fox, Memphis, MO*

# HASH BROWNS I

| | |
|---|---|
| Cooking oil | Salt |
| Grated raw potatoes | Pepper |

Preheat a skillet filled with 1/8" oil. Spread potatoes 1/2 to 3/4 inch thick in hot oil. Sprinkle generously with salt. Pepper as desired. Cover and fry till brown. Cut into serving pieces and turn, leaving the lid off so potatoes get crisp. Add oil if needed. Season. Fry till golden brown. This recipe doesn't work well with fresh potatoes.

*Mrs. LaVerne (Virginia) Hoover, Goshen, IN*

# HASH BROWNS II

3 cups cooked, shredded
   potatoes
3 T. flour
1/4 cup chopped onion

1 tsp. salt
1/8 tsp. pepper
1 T. milk
Cooking oil

Combine everything but oil. Heat oil in skillet and pack potato mixture into it. Brown on both sides over medium low heat.

# GRILLED POTATOES

**Slice well scrubbed potatoes and place on tin foil sprayed with no-stick cooking spray. Spread out evenly and sprinkle with salt, pepper, onion salt and garlic salt. Spray another sheet of foil and lay on top of potatoes. Seal the edges. Grill over medium heat for 25 minutes or until soft.**

# CARAMEL SWEET POTATOES

2-16 oz. cans whole sweet
   potatoes
3/4 cup brown sugar
1/2 cup light corn syrup

3/4 cup butter
1 tsp. cinnamon
1/4 tsp. salt

Arrange sliced sweet potatoes in baking dish (11/2 quarts cooked, lightly salted sweet potatoes can be used). Bring remaining ingredients to a boil. Reduce heat; simmer 5 minutes. Pour over sweet potatoes. Bake at 350° for 20 to 25 minutes, basting often.

*Mary Ann Martin, Sauk Centre, MN*

# GLAZED SWEET POTATOES

1/2 cup brown sugar
1/4 cup butter
1/8 tsp. cinnamon

1/4 tsp. salt
2 lb. cooked sweet potatoes

Combine all but sweet potatoes in a skillet and cook over medium heat, stirring constantly, until mixture bubbles. Arrange sweet potatoes in skillet. Cover and cook 10 over low heat. Uncover and cook 5 minutes more, basting frequently.

*Mrs. Ray (Elsie) Hoover, Stratford, WI*

*The most dangerous of all falsehoods is a slightly distorted truth*

# SWEET POTATO CASSEROLE

| | |
|---|---|
| 4 cups cooked, mashed sweet potatoes | 1 1/2 tsp. pumpkin pie spice, opt. |
| 3/4 cup sugar | 3/4 cup brown sugar |
| 2 eggs, beaten | 1 cup chopped nuts |
| 1/4 cup melted butter | 1/2 cup flour |
| 2/3 cup evaporated milk | 1/3 cup melted butter |
| 2 tsp. vanilla | 1 cup coconut, opt. |

Mix first 7 ingredients. Place in casserole dish. Combine brown sugar with remaining ingredients. Mix well and sprinkle on top. Bake at 350° for 45 minutes.

*Cindy (Lee) Hilty, Brooksville, MS*     *Miriam Hooley, Elkhart, IN*

# SPINACH BALLS

| | |
|---|---|
| 1 pint frozen spinach, drained or 10 oz. pkg. | 1 chicken bouillon cube, dissolved in 1/4 c. water |
| 6 eggs | 1 T. parsley |
| 2 cups bread crumbs | 1/2 T. Accent |
| 1 cup shredded cheese | 1/2 tsp. thyme |
| 2 small onions, chopped | 1/2 tsp. pepper |
| 1/4 cup melted butter | |

Mix all ingredients until well blended. Form into walnut-sized balls and place in a 12x8 pan. Bake at 350° for 30 to 35 minutes. This recipe can be frozen before baking. It can also be shaped into a loaf.

*Donna Hoover, Goshen, IN*

# BAKED ACORN SQUASH

| | |
|---|---|
| 2 acorn squash | 1/2 cup brown sugar |
| 2/3 cup cracker crumbs | 1/2 tsp. salt |
| 1/3 cup soft butter | 1/2 tsp. cinnamon |

Cut squash in half; remove seeds and fibers. Stir together remaining ingredients. Spoon 1/4 of mixture into each squash half. Place squash, cut side up, in a baking dish with 1/4 inch of water. Bake at 400° for 40 minutes or until tender.

**Take care of your life and the Lord will take care of your death.**

## SQUASH CONTINENTAL

1/4 cup butter
1 1/2 cups sliced zucchini or
   other summer squash
1 T. water

1/2 tsp. salt
1/2 tsp. pepper
1 clove garlic, crushed
1/3 cup grated cheese

Melt butter in skillet. Add squash, water and seasoning; sauté for 1 or 2 minutes. Cover skillet and simmer for 6 to 8 minutes until squash is crisp-tender. Stir in grated cheese until it melts.

*Connie Rodes, Milford, IN*

## SUMMER SQUASH CASSEROLE

4 cups diced, cooked squash
2 1/2 tsp. salt
1/4 tsp. pepper
2 T. butter or margarine
1 1/2 cups scalded milk

30 soda crackers, small squares
2 beaten eggs
1 medium onion, chopped
Velveeta cheese slices

Drain squash well. Add salt, pepper and butter to milk. Pour milk over crackers; add squash, eggs and onion. Bake in a covered casserole at 350° for an hour, then put cheese slices on top and bake till melted.

*Mrs. Lloyd E. Troyer, Stella, MO*

## STUFFED ZUCCHINI

3 medium zucchini
Salt and pepper
1 T. butter
1/2 lb. lean ground beef
1/2 cup chopped celery

1/4 cup chopped onion
8 oz. tomato sauce
1/2 cup soft bread crumbs
1/4 cup Parmesan cheese

Wash squash. Cook in boiling salted water 5 minutes. Cut squash in half lengthwise. Scoop out seeds. Sprinkle cavities with salt and pepper; set aside. Melt butter in skillet; add beef, celery and onion. Cook and stir until beef is browned. Add tomato sauce and bread crumbs; stir well. Spoon into squash. Place squash in shallow baking dish and sprinkle with cheese. Bake uncovered at 375° for 30 minutes or until squash are tender.

*Mary Ann Martin, Sauk Centre, MN*

***Discontentment makes rich men poor while contentment makes poor men rich.***

## ZUCCHINI PUFFS

1 cup grated zucchini
1 egg
2/3 cup Bisquick biscuit mix

1/2 cup grated cheese
Chopped onion
Salt and Pepper to taste

Mix all ingredients. Form into patties and fry in oil.

*Alice Moser, Tyrone, NM*

## ZUCCHINI QUICHE I

1 can crescent rolls
4 cups thin zucchini slices
1/2 cup chopped onion
1/2 cup butter
2 eggs
2 T. parsley

1/2 tsp. salt
1/2 tsp. pepper
1/2 tsp. garlic powder
1/2 tsp. oregano
1/4 tsp. basil
2 cups grated mozzarella cheese

Line a 9" pie pan with roll mix. Sauté zucchini and onion in butter for 10 minutes. Beat eggs well; add zucchini and remaining ingredients. Pour into dough lined pan. Bake at 375° for 18 to 20 minutes. Let stand 10 minutes before serving.

*Mrs. Dale (Margaret) Love, Goshen, IN*

## ZUCCHINI QUICHE II

1 cup chopped onion
1 cup Bisquick biscuit mix
4 eggs
1/2 cup cooking oil
1/2 cup Parmesan cheese

1 tsp. parsley
1/4 tsp. salt, or to taste
3 to 3 1/2 cups diced or grated
   zucchini

Mix all ingredients except zucchini in a bowl. Stir in zucchini and pour into a buttered 9" pie pan. Bake at 350° for 30 to 40 minutes or until brown. Parmesan cheese may be omitted.

*Mrs. James Horst, East Earl, PA*          *Mrs. James Kulp, Unity, WI*

*When life's pathway is shadowed and dark clouds dip low,*
*And the winds of difficulty and adversity blow,*
*What comfort to trust, though we don't understand,*
*In the safety and guidance of God's loving hand.*

# TOMATO BAKE

8 cups tomato chunks
1/3 cup sugar
1 1/2 tsp. salt
Dash of pepper

3 T. butter
2 cups bread cubes
1/2 cup grated cheese or 6 slices
    American cheese

Squeeze seeds out of tomatoes and place in a greased 12x8 glass baking dish. Sprinkle with sugar, salt and pepper. Lightly toast bread cubes in melted butter. Top tomato mixture with bread cubes. Bake at 350° for 30 minutes. Add cheese and bake 10 to 15 minutes longer.

*Mary Ann Martin, Sauk Centre, MN*

# CREAMED VEGETABLES

1/4 cup butter
1/4 cup flour
1/2 cup vegetable liquid
1/2 cup light cream or milk

1 tsp. sugar
1/4 tsp. pepper
2 lb. salted, cooked vegetables

Melt butter; add flour and stir until smooth. Blend in liquid and milk; cook till thickened. Stir in sugar and pepper. Combine with vegetables. Heat through before serving.

# QUICK AU GRATIN VEGETABLES

Vegetables of choice
Butter

Bread crumbs
Grated cheese

Cook vegetables. Pour in a shallow baking dish. Dot with butter. Cover with bread crumbs and grated cheese. Bake at 375° until golden brown.

*Nancy Kilmer, California, MO*

# ROASTED VEGETABLES

8 cups assorted vegetable pieces
1/4 cup olive oil

1 1/2 tsp. salt

Toss together and place in a baking pan. Bake at 375° until vegetables are tender.

152

## VEGETABLE PIZZA I

Favorite pizza crust
16 oz. cream cheese
1 pkg. Hidden Valley Ranch salad
    dressing mix or 3 T.
1 cup mayonnaise or salad
    dressing
Chopped cauliflower

Chopped broccoli
Chopped carrots
Chopped celery
Chopped onion
Chopped lettuce
Shredded cheese

Bake and cool pizza crust. Mix cream cheese, dressing mix, and salad dressing. Spread on cooled pizza crust. Top with any or all of the vegetables. Sprinkle with cheese.

*Elaine Martin, Nappanee, IN*

## VEGETABLE PIZZA II

2-8 oz. tubes crescent rolls
16 oz. sour cream
1 pkg. Hidden Valley Ranch salad
    dressing mix or 3 T.
Chopped carrots
Chopped cauliflower

Chopped broccoli
Chopped peppers
Chopped radishes
Chopped tomatoes
Fried bacon, crumbled
Shredded cheese

Press rolls into an 18 x 12 cookie sheet and bake. Cool. Mix sour cream and dressing mix and spread on cooled crust. Sprinkle with any or all of the following vegetables. Top with bacon and shredded cheese.

*Rebecca Glick, Spencer, WI*

***It takes two to quarrel,
but only one to apologize.***

# ADDITIONAL RECIPES

*Children need parents' presence more than their presents.*

# STOVETOP
# MAIN
# DISHES

# STIR-FRY AND RICE DISHES

## VEGETABLE STIR-FRY WITH RICE

1 1/2 cups brown rice
3 cups water
3/4 tsp. salt, opt.
3 quarts fresh vegetables

1/2 lb. slivered chicken breast or
   beef steak
1/4 cup cornstarch
1/4 cup soy sauce

Bring rice, water and salt to a boil; stir and put a tight lid on. Reduce heat and don't uncover for 45 minutes. If it boils over turn heat lower. Wash and cut up a large variety of vegetables, using as many different colors and shapes as possible. Sliver meat; cutting while still partially frozen is easiest. Using a large skillet, fry meat in a little oil until almost done. Add vegetables and stir-fry until vegetables are crisp-tender. If you prefer softer vegetables, put the lid on and steam a bit. Combine cornstarch and soy sauce. When vegetables are as you like them, stir in cornstarch mixture; cook till sauce is clear and thickened. Add water if necessary. Fluff rice and place on a platter, mounding edges slightly. Pour meat and vegetables in the center. Cooked meat may be used; add after vegetables are cooked.

*Vera Witmer, Goshen, IN*

## SUMMER VEGETABLE MEAT STIR-FRY

1 1/2 T. cornstarch
3 T. soy sauce
1/2 tsp. dry mustard, opt
1/2 to 1 lb. beef, pork or turkey
   breast strips
3 T. cooking oil

2 cups broth or bouillon
3 cups fresh green beans
5 ribs celery, sliced
1 cup sliced zucchini
1 cup sliced mushrooms
Garlic powder

Combine first 3 ingredients; add meat and coat well. Heat skillet for 1 minute; add oil. Heat 30 seconds then add meat. Stir meat till no longer pink. Add broth slowly, stirring until it begins to thicken. Add vegetables and mix well. Cover and simmer 10 minutes or until vegetables are crisp-tender.

*Mary Ann Martin, Sauk Centre, MN*

*Meekness is not weakness but strength harnessed for service.*

155

## GARDEN VEGETABLE STIR-FRY

2 medium carrots
2 cups green beans
2 cups sliced cauliflower
2 T. cold water
1 1/2 tsp. cornstarch
2 T. soy sauce

1 T. dry sherry or water
2 tsp. sugar
Dash of pepper
2 T. cooking oil
1 onion cut into wedges
1 cup sliced zucchini

Cut carrots into thirds, then into thin sticks. Bias slice green beans. Cover and cook carrots and green beans in boiling salted water for 3 minutes. Add cauliflower; cover and cook 2 minutes more. Drain well. Blend water and cornstarch. Stir in next 4 ingredients; set aside. Preheat a large skillet or wok over high heat; add oil. Stir-fry thin onion wedges for 1 minute. Add carrots, beans, cauliflower and zucchini; stir-fry 2 minutes or until vegetables are crisp-tender. Stir and add soy sauce mixture. Cook and stir 3 to 4 minutes or until mixture thickens and bubbles.

*Connie M. Rodes, Milford, IN*

## SHRIMP STIR-FRY

1 cup ketchup
1 T. sugar
1 T. chili powder
1 T. Worcestershire sauce
2 T. cooking oil, divided
1 cup coarsely chopped red or
    green pepper

1 cup coarsely chopped onion
1 cup snow peas
1 lb. large shrimp
20 oz. can pineapple chunks,
    drained

Combine first 4 ingredients. Heat 1 tablespoon of oil in a wok or large skillet. Add peppers and onion; cook 1 to 2 minutes. Add peas and cook 2 more minutes, or until vegetables are crisp-tender. Remove vegetables. Add remaining oil; add shrimp; cook 3 minutes or until shrimp turn pink. Stir in ketchup sauce, vegetables and pineapple. Heat through.

## CHOP SUEY OR CHOW MEIN

1/4 cup butter
1 medium onion, chopped
2 cups diced celery
1 tsp. salt
Dash of pepper
1 1/2 cups hot water
1 1/2 cups mushrooms

2 to 3 cups bean sprouts
2 cups cooked pork, beef or
    chicken strips
2 T. cold water
2 T. cornstarch
2 tsp. soy sauce
1 tsp. sugar

Cook onion in butter 3 minutes. Add celery, salt, pepper and hot water. Cover and cook 5 minutes. Add mushrooms, bean sprouts and meat. Mix well and cook 5 minutes. Combine remaining ingredients and add to meat mixture. Mix lightly; cook 1 minute. Serve hot over cooked rice for chop suey or over chow mein noodles for chow mein.

*Mrs. Ray (Elsie) Hoover, Stratford, WI*

## COLOMBIAN CHICKEN AND RICE

| | |
|---|---|
| 2 T. butter or margarine | Salt and garlic to taste |
| 3 fresh tomatoes, peeled and | 1 cup dry rice |
| chopped | 2 cups chicken broth |
| 1/2 cup chopped onion | 1 1/2 cups cooked chicken |
| 1 green pepper, chopped | 1 T. chopped olives |

In skillet, stew first 5 ingredients a few minutes. Add rice and stir 5 minutes. Add broth; cook on low heat till rice is done and broth absorbed. Add chicken and olives and heat through.

## CENTRAL AMERICAN FRIED RICE

| | |
|---|---|
| 3 T. butter or margarine | 1 cup celery |
| 1 cup rice | 2 cups chicken broth or bouillon |
| 2 cups peas | 2 cups chopped chicken |
| 1 cup carrots | Salt and pepper to taste |

Fry rice and butter slowly in skillet until light brown and puffed up; about 15 to 20 minutes. Stir often. Add rest of ingredients and steam slowly on low heat until rice is dry, about 1/2 hour.

*Beverly Stauffer, New Paris, IN*

## SPEEDY SPANISH RICE

| | |
|---|---|
| 1/2 lb. ground beef | 1/4 tsp. pepper |
| 2 medium onions, chopped | 2 cups water |
| 1 1/2 tsp. salt | 2 cups tomato juice |
| 1 cup dry rice | 1 cup diced cheese |

Brown meat and onion in skillet. Add remaining ingredients, except cheese. Cover and simmer 20 minutes or until rice is soft. Add more water if needed. Stir in cheese the last 5 minutes.

*Mrs. Isaac Martin, Martinsburg, PA*

# FRIED RICE

| | |
|---|---|
| 1/4 cup butter | 1/8 tsp. pepper |
| 1/4 cup chopped onion | 2 T. minced parsley |
| 4 cups cooked rice | 1 tsp. garlic salt |
| 3 T. soy sauce | 1 egg, well beaten |

Fry onion in butter until tender. Add all but the egg and cook over low heat 5 to 10 minutes, stirring occasionally. Add egg, stirring constantly. Cook on low heat 5 minutes more. This is good without the egg, too.

*Mrs. Ray (Elsie) Hoover, Stratford, WI*

# STIR-FRIED RICE CONFETTI

| | |
|---|---|
| 6 T. butter | 1/2 tsp. sugar |
| 1/2 cup minced green onions with tops | 1/2 tsp. salt |
| | 1/4 tsp. garlic powder |
| 4 cups cooked rice | 1 cup leftover vegetables like |
| 8 slices bacon, fried and crumbled | peas, carrots or broccoli |

Sauté onion in butter 5 minutes. Add remaining ingredients. Heat, uncovered over medium heat about 10 minutes, or until rice is golden. Sprinkle with roasted, salted sunflower seeds if desired. Rice can be cooked in large amounts and kept in refrigerator a while or can be frozen. If frozen be sure to thaw completely before using in stir-fry recipes.

*Mary Ann Martin, Sauk Centre, MN*

# HERB FRIED RICE

| | |
|---|---|
| 1/4 cup chopped onion | 3 cups cooked, salted rice |
| 2 T. butter | 1/4 to 1/2 tsp. poultry seasoning |

Sauté onion in butter. Add rice and seasoning. Cook 5 minutes.

*Mrs. Ray (Elsie) Hoover, Stratford, WI*

# RICE WITH BROCCOLI

| | |
|---|---|
| 1/2 cup butter or margarine | 2 cups Minute rice |
| 1 medium onion, chopped | 1 pkg. broccoli, thawed |
| 2 sticks celery, chopped | 10.5 oz. can cream of mushroom soup |
| 8 oz. jar Cheez Whiz or Velveeta cheese | 1 soup can of water |
| 2 tsp. salt | |

Mix all in a 2 1/2 quart casserole. Bake at 350° for 45 minutes.

*Charlene Ramer, Goshen, IN*

# MONTEREY BEEF RICE SKILLET

1 lb. ground beef
1 cup dry rice
2 1/2 cups water
1 cup chopped onion

1 tsp. salt
3 oz. cream cheese, cubed
15 oz. can tomato sauce
1 tsp. chili powder

Brown beef in 10" skillet; drain. Stir in rice, water, onion and salt. Cover and simmer 25 minutes or till water is absorbed. Stir in cheese, tomato sauce and chili powder. Cover and heat through.

*Mary Zook, Virginia Beach, VA*

# SAUSAGE AND RICE SKILLET

1 lb. bulk sausage
2 cups canned tomatoes,
    undrained
16 oz. can kidney beans

1 cup dry rice
1 cup water
2/3 cup salsa
Salt to taste

Brown sausage; drain. Add remaining ingredients and bring to a boil. Reduce heat; cover and simmer 20 to 25 minutes or until rice is tender. Ground beef can be used but will need more salt. Add more water if needed.

# HAMBURGER RICE DISH

1 lb. ground beef
1 medium onion, chopped
1 1/2 cups dry rice

1 pkg. Lipton chicken soup
1/2 T. poultry seasoning
4 cups water

Brown ground beef and onion in a 4 quart pressure saucepan. Add remaining ingredients and pressure 3 to 5 minutes.

*Gladys Hoover, Sheldon, WI*

# KOREAN GOULASH

1 lb. ground beef, pork or turkey
1 small onion
Salt and pepper to taste
4 cups chopped cabbage
2 ribs celery, sliced

1/2 green pepper, chopped
4 oz. can mushrooms, drained
1 cup bean sprouts, opt.
1/2 cup sliced water chestnuts,
    opt.

Brown meat with onion and season with salt and pepper. Set aside. In a large skillet cook a very small amount of water with remaining ingredients. Season with salt and pepper. Cook just until crisp-tender. Add meat and heat through. Serve over hot rice with chow mein noodles. Season with Worcestershire sauce.

*Connie M. Rodes, Milford, IN*

# FAST CASSEROLE

| | |
|---|---|
| 1 lb. ground beef or sausage | 10 oz. can mushroom soup |
| 1 small onion, diced | 1 cup water |
| 1 tsp. salt | 3/4 cup instant rice |
| 1/4 tsp. pepper | 4 slices Velveeta cheese |
| 2 cups peas or corn | |

Brown ground beef and onion; add salt, pepper, peas, mushroom soup and water. Cook until boiling; add rice. Turn heat low and stir occasionally. Cover until rice is tender, then add cheese.

*Rita Martin, Nappanee, IN*

# KUSHERIE (EGYPTIAN RICE AND LENTILS)

| | |
|---|---|
| 2 T. cooking oil | 1 green pepper |
| 1 1/4 cups lentils | Chopped celery leaves |
| 3 cups boiling water or stock | 1 T. sugar |
| 1 tsp. salt | 1/2 tsp. salt |
| Dash of pepper | 1 tsp. cumin |
| 1 1/2 cups rice | 1/4 tsp. cayenne pepper |
| 1 cup boiling water or stock | 2 T. cooking oil |
| 3/4 cup tomato paste | 3 onions, sliced |
| 3 cups tomato juice or sauce | 4 cloves garlic, minced |

Heat oil in skillet; add lentils and brown 5 minutes, stirring often. Add boiling water, salt and pepper. Cook, uncovered, for 10 minutes. Stir in rice and 1 cup boiling water. Bring to a boil; reduce heat to low; cover and simmer 25 minutes without stirring. Make sauce by heating tomato paste and sauce, green pepper, celery, sugar, salt, cumin and cayenne pepper. Bring to a boil; reduce heat and simmer 20 to 30 minutes. In a small skillet brown onions and garlic in oil. To serve, put rice and lentil mixture on a platter. Pour tomato sauce over it. Top with browned onions.

*Kent Martin, W. Liberty, OH*

*God is before me, He will be my guide;*
*God is behind me, no ill can betide;*
*God is beside me, to comfort and cheer;*
*God is around me, so why should I fear?*

# PASTA DISHES

## MACARONI, SPAGHETTI, OR NOODLES

2 quarts water
2 tsp. salt

8 oz. macaroni, spaghetti or
noodles

Bring water and salt to a rapid boil. Add pasta slowly. Boil uncovered 7 to 10 minutes, stirring occasionally. Drain water. Eat plain or add butter or cheese.

## PARMESAN GARLIC NOODLES

8 oz. noodles
2 T. butter
1/2 cup Parmesan cheese

1 tsp. dried parsley
1/2 tsp. garlic salt
1/8 tsp. pepper

Cook noodles in salt water. Drain well. Toss with remaining ingredients.

## ZIPPY MACARONI AND CHEESE

1 lb. ground beef
1 onion, chopped
2 cups salsa
4 cups water

1 tsp. salt or to taste
2 cups dry macaroni
1/2 lb. Velveeta, cubed

Brown beef and onion in a large skillet. Drain excess grease. Add salsa, water and salt; bring to a boil. Stir in macaroni. Reduce heat and cover. Simmer 10 minutes or until macaroni is tender. Add cheese and stir until it melts.

## GOULASH

1 lb. ground beef
1 medium onion, chopped
1 clove garlic, minced
6 cups tomato juice
2 tsp. chili powder
1 tsp. Worcestershire sauce
1 1/4 cups dry macaroni
3 T. brown sugar

1/4 cup ketchup
1/2 T. mustard
1/2 tsp. seasoning salt
1/2 tsp. salt
1/8 tsp. pepper
1 tsp. liquid smoke, opt.
Velveeta cheese slices

Brown hamburger, onion and garlic in large skillet. Add remaining ingredients. Simmer, covered, 20 to 30 minutes, stirring occasionally. Top with cheese slices if desired. Stir till melted.

*Mrs. LaVerne (Virginia) Hoover, Goshen, IN*

# SKILLET SPAGHETTI

1 lb. ground beef
1/4 cup chopped celery
1 onion, chopped
5 cups tomato juice
3/4 cup ketchup or 6 oz. tomato
   paste
1 1/2 tsp. chili powder, opt

1 tsp. garlic salt
1 tsp. salt
1 1/2 tsp. oregano
1/2 tsp. pepper
1 bay leaf
1/4 cup brown sugar
8 oz. spaghetti

Cook ground beef, celery and onion in a large skillet. Pour off fat; add remaining ingredients, except spaghetti and simmer, uncovered, 30 minutes. Remove bay leaf. Add spaghetti and simmer, covered, until tender, about 20 minutes, or cook spaghetti separately and top with sauce. Serve with Parmesan cheese.

*Donna Hoover, Goshen, IN    Vera Witmer, Goshen, IN*

# QUICK SKILLET SUPPER

1 lb. ground beef
1 cup chopped onion
1 T. cooking oil
3 cups whole wheat or regular
   noodles
3 cups tomato juice

1/2 cup sour cream
2 tsp. salt
1/8 tsp. celery salt
2 tsp. Worcestershire sauce
1/2 cup water

Cook beef and onion in hot oil. Place dry noodles on top of meat. Combine remaining ingredients; mix well. Pour over noodles, moistening well. Do not stir; bring to a boil. Turn heat low; cover and simmer for 30 minutes or until noodles are tender.

*Hannah Kulp Family, Mt. Hermon, KY*

> **As a rule of thumb 1 cup dry macaroni equals 2 cups cooked; a cup of dry noodles equals 1 cup cooked noodles.**

# EASY HAMBURGER SKILLET

1 lb. ground beef
1 small onion, chopped
1 tsp. salt
4 cups water

2 cups shells
4 oz. can mushrooms
2 cups 1/2" cubes Velveeta
   cheese

Brown beef and onion. Drain excess grease. Add salt. Add water and bring to a boil. Add shells or other pasta. Reduce heat and simmer 10 to15 minutes until shells are tender and just a little water remains. Stir in cheese.

# ITALIAN CHICKEN SKILLET

*For added calcium, mix in a cup or two of shredded mozzarella cheese when ready to serve—or sprinkle some cheese on top.*

4 skinless boneless chicken
    breasts halves, cut into bite-
    size pieces
1 T. cooking oil
1 1/2 cups water or bouillon
1 tsp. oregano
1/2 tsp. garlic powder

2 cups canned tomatoes or
    spaghetti sauce
1 green pepper, sliced
1 coarsely chopped onion
2 1/2 cups medium shells or 2
    cups macaroni

Cook chicken in oil 10 minutes or until browned.  Set aside. Add all but pasta. Bring to a boil; add shells.  Cover and cook over low heat 10 minutes, stirring often.  Return chicken to pan.  Heat through or cook till chicken is no longer pink.

# CHICKEN BROCCOLI NOODLE DINNER

1 lb. skinless boneless chicken
    breast, cut into bite-size
    pieces
1 T. cooking oil
1/2 tsp. garlic salt
Pepper

1 3/4 cups chicken broth or water
1/2 tsp. salt or to taste
6 oz. dry noodles
2 cups chopped broccoli
1 cup shredded cheese

In a large kettle, cook chicken in oil until no longer pink, about 5 minutes. Sprinkle with garlic salt and pepper.  Add broth; bring to a boil.  Stir in noodles and broccoli.  Return to boil then reduce heat.  Cover; simmer 10 minutes or until noodles are tender, stirring frequently.  Remove from heat; stir in cheese.

# BEEF STROGANOFF

2 lb. sirloin or round steak
2 cups fresh mushrooms
2 medium onions, sliced
2 T. cooking oil
2 cubes beef bouillon
1 cup hot water

1/2 tsp. salt
2 T. ketchup
2 tsp. mustard
2 T. flour
1/2 cup water
1 cup sour cream

Cut beef into strips.  Brown beef, sliced mushrooms and onion in oil.  Add bouillon, water, salt, ketchup and mustard.  Cover; simmer 30 minutes or until tender.  Combine flour and water.  Stir into meat mixture. Bring to a boil, stirring constantly.  Reduce heat; stir in sour cream. Heat but do not boil. Serve over rice or noodles.

# ONE PAN STROGANOFF

1 lb. ground beef or beef strips
1/2 cup onion
1 clove garlic
1 tsp. salt
2 beef bouillon cubes
1 T. lemon juice, opt.

1/2 cup mushrooms, opt.
1/4 tsp. pepper
4 oz. dry noodles
3 to 3 1/2 cups water
2 T. parsley
1 cup sour cream

Brown meat, onion and garlic. Stir in all but last two ingredients. Simmer 20 minutes or until noodles are soft and liquid mostly absorbed. Stir in parsley and sour cream; heat but don't boil.

*Mrs. Cliff Schalliol, Elkhart, IN*

# HAM, PEAS AND PASTA

16 oz. bowties
2 T. cooking oil
1 onion, chopped
2 cups fresh mushrooms
2 cloves garlic, minced

2 cups cubed, cooked ham
2 cups peas, thawed
1/2 cup broth or water
1 T. lemon juice
1/2 cup Parmesan cheese

Cook bowties or other pasta in salt water. Drain. Heat oil and sauté onion, mushrooms and garlic for 3 minutes. Stir in ham, peas, broth and lemon juice. Cook and stir on high heat until half of the liquid evaporates. Add to pasta and toss with cheese.

Two cups dry macaroni weigh approximately 8 ounces. Two cups dry noodles weigh about 4 ounces.

# FRANKFURTER SUPPER

2 T. butter
1 onion, chopped
2 1/2 cups tomatoes
2 1/2 cups tomato juice
1 T. brown sugar
1 salt

1 bouillon cube
1/4 cup hot water
8 oz. wide noodles
1 lb. hot dogs
1/2 cup grated cheese

Combine everything but cheese in a skillet. Cook until noodles are done. Sprinkle cheese on top before serving.

*Rebecca Ringler, Fleetwood, PA*

# MEAT AND VEGETABLE DISHES

## MEAT, BEANS AND POTATOES

5 potatoes, peeled
1 lb. ground beef
1 medium onion, chopped
10 oz. can mushroom soup

4 oz. can mushrooms
2 cups canned green beans
8 slices cheese, opt

Slice potatoes; cook in salt water till done. Brown meat and onion. Drain grease if necessary. Add soup and *undrained* mushrooms. Stir and heat until bubbly. Add potatoes and green bean; mix well. Heat through. Top with cheese slices and stir.

## HOT DOGS, BEANS AND POTATOES

1 lb. hot dogs
5 potatoes, peeled and cubed
2 cups green beans
10 oz. can mushroom soup

2 cups water
1/2 tsp. salt
1/8 tsp. pepper

Cut hot dogs in chunks. Bring everything to a boil; reduce heat and simmer for 30 minutes or until potatoes are soft. Stir occasionally.

## GREEN BEANS AND GROUND BEEF

1 lb. ground beef
1/2 cup chopped onion
1 T. butter
4 cups green beans
1 or 2 beef bouillon cubes
1 tsp. salt

1 tsp. Worcestershire sauce
1/8 tsp. garlic powder
1/8 tsp. pepper
1 cup tomato juice
1 T. cornstarch

Brown beef and onion in butter. Add fresh or frozen beans; brown a little more. Add cubes, sauce and seasonings. Combine tomato juice and cornstarch; add while stirring. Cook till beans are soft.

*Ellen Newswanger, Kutztown, PA*

***Offering good advice may be noble and grand,***
***But it's not the same as a helping hand.***

## BLACK-EYED PEAS AND BEEF SKILLET

| | |
|---|---|
| 2 1/4 cups black-eyed peas | 1/2 tsp. salt |
| 1 lb. ground beef | 1/8 tsp. pepper |
| 1/4 cup chopped onion | 1/2 cup ketchup |
| 1 clove garlic, minced | 1 T. flour |
| 2 cups canned tomatoes | 1/2 cup shredded sharp American |
| 1 tsp. Worcestershire sauce | cheese |

Put 8 cups water and 1 teaspoon salt in a large kettle. Add peas; cook covered for 40 minutes or till tender. Drain and set aside. In large skillet, cook beef, onion and garlic till meat is browned; drain fat. Stir in drained peas, cut up tomatoes, Worcestershire sauce, salt and pepper. Bring to a boil; reduce heat. Simmer 15 minutes. Blend ketchup and flour; stir in. Cook and stir till thick and bubbly. Sprinkle cheese on top. Heat till cheese melts.

*Connie Rodes, Milford, IN*

## HAMBURGER GRAVY WITH PEAS

*For plain hamburger gravy, delete peas and carrots.*

| | |
|---|---|
| 1 lb. ground beef | 1 cup water |
| 1/4 cup chopped onion | 2 cups peas |
| 1 tsp. salt | 1/4 cup cooked diced carrots, opt. |
| 1/4 tsp. pepper | 2 T. cornstarch |
| 1 beef bouillon cube | 1/4 cup water |

Brown beef, onion, salt and pepper. Drain excess grease. Dissolve bouillon cube in 1 cup water. Add to meat along with peas and carrots. Simmer until peas are tender. Make a paste of cornstarch and water. Gradually add to meat mixture. Serve on mashed potatoes.

*Esther Burkholder, New Providence, PA*

## HAMBURGER ZUCCHINI SKILLET

| | |
|---|---|
| 1 lb. ground beef | 1 tsp. salt or to taste |
| 1/2 onion, chopped | Pepper |
| 1 tomato, chopped | 2 to 3 slices Velveeta cheese |
| 3 small zucchini, sliced | |

Fry ground beef and onion. Drain excess grease. Stir in tomato, zucchini, and seasoning. Cover and simmer till zucchini is tender. Stir in cheese. Cover till melted.

*Mrs. LaVerne (Virginia) Hoover, Goshen, IN*

## FRIED CABBAGE WITH HAMBURGER

1 lb. ground beef
1 small head cabbage

1 1/2 tsp. salt or to taste
1/4 tsp. pepper

Brown meat in a large skillet. Drain excess grease. Add shredded or coarsely cut cabbage and seasonings. Cover and simmer slowly till cabbage is tender, stirring occasionally. Serve with cheese sauce or over mashed potatoes or eat it plain. Cooked chopped ham sautéed in 2 tablespoons of butter may be substituted for ground beef; reduce salt.

*Mrs. LaVerne (Virginia) Hoover, Goshen, IN*

## GERMAN PIZZA

*Substitute hash browns for potatoes and ham or sausage for ground beef to make a breakfast pizza.*

2 T. butter
6 medium potatoes
1 lb. ground beef
Salt and pepper
1/2 cup chopped onion

1/2 cup chopped green pepper
3 eggs
1/3 cup milk
Grated cheese

Melt butter in skillet. Arrange sliced or grated potatoes in bottom of skillet for crust. Add meat, seasoning, onion and pepper. Combine eggs and milk and pour over pizza. Top with cheese; cook or simmer until done.

*Laura Kulp, Stratford, WI*

# CHIP AND MISCELLANEOUS DISHES

## STRAW HATS

*In a hurry? Brown 2 pounds of ground beef and add a 16 ounce can or two of pinto or chili beans. Cut seasoning in half or to taste.*

1 lb. dry pinto beans
7 cups water
1 onion, chopped
2 cloves garlic, minced or 1/2 tsp.
   garlic powder
2 T. chili powder
1 T. salt

1 T. cumin
1 T. oregano
Corn chips
Tomatoes, lettuce, onions, olives
   and cheese
Sour cream and taco sauce or
   salsa

Simmer first column plus cumin and oregano until beans are soft. Uncover and cook to desired thickness. Ground beef or other meat may be added. Serve on slightly crushed corn chips and top with any or all of the remaining ingredients.

*Mrs. Ray (Elsie) Hoover, Stratford, WI*

# NACHOES

1 bag tortilla chips
1 lb. ground beef or turkey
1/2 cup diced onion

1 lb. Mexican Velveeta cheese
3/4 cup milk

Line individual plates with chips. Brown meat and onion; drain fat. Put cheese and milk in microwave for 6 minutes, stirring every 2 minutes. Mixture is thin but thickens quickly. Sprinkle meat over chips and drizzle heavily with cheese.

*Faith Mobley, Sapulpa, OK*

# MEXICAN FIESTA BUFFET

1 lb. rice
3 lb. ground beef
1 large onion
1 large can tomato sauce
2 pkg. Chili-O-Mix
Salt and pepper
1 large head lettuce

8 to 10 large tomatoes
2 large onions, chopped
2-10 oz. cans cheddar cheese
 soup
1/2 can milk
1 cup taco sauce or salsa
1 1/2 large bags corn chips

Cook rice. Brown meat and onion. Add sauce, mix (or taco seasoning), salt and pepper. Cut up lettuce and tomatoes. Make sauce with soup, milk and taco sauce. Place in this order: Chips, rice, meat mixture, lettuce, tomatoes, onions, and cheese sauce.

*Cindy (Lee) Hilty, Brooksville, MS*

# TACO SKILLET

1 lb. ground beef
1 onion, chopped
2 cloves garlic, minced
15 oz. tomato puree
15 oz. red kidney beans, drained
1/4 cup water
1 1/2 tsp. chili powder

3/4 tsp. ground cumin
1/2 tsp. salt
1/2 tsp. coriander
1/8 tsp. red pepper
8 oz. nacho chips
1 cup shredded Monterey Jack
 cheese

Fry meat, onion and garlic. Add remaining ingredients except chips and cheese. Cover and simmer 15 minutes. Put chips on top and top with cheese. Cover just long enough to melt cheese.

*Mrs. LaVerne (Virginia) Hoover, Goshen, IN*

*A good thing to remember, a better thing to do—*
*Work with the construction gang, not with the wrecking crew.*

# CREAMED CHIPPED BEEF

5 oz. dried beef
3/4 cup boiling water
2 T. minced onion or shallots
1/4 cup butter
1/4 cup flour

1 cup hot chicken broth or
   bouillon
3/4 cup cream
1/2 tsp. dry mustard
1/4 tsp. ginger, opt.
Dash of red pepper sauce

Place beef in boiling water 5 minutes; drain and chop (disregard if using sliced packaged dried beef). Sauté onion in butter. Stir in flour. Cook and stir 2 minutes; add broth gradually. Cook 3 minutes, stirring constantly. Reduce heat. Stir in remaining ingredients. If too thick add a tablespoon or two of water. Serve over biscuits, baked potatoes or toast. For a different flavor brown in butter pretty dark before adding the rest.

*Mrs. LaVerne (Virginia) Hoover, Goshen, IN*

# BEEF AND CORN BREAD RING

1 cup corn meal
1 cup flour
1 cup shredded cheese
1/4 cup brown sugar
2 T. fresh parsley
4 tsp. baking powder
1/2 tsp. salt
1 cup milk
1/4 cup cooking oil
1 egg, beaten

1/2 cup water
1/4 tsp. salt
10 oz. corn
1/4 cup chopped black olives
1 lb. ground beef
1 onion, chopped
2 cloves garlic, minced
1/2 cup ketchup
1/2 tsp. salt
1/4 tsp. pepper

To make corn bread, mix first 7 ingredients. Stir in next three ingredients just till moistened; set aside. Bring water and 1/4 tsp. salt to a boil in 10" skillet. Add corn. Simmer, uncovered for 5 minutes. Put in bowl, undrained. Stir in olives. Brown beef, onion and garlic. Drain fat. Stir in ketchup, salt and pepper. Push beef to sides to form 1 3/4" ring. Pour corn with liquid into center. Bring to a boil. Pour corn bread batter evenly over all. Cover. Simmer 20 to 25 minutes. Test with a toothpick. Uncover. Let stand 5 minutes. Invert on platter.

*Mrs. LaVerne (Virginia) Hoover*

*A person without patience is like a car without brakes.*

# ADDITIONAL RECIPES

*Enjoy the little things, for someday you may look back
and realize they were the big things.*

# MAIN
# DISHES

# PASTA AND NOODLE DISHES

## BAKED MACARONI AND CHEESE

1 lb. or 4 cups dry macaroni
1/2 cup butter or margarine
1 onion chopped, opt.
1/2 cup flour

1 tsp. salt
4 cups milk
1 to 1 1/2 lb. Colby cheese,
   grated (4 to 6 cups)

Bring 4 to 5 quarts water to a boil. Add a tablespoon of salt. Add macaroni; cook uncovered 10 minutes or until tender. Stir occasionally; drain. Melt butter; add chopped onion and cook several minutes. Blend in flour and salt. Gradually stir in milk. Boil one minute. Add most of cheese (if using Velveeta delete flour); stir till melted. Add macaroni. Bake uncovered at 350° for 30 minutes, or until hot. Sprinkle with remaining cheese the last 15 minutes of baking. Can be made the night before. Serves 15.

*Mrs. Larry Zimmerman, Elkhart, IN*

**Leftover macaroni and cheese tastes great in tuna or chicken salad.**

## MACARONI FRANK BAKE

1 lb. hot dogs, sliced
1 cup chopped onion
2 T. shortening
1 3/4 cups dry macaroni
2-10 oz. cans cream of mushroom
   soup

1 cup water
2 cups shredded Velveeta
   cheese
Salt and pepper to taste
1 cup bread crumbs tossed
   with 2 T. melted butter

Brown hot dogs and onion in shortening. Cook macaroni in boiling water till soft; drain. Combine all but crumbs and butter. Top with crumbs. Bake at 350° for 30 minutes or until hot and bubbly.

*Sheryl Weaver, Goshen, IN*

## CHEDDAR CHEESE CASSEROLE

2 cups dry macaroni
2 cups shredded cheddar
   cheese, divided

10 oz. can mushroom soup
1/2 cup milk
1/2 cup canned tomatoes

Cook macaroni in salt water till tender; drain. In a shallow baking dish combine 1 1/2 cups cheese with remaining ingredients. Top with 1/2 cup cheese. Bake at 350° for 30 minutes. Browned ground beef may be added.

*Mrs. Edwin Nolt, Liberty, KY*

# GROUND BEEF CASSEROLE I

1 onion, chopped
1/2 cup diced celery
3 T. chopped pepper
1/4 cup butter
1 lb. ground beef
1 tsp. salt
Dash of pepper

10 oz. can mushroom soup
10 oz. can cream of chicken
  soup
1/2 cup milk
1/4 cup mayonnaise
6 oz. noodles
3/4 cup grated cheese

Brown onion, celery, and pepper in butter; add meat, salt and pepper. Fry until browned. Mix soup, milk, mayonnaise and add to meat mixture. Cook noodles; drain and add. Place in a large greased casserole. Top with cheese. Bake at 350° for 1 hour.

*Mrs. John (Twila) Kulp, Stratford, WI*

# GROUND BEEF CASSEROLE II

*This recipe can easily be multiplied for large groups.*

1 lb. noodles
2 lb. ground beef
1 onion, chopped
1 lb. Velveeta cheese
2 cups peas, thawed
10 oz. cream of celery soup

2-10 oz. cans cream of
  mushroom soup
10 oz. can cream of chicken
  soup
Bread crumbs

Cook and drain noodles. Brown meat and onion. Grate cheese. Combine all but crumbs. Top with bread crumbs. Bake 1 hour on low heat.

*Mrs. Lloyd E. Troyer, Stella, MO*

**Pasta is made from durum wheat which contains a large proportion of gluten, or elastic protein.**

# CORN CASSEROLE

1 lb. ground beef
1 cup macaroni
2 cups corn
8 oz. cream cheese
10 oz. can cream of mushroom
  soup

1 cup milk
Salt and pepper, to taste
1/2 cup chopped onion
1/4 cup chopped pimento
Buttered bread crumbs

Brown meat. Cook macaroni or 8 oz. noodles. Thaw corn. Mix all together in baking dish. Top with bread crumbs. Bake at 350° for 30 minutes.

*Edith Martin, New Market, VA*     *Mrs. Lester Weaver, Manheim, PA*

# WIGGLES

3 lb. ground beef
3 onions, chopped
3 cups diced potatoes
3 cups diced celery
3 cups diced carrots
3 cups peas

2 cups spaghetti
3 cans mushroom soup
4 cups tomato juice
Salt and pepper to taste
9 slices bacon, fried
4 cups grated cheese

Brown beef and onions. Cook vegetables and spaghetti. Combine all but bacon and cheese. Layer in a large roaster with seasoning, bacon and cheese. Bake at 350° for 1 1/2 hours.

*Mrs. Harvey Mazelin, Cincinnati, IA*

# CHEESY CABBAGE CASSEROLE

2 T. butter or margarine
3 T. flour
1 1/2 cups milk
1/2 tsp. salt

1 1/2 cups grated cheese
1 cup broken-up spaghetti
1 lb. ground beef, browned
3 cups shredded cabbage

Melt butter; stir in flour. Slowly add milk and salt. Stir in cheese. Cook spaghetti until tender. Layer spaghetti with meat and raw cabbage in a casserole. Make holes and pour sauce over all. Top with buttered bread crumbs. Cover and bake at 350° for 30 minutes. Uncover and bake 15 minutes longer.

*Charlene Ramer, Goshen, IN*          *Sheryl Weaver, Goshen, IN*

# HAM AND GREEN BEAN CASSEROLE

2-4 oz. cans mushrooms
1 medium onion, chopped
1/4 cup butter or margarine
1/4 cup flour
3 cups thin cream or milk
2-10 oz. cans cheddar cheese soup
2 T. soy sauce

1/4 tsp. Tabasco sauce
2-5 oz. cans water chestnuts
12 oz. noodles, cooked
3 pkg. frozen green beans,
   cooked 6 minutes
2 to 4 cups cubed, cooked ham

Fry mushrooms and onion in butter. Combine flour and cream. Combine everything; place in casserole. Bake at 300° for 1 hour.

*Mrs. Luke Hoover, Goshen, IN*

*Yesterday is already a dream, and tomorrow is only a vision;*
*But today, well lived,*
*Makes every yesterday a dream of happiness,*
*And every tomorrow a vision of hope.*

173

## EASY CHEESY NOODLES

| | |
|---|---|
| 3 T. butter or margarine | 1 tsp. salt |
| 8 oz. homemade noodles | 1/4 tsp. black pepper |
| 8 oz. Velveeta cheese | 4 cups cold milk |

Melt butter in an 11x9 pan. Pour in noodles and stir until well coated. Cover with sliced cheese. Add seasoning and milk. Bake uncovered at 325° for 1 1/2 hours; do not stir. Sliced hot dogs or drained canned peas may be added.

*Nancy Kilmer, California, MO*

## DRIED BEEF AND NOODLE CASSEROLE

| | |
|---|---|
| 12 oz. noodles | 3-10 oz. cans mushroom soup |
| 8 oz. dried beef | 3 oz. cream cheese |
| 3 T. butter | 2 cups grated cheese |
| 4 cups green beans | 1 cup sour cream |
| 1 1/2 cups milk | |

Cook noodles in boiling water until tender. Drain. Sauté beef in butter until edges curl. Fry green beans in butter until shriveled and slightly brown. Combine milk, soup, and cheeses. Heat until melted. Mix in sour cream, noodles, beef and beans. Add more milk if too dry. Bake at 350° for 45 minutes.

*Mrs. Larry Zimmerman, Goshen, IN*

# MEAT AND VEGETABLE DISHES

## MIXED VEGETABLE CASSEROLE

*No mixed vegetables? Use a quart of green beans or any combination of leftover vegetables.*

| | |
|---|---|
| 1 1/2 lb. ground beef | 10 oz. can cream of mushroom soup |
| 1 onion, chopped | |
| 1/2 cup milk | 10 oz. can cream of chicken soup |
| 8 oz. Velveeta cheese | |
| 16 oz. bag mixed vegetables | Tator Tots |

Brown meat and onion. Season to taste. Melt cheese with milk. Cook vegetables. Combine everything. Add more milk if dry. Place in casserole; top with Tator Tots. Bake at 350° for 30 minutes or until hot through.

*Mrs. Larry Zimmerman, Elkhart, IN*

## DINNER IN A DISH

1/4 cup butter
1 medium onion, chopped
2 green peppers, chopped
1 lb. ground beef
1 1/2 tsp. salt

1/4 tsp. pepper
2 eggs
2 cups fresh corn
4 medium tomatoes
1/2 cup dry bread crumbs

Fry onion and peppers in butter for 3 minutes. Add meat; mix well. Add seasonings. Remove from heat. Stir in eggs; mix well. Put 1 cup corn in casserole then half of meat topped with sliced tomatoes. Repeat. Cover with crumbs. Dot generously with butter. Bake at 325° approximately 35 minutes.

*Hannah Kulp Family, Mt. Hermon, KY*

## HAMBURGER HOT DISH

1 1/2 lb. ground beef
1 onion, chopped
2-10 oz. cans vegetable or cream
    soup

1/2 soup can water
Tator Tots

Brown ground beef and onion. Put in the bottom of a casserole dish. Pour soup on top. Pour water over all. Cover with Tator Tots. Bake at 325° until browned.

*Ruth (Ramer) Strumland, Harrison, AR*

## BAKED BEEF STEW

3 lb. stew meat
10 oz. can tomato soup
2-10 oz. cans mushroom soup

2-10 oz cans onion soup
8 medium potatoes, diced
4 carrots, diced

Combine everything adding no water or salt. Bake at 300° for 3 hours.

*Rita Martin, Nappanee, IN*

## QUICK AND EASY CASSEROLE

1 lb. ground beef
1 tsp. salt
1 onion, chopped
1 cup diced celery

2 cups kidney beans
4 potatoes, French fry cut
1 can tomato soup

Layer all ingredients in a greased casserole. Pour soup over top and dot with butter. Bake at 350° for 1 hour.

*Mrs. Susan Martin, Romulus, NY*

# LIMA BEAN CASSEROLE

*One inch smoked sausage chunks may be substituted for meatballs.*

1 1/2 lb. ground beef
1 onion, chopped fine
1/2 tsp. salt
1/2 tsp. pepper
1/4 garlic powder

3 medium potatoes, diced
2 cups lima beans
2 cups tomato juice
1 cup diced celery, opt.
2 beef bouillon cubes

Mix first 5 ingredients.  Form into 20 small balls; put into cake pan and bake at 350° for 15 minutes.  Mix remaining ingredients in a kettle; stir in meatballs and bring to a boil.  Put into baking dish.  Cover.  Bake at 350° for 30 minutes; stir; bake till vegetables are done.

*Mrs. Isaac Kulp, Millersburg, IN*

# MASHED POTATO CASSEROLE

*Leftover mashed potatoes work great!*

1 lb. ground beef
1/2 cup finely chopped onion
2 T. shortening
2 cups tomatoes or 1 can tomato
   soup

1 can green beans
1 tsp. salt
1/4 tsp. pepper
3/4 cup grated cheese
2 cups mashed potatoes

Brown meat and onion in shortening.  Add tomatoes, beans and seasoning.  Pour into a 2-quart casserole.  Fold cheese into potatoes. (Cheese may be omitted and an egg stirred into the potatoes instead.) Arrange potatoes on top of other ingredients.  Bake at 350° for 30 to 40 minutes.

*Mrs. Cleon (Carol) Bauman, Elmira, Ont. Canada*     *Mrs. Isaac Brubacker, Versailles, MO*

# DRIED BEEF AND POTATO CASSEROLE

8 to 10 boiled potatoes
4 oz. dried beef
2 T. butter
2 T. flour

2 cups milk
1 cup shredded cheese
2 T. butter bread crumbs

Slice half of the potatoes into a 2 1/2 quart casserole.  Fry beef slightly in butter.  Blend in flour.  Stir in milk, then cheese.  Cook till thickened.  Pour half of sauce over potatoes.  Add remaining potatoes; pour on remaining sauce.  Top with crumbs.  Bake at 350° for 30 minutes.

*Mrs. Elmer Sensenig, Quarryville, PA*

***Those who fear God most fear men least.***

176

# CHEESY CASSEROLE

Slice cooked potatoes in the bottom of a buttered casserole. Add a layer of browned ground beef. Add a layer of cooked green beans. Top each layer with slices of Velveeta cheese. Pour mushroom soup over all. Bake at 350° for 1 hour.

*Karen Weaver, Milford, IN*

# HAM CASSEROLE

*This is a very versatile recipe. Delete mashed potatoes and place cubed cooked potatoes on the bottom of the casserole or substitute cooked broccoli for beans and 4 cups cooked noodles for potatoes.*

3/8 cup butter or margarine
3/8 cup flour
3 cups milk
1 1/2 cups grated cheese

4 cups green beans
3 cups cooked diced ham
5 medium potatoes, cooked
   and mashed

Melt butter; stir in flour. Add milk, stirring till thickened. Add cheese; stir till melted. Put beans in greased casserole; pour on half of cheese sauce. Add ham and pour on remaining sauce. Spread potatoes on top. Sprinkle with cheese if desired. Instant potatoes may be used. Bake at 350° for 30 minutes or until slightly browned.

*Mrs. Larry Zimmerman, Elkhart, IN*

# HAM AND ASPARAGUS CASSEROLE

1 lb. fresh asparagus
4 hard-cooked eggs
1 cup cubed cooked ham
2 T. tapioca
1/4 cup grated American cheese
2 T. chopped onion

1/2 tsp. parsley
1/2 cup light cream or
   evaporated milk
1 T. lemon juice
10 oz. can mushroom soup
Buttered bread crumbs

Cut asparagus into 1 inch pieces. Blanch for 3 minutes. Drain. Mix with chopped eggs and ham. Pour into a 2 1/2 quart baking dish. Sprinkle with tapioca, cheese, onion and parsley. Thoroughly mix cream, lemon juice and mushroom soup; pour on top. Sprinkle with bread crumbs. Bake at 375° for 30 minutes.

*Anna Mae Hoover, Reinholds, PA*

*Not so in haste, my heart; have faith in God and wait;
Although He linger long, He never comes too late.*

## POTATOES AU GRATIN WITH HAM

4 cups sliced potatoes
1 to 2 cups cooked cubed ham
8 oz. Velveeta cheese cubes
1/2 cup chopped onion

1 tsp. dry mustard
1/2 tsp. salt
1/4 tsp. pepper

Cook potatoes 8 to10 minutes or until fork-tender; drain. Toss with remaining ingredients. Bake, covered, at 350° for 20 to 25 minutes or until potatoes are tender. Stir before serving.

## EASY HAM CASSEROLE FOR A CROWD

7-32 oz. bags frozen cubed hash
   browns
10 lb. cooked ham
1 1/3 cups chopped onion
10 cups shredded cheese
2 1/2 cups milk

6-10 oz. cans cream of chicken
   soup
8 cups sour cream
1 1/4 cups butter
Pepper to taste

Use unbrowned, no oil added, hash browns. Combine ingredients in a big container. Do not add salt. Pour into an 18 quart roaster. Bake at 350° for 2 1/2 to 3 hours. Turn to 300° for the last 30 minutes. Serves approximately 80 people.

*Mrs. James Kulp, Unity, WI*

## BROCCOLI, HAM AND CHEESE BAKE

6 slices frozen bread
12 slices cheese
10 oz. frozen broccoli
2 cups diced cooked ham or
   bologna

5 eggs
3 1/2 cups milk
2 tsp. minced onion
1/2 salt
1/4 tsp. dry mustard

Layer bread, 6 slices cheese (Velveeta works fine), broccoli and ham in a pan. Beat eggs; add milk, onion, salt and mustard. Pour over everything. Top with remaining cheese. Refrigerate 6 hours or overnight. Bake at 325° for 50 or 60 minutes.

*Edith (Hoover) Martin, Sauk Center. MN*

## PORK CHOPS AND POTATOES

4 pork chops (1/2" thick)
2 T. flour
2 tsp. salt
1/8 tsp. pepper

4 cups sliced potatoes
2 cups milk
1 T. butter
Velveeta or other cheese

178

Brown and season chops. Combine flour, salt and pepper. Alternate layers of potatoes and flour mixture in a buttered casserole. Pour milk on. Dot with butter. Lay cheese slices over potatoes. Top with chops. Cover. Bake at 375° for 45 minutes. Uncover and bake15 minutes longer.

*Mrs. Susan Martin, Romulus, NY*

## SAUSAGE AND SQUASH CASSEROLE

1 lb. sausage, fried
5 cups cubed or shredded summer
    squash
3 eggs, beaten

1 1/2 cups cracker crumbs
1/3 cup melted butter
1/2 tsp. salt
2 cups shredded sharp cheese

Mix all together. Bake at 350° for 40 to 45 minutes.

*Susan Hilty Hoover, Elida, OH*

## KRAUT, FRANK AND APPLE CASSEROLE

1/4 lb. bacon, diced
8 frankfurters
1/2 cup chopped onion
1 clove garlic, minced
3 cups cooked cubed potatoes
1/2 tsp. salt

Pepper to taste
3 T. brown sugar
2 1/2 cups sauerkraut
2 medium apples, chopped
1 cup grated Swiss cheese

Fry bacon. Cut franks in pieces. Mix together all but bacon, using *undrained* sauerkraut. Pour in a 2 1/2 quart casserole. Top with cheese if desired, and bacon. Bake at 350° for 45 minutes.

*Connie Rodes, Milford, IN*

## HOT DOG BOATS

1 lb. hot dogs
3 cups mashed potatoes

Cheese
Pepper, opt.

Slit hot dogs lengthwise without cutting in half. Fold open and mound with mashed potatoes, leftover potatoes are fine. (Warm potatoes speed up the process.) Top with long narrow cheese slices and sprinkle with pepper. Bake at 350° till cheese melts and hot dogs sizzle. Bologna slices may be used instead of hot dogs.

*Mrs. Ray (Elsie) Hoover, Stratford, WI    Esther Martin, Decker, MI*

*If Christ is the center of our lives, the circumference will take care of itself.*

# RICE AND CHINESE DISHES

## HAMBURGER-CABBAGE-RICE CASSEROLE

1 lb. ground beef
2 onions, chopped
1/4 green pepper, diced, opt.
1 tsp. salt

4 cups cut-up cabbage
3/4 cup dry rice
3 cups tomato juice

Brown beef, onion and pepper. Add salt. Heat cabbage, rice, and tomato juice; mix with ground beef. Place in a greased casserole and bake at 350° for 1 hour. Serve with sour cream, if desired.

*Mrs. Larry Zimmerman, Elkhart, IN*

## SHIPWRECK CASSEROLE

2 onions, chopped
2 medium potatoes, cubed
1 lb. ground beef
1/3 cup dry rice
1 cup diced celery

1 cup diced carrots
1 can tomato soup
1 cup boiling water
Salt and pepper, to taste

Layer all but soup and water. Sprinkle each layer with salt and pepper. Mix soup and boiling water; pour on top. Bake, covered, at 250° to 300° for 3 to 4 hours.

*Mrs. Cleon (Carol) Bauman, Elmira, Ont. Canada*

## STUFFED GREEN PEPPER

6 medium green peppers
1 lb. ground beef
1 onion, chopped
1 tsp. salt
1/8 tsp. pepper
1/2 cup water

2 cups canned tomatoes or
    1 1/2 cups tomato juice
1/2 cup dry rice
1 tsp. Worcestershire sauce
1 cup shredded cheese

Cut tops off peppers; remove membrane. Precook peppers in boiling salt water for 5 minutes; drain. For crisp peppers omit precooking. Brown meat and onion. Season. Add water, tomatoes, rice and Worcestershire sauce. Cover and simmer until rice is tender; add water if needed. Stir in cheese. Stuff peppers; stand upright in baking dish. Bake, uncovered, at 350° for 20 to 25 minutes.

*Mrs. Larry Zimmerman, Elkhart, IN*

# PORK CHOP AND RICE CASSEROLE

4 to 6 pork chops
1/4 cup chopped onion
1/4 cup chopped green pepper
1 1/2 cups dry rice

1 1/2 cups beef broth or
   bouillon
2 1/2 cups tomato juice
Salt and pepper

Brown chops; place in 2-quart casserole. Mix onion, peppers and rice and pour over chops. Mix remaining ingredients and pour over everything. Cover. Bake at 375° for 45 minutes or until rice is soft.

# SWEET AND SOUR PORK

*If you don't want to deep fry, just brown pork in a skillet. Strips or chunks of chicken breast may be used instead of pork.*

1 1/2 lb. cubed pork
2 cups water
1/4 cup soy sauce
2 T. sugar
2 tomatoes cut in wedges
1 green pepper, diced
1/2 cup chopped green onions
1 cup pineapple chunks
1/4 cup butter
1 egg, beaten

2/3 cup milk
1 cup flour
2 tsp. baking powder
1/2 tsp. salt
1/2 cup vinegar
1/2 cup water
1/4 cup sugar
1/4 cup brown sugar
1/4 cup cornstarch
1/2 cup pineapple juice

Simmer pork in water, soy sauce and sugar for 45 minutes; drain. Seed tomato wedges then cook vegetables and pineapple in butter briefly, keeping vegetables crisp. To make batter combine egg, milk, flour, baking powder and salt. Beat till smooth. Dip pork in batter and deep fry at 360° until golden brown. To make sauce bring vinegar, water and sugars to a boil. Combine cornstarch and pineapple juice. Add and cook until thickened. Arrange pork and vegetables on platter and pour sauce over all. This is good served over rice.

*Mrs. Ray (Elsie) Hoover, Stratford, WI*

# MOCK CHOP SUEY

1 lb. ground beef
1 onion chopped
2 cups chopped celery
10 oz. can mushroom soup

1 soup can of water
1/4 cup soy sauce
1 can chow mein noodles

Brown meat, onion and celery. Add soup, water and soy sauce. Do not add salt. Simmer 30 minutes. Add half of noodles and pour into baking dish. Sprinkle remaining noodles on top. Bake 30 minutes at 300°.

*Mrs. Luke Hoover, Goshen, IN*

181

# HAMBURGER CHOW MEIN

1 to 1 1/2 lb. ground beef
1/2 cup chopped onion
10 oz. can cream of chicken soup
10 oz. can cream of mushroom
   soup

2 cups water
1 to 2 cups chopped celery
1 cup dry rice
2 to 4 T. soy sauce
Chow mein noodles

Fry meat and onion. Add remaining ingredients and pour into casserole. Bake at 350° approximately 1 hour. Add a generous topping of noodles for last 20 minutes of baking time. This can also be made using only 1/2 cup of rice and decreasing water to 1/2 cup.

*Mrs. Lloyd E. Troyer, Stella, MO*

# EGG ROLLS

1 lb. ground beef
1/4 cup butter
4 cups finely shredded cabbage
1/2 cup chopped green onion
1 1/2 cups finely diced celery
2 cups bean sprouts
1/4 cup soy sauce
1 tsp. salt

2 T. sugar
2 cups flour
2 T. cornstarch
1 tsp. salt
1 egg, beaten
1 tsp. sugar
2 cups water

Brown beef in butter. Add vegetables, soy sauce, salt and sugar; cook 5 minutes. Drain and cool. To make batter mix flour, cornstarch and salt; add egg and sugar. Gradually beat in water until smooth batter is formed. Lightly grease a 6" skillet. Pour 1/4 cup batter in the center, tilting pan to spread evenly. Cook over low heat until edges pull from sides. Carefully turn pancake with fingers and cook other side. Cool. Put heaping tablespoon of filling in the center and spread filling to within 1/2 inch of edges. Roll, folding in sides and seal with a mixture of 1 T. flour and 2 T. water. Deep fry egg rolls in 360°oil until golden brown.

*Mrs. Ray (Elsie) Hoover, Stratford, WI*

*I know not by what methods rare,*
*But this I know: God answers prayer.*
*I know not if the blessing sought*
*Will come in just the guise I thought.*
*I leave my prayer to Him alone*
*Whose will is wiser than my own.*
*Eliza M. Hickok*

# MEXICAN AND ITALIAN DISHES

## BURRITOS

1 cup flour
1/2 tsp salt
2 T shortening
1/4 cup water
Fried ground beef

Refried or other beans
Shredded cheese
Onions, olives, sour cream,
   taco sauce, tomatoes,
   lettuce

To make tortillas mix flour and salt; cut in shortening and add water. Mix till stiff dough forms. Knead until smooth; divide into 5 balls. Roll into 8 or 9 inch circles. Fry one tortilla at a time over medium heat; 1 minute per side. Place between foil so they don't dry out. Coat each tortilla with beans and sprinkle with cheese. Spoon seasoned meat down the center; top with any or all of the remaining ingredients. Fold up bottom then roll up sides.

## WET BURRITOS

*Busy day coming up? Make this the evening before.*

1 1/2 lb. ground beef
1 small onion, chopped
1 pkg. or 1/4 cup taco seasoning
16 oz. can chili or refried beans

10 flour tortillas
2 cups sour cream
10 oz. can mushroom soup
Grated cheese

Brown meat and onion. Add seasoning and beans. Spoon mixture down center of tortillas. Roll up and place in 13x9 pan. Mix soup and sour cream together; spread over tortillas. Sprinkle with grated cheese. Bake at 350° for 35 minutes or until bubbly. Bake longer if cold. Good served with lettuce, tomatoes and salsa.

*Mrs. James Kulp, Unity, WI*

## TACO CASSEROLE

1 1/2 lb. ground beef
15 oz. can chili beans
1 cup salsa
2 tsp. chili powder
1 tsp. garlic salt

Broken tortilla chips
1 cup sour cream
1 onion, chopped
1 tomato, chopped
1 to 2 cups grated cheese

Brown meat; drain excess fat. Add beans, salsa, chili powder and garlic salt. Bring to a boil. Spread about 2 cups chips in a 13x9 pan. Top with beef mixture. Spread with sour cream. Sprinkle with onion, tomato and cheese. Top with more chips. Bake, uncovered, at 350° for 30 minutes.

# ENCHILADA CASSEROLE

*For a different taste use 2 cups chopped cooked chicken, and flour tortillas. Replace part of the salsa or taco sauce with a can of cream of mushroom soup.*

1 1/2 lb. ground beef
1 cup chopped onion
2 garlic cloves or 1/4 tsp. garlic
   powder
4 tsp. chili powder
1 1/2 tsp. cumin
1 1/2 tsp. salt

1/2 tsp. pepper
1 cup water
2 cups salsa or taco sauce
12 6-inch corn tortillas
1 cup sour cream
4 cups (1 lb.) shredded cheese

Brown beef, onion and garlic. Simmer all but the last 4 ingredients for 10 minutes. Pour 1/2 cup salsa in the bottom of a 13x9 pan. Lay 6 tortillas in and cover with another 1/2 cup salsa. Add beef mixture and top with sour cream and half of the cheese. Place remaining 6 tortillas on; cover with remaining salsa; top with the remaining cheese. Bake at 350° for 40 minutes. Good with sour cream, olives, chopped lettuce and chopped tomatoes. Can be made a day ahead.

*Mrs. Ray (Elsie) Hoover, Stratford*

# AMERICAN-STYLE ENCHILADAS

6 eggs
3 cups milk
2 cups flour
3/4 tsp. salt
1 lb. ground beef
1 lb. bulk pork sausage
1/2 cup chopped green pepper
2 cloves garlic, minced

1 2/3 T. chili powder
1 tsp. salt
10 oz. frozen spinach, cooked,
   drained and chopped
4 cups spaghetti sauce
1 cup water
1 T. chili powder
2 cups shredded cheese

Combine eggs with milk. Add flour and salt; beat well. Pour 1/4 cup batter into a hot 6 or 7" skillet, tilting so batter covers surface. Turn pancakes when surface looks dry. Stack pancakes while making the remaining pancakes. This makes about 30 pancakes. Brown the meat; pour off fat. Add pepper, garlic, chili powder and salt. Simmer 10 minutes. Add spinach. Spoon scant 1/4 cup meat mixture into center of each pancake. Fold the sides in and roll up. Place in two 13x9 pans. Combine remaining ingredients and pour over both pans. Top with cheese. Bake at 325° for 30 minutes. To reheat, if frozen, bake at 375° for 45 minutes.

*Vera Witmer, Goshen, IN*

**The truth of a matter is not determined by how many people believe it.**

# $25,000 MEXICAN DISH

2 cups biscuit mix
1 cup water
2-15 oz. cans refried beans
2 lb. ground beef
2 cups salsa

3 cups shredded cheddar
  cheese
2 cups sour cream
Chopped lettuce and tomato

Mix biscuit mix, water and beans; spread in greased 13x9 pan. Sprinkle fried and seasoned meat on top. Spread salsa and cheese on top. Bake at 350° for 30 minutes. Top with sour cream, lettuce and tomatoes just before serving.

*Mary Zook, Virginia Beach, VA*

# SOUTHWESTERN CASSEROLE

1 lb. ground beef
1 onion, chopped
1 green pepper, chopped
1 tsp. salt
2 tsp. chili powder
1 tsp. cumin
1/2 tsp garlic powder

4 cups tomato juice
4 cups canned kidney beans
2 cups water
1 1/2 cups dry rice
1 to 2 cups shredded cheese
1/4 cup sliced olives

Brown beef, onion and green pepper; drain fat. Add all but cheese and olives. Bake, covered, at 350° at least 1 hour. Uncover and sprinkle with cheese and olives; bake 15 minutes longer.

# MEXICAN CORNBREAD

1 lb. ground beef
1 onion, chopped
1 tsp. hot pepper, chopped
2 eggs
1 1/4 cups cornmeal

1 tsp. soda
1 tsp. salt
1 cup buttermilk
16 oz. can cream-style corn
8 oz. (2 cups) grated cheese

Cook meat, onion, and pepper till meat is brown. Sprinkle with a little salt. Mix eggs, cornmeal, soda, salt and buttermilk; add corn and mix well. Put half of batter in a greased casserole. Add meat mixture and a layer of cheese. Top with remaining batter. Bake at 375° for 45 minutes or until cornbread is brown.

*Janice Weaver, Unity, WI*

*Disappointment to a noble soul is what cold water is to burning metal; it strengthens, tempers, intensifies, but never destroys it.* E. Tabor

## CHILI CON CARNE WITH CORN BREAD

1 onion, chopped
1 lb. ground beef
1 tsp. powdered garlic or 4 cloves
   garlic, crushed
2 cups cooked kidney beans
2 cups whole tomatoes
1 T. chili powder
1/2 tsp. oregano
1/2 tsp. cumin

Salt and pepper to taste
1/2 cup cornmeal
1/2 cup flour or wheat flour
2 tsp. baking powder
1 T. cooking oil
1/2 tsp. salt
1 egg
3/4 cup milk or buttermilk

Fry onion with meat; add garlic. Add beans, tomatoes, spices, salt and pepper. Pour into a 9x9 cake pan or a 1 1/2 quart casserole. Combine dry ingredients; beat together and add remaining ingredients. Spoon over meat mixture. Bake at 400° for 30 minutes.

*Rachel Ramer, Cazenovia, WI*

## CORNMEAL BEAN SQUARES

5 1/2 cups water
2 cups yellow cornmeal
2 cups cold water
2 tsp. salt
2 tsp. sugar
1/3 cup chopped onion
2 T. butter
2 cups sharp cheddar cheese,
   shredded
3 cups cooked kidney beans
3/4 lb. ground beef

1/3 cup cooking oil
1/3 cup chopped onion
1 clove garlic, minced
1 bay leaf
1/2 tsp. oregano
1/2 tsp. salt
1/4 tsp. pepper
Dash cayenne pepper
2 lb. can tomatoes
15 oz. can tomato sauce
1/2 tsp. sugar

Bring 5 1/2 cups water to a boil in a 4-quart saucepan. Combine next four ingredients; gradually stir into boiling water. Cook until thick. Reduce heat to low. Cook for 25 minutes, covered, stirring occasionally. Sauté onion in butter then stir onion and 1 cup of cheese into cornmeal. Add beans. Pour into 13x9 pan and refrigerate until mixture sets. Cut into 24 pieces and place 12 each in two 12x7 glass pans. To make sauce, brown beef in oil; add onion, garlic and seasonings. When done, add tomatoes, sauce and sugar. Simmer 50 minutes. Pour over cornmeal squares. Bake at 350° for 30 minutes or until well heated.

*Edith Martin, New Market, VA*

***I would no more permit myself to worry than to swear.***    *John Wesley*

# DEEP DISH TACO SQUARES

| | |
|---|---|
| 1/2 lb. ground beef | 1 cup biscuit mix |
| 1/2 cup sour cream | 1/4 cup cold water |
| 1/3 cup salad dressing | 1 to 2 fresh tomatoes, sliced thin |
| 1/2 cup shredded cheese | 1/2 cup chopped green pepper |
| 2 T. chopped onion | |

Cook beef till brown; drain. Mix sour cream, salad dressing, cheese and onion. Set aside. Mix biscuit mix and water till soft dough forms. Pat dough into a greased 8x8" pan pressing 1/2 inch up the sides. Layer beef, tomatoes and green pepper in pan; spoon sour cream mixture over top. Sprinkle with paprika if desired. Bake at 375° for 25 to 30 minutes.

# LASAGNA

*For added nutrition mix one cup chopped spinach with cottage cheese.*

| | |
|---|---|
| 1 lb. ground beef | 1 tsp. basil |
| 1/2 cup chopped onion | 1/4 tsp. pepper |
| 1 clove garlic, minced | 8 oz. lasagna noodles, cooked |
| 6 oz. can tomato paste | 16 oz. cottage cheese |
| 1 1/2 cups water | 12 oz. mozzarella cheese slices or |
| 1 tsp. salt | 3 cups shredded |
| 3/4 tsp. oregano | 1/2 cup parmesan cheese, opt. |

Brown meat, onion and garlic. Stir in next 6 ingredients. Cover and simmer 30 minutes. In 12x8 inch pan layer half of noodles, meat sauce, cottage cheese and mozzarella cheese; repeat layers. Sprinkle with parmesan cheese, if desired. Bake at 375° for 30 minutes. Let stand 15 minutes after baking for easier cutting. If refrigerated overnight, bake 40 minutes.

*Mrs. LaVerne (Virginia) Hoover, Goshen, IN*

# EASY LASAGNA

| | |
|---|---|
| 8 oz. lasagna noodles | 1 tsp. oregano |
| 2 lb. ground beef | 16 oz. cottage cheese |
| 2 onions, chopped | 1 to 2 cups grated cheddar |
| 32 oz. spaghetti sauce | cheese |

Cook noodles according to instructions. Drain. Brown beef and onions. Add sauce, oregano and cottage cheese. In a 13x9 pan put a layer of noodles, then spoon on sauce. Repeat twice. Top with cheese. Bake at 350° for 1 hour.

*Thelma Martin, Osceola, IN*

# OVEN-READY LASAGNA

*Uncooked regular lasagna noodles can be used instead of oven-ready lasagna noodles, but they will be firmer.*

| | |
|---|---|
| 1 lb. ground beef | 1 tsp. oregano |
| 1 onion, chopped | 8 oz. oven-ready lasagna noodles |
| 4 cups spaghetti sauce | 16 oz. cottage cheese |
| 1 tsp. garlic salt | 4 cups shredded cheese |

Brown beef and onion; drain excess fat.  Stir garlic salt and oregano into spaghetti sauce.  Spread one cup of sauce on the bottom of a 13x9 pan.  Add 1/2 of the noodles.  Top uncooked noodles with another cup of sauce.  Add all of the meat and cottage cheese.  Add 1/2 of the cheese.  Top cheese with 3/4 cup of sauce.  Add remaining noodles and rest of sauce.  Top with remaining cheese.  Cover with foil.  Bake at 350° for 1 hour.  Let stand 15 to 20 minutes before serving.  Make the day before if possible.

# LASAGNA WITH VEGETABLES

*Vegetable suggestions are beans, broccoli, carrots, peas, spinach or zucchini.*

| | |
|---|---|
| 2 cups spaghetti or pizza sauce | 1 cup cottage cheese |
| 1 1/2 cups cooked meat of choice | 1 egg, beaten |
| 1 cup any cooked vegetable | Lasagna noodles |
| 1/2 tsp. oregano or basil | 4 oz. thinly sliced cheese |
| 1/2 tsp. pepper | 2 to 3 T. grated parmesan cheese |

Combine sauce, meat, vegetables, oregano and pepper.  Simmer, covered, about 10 minutes, stirring occasionally.  Combine cottage cheese and egg.  Place half of cooked noodles in a 10x6 pan.  Spread with half of cheese-egg mixture.  Top with half the cheese, then half of meat-vegetable mixture.  Repeat layers.  Sprinkle with parmesan cheese.  Bake, covered, at 375° for 40 minutes or until bubbly.  Let stand 10 minutes before serving.

*Lizzie Hoover, Goshen, IN*

# DO-AHEAD SPAGHETTI

| | |
|---|---|
| 5 T. cooking oil | 1/2 cup olives |
| 1 onion, chopped | 1 1/2 tsp. salt |
| 1 green pepper, chopped | 1/2 cup Velveeta cheese |
| 1 clove garlic, minced | 8 oz. spaghetti |
| 1 medium can mushrooms | 10 oz. can tomato soup |
| 1 lb. ground beef | 2 tsp. Worcestershire sauce |
| 1 large can tomatoes, chopped | |

Sauté onion, pepper, garlic and mushrooms in oil. Add meat and brown. Add tomatoes, olives, salt and cheese. Cover and cook on low for 30 minutes. Meanwhile cook spaghetti. Add spaghetti, tomato soup and Worcestershire sauce to meat sauce. Place in baking dish. Cover and keep refrigerated up to 2 days. Bake at 350° for 1 hour.

*Esther Martin, Decker, MI*

## SPAGHETTI BAKE

2 lb. ground beef
1 cup chopped onion
1/4 cup cooking oil
2 tsp. salt
1/4 tsp. pepper
1 tsp. parsley flakes
1 T. Worcestershire sauce

3 cups tomato juice
8 oz. can tomato sauce
3 bay leaves
16 oz. spaghetti
12 oz. sharp cheese, diced
3 oz. bottle stuffed olives, sliced

Brown beef and onion in oil. Add next 7 ingredients; simmer slowly 15 minutes, then remove bay leaves. Meanwhile, cook spaghetti in boiling water till tender. Drain and mix with meat sauce and remaining ingredients. Turn into large, greased casserole. Bake at 350° for 1 hour.

*Mrs. Vernon Kurtz, Ewing, IL*

## CHEESE TETRAZZINI

*This can be made ahead. Bake directly from refrigerator, uncovered, for 40-45 minutes.*

1 T. butter
1/2 cup chopped onion
1 1/2 lb. lean ground beef
1 tsp. salt
1/4 tsp. pepper
15 oz. can tomato sauce
8 oz. cream cheese

1 cup cottage cheese
1/4 cup sour cream
1/4 cup chopped green pepper
1/4 cup sliced green onions
8 oz. spaghetti, cooked and
    drained
1/4 cup grated parmesan cheese

Melt butter in a large skillet; add onion and sauté until tender. Add beef and cook until lightly browned and crumbly. Drain off drippings. Add salt, pepper and tomato sauce. Simmer 5 minutes. Remove from heat. Beat together cream cheese, cottage cheese and sour cream. Add green pepper, onion and spaghetti. Spread spaghetti mixture in bottom of buttered 3-quart shallow casserole. Pour meat sauce over top; sprinkle with cheese. Bake at 325° for 30 to 35 minutes. Garnish with green pepper rings and cherry tomatoes, if desired.

*Elizabeth B. Hoover, Fort Wayne, IN*

**When we sing our own praises, we generally get the pitch too high.**

# ITALIAN DELIGHT

1 onion, chopped
1 green pepper, chopped
1 garlic clove, minced
1 lb. ground beef
Salt and pepper
1 can cream-style corn

4 oz. can mushrooms
10 oz. can mushroom soup
8 oz. can tomato sauce
1 pkg. noodles
Velveeta cheese

Brown slightly, onion, green pepper, garlic and beef. Add all but noodles and cheese. Cook noodles and mix with other ingredients. Add salt and pepper to taste. Pour into 13x9 pan and bake 30 minutes. Top with thin slices of Velveeta cheese for last 15 minutes.

*Sarah Nolt, Fortuna, MO*

# BEEFY TOMATO NOODLE CASSEROLE

*No tomato paste? Substitute a pint of spaghetti sauce for juice, paste and water.*

4 oz. noodles
1 lb. ground beef
1 onion, chopped
1/2 cup chopped green pepper
1 cup mushrooms
1 T. Worcestershire sauce

1 tsp. salt
1/4 tsp. pepper
1 cup tomato juice
6 oz. can tomato paste
1/3 cup water
8 oz. grated cheese (2 cups)

Boil noodles in 1 1/2 quarts of boiling water and 1/2 teaspoon salt. Brown beef, onion, green pepper and mushrooms. Mix the rest of the ingredients, except cheese, to make sauce. Put in layers: noodles, meat, sauce and cheese. Repeat. Bake at 350° for 45 minutes.

*Mrs. Ray (Elsie) Hoover, Stratford, WI*

# SEA SHELLS, GROUND BEEF AND TOMATOES

8 oz. (2 cups) shell macaroni
2 T. butter
1 onion, chopped
2 cups ground beef
1/2 tsp. salt
1/8 tsp. pepper

1 T. parsley
Dash of oregano and marjoram
1 tsp. sugar, opt.
2 to 3 cups tomatoes
1 cup grated cheese

Cook macaroni in salted water. Drain. Sauté onion in butter till soft. Add beef, seasonings and tomatoes; simmer until blended. Alternate layers of meat, macaroni and cheese in a casserole. Top with cheese. Bake, uncovered, at 350° for 50 minutes. You can use jumbo shells and stuff them with meat mixture.

*Mrs. Lawerence Newswanger, Carson City, MI*

## CHEESERONI

2 cups macaroni
1 lb. ground beef or sausage
10 oz. can tomato soup
10 oz. can mushroom soup

1 green pepper, diced
1/4 cup pimento, opt.
2 cups cubed or grated cheese
3 oz. can French-fried onions

Cook macaroni; drain. In a large skillet brown meat; season with onion, oregano, basil or Italian seasoning, if desired. Add *undiluted* soups, green pepper, pimento and macaroni; mix. Place half of the mixture in a greased 2 1/2 quart casserole. Sprinkle with half of the cheese and onions. Top with remaining macaroni mixture and cheese. Bake at 350° for 25 minutes. Sprinkle on remaining onions and bake another 5 minutes.

*Carol Hoover, Plymouth, IN*

## PIZZA CASSEROLE I

1 1/2 lb. ground beef or sausage
1 onion, chopped
1 cup mushrooms
1 tsp. oregano
1/2 tsp. pepper
1/2 tsp. salt

1 1/2 cups macaroni
2-15 oz. cans spaghetti sauce
1 lb. shredded mozzarella cheese
   (4 cups)
1 pkg. pepperoni

Brown meat and onion. Add mushrooms, oregano, pepper and salt. Cook macaroni in salt water; drain. Add to meat. Put half of mixture in baking dish or a 13x9 cake pan. Add half of sauce, cheese and pepperoni. Repeat. Bake at 350° for 30 minutes.

*Mrs. James Kulp, Unity, WI*     *Mrs. John (Twila) Kulp, Mosinee, WI*

## PIZZA CASSEROLE II

1 lb. ground beef
1/3 cup chopped onion
1 tsp. oregano
1/2 tsp. salt

10 oz. can tomato soup
1/3 cup water
2 cups cooked wide noodles
1/2 cup cheese, shredded

Brown meat and onion; add seasoning. Combine remaining ingredients, except cheese. Place in a baking dish. Cheese can be mixed in or sprinkled on top. Bake at 350° for 30 minutes.

*Mrs. Clarence Martin, Snover, MI*     *Mrs. Marvin Sensenig, Penn Yan, NY*

***Never doubt in the valley what you found to be true on the mountain.***

# PIZZA RICE CASSEROLE

3/4 lb. ground beef
1 onion, chopped
2 cups tomato sauce
1/4 tsp garlic salt
1 tsp. sugar
1 tsp. salt

Dash of pepper
1/4 tsp. oregano
1 tsp. parsley
1/2 cup cottage cheese
2 cups cooked rice
Shredded cheese

Brown beef and onion. Add next 7 ingredients; cover and simmer 15 minutes. Mix cottage cheese and rice. Layer rice mixture and meat mixture in buttered 6 quart casserole. Sprinkle with cheese. Bake at 350° for 30 minutes or till bubbly.

*Mrs. Sam Newswanger, Goshen, IN*

# ZUCCHINI PIZZA CASSEROLE

4 ten-inch zucchini squash
1 lb. ground beef
1 onion, chopped
1 tsp. oregano
1 tsp. salt

1/4 tsp. pepper
2 cups pizza or spaghetti sauce
2 cups shredded mozzarella
　　cheese

Cut squash into 1/4 inch slices. Cook slightly in water and a teaspoon or so of salt. Drain well. Fry meat and onion; season and add pizza sauce. Mix with squash or layer in a casserole. Top with cheese. Bake at 350° for 30 minutes.

*Mrs. Ray (Elsie) Hoover, Stratford, WI*

# PIZZA

*To speed up the process, substitute a cup of ready made pizza or spaghetti sauce for sauce ingredients. This recipe is easily doubled.*

1 pkg. (1 T.) yeast
1 cup warm water
1 tsp. sugar
1 tsp. salt
2 T. cooking oil
2 1/2 cups flour
8 oz. tomato paste
1 tsp. seasoned salt
1 tsp. oregano

1 tsp. Italian seasoning
1/8 tsp. garlic powder
Dash of pepper
1 T. dried onion
1 T. dried green pepper
4 oz. mushrooms
1 lb. sausage, browned
4 oz. sliced pepperoni
2 cups shredded cheese

Dissolve yeast in water; add sugar, salt and oil. Add flour and mix well. Cover and let rise in a warm place at least 5 minutes. Combine paste and seasonings. Grease pan; flour fingers and spread crust. Pour on sauce. Sprinkle last 6 ingredients on in order given. Bake at 425° for 18 to 20 minutes.

*Anna Mary Evans, MO*　　*Karen Meador, Rossville, IN*

# PASTA PIZZA

*Add mushrooms, olives or other favorite pizza toppings.*

1 to 2 lb. sausage or ground beef
3 to 4 cups cooked spaghetti
1/2 cup parmesan cheese
3 T. butter
2 cups shredded mozzarella
   cheese

2 cups pizza or spaghetti sauce
1 tsp. Italian seasoning or
   oregano
1 onion, chopped
1 green pepper, chopped

Brown sausage. Combine hot, salted spaghetti or other pasta with parmesan cheese and butter. Press into a 13x9 pan. Top with half of cheese. Mix sauce and seasoning and pour over cheese. Top with sausage, sprinkle with onion and pepper. Top with remaining cheese. Bake at 350° for 30 minutes

**All baking times in this cookbook, unless stated otherwise, assume you are starting with a preheated oven. If the oven is not preheated it will require longer cooking time.**

# EASY DEEP DISH PIZZA

3 cups biscuit mix
3/4 cup water
1 lb. ground beef
1/2 cup chopped onion
1/2 tsp. salt
2 cloves garlic, crushed

15 oz. can tomato sauce
1 tsp. Italian seasoning
4 oz. can sliced mushrooms
1/2 cup chopped green pepper
2 cups (8 oz.) shredded
   mozzarella cheese

Combine biscuit mix and water. Knead 20 times on floured surface. Pat dough into and up the sides of a 15x10 lightly greased pan. Brown beef, onion, salt and garlic; drain. Mix tomato sauce and Italian seasoning; spread over dough. Spoon beef mixture evenly over sauce. Top with mushrooms, green peppers and cheese. Bake at 425° approximately 20 minutes.

*Mrs. Norman Burkholder, Mertztown, PA*

# PIZZA WITH HAMBURGER CRUST

1 lb. ground beef or turkey
1/2 cup dry bread crumbs
1 tsp. salt
1/2 tsp. oregano

1 cup tomato sauce
1 cup kidney beans
3 slices cheese

Mix first 4 ingredients; add 1/2 cup tomato sauce. Spread in ungreased 10" pizza pan or pie plate. Pour on 1/2 cup tomato sauce and kidney beans. Put cheese on top. Bake at 375° for 20 minutes.

*Edna Miller, Snover, MI*

193

# YORKSHIRE PIZZA

1/4 cup butter
1 cup flour
2 eggs

1 cup milk
1/4 tsp. salt

Melt butter in a 12x8 glass pan in a 425° oven. Beat flour, eggs, milk and salt until smooth. Pour into hot pan. Top with pizza sauce and other toppings. Sprinkle with oregano and top with cheese. Bake at 400° for 15 to 20 minutes.

*Donna Hoover, Goshen, IN*

# PIZZA SAUCE

4 cups tomato juice
2 tsp. oregano
2 tsp. garlic powder, scant
2 tsp. salt
1 tsp. pepper

1/2 cup chopped onion
1/3 tsp. ground cloves
1/3 tsp. sweet basil
Sprinkle of brown sugar
1 T. cornstarch, heaping

Bring all but cornstarch to a boil. Add cornstarch and boil another 30 minutes.

*Rita Martin, Nappanee, IN*

# NO-YEAST PIZZA DOUGH

1 3/4 cups flour
1 tsp. baking powder
1 tsp salt

2/3 cup milk
1/4 cup cooking oil

Combine dry ingredients. Add milk and oil. Knead about 10 times. Press into a 12 or 14 inch pizza pan. Top as desired.

# WHOLE GRAIN PIZZA DOUGH

1 pkg. yeast
1/2 cup warm water

2 1/4 cups whole grain mix (found in Biscuits and Muffins)

Soften yeast in water. Stir in grain mix. Knead 25 strokes. Let rest 10 minutes. Pat out on greased 14" pizza pan. Top as desired. Bake at 425° for 10 to 15 minutes.

*Rhoda Schultz, West Salem, OH*

***God's part we cannot do; our part God will not do.***

## STROMBOLI

*Replace any or all of the meat with cooked Italian sausage or ground beef. Slices of pepperoni add flavor.*

1 loaf frozen bread dough, thaw
1/4 lb. thin sliced hard salami
1/4 lb.  sliced cooked salami
1/2 lb. thin sliced ham
1/4 lb. mozzarella cheese
1/2 lb. white American cheese

1 cup cooked mushrooms
1 cup sliced green peppers
1 cup sliced onion
1/2 cup parmesan cheese
Oregano and sweet basil

Divide thawed dough in half.  Grease 2 large cookie sheets.  Roll out dough to cover pans.  Sprinkle with oregano and basil.  Arrange meat, cheese and vegetables in alternate layers up center of dough.  Sprinkle last layer with parmesan cheese and moderate amount of oregano and basil.  Fold one side of dough over center, then fold in one end.  Cover with other side and last end.  Pinch tightly to seal.  Bake at 375° approximately 30 minutes.

*Margaret Zimmerman, Ephrata, PA*

# PIES, QUICHES AND SOUFFLÉS

## CHEESEBURGER PIE

1 lb. ground beef
1/4 cup minced onion
1/2 tsp. salt
1/4 tsp. pepper
1/2 cup tomato juice
1 unbaked pie crust

1 cup shredded cheese
1/3 cup milk
1/2 tsp. dry mustard
1 egg, beaten
1/2 tsp. Worcestershire sauce

Brown meat and onion; drain.  Add salt, pepper and tomato juice.  Mix and pour into pie shell.  Mix remaining ingredients and warm on stove until cheese melts.  Pour over meat mixture.  Bake at 375° for 35 minutes.

*Ellen Newswanger, Kutztown, PA*

*He who cannot forgive others burns the bridge over which he himself must pass.*

## IMPOSSIBLE CHEESEBURGER PIE

*To make taco pie, delete salt and pepper and add a package of taco seasoning and a half cup of chopped green pepper.*

1 lb. ground beef
1 cup chopped onion
1 1/2 cups milk
3 eggs
3/4 cup biscuit mix

1/2 tsp. salt
1/4 tsp. pepper
2 tomatoes, sliced
1 cup shredded cheddar cheese

Brown beef and onion; drain. Spread in a greased 10-inch pie plate. Beat milk, eggs, biscuit mix, salt and pepper 15 seconds in blender on high or a minute with a hand beater. Pour into plate. Bake 25 minutes. Top with tomatoes and cheese. Bake until knife inserted in center comes out clean, 5 to 8 minutes longer.

*Pauline Kulp, Stratford, WI*     *Mrs. Carlton Zimmerman, Brooten, MN*

## CHEESEBURGER CASSEROLE

1 lb. ground beef
1 small onion, chopped
Salt and pepper to taste
1/2 cup ketchup

10 oz. can tomato soup
American cheese slices
1 can Pillsbury biscuits

Fry meat and onion; season. Add ketchup and soup; heat thoroughly. Pour into baking dish and top with cheese slices. Top cheese slices with biscuits. Bake at 375° for 25 minutes.

*Anna Mae Hoover, Reinholds, PA*

## HAMBURGER CHEESE PIE

*A little garlic salt and parsley can be added to the dough when making the pie crust.*

1 lb. ground beef
1/2 cup chopped onion
1 1/3 cups shredded cheese
9-inch unbaked pie shell
3/4 cup mayonnaise

3/4 cup milk
1 T. cornstarch, slightly rounded
3 eggs
1/2 tsp. salt
1/8 tsp. pepper

Brown meat and onion; drain excess fat. Arrange meat and cheese in pie crust. Beat remaining ingredients and pour into pie shell. Bake at 350° for 35 minutes.

*Edith Hoover Martin, Sauk Centre, MN*

***There is no better exercise for the heart than reaching down and lifting people up.***

# CHEESE-TATO TOPPER

*Try using your favorite meat loaf recipe for the meat filling. For a different taste pour cream of mushroom soup over the potatoes.*

1/2 cup milk
1 cup bread crumbs
1 egg
1 tsp. salt
1 tsp. dry mustard
1/4 tsp. pepper

1/4 tsp. thyme
1/3 cup minced onion
1 lb. ground beef
4 slices Velveeta cheese
3 or more cups seasoned mashed
  potatoes

Mix milk with bread crumbs. Beat in next 6 ingredients. Mix in raw meat. Turn into 9" pie plate. Bake at 350° for 30 minutes. Remove. Place cheese slices on meat and top with hot potatoes. Place under broiler for a few minutes.

*Sharon Fox, Baring, MO        Linda Hoover Shaum, Roann, IN        Mrs. Vernon Kurtz, Ewing, IL*
*Elaine Martin, Nappanee, IN*

# JUMBO CORNBURGER

1 1/2 lb. ground beef
2 eggs, slightly beaten
8 oz. can tomato sauce or 1 cup
  tomato juice
1/2 tsp. salt
Dash of pepper
1 tsp. Worcestershire sauce
1/4 tsp. sage

12 oz. can corn
1/2 cup cracker crumbs
1 egg, slightly beaten
1/4 cup diced green pepper
1/4 cup chopped onion
1/2 tsp. salt
4 oz. can mushrooms
1/2 cup shredded cheese

Combine ingredients in first column. Spread half of the mixture in an 8-inch pie plate or square pan. Combine remaining ingredients, except cheese. Spoon over meat and cover with remaining meat mixture. Bake 375° for 1 hour. Sprinkle cheese on top for the last 5 minutes of baking time.

*Mrs. Larry Zimmerman, Elkhart, IN*

# DEEP DISH PIZZA PIE

2 cups ground beef
2 eggs
3/4 cup milk
1 tsp. salt
1/8 tsp. pepper

1/2 tsp. oregano
2 cups cooked peas or corn
1 unbaked pie shell
2 cups pizza sauce
1 cup shredded cheese

Brown beef. Beat eggs; add milk, salt, pepper, oregano and peas. Add to beef and simmer a few minutes. Pour into pie shell. Pour pizza sauce on; top with cheese. Bake at 350° for 35 minutes.

*Mrs. Marvin (Lydia) Sensenig, Penn Yan, NY*

197

# SPAGHETTI PIE

6 oz. spaghetti
2 T. butter
1/3 cup parmesan cheese
2 eggs, well beaten
1 lb. ground beef or sausage
1/2 cup chopped onion
15 oz. can tomato sauce

1 tsp. sugar
1 tsp. oregano
1/2 tsp. garlic salt
1 cup cottage cheese
1/2 cup shredded mozzarella
    cheese

Cook and drain spaghetti. Stir in butter, parmesan cheese and eggs. Press into a 10" pie plate to form crust. Brown meat and onion; drain grease. Add tomato sauce, sugar, oregano and garlic salt. Heat through. Spread cottage cheese into crust. Add meat mixture and top with cheese. Bake at 350° for 20 minutes.

*Gail (Martin) Blum, Elkhart, IN     Rachel Ramer, Cazenovia, WI*

# WESTERN BEEF AND CORN PIE

1 lb. ground beef
1 onion, chopped
1/2 tsp. salt
1/2 tsp. chili powder
1 cup shredded cheese
1/2 cup barbeque sauce
1 1/2 cups canned corn or frozen
    corn
3/4 cup tomato paste

1 cup flour
1/2 cup cornmeal
2 T. sugar
1 tsp. baking powder
1 tsp. salt
1/2 cup milk
1/4 cup butter or margarine
1 egg
1 cup shredded cheese, divided

Brown meat and onion; drain. Stir in salt, chili powder, cheese, sauce, corn and paste. Combine all remaining ingredients except 1/2 cup cheese. Press dough over bottom and sides of a greased 10" pie plate. Pour filling into crust. Sprinkle with reserved cheese. Bake at 400° for 25 to 30 minutes.

*Mrs. Jacob Oberholtzer, Liberty, KY*

# DRIED BEEF PIE

1 cup chopped onion
6 oz. thin sliced dried beef
1/4 cup cooking oil
2 T. flour
1/4 salt
1/4 tsp. pepper
2 cups sliced cooked potatoes

2 cups sliced cooked carrots
2 cups water
1 bouillon cube
1 cup flour
1/2 tsp. salt
1/3 cup shortening
2 T. water

Sauté onion and dried beef in oil; stir in flour and seasonings. Add vegetables, water and bouillon cube; bring to a boil. Cover and simmer 5 minutes. Pour into 2-quart casserole. To make pastry, combine flour and salt. Cut in shortening until crumbly. Add water a little at a time. Roll out to fit casserole. Place on mixture in casserole. Bake at 425° for 25 to 30 minutes.

*Mrs. Larry Zimmerman, Elkhart, IN*

## DELUXE MEAT PIE

1/2 cup chopped onion
1/4 cup shortening
1 lb. ground beef
1 tsp. salt
1/8 tsp. pepper
1 cup tomato juice
3 ribs celery, chopped fine
2 medium carrots, diced
3 drops Tabasco sauce

1/2 cup tomato juice
1/3 cup flour
1/2 cup ketchup
1 cup flour
1 1/2 tsp. baking powder
1/4 tsp. salt
2 T. shortening
Reserved onions
1/3 cup milk

Fry onion in shortening. Reserve half of onions for topping. Add beef, salt and pepper to remaining onions; brown. Add 1 cup tomato juice, celery, carrots and sauce. Simmer 5 to 10 minutes. Combine 1/2 cup tomato juice, 1/3 cup flour and ketchup. Add to beef mixture; stir till thickened. Pour into a 9x9 pan. Combine flour, baking powder and salt for biscuit topping. Cut in shortening. Add reserved onions. Add milk, mixing just till flour is moistened. Knead a little. Roll out to fit top of baking dish. Bake at 450° for 12 to 15 minutes.

*Mrs. Norman Burkholder, Mertztown, PA*

## EASY SAUSAGE PIE

1 1/2 cups flour
1 tsp. salt
3/4 cup shortening
1/4 cup ice water
1 lb. sausage

1 onion, chopped
3 T. butter
3 T. flour
1 cup milk
1 1/2 cups shredded cheese

Combine flour and salt. Work in shortening. Work water in lightly. Roll a little more than half of the dough into a 1/8 inch thick circle to fit a 9-inch pie pan. Press into pie plate. Brown sausage and onion; drain. Add butter to sausage and sprinkle flour over meat. Mix well. Add milk and stir till smooth. Add cheese and stir until melted. Pour into pastry lined plate. Roll out remaining dough for a top crust. Seal the edges and cut slits in the top. Bake at 375° for 35 minutes. Let stand 10 minutes before serving.

# CHILI SAUSAGE PIE

1 lb. sausage
1/2 cup chopped onion
1/2 cup chopped green pepper
16 oz. can kidney beans
1 tsp. seasoned salt

1 tsp. chili powder
1 tsp. parsley
1/3 cup chili sauce
9-inch unbaked pie shell
1 cup shredded cheddar cheese

Brown sausage, onion and green pepper; drain. Stir in beans, seasonings, parsley and sauce. Spoon into pie shell and top with cheese. Bake at 400° for 40 minutes.

# SAVORY SAUSAGE AND POTATO PIE

5 medium potatoes
1 tsp salt
1 egg, beaten
1/2 cup chopped onion
1/2 cup cornflakes
2 tsp. parsley flakes

1 lb. sausage
1/2 cup green pepper strips
2 tsp. cornstarch
10 oz. can mushroom soup
1 can corn, drained
1 cup shredded cheese

Cook potatoes in boiling salted water until tender. Drain and mash (or use leftover mashed potatoes). Stir in egg. Add onion, cornflakes and parsley. Spread evenly in 10" pie plate. Brown sausage in skillet. Remove sausage but save 1 tablespoon fat. Add pepper strips; sauté for 5 minutes. Stir in sausage and cornstarch. Add soup and corn. Heat through. Pour into potato shell. Sprinkle cheese on top. Bake at 400° for 25 minutes.

*Laura Kulp, Stratford, WI*

# PASTIES

3 cups flour
1 tsp. salt
1 cup shortening
1/4 cup ice water
2 T. butter

2 cups cubed beef or pork
1 cup chopped onion
1 cup cooked diced potatoes
1 tsp. salt
1/8 tsp. pepper

Combine flour and salt. Cut in shortening. Gently work in ice water. Divide dough into 16 portions and roll each into a 5 inch circle. Brown meat and onion in butter. When done, add potatoes, salt and pepper. Place 2 tablespoons of meat mixture on each circle. Fold over and press edges together to seal. Moisten edges if necessary. Place on a cookie sheet and bake at 375° for 20 minutes.

# CHUCKWAGON TURNOVERS

1 lb. ground beef
1/2 cup chopped onion
2/3 cup Swiss cheese, shredded
1 egg, beaten
1/4 tsp. Tabasco sauce
1 tsp. salt

2 T. snipped fresh parsley
2 cups flour
1 tsp. salt
2/3 cup plus 2 T shortening
4 to 5 T. cold water

Brown meat and onion. Cool slightly. Stir in cheese, egg, sauce and salt and parsley; set aside. Mix flour and salt. Cut in shortening. Sprinkle in water. Divide dough in half. Roll each into 10" circle on floured surface. Place 1 1/2 cups meat filling on half of each circle. Fold pastry over and seal edges securely. Prick a few times with fork. Place on ungreased cookies sheet. Bake at 425° for 20 to 25 minutes. Eat plain or serve with the following recipe of tomato gravy.

*Mrs. LaVerne (Virginia) Hoover, Goshen, IN*

# TOMATO GRAVY

2 T. butter
2 T. flour
1/2 cup milk

1 cup tomato juice
1/4 tsp. salt
1 T. sugar

Melt butter and add flour. Cook 2 minutes. Blend in milk; add tomato juice. Stir in salt and sugar.

*Mrs. LaVerne (Virginia) Hoover, Goshen, IN*

# MEAT AND POTATO QUICHE

3 T. cooking oil
3 cups coarsely shredded raw
    potatoes
1 cup shredded cheese
3/4 cup cooked meat
1/4 cup chopped onion

1 cup thin cream
2 eggs
1/2 tsp. salt
1/8 tsp. pepper
1 T. parsley flakes

Stir together oil and potatoes in a 9" pie pan or an 8x8 pan. Press evenly onto the bottom and sides. Bake at 425° for 15 minutes or until beginning to brown. Remove from oven and layer on cheese, meat and onion. Combine cream, eggs, salt and pepper. Pour on top. Sprinkle with parsley. Bake at 425° for 30 minutes or until knife inserted an inch from the edge comes out clean. Cool 5 minutes before cutting.

*Mrs. Lawrence Newswanger, Carson City, MI*          *Vera Witmer, Goshen, IN*

## CHEESY MUSHROOM QUICHE

3 eggs, slightly beaten
1 1/2 cups thin cream
8 oz. bacon, fried and crumbled
8 oz. shredded Swiss cheese

1 can mushrooms or spinach
1/2 tsp. salt
1/8 tsp. pepper
2 9-inch unbaked pie shells

Mix everything together, using well drained mushrooms or spinach, and pour into pies shells. Bake at 350° for 30 minutes or until done.

*Anna Mary Evans, MO*

## SAUSAGE SOUFFLÉ

1 lb. sausage
6 eggs
2 cups milk
1 tsp. salt

1 tsp. dry mustard
1 cup shredded cheese
6 slices white bread

Brown sausage; drain. Beat eggs. Add remaining ingredients; beat well. Place in a buttered 12x8 pan. Refrigerate overnight. Bake at 350° for 45 minutes.

*Rita Martin, Nappanee, IN*

*Difficulties in life should make us better, not bitter.*

# MEATS

Elsie
Hoover

# TIME TABLE FOR MEAT & POULTRY

| | OVEN TEMP. | TIME |
|---|---|---|
| Standing Ribs of Beef | 300° | 35 minutes per pound |
| 5 Pound Rolled Rump | 325° | 35 minutes per pound |
| Large Uncooked Ham | 300° | 20 minutes per pound |
| Medium Uncooked Ham | 300° | 25 minutes per pound |
| Small Uncooked Ham | 300° | 27 minutes per pound |
| Ready to Eat Ham | 300° | 15 minutes per pound |
| Small Chicken | 325° | 30 minutes per pound |
| Large Chicken | 325° | 22 minutes per pound |
| Small Roasting Chicken | 300° | 45 minutes per pound |
| Large Roasting Chicken | 300° | 30 minutes per pound |
| 8 to 10 Pound Turkey | 300° | 20 to 25 minutes per pound |
| 10 to 15 Pound Turkey | 300° | 18 to 20 minutes per pound |
| 18 to 25 Pound Turkey | 300° | 15 to 18 minutes per pound |

# ROASTS, STEAKS, ETC.

## SAVORY SWEET ROAST

3 to 4 lb. blade roast
1 onion, chopped
10 oz. can mushroom soup
1/2 cup water
1/4 cup sugar

1/4 cup vinegar
2 tsp. salt
1 tsp. mustard
1 tsp. Worcestershire sauce

Brown meat on both sides in a skillet. Add onions. Blend together remaining ingredients. Pour over meat. Cover and simmer for 2 1/2 to 3 hours or until tender. The juice is good for gravy or to cook noodles in after the roast is done. This can also be put in a slow cooker on low for 12 to 16 hours.

*Laura Kulp, Stratford, WI     Ada Mae Miller, Nappanee, IN*

## GRAVY

2 cups meat drippings
1/4 cup flour

1/2 cup cold water
Salt and pepper to taste

Remove cooked meat from pan or roaster. Skim fat from drippings. Add water if you don't have 2 cups of pan liquid. Combine flour with cold water, stir until smooth. Slowly stir into drippings. Stir constantly while bringing to a boil. Simmer several minutes. Add salt and pepper to taste. For thicker gravy use less water, for thicker gravy add more.

## BOUILLON GRAVY

1 cup hot water
1 to 2 beef bouillon cubes
1 tsp. Worcestershire sauce
1/4 tsp. salt or to taste

1/8 tsp. pepper
3 T. butter
3 T. flour
1 cup milk

Dissolve cubes in hot water. Add Worcestershire sauce, salt and pepper. Melt butter in a skillet and add flour. Stir constantly until mixtures bubbles and brown slightly. Add broth and milk while stirring. Stir until gravy thickens. Simmer several minutes. Leftover cooked meat can be added for extra flavor.

*God gives birds their food, but He doesn't throw it into their nests.*

# EASY BEEF ROAST

*For an even easier roast, delete mushroom soup and use only onion soup mix.*

3 to 4 lb. chuck roast
10 oz. can mushroom soup

1 pkg. onion soup mix or 1/4 cup
(or more) bulk onion soup mix

Place roast in pan and cover with mushroom soup. Sprinkle soup mix on top. Cover. Bake at 300° for 3 hours. Makes good gravy.

*Mrs. Ray ((Elsie) Hoover, Stratford, WI*

# SMOKED ROAST

2 T. liquid smoke
1 tsp. salt
1 tsp. celery salt
1 tsp. garlic salt

1 tsp. onion salt
1 tsp. pepper
4 lb. beef or pork roast

Combine first 6 ingredients and marinate roast overnight. Bake at 275° for 4 hours. For barbecued roast pour 1 to 2 cups of barbecue sauce over roast an hour before done. This can also be baked at a higher temperature for less time.

# SWISS STEAK

*Tomatoes and peppers can be deleted. Just add a chopped onion or two and a cup of hot water right with the meat.*

2 lb. round steak
1/4 cup flour
1/2 tsp. salt
1/4 tsp. pepper
2 T. shortening

1/2 cup chopped green pepper
1 1/4 cups chopped onion
2 cups tomatoes or tomato juice
1 tsp. salt
1/4 tsp. pepper

Lightly score surface of meat and cut into serving pieces. Mix next 3 ingredients. Sprinkle one side of meat with half of flour mixture. Pound in well. Repeat on other side. Melt shortening in large skillet. Brown meat. Cover and simmer 1 hour. Add small amount of water as needed. Combine remaining ingredients and pour over meat. Cover and simmer 30 minutes or until meat is tender.

*Mrs. LaVerne (Virginia) Hoover, Goshen, IN*

*I long to accomplish a great and noble task, but it is my chief duty to accomplish tasks as though they were great and noble.* Helen Keller

# QUICK SWISS STEAK

1 lb. boneless sirloin or round
   steak
2 T. cooking oil, divided
1 onion, coarsely chopped
1 rib celery, sliced

1/2 tsp. garlic powder
1 cup canned or fresh tomatoes
2 cups broth or water
3 T. cornstarch
1 tsp. Worcestershire sauce

Slice beef into very thin strips. Heat 1/2 of oil and brown beef in 2 batches, stirring often. Set aside. Heat remaining oil; add onion, celery and garlic powder. Cook several minutes. Add tomatoes. Combine broth and cornstarch; add. Stir until mixture thickens. Add beef and heat through. Good over rice.

**As a rule of thumb use approximately one teaspoon of salt to one pound of meat.**

# SWISS CREAM STEAK

6 T. butter or margarine
2 cups sliced onion
2 lb. round steak, cut into serving
   sized pieces
1/2 cup flour

1 T. salt
1 tsp. pepper
1 tsp. paprika
1 cup water
1/2 cup sour cream

Melt 4 tablespoons butter in large skillet. Sauté onion; remove from skillet. Pound steak and dredge in flour seasoned with salt, pepper and paprika. Melt remaining butter in skillet. Brown meat. Stir in onions, water and sour cream. Cover and cook 35 to 40 minutes. Uncover and cook until sauce thickens. Good over noodles.

*Mrs. LaVerne (Virginia) Hoover, Goshen, IN*

# SWISS-STYLE PORK STEAK

4 pork steaks
1 T. cooking oil
2 cups canned tomatoes, cut up
1 cup chopped onion
1/2 cup chopped celery
1 T. Worcestershire sauce

1 tsp. salt
1 tsp. basil
1 clove minced garlic or 1/8 tsp.
   garlic powder
1/4 tsp. pepper

Brown steaks in oil and pour off drippings. Stir in undrained tomatoes. Add remaining ingredients. Bring to a boil. Cover and reduce heat. Simmer till pork is tender, approximately 45 to 60 minutes.

# PEPPER STEAK

**2 to 3 lb. 1-inch thick round steak**
**1/2 cup soy sauce**
**2 cups water**
**1/4 cup cooking oil**
**1/4 cup sugar**
**1/4 cup cornstarch**

**1/2 tsp. ginger, opt.**
**1 tsp. garlic salt**
**2 medium onions, sliced 1/4-inch thick**
**2 medium green peppers**
**2 medium tomatoes**

Trim fat from meat. Slice 1/4 inch or thinner while meat is partially frozen. Mix soy sauce and water and pour on meat. Refrigerate 2 hours if you have time. Drain soy sauce from meat; reserve. Heat oil in skillet. Cook meat, turning frequently, until it looses its red color. Pour soy sauce and water over meat. Mix sugar, cornstarch, ginger and garlic salt. Stir into meat. Top with onions and peppers. (For crisp peppers wait to add till the last 7 to 8 minutes.) Cover and bring to a boil. Simmer 15 minutes. Top with tomato slices and cook 5 minutes more. Good over hot rice.

*Mrs. LaVerne (Virginia) Hoover, Goshen, IN*

# FRIED STEAK

**Fresh steaks**
**Flour**
**Beaten egg**

**Fine cracker crumbs**
**Salt and pepper**

Slice steaks thin and tenderize, pounding very thin. Roll in flour, then eggs, then cracker crumbs. Fry in deep fat until golden brown. Season both sides with salt with salt and pepper.

*Mrs. Ivan Zimmerman, Scottsville, KY*

# STEAK ROLLS

**1 to 2 round steaks, cubed and tenderized**
**Salt and pepper**
**Garlic powder**
**Bacon slices**

**Onion chunks**
**Flour**
**Beef broth**
**Fresh mushrooms**
**Green pepper slices**

Trim fat off steaks and cut into 7x 1 1/2 inch strips. Sprinkle with salt, pepper and garlic powder. Top each strip with a slice of bacon and a chunk of onion. Roll up strips, securing ends with toothpicks. Coat with flour and brown in skillet. Cover with beef broth; add mushrooms and green pepper. Simmer on low heat 1 1/2 hours, adding water as needed. When meat is tender, remove steak rolls and thicken remaining broth for gravy. Steak rolls also may be cooked in pressure cooker for 15 minutes at 15 pounds of pressure.

*Linda Hoover Shaum, Roann, IN*

# GLORIFIED PORK CHOPS

6 pork chops
10 oz. can mushroom soup

1/4 cup water

Brown chops in skillet.  Pour off fat.  Stir in soup and water.  Cover; simmer 30 minutes or until done.  Stir often.

*Laura Kulp, Stratford, WI*

# ORANGE PORK CHOPS

4 pork chops
1/2 cup orange juice
1 tsp. salt

1/4 tsp. pepper
1/2 tsp. dry mustard
1/4 cup brown sugar

Place chops in a baking pan.  Mix other ingredients and pour over chops.  Bake at 350° for 1 hour, basting occasionally.

# PORK CHOPS AND ONIONS

2 T. cooking oil
2 onions, chopped
6 pork chops
Flour

1/2 cup water
1 1/2 tsp. salt
1 tsp. parsley
1/2 tsp. oregano

Cook onion in oil about 5 minutes.  Remove from skillet and brown flour coated chops, turning once.  Add remaining ingredients.  Cover and simmer 25 to 30 minutes or until meat is tender.

# BARBECUED SPARERIBS

2 lb. spareribs, cut up
1/2 cup chopped onion
1/2 cup water
2 T. Worcestershire sauce
1/4 cup lemon juice

2 T. brown sugar
1 cup chili sauce or ketchup
1/2 tsp. salt
1/4 tsp. paprika

Place ribs in a 13x9 pan, covered with waxed paper.  Bake at 500° for 15 minutes.  Drain and reduce heat to 350°.  Use 1 tablespoon drippings and sauté onion.  Add remaining ingredients and simmer 20 minutes.  Remove wax paper and pour sauce over meat.  Bake 1 hour.  Baste frequently.

*Rita Martin, Nappanee, IN*

## SHISH KABOBS

1/2 cup cooking oil
1/4 cup vinegar
1/4 cup ketchup
1 tsp. salt
1/2 tsp. oregano
1/4 tsp. pepper
2 T. Worcestershire sauce
1/2 cup chopped onion

2 cloves garlic, peeled and
   crushed
3 lb. beef, cut in 1-inch cubes
Green pepper squares
Small onions
Tomato wedges or cherry
   tomatoes
Mushrooms

Combine oil, vinegar, ketchup, seasoning, onion and garlic in a large bowl. Add meat; stir to coat. Cover tightly and refrigerate 4 hours or overnight. On skewers, alternate cubes of meat with desired vegetables. Before lighting grill, spray with no-stick cooking spray. When grill is ready for cooking, place kabobs about 5 inches above hot coals. Turn often until meat is done.

# GROUND MEAT

## POOR MAN'S STEAK

3 lb. ground beef
1 cup cracker crumbs
1 cup cold water or milk
1 T. salt

1/4 tsp. pepper
1 onion, chopped
Oregano and sage, opt.
10 oz. can mushroom soup

Combine all ingredients, except soup. (Two cups each of crumbs and milk may be used.) Press onto a cookie sheet, 1/2 inch thick or shape into balls. Refrigerate several hours or overnight. Roll in flour and brown on both sides. Put into roaster, top with diluted or undiluted soup. Bake at 325° for 1 1/2 hours.

*Mrs. Allen Garman, Roaring Spring, PA     Esther Horst, East Earl, PA     Mrs. William (Lena) Kilmer
Rachel Newswanger, Barnett, MO     Mrs. Phillip Zimmerman, Versailles, MO*

## SALISBURY STEAK

1 lb. ground beef
1 egg, beaten
1 onion, chopped
1/2 cup milk

1 tsp. salt
1/2 tsp. pepper
1 cup crushed cornflakes
10 oz. can mushroom soup

Mix together everything but soup. Make patties; roll in flour and brown. Put in casserole and pour soup on top. Bake at 350° for 30 to 45 minutes.

*Mrs. Ernest Newswanger, Kutztown, PA*

# HAMBURGER STEAK

| | |
|---|---|
| 1/2 chopped onion | 1 tsp. parsley |
| 1/2 cup minced green pepper | 1 tsp. salt |
| 1/3 cup chopped celery | 1/2 tsp. pepper |
| 4 T. butter, divided | 1/2 tsp. dry mustard |
| 2 lb. ground beef | Dash each marjoram, thyme and |
| 2 T. minced chives | paprika, opt. |

Sauté onion, peppers and celery in 2 tablespoons butter. Add to remaining ingredients and mix well. Shape into six 1-inch thick patties. Fry in remaining butter on both sides until done.

*Mrs. Ray (Elsie) Hoover, Stratford, WI*

# BAKED HAMBURGERS

| | |
|---|---|
| 1 lb. ground beef | 3/4 cup water |
| 1/2 cup bread crumbs | 1/4 cup ketchup |
| 1/2 cup milk | 1/4 cup sugar |
| 1 small onion, chopped | 1 tsp. mustard |
| 1 tsp. salt | 1 tsp. vinegar |
| 1/4 tsp. pepper | |

Mix first 6 ingredients and form into patties. Brown in skillet and place into baking dish. Mix remaining ingredients and pour over burgers. Cover. Bake at 325° for an hour. Baking longer enhances flavor.

*Rachel Weirich, Stone Lake, WI*

As a time-saver, put your favorite meat loaf recipe in muffin pans, filling level full. Bake at 450° for 15 to 18 minutes.

# MEAT LOAF

*For a firmer loaf, delete egg and substitute 3/4 cup dry oatmeal for crumbs.*

| | |
|---|---|
| 1 3/4 lb. ground beef | 1 1/2 tsp. salt |
| 1 cup bread or cracker crumbs | 1 small onion, chopped |
| 1 cup milk | 1/4 tsp. pepper |
| 1 egg | |

Mix all ingredients. Form into a loaf. Bake at 350° for 1 1/2 hours. This stays together nice for cutting.

*Mrs. Ray (Elsie) Hoover, Stratford, WI*   *Mrs. Amos Horst, Ephrata, PA*

# PIZZA MEAT LOAF

1 cup pizza sauce, divided
1 egg, beaten
2 tsp. seasoned salt
3/4 tsp. onion powder
3/4 tsp. oregano
1/8 tsp. pepper

1/2 cup chopped green pepper
3 cups cornflakes
2 lb. ground beef
1/2 cup shredded mozzarella
   cheese

Combine 2/3 cup pizza sauce with egg, seasoning, and green pepper. Crush cornflakes and add. Mix in ground beef. Shape in shallow baking pan. Bake at 350° for an hour. Brush on half of reserved sauce. Bake 20 minutes. Brush on remaining sauce. Sprinkle cheese on top. Bake 15 minutes longer. Let stand a little before cutting.

*Mrs. James Kulp, Unity, WI*

# ZUCCHINI MEAT LOAF

3 cups chopped zucchini
1 1/2 lb. ground beef
1 small onion, chopped
2 tomatoes, chopped
1 egg, beaten

1 T. Worcestershire sauce
1 tsp. salt
1/2 tsp. pepper
1/2 tsp. sage
1/2 cup bread crumbs

Combine all ingredients. Bake at 325° for 1 1/2 hours. Let stand 15 minutes before cutting.

*Mrs. Elmer Sensenig, Quarryville, PA*

# POTATO-FROSTED MEAT LOAF

2 lb. ground beef
2 cups bread crumbs
1/2 cup chopped onion
2 T. parsley
2 tsp. marjoram
2 tsp. salt
1/4 tsp. pepper

2 eggs, beaten
1 cup tomato juice
6 medium potatoes, peeled
1/4 cup melted butter
1/3 cup hot milk
1 egg, beaten
1 cup shredded cheese

Combine first 9 ingredients in a bowl. Mix lightly, but well. Shape into a 9 inch loaf. Bake at 350° for 50 minutes. Meanwhile, cook cut potatoes in boiling salted water for 25 minutes or until tender. Drain well. Mash. Beat in butter and milk. Stir in egg. Spread hot meat loaf with hot potatoes. Sprinkle with cheese. Place in broiler 9 inches from heat till cheese melts and surface is lightly browned. Let stand 5 minutes before slicing.

*Suetta Hoover, Tipton, MO*

# MEAT LOAF GLAZE I

1/2 cup mustard          1/2 cup brown sugar
1/2 cup ketchup

Mix ingredients and pour over your favorite meat loaf 10 minutes before it's done. This is enough for a 13x9 pan.

*Mary Zook, Virginia Beach, VA*

# MEAT LOAF GLAZE II

3/4 cup ketchup          1 T. mustard
1/4 cup brown sugar

Combine and spread on top of meat loaf. Just plain ketchup is good too.

# HAM LOAF

1 lb. ground ham               Salt and pepper if desired
1 1/2 lb. ground pork          1 cup brown sugar
1 cup milk                     1/4 cup vinegar
1 cup bread crumbs             1 tsp. mustard
2 eggs                         1/4 cup water

Mix meats, milk, crumbs, eggs and seasoning. Shape into loaves. Bake at 350° for 1 hour or until done. Heat remaining ingredients. Pour over loaves and baste occasionally.

*Rachel Newswanger, Barnett, MO*

# MOCK HAM LOAF

1 lb. ground beef              1/8 tsp. pepper
1/2 lb. hot dogs, ground       3/4 cup brown sugar
1 cup cracker crumbs           3/4 cup water
1 egg                          1 T. vinegar
1 tsp. salt                    1/2 tsp. dry mustard

Mix beef, hot dogs, crumbs, egg, salt and pepper. Bring remaining ingredients to a boil. Mix half of the syrup into the meat. Shape in pan. Put the other half on top of the loaf. Bake at 350° for 1 to 1 1/2 hours.

*Mrs. Luke Hoover, Goshen, IN      Sarah Imhoff, Sheridan, MI      Velma Martin, Nappanee, IN*
*Mrs. Sam Newswanger, Goshen, IN*

# HAM BALLS

| | |
|---|---|
| 1 1/2 lb. ground beef | 1 cup brown sugar |
| 1 1/2 lb. ground ham | 1 T. mustard |
| 1 3/4 cups graham cracker | 1/3 cup water |
|    crumbs | 1/2 cup vinegar |
| 3 eggs | 4 oz. crushed pineapple with juice |
| 1 cup milk | |

Mix the first column and shape into balls. Place into a baking dish. Bring remaining ingredients to a boil; pour over ham balls. Bake 350° for 1 1/2 hours.

*Mrs. Isaac Martin, Martinsburg, PA*

# MEATBALLS AND SAUCE

*A good quick sauce can be made using 2 cups ketchup mixed with 3/4 cup brown sugar.*

| | |
|---|---|
| 1 1/2 lb. ground beef | 1/4 tsp. pepper |
| 2/3 cup milk | 12 oz. can tomato paste |
| 3/4 cup oatmeal | 1 cup water |
| 1/4 cup chopped onion | 1 tsp. oregano |
| 1 tsp. salt | 1 tsp. salt |

Mix beef, milk, oatmeal, onion, salt and pepper. Shape into 16 balls. Brown in a small amount of oil and drain. Combine remaining ingredients and pour over meatballs. Simmer 30 minutes. Cooked rice can be used instead of oatmeal.

*Mrs. Ray (Elsie) Hoover, Stratford, WI*

**Using an ice cream scoop when making meat balls cuts back on the time and mess.**

# PRICKLY MEATBALLS

| | |
|---|---|
| 1 lb. ground beef | 1/4 tsp. salt |
| 1/2 cup dry rice | 1/8 tsp. pepper |
| 1/4 cup chopped onion | 10 oz. can tomato soup |
| 2 T. minced parsley | 1 soup can of water |

Combine all but tomato soup and water. Mix well. Shape into small 1-inch balls and put into a greased casserole. Pour tomato soup and water over meatballs. Bake at 350° for 30 minutes. Remove cover and bake another 30 minutes.

*Mrs. Cleon (Carol) Bauman, Elmira, Ont. Canada*

***When the truth is spoken in anger, people respond to the anger
rather than the truth.***

# NORWEGIAN MEATBALLS

1/4 cup milk
1/2 cup cornstarch, divided
1 lb. ground beef
1 medium onion chopped
3/4 tsp. salt

1/2 tsp. ground nutmeg
1/4 tsp. pepper
1 egg
2 T. cooking oil
2-13 oz. cans beef broth

In a large bowl combine milk and 1/4 cup cornstarch until well blended. Add meat, onion, salt, nutmeg, pepper and egg. Mix well; chill for 20 minutes. Shape into 1-inch balls. In 12-inch skillet heat oil; cook meatballs until brown 8 to 10 minutes. Remove; drain on towel. Keep 1/4 cup drippings in skillet. In medium bowl mix broth and 1/4 cup cornstarch until well blended. Pour into skillet. Cook over medium heat, stirring constantly, until broth boils and thickens. Add meatballs; reduce heat and simmer for 15 minutes. Spoon hot mashed potatoes in middle of platter. With slotted spoon add meatballs around potatoes. Serve gravy on the side.

*Linda Hoover Shaum, Roann, IN*

# CHEESY BARBECUED MEATBALLS

2 cups cornflakes
2 eggs
1/3 cup milk
1/2 tsp. salt
1/8 tsp. pepper
1/2 lb. ground beef
1 cup (4oz.) shredded cheese

1 cup ketchup
3/4 cup water
2 T. vinegar
3 T. packed brown sugar
1 T. minced onion
1 tsp. salt
1 tsp. celery seed

Crush cornflakes slightly. Add eggs, milk, salt and pepper. Mix well. Let stand 5 minutes or until cereal softens. Add ground beef and cheese, mix well. Shape into 1-inch balls. Place in a single layer on greased shallow pan. Bake at 350° for 10 minutes or until brown. While meatballs are baking combine remaining ingredients in a large saucepan. Bring to a boil; reduce heat. Remove meatballs from oven and immediately put in skillet with sauce. Cook, uncovered, for 15 minutes. Serve on spaghetti or noodles.

*Mrs. Elias Martin, Goshen, IN*

*Oh, loving words are not hard to say*
*If the heart be loving too,*
*And the kinder the thoughts you give to others,*
*The kinder their thoughts of you*

# SWEET-SOUR MEATBALLS

5 beef bouillon cubes
1/4 cup hot water
1 1/2 lb. ground beef
1 cup soft bread crumbs
3/4 cup finely chopped onion
1 egg
20 oz. can pineapple chunks,
    reserve juice

1/3 cup lemon juice
3 T. brown sugar
2 T. soy sauce
1 tsp. ginger
2 T. cornstarch
1 large green pepper, chopped
Hot rice

Dissolve 2 bouillon cubes in hot water. Combine beef, crumbs, onion, bouillon liquid and egg; mix well. Shape into 18 meatballs. Brown meatballs and drain. Combine 1/4 cup pineapple juice, lemon juice, sugar, soy sauce, remaining bouillon and ginger. Add to meatballs. Cover and simmer 20 to 25 minutes. Cook and stir until thickened. Add pineapple and green pepper. Heat through. Serve on rice.

# MAKE-AHEAD MEATBALLS

3 lb. ground beef
12 oz. can evaporated milk
    or 1 1/2 cups milk
1 cup oatmeal
1 cup cracker crumbs
2 eggs
1/2 cup chopped onion
1/2 tsp. garlic powder

2 tsp. salt
1/2 tsp. pepper
2 tsp. chili powder
2 cups ketchup
3/4 cup brown sugar
1/2 tsp. liquid smoke
1/2 tsp. garlic powder
1/4 cup chopped onion

Combine beef, milk, crumbs, eggs, onion, garlic powder, salt and pepper. Mix well. Divide into 8 equal parts then shape each part into 10 meatballs. Freeze in a single layer then store in airtight container. When ready to bake combine remaining ingredients. Heat and stir until sugar dissolves. Place frozen meatballs in 13x9 pan. Pour on hot sauce. Bake at 350° for 1 hour or until done.

*Jenifer Horst, Colby, WI*

# SPINACH MEAT ROLL

10 oz. pkg. frozen spinach
2 lb. ground beef
2 eggs
1/4 cup ketchup
1/4 cup milk
3/4 cup soft bread crumbs
1/2 tsp. salt

1/4 tsp. pepper
1/4 tsp. oregano
1 tsp. salt
3 oz. smoked sliced ham
3 slices mozzarella cheese, sliced
    diagonally in half

Thaw spinach quickly by rinsing with running hot water. Mix next 8 ingredients. Pat into 10x12 inch rectangle on a piece of tin foil. Arrange spinach evenly on top of meat, leaving a 1/2 inch margin around edge. Sprinkle with 1 teaspoon salt. Arrange ham on top. Carefully roll up, beginning at narrow end and using foil to lift meat. Press edges and ends of roll to seal. Place on ungreased 13x9 pan. Bake at 350° for 1 hour and 15 minutes. Overlap cheese triangles on roll. Bake 5 minutes more.

*Mrs. LaVerne (Virginia) Hoover, Goshen, IN*

# MISCELLANEOUS MEATS

## BARBECUED HOT DOGS

| | |
|---|---|
| 1/2 green pepper | 2 T. brown sugar |
| 2 T. mustard | 1 T. Worcestershire sauce |
| 1/8 tsp. salt | 1 to 2 cups water |
| 3/4 cup ketchup | 1 lb. hot dogs |
| 1 small onion, chopped | |

Combine first 7 ingredients; add water. Cook 15 minutes. Add whole or sliced hotdogs and heat through. Good served over mashed potatoes.

*Mrs. Clarence Martin, Snover, MI*

## STUFFED HOT DOGS

| | |
|---|---|
| Hot dogs | Dill pickle strips |
| Ketchup or mustard | Cheese strips |

Split hot dogs lengthwise. Spread with ketchup or mustard. Fill each hot dog with a long strip of pickle and cheese. Fasten with toothpicks. Broil or bake until hot.

## BAKED LIVER

| | |
|---|---|
| 1 large onion, chopped | Dash of Tabasco sauce, opt. |
| 1 T. butter | 1/3 cup chili sauce or ketchup |
| 1 tsp. paprika, opt. | 2 T. vinegar |
| 1 tsp. dry mustard, opt. | 1/2 cup water, opt. |
| 4 tsp. sugar | 1 lb. thinly sliced liver |
| 2 tsp. Worcestershire sauce | Salt, pepper and flour |

Mix together everything but liver, salt, pepper and flour and cook 10 minutes. Dip liver in flour; season with salt and pepper. Brown, then place into casserole. Pour sauce over liver. Bake at 350° for 30 minutes.

*Mrs. Cleon (Carol) Bauman, Elmira, Ont. Canada*

# GLORIFIED LIVER

4 slices bacon, diced
1/2 cup chopped onion
3 T. chopped green pepper
1/2 cup brown sugar
6 T. vinegar

2 tsp. salt
Pepper to taste
Dash of marjoram and rosemary
1 lb. liver

Brown bacon; add onion and pepper. Cook till tender. Add all except liver. Remove membrane from liver. Place in baking dish. Add sauce. Bake at 350° for 25 to 30 minutes.

# LIVER CREOLE

1/2 lb. liver
1 large onion, chopped
1 tsp. paprika
1 tsp. dry mustard
4 tsp. sugar
2 tsp. Worcestershire sauce

Several drops Tabasco sauce
1/2 cup chili sauce or tomato
 juice
1/4 tsp. garlic powder
2 T. vinegar

Roll liver in flour; sauté till lightly browned. Mix other ingredients and bring to boil. Reduce heat. Add liver. Simmer 30 minutes.

*Ethel Hoover, Goshen, IN*

# SPANISH LIVER

1 to 2 lb. liver
Flour, salt and pepper
10 oz. can tomato soup
1/2 cup water

1/2 cup chopped celery
2 T. chopped green pepper
1 T. sugar
1 T. finely chopped onion

Dredge liver in flour seasoned with salt and pepper. Brown quickly on both sides in hot fat. Add remaining ingredients and simmer 15 to 20 minutes.

*Connie Rodes, Milford, IN*

# LIVER PATTIES

1 lb. beef liver
1 to 3 cups chopped onion
1/4 to 1 cup oatmeal
1 tsp. salt

1/8 pepper
2 T. light cream or milk
2 eggs, slightly beaten

Grind liver or chop fine. Add remaining ingredients and mix thoroughly. Mixture should be quite moist. Drop by rounded tablespoons into skillet containing hot oil. Fry until nicely browned on both sides. These can also be made by removing patties and making gravy from drippings. Place patties in baking dish; top with gravy and bake at 325° for 30 minutes.

*Ruth Weaver, Nappanee, IN*

## PICKLED HEART AND TONGUE

1 tongue
1 heart
1 T. salt

1 cup water
1 cup vinegar
1/4 to 1 cup sugar

Scald and skin tongue. Cook heart and tongue using 1 tablespoon salt, until tender. Slice thin and cover with water and vinegar sweetened to taste with sugar. Refrigerate. Good in sandwiches.

*Rita Martin, Nappanee, IN*        *Edna Miller, Snover, MI*

**There may be a lot of Christians who do nothing,**
**but there are no Christians**
**who have nothing to do.**

# ADDITIONAL RECIPES

*What is right isn't always popular,*
*And what is popular isn't always right.*

# CHICKEN
## and
# FISH

Elsie Hoover

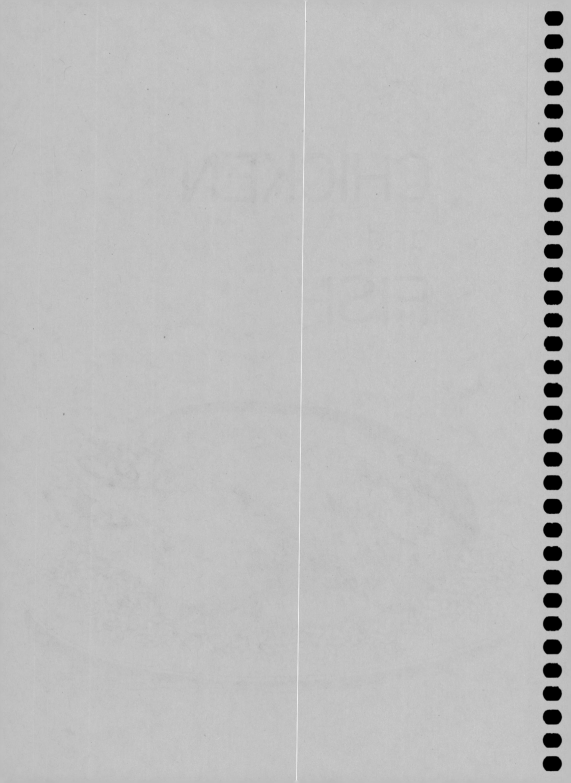

# FRIED OR BAKED CHICKEN

## FRIED CHICKEN

3 lb. frying chicken
1 cup flour
1 T. salt

1/2 tsp. pepper
1 cup shortening or cooking oil

Cut chicken into serving pieces. Combine flour, salt and pepper. Roll chicken in flour mixture. Heat oil in skillet and brown chicken 5 minutes per side. Reduce heat to low and remove all but several tablespoons of oil from skillet. Cook, covered, for 30 minutes. Uncover and cook another 15 minutes.

## CHICKEN DENISE

2 T. butter
3 lb. frying chicken, cut up
Paprika
4 onions, sliced 1/8" thick

8 oz. fresh mushrooms, sliced
  1/8" thick
2 cups heavy cream
1/2 tsp. salt

Melt butter in a 12-inch skillet; add chicken skin side down; sprinkle liberally with paprika. Fry at moderate heat until browned, about 15 minutes. Turn chicken skin side up; sprinkle with more paprika. Fry another 15 minutes. Remove chicken; drain fat, reserving 2 tablespoons. In reserved fat cook onions until translucent. Layer mushrooms over onions; add chicken. Pour cream over chicken and baste once. Add salt and enough more paprika to make sauce a pale orange. Cover skillet and simmer, stirring occasionally, until sauce is desired consistency, 30 to 60 minutes. Serve over cooked noodles.

*Connie Rodes, Milford, IN*

## TENDER CRUSTY CHICKEN

1 frying chicken, cut up
1 cup flour
1 T. salt
1/2 tsp. seasoned salt

1/4 tsp. pepper
1 1/2 tsp. paprika
2 T. melted butter
2 T. milk

Combine flour, salt, seasoned salt, pepper and paprika. Work mixture into chicken pieces, leaving no moist spots. Brown chicken in 1/2" hot fat, then place in pan. Do not stack pieces. Drizzle melted butter and milk over pieces. Bake, uncovered, at 350° for 30 to 40 minutes or until tender. Pour extra milk over chicken during baking if chicken looks dry.

*Rachel Newswanger, Barnett, MO*

219

## OVEN-FRIED CHICKEN I

2 frying chickens, cut up
1/2 cup melted butter
2 tsp. salt

1 1/2 cups crushed cornflakes
1/2 cup parmesan cheese
1/4 tsp. pepper

Dip chicken pieces into butter, then in mixture of remaining ingredients. Arrange in two 13x9 pans, allowing space between pieces. Bake, uncovered. Bake at 350° for 1 1/2 hours or until tender. Chicken can be covered with Miracle Whip salad dressing instead of butter.

*Karen Meador, Rossville, IN*    *Mrs. Elmer Sensening, Quarryville, PA*

## OVEN-FRIED CHICKEN II

4 cups flour
2 T. baking powder
2 1/2 T. salt

8 tsp. paprika
3/4 cup shortening

Combine first 4 ingredients then cut in shortening. Roll or shake chicken in mixture. Bake skin side down at 450° for 45 minutes. Turn and brown another 15 minutes. Store leftover crumbs in freezer.

*Susan Hilty Hoover, Elida, OH*

A quick yet delicious way to bake chicken is to sprinkle serving-size pieces liberally with seasoned salt and bake, covered or uncovered.

## CRISP GOLDEN CHICKEN

1 1/4 cups whole wheat flour
1/2 cup parmesan cheese
1 1/2 tsp. poultry seasoning
2 tsp. paprika
2 tsp. seasoned salt
1 tsp. celery salt

1 tsp. black pepper
3 tsp. salt
1 egg
1/2 cup water
2 frying chickens, cut up
1/2 cup butter or margarine

Mix dry ingredients in a large plastic bag. Mix egg with water. Dip chicken in egg mixture, then in flour mixture. Place chicken in single layer on a pan with sides in which butter was melted. Bake at 400° for 1/2 hour, then turn chicken, reduce heat to 375° for home-grown chickens and to 350° for store-bought chickens. Bake another half hour or until tender.

*Mrs. William (Lena) Kilmer, California, MO*

# SOUR CREAM CHICKEN

| | |
|---|---|
| 12 fryer pieces | 2 T. butter |
| 1/2 cup chopped celery | 16 oz. sour cream |
| 1/2 cup chopped onion | 10 oz. can mushroom soup |
| 1/2 cup chopped green pepper | 4 oz. can mushrooms |

Bake chicken in a single layer till tender. Sauté celery, onion and pepper in butter till tender. Combine sour cream, soup and mushrooms. Add vegetables and spread over baked chicken. Bake 30 minutes longer at 350°. Serve with steamed rice.

*Mary Zook, Virginia Beach, VA*

# PARMESAN CHICKEN

| | |
|---|---|
| 1 1/4 cups parmesan cheese | 3 lb. frying chicken, cut up |
| 1 tsp. salt | 1/3 cup melted butter |
| 1/4 tsp. pepper | |

Combine cheese, salt and pepper. Dip chicken into butter then into cheese mixture. Place in a greased 13x9 pan with skin down. Pour any remaining butter over chicken. Bake uncovered at 425° for 30 minutes. Turn chicken and bake an additional 20 minutes or until done.

# PLANTATION-STYLE CHICKEN

| | |
|---|---|
| 10 T. butter or margarine | 3 T. flour |
| 1/3 cup flour | 1/2 cup broth |
| 1 tsp. seasoned salt | 1 cup milk |
| 1/8 tsp. pepper | 1/4 tsp. salt |
| 3 lb. frying chicken, cut up | 1/4 tsp. pepper |
| 1 2/3 cups crushed cracker crumbs or Chex | 1 tsp. parsley |

Combine butter, flour, seasoned salt and pepper. Dip chicken into mixture and roll into cracker crumbs. Let stand 10 minutes. Bake at 400° for an hour or until tender. Remove from oven and reserve 2 tablespoons drippings. Combine drippings and flour over medium heat. Gradually stir in remaining ingredients in order given; stir till thick and bubbly. Pour over chicken and serve immediately. The sauce can be passed with chicken instead of pouring it on top. The chicken is good without the sauce too.

*Mrs. Ray (Elsie) Hoover, Stratford, WI*

***Praise is to a child like water is to a thirsty plant.***

# TENNESSEE WALTZING CHICKEN

1/2 cup flour
2 tsp. Accent flavor enhancer
1 tsp salt
1 tsp paprika
1/2 tsp. poultry seasoning
1 frying chicken, cut up

3/4 cup cooking oil
1/2 cup ketchup
1/4 cup orange juice
1 T. honey
1 tsp. mustard
1 tsp. Worcestershire sauce

Mix first 5 ingredients in a paper bag. Add chicken; shake to coat. Heat oil and fry chicken on both sides. Heat remaining ingredients in saucepan. Simmer 5 minutes, stirring occasionally. Place chicken skin side up in a shallow pan. Spoon half of sauce over chicken. Bake uncovered at 350° for 20 minutes. Spoon remaining sauce on; bake 20 minutes longer, or until chicken is tender.

*Nora Fox, Novelty, MO*

# COMPANY CHICKEN

2-3 lb. frying chickens (use drum-
   sticks, thighs and halved
   breasts)
1 cup flour
3 T. salt
1/4 tsp. pepper
2 tsp. paprika
1/4 cup butter
1/4 cup shortening

3 cups celery chunks
10 oz. can cream of chicken soup
1/2 cup light cream
2 tsp. diced pimento
1 cup finely chopped American
   cheese
2 cups soft bread crumbs
2 T. melted butter
1/2 cup slivered almonds, opt.

Coat chicken with dry ingredients. Lightly brown in butter and shortening. Put celery in greased 13x9 casserole with chicken on top. Combine soup, cream, pimento and cheese. Pour over chicken. Cover with bread crumbs and almonds. Bake at 350° for an hour.

*Mary Ellen Hission, Plymouth, IN     Lizzie Hoover, Goshen, IN     Rita Martin, Nappanee, IN*

# OVEN BARBECUED CHICKEN

3 lb. fryer
2/3 cup ketchup
1/2 cup sugar

1/4 cup vinegar
1/4 tsp. chili powder
1/4 tsp. paprika

Roll chicken in flour and brown. Put into roaster and pour combined sauce ingredients over chicken. Bake at 300° until chicken is soft.

*Mrs. LaVerne (Virginia) Hoover, Goshen, IN*

# SWEET AND SMOKY CHICKEN

1 chicken cut up
1 small onion, sliced
1/4 tsp. pepper
1/2 cup ketchup

1/2 cup molasses
1/4 cup vinegar, (scant)
1 tsp. hickory smoke salt

Place chicken in a 13x9 pan. Combine remaining ingredients and pour over chicken. Do not cover. Bake at 350° for 1 hour or until tender.

*Mrs. Elmer Sensenig, Quarryville, PA*

# SWEET-SOUR CHICKEN I

*To make in a slow cooker, put chicken and onions on the bottom and pour sauce over it placing pineapples and peppers on top. Cook on low for 8 to 10 hours.*

1/4 cup butter
1/2 cup chopped onion
1/2 cup chopped green pepper
3/4 cup pineapple juice
3/4 cup ketchup
1/4 cup brown sugar
2 T. vinegar

2 tsp. soy sauce
1/2 tsp. garlic salt
1/2 tsp. salt
1/4 tsp. pepper
15 oz. can pineapple chunks,
    drained
3 lb. chicken, cut up

Cook onion and green pepper in butter 5 minutes, stirring occasionally. Drain pineapple. Combine juice with all but pineapple and chicken; add to onions. Stir constantly until mixture boils. Add pineapple. Arrange chicken pieces skin side up in a 13x9 pan. Pour sauce over chicken. Cover pan with foil. Bake at 400° for 45 minutes. Remove foil and bake 35 minutes longer, basting occasionally.

*Ray Hoover, Stratford, WI*

# SWEET-SOUR CHICKEN II

4 lb. fryer chickens
1 T. cornstarch
1 T. cold water
1/2 cup sugar
1/2 soy sauce
1/4 cup vinegar

1 clove garlic, minced
1/2 tsp. Accent
1/2 tsp. ginger
1/4 tsp. pepper
1/2 cup drained pineapple

Cut up chickens. Cook together remaining ingredients, except pineapple, until mixture thickens and bubbles. Brush chicken with glaze. Place skin side down in greased pan. Bake at 425° for 30 minutes. Brush with glaze every 10 minutes. Then turn skin side up. Bake 30 minutes more and keep brushing. Add pineapple during the last 10 minutes of baking.

*Susan Miller, Nappanee, IN*

# CHINESE HONEYED CHICKEN

2 chickens, cut up
2 egg yolks, slightly beaten
1/4 cup melted butter
1/4 cup soy sauce

1/4 cup lemon juice
1/2 cup honey
1 small onion, chopped
Salt and pepper to taste

Place chicken pieces into roaster. Mix remaining ingredients and pour over chicken. Bake, uncovered, at 325° for 1 1/2 hours. Baste occasionally.

*Erla (Horst) Horning, Penn Yan, NY*

# CHICKEN AND RICE DISH

1 pkg. dry onion soup mix
10 oz. can golden or regular
    mushroom soup
1 cup dry rice

1 1/2 soup cans water
1 chicken, cut up
4 oz. can mushrooms
Seasoned salt

Mix first 4 ingredients. Put on bottom of 13x9 pan. Place chicken pieces on top. Sprinkle with seasoned salt. Bake at 350° for 1 1/2 hours, covered. If using brown rice double the water. Serve with soy sauce if desired.

*Gladys Hoover, Sheldon, WI      Mrs. Luke Hoover, Goshen, IN*

# CHICKEN MAKE AND BAKE

1 cup fine bread crumbs
1/2 cup flour
1 tsp. cornstarch
1/4 tsp. salt

1 tsp. sugar
1 tsp. paprika
1 3/4 tsp each: poultry seasoning,
    onion powder, garlic powder

Combine ingredients; mix well. Rub cut-up chicken with oil then roll in crumbs. Bake covered at 400° for 30 minutes then uncovered for 30 minutes more.

*Connie Rodes, Milford, IN*

# SMOKED TURKEY

1 cup Tenderquick
8 to 10 cups water

1 turkey
3 T. liquid smoke

Dissolve Tenderquick in water. Pour over turkey, covering completely. Refrigerate 2 days then drain. Rub on liquid smoke. Let stand overnight. Bake at 350°, 18 to 20 minutes per pound for a 15 pound turkey. Allow 15 to 18 minutes per pound for a larger bird. Bake, covered, or baste every 20 minutes. Brine recipe may need to be doubled to completely cover turkey.

*Ella Horning, Penn Yan, NY*

# RECIPES USING SKINLESS, BONELESS CHICKEN BREAST HALVES

## BAKED CHICKEN FINGERS WITH HONEY MUSTARD SAUCE

1 cup seasoned bread crumbs
2 T. parmesan cheese
1/4 cup cooking oil
1 clove garlic, minced or 1 tsp.
   dried minced garlic

6 chicken breast halves
2 T. cornstarch
1 cup water, divided
1/2 cup honey
1/4 cup mustard

Combine seasoned bread crumbs and parmesan cheese. Add garlic to oil. Flatten chicken to 1/2 inch thickness and cut into 1-inch wide strips. Dip strips into oil; roll in crumbs. Place on a greased cookie sheet. Bake at 350° for 20 minutes, or until golden brown. To make sauce dissolve cornstarch in 1 tablespoon water in a sauce pan. Add honey, mustard and rest of water. Bring to a boil over medium heat. Boil for 1 minute, stirring constantly. Serve sauce with chicken for dipping.

*Melinda Weaver, Spencer, WI*

To grill chicken breasts, flatten thick ends, then marinate 30 to 60 minutes. Grill 6 to 8 minutes on each side or until cooked through. Brush with barbeque sauce the last few minutes of grilling time.

## CHICKEN ALOHA

4 chicken breast halves
1 green pepper
8 oz. can pineapple chunks
2 T. cornstarch
1/4 cup apricot preserves
3 T. soy sauce
1/2 tsp. instant chicken bouillon

1/8 tsp. pepper
1 cup sliced celery
2 T. butter or margarine
Chow mein noodles or hot rice
Slivered almonds
Coconut

Cut chicken into 1 inch pieces. Cut green pepper into strips. Drain pineapple, saving syrup. Add water to syrup to make 1 1/4 cups. In small bowl blend syrup and cornstarch; stir in preserves, soy sauce, bouillon and pepper. In 10-inch skillet cook celery and green pepper in butter; about 2 minutes. Remove from skillet. Add chicken; cook and stir 2 minutes. Stir soy sauce mixture; blend into chicken. Cook and stir till thickened and bubbly. Add pineapple and pepper mixture. Cover and cook 1 minute. Serve over chow mein noodles or rice. Pass almonds and coconut.

*Connie Rodes, Milford, IN*

## CHICKEN CORDON BLEU CASSEROLE

6 chicken breast halves
6 slices boiled ham
6 slices Swiss cheese
10 oz. can cream of chicken soup

1/4 cup water
2 cups croutons or bread crumbs
1/2 cup melted butter

Layer chicken, ham and cheese in a 13x9 pan. Mix soup and water and pour on top. Mix croutons and butter; sprinkle on top. Bake, uncovered, at 325° for 1 1/2 hours.

## QUICK SAUCY CHICKEN STIR-FRY

2 T. cooking oil
1 cup broccoli
1 cup cauliflowerets
3/4 cup 2" julienne-cut carrots
1/4 cup green onion slices
1 garlic clove, minced

3 chicken breast halves, cut into
    bite-sized pieces
1/2 cup Miracle Whip salad
    dressing
1 T. soy sauce
1/2 tsp. ground ginger

In large skillet heat 1 tablespoon oil over medium-high heat. Stir-fry vegetables 4 to 5 minutes or until tender-crisp; remove from pan. Add remaining oil and stir-fry chicken 4 minutes or until tender. Return vegetables and remove from heat. Add combined remaining ingredients; mix well. Serve over hot rice.

*Laura Kulp, Stratford, WI        Rachel Ramer, Cazenovia, WI*

## SALSA CHICKEN

4 chicken breast halves
1 T. cooking oil
1 onion, coarsely chopped

1 green pepper, coarsely
    chopped
1 1/2 cups salsa

Cut chicken into thin strips; sauté in oil 3 minutes. Add vegetables; cook 3 to 4 minutes. Add salsa and simmer 2 minutes. Good over rice.

## SAUCY CHICKEN BREAST WITH FRESH MUSHROOMS

1/4 cup flour
1 tsp. salt
1 tsp. Italian seasoning
4 chicken breast halves
2 T. cooking oil

2 cups fresh mushrooms
1/2 cup chopped onion
3 cups spaghetti or pizza sauce
1 cup shredded mozzarella
    cheese

Combine flour, salt and seasoning; coat chicken. Brown chicken in hot oil. Remove chicken. Add sliced mushrooms and onion; cook and stir until tender. Add sauce and chicken. Cover and simmer 15 or until chicken is fully cooked. Sprinkle each chicken breast with cheese. Serve with hot pasta if desired.

## SPICY BROILED CHICKEN

1/2 cup oil
2 cloves garlic, minced
2 tsp. chili powder
1/2 tsp. salt

1/2 tsp. oregano
1/4 tsp. red pepper
4 chicken breast halves

Blend together all but chicken. Place chicken on a broiler pan that has been sprayed with no-stick spray. Spoon 1/2 of mixture over chicken. Broil six minutes 4 to 6 inches from heat. Turn chicken and top with remaining mixture. Broil 5 minutes longer or until juice runs clear.

Recipes using
# COOKED CHICKEN

## CHICKEN-ETTI

8 oz. spaghetti
3 to 4 cups cooked and chopped
    chicken
1/4 cup chopped green pepper
1 cup chicken broth

1/4 tsp. celery salt
1/4 tsp. pepper
3/4 lb. grated Velveeta cheese
2-10 oz. cans mushroom soup

Cook and drain spaghetti. Mix with remaining ingredients, reserving 1 cup cheese. Put in casserole and top with reserved cheese. Bake at 350° for 1 hour.

*Erla (Horst) Horning, Penn Yan, NY*

## HUNTINGTON CHICKEN

1 hen, cooked and boned
2 cups macaroni, cooked
8 T. flour
3/4 to 1 cup milk

1 T. poultry seasoning
Salt and pepper to taste
4 cups chicken broth
1 cup grated cheese

Place chicken and drained macaroni into casserole. Combine flour, milk and seasonings with broth. Heat, stirring constantly, until it thickens. Stir in cheese. Add to chicken; do not overstir or chicken will get stringy. Top with buttered bread crumbs if desired. Bake at 350° for 30 minutes or until bubbly.

*Mrs. Leonard Weaver, Orrville, AL*

## CHICKEN CHINESE

1 1/2 cups water
1 1/2 cups sliced carrots
1 1/2 cups sliced celery
2 T. dry onion
2 T. soy sauce

1/8 tsp. ginger
1/8 tsp. pepper
2 T. cornstarch
1 cup broth
24 oz. canned or cooked chicken

Put first 7 ingredients in a saucepan and cook until tender. Combine cornstarch and broth and add. Cook and stir till thick. Add chicken; heat. Serve over rice.

*Edna Miller, Snover, MI*

## CHICKEN CHOW MEIN

1 large chicken, cooked, boned
   and chopped
1 1/2 pkg. fine noodles
2 cups chopped celery

2 cups chopped onion
2 green peppers, chopped
10 oz. can mushroom soup
Buttered bread crumbs

Boil noodles in chicken broth. Add water if necessary. Cook vegetables; stir in mushroom soup. Add drained noodles and chicken. Put in casserole; top with bread crumbs. Bake at 375° until brown.

*Mrs. Edwin Nolt, Liberty, KY*

## CHICKEN CASSEROLE

3 cups cooked, diced chicken
1/2 cup chopped celery
1/2 cup chopped green pepper
1/2 cup chopped onion
1/2 cup salad dressing
1 tsp. pepper

1 tsp. salt
6 slices bread
1/2 cup milk
2 to 3 eggs
10 oz. mushroom soup
1/4 cup cheese

Mix first 7 ingredients. Cube bread, putting 1/2 of it into a well-greased casserole. Add chicken mixture. Put remaining bread on top. Beat milk and eggs well and pour over casserole. Refrigerate overnight. Top with soup and cheese before baking at 350° until done.

*Mrs. Harvey Mazelin, Cincinnati, IA*

## CORNY CHICKEN CASSEROLE

1/3 cup butter
1/2 cup flour, scant
2 cups milk
1/2 tsp. celery salt
1/2 tsp. salt

1/4 tsp. pepper
2 cups diced cooked chicken or
   turkey
2 cups canned or frozen corn
Buttered bread crumbs

Melt butter in skillet. Add flour to butter and simmer 1 minute. Remove pan from heat to stir in milk. Return to medium heat and cook and stir to thicken white sauce. Add seasonings and cooked meat to sauce. Stir in corn. Pour into buttered 2-quart casserole; top with bread crumbs. Bake at 350° for 30 minutes or until bubbly and browned.

*Mrs. Cleon (Carol) Bauman, Elmira, Ont. Canada*

## HERB AND CHICKEN CASSEROLE

6 chicken breast halves or small
   chicken, cooked
10 oz. can cream of celery soup
10 oz. can mushroom soup

2/3 cup milk
1/2 cup butter or margarine
1/2 cup broth or water
1 pkg. herb stuffing or croutons

Cube or chop cooked chicken and place in a greased casserole. Mix soups with milk and pour over chicken. Melt butter and mix with broth. Mix with stuffing. Place on top. Bake at 350° for 30 minutes. Two cups noodles may be added.

*Susie St. John, Alvordton, OH*

## CHICKEN AND RICE CASSEROLE

1/4 cup finely chopped onion
1/4 cup finely chopped celery
1/4 cup butter
10 oz. can cream of celery soup
10 oz. can mushroom soup
2 cups cooked chicken or turkey

1 cup dry long grain rice
1/2 tsp. poultry seasoning
1 tsp. salt
2 cups milk
2 cups chicken broth

Sauté onion and celery in butter. Add other ingredients and mix well. Bake in a 13x9 pan, uncovered, at 325° for 2 hours. Stir occasionally.

*Edith (Hoover) Martin, Sauk Centre, MN*

## BROCCOLI, RICE AND CHICKEN CASSEROLE

1/2 cup butter or margarine
10 oz. pkg. frozen broccoli
1 cup dry minute rice
8 oz. jar Cheez Whiz

10 oz. can mushroom soup
2 cups cooked chicken
French-fried onion rings

Melt butter and add broccoli to thaw and break apart. Add rice. Melt cheese and stir in soup. Mix together with broccoli in casserole. Top with chicken chunks. Bake at 350° for 30 minutes. Top with onion rings during the last 5 to 10 minutes.

*May BeMiller, Wakarusa, IN*

## BROCCOLI, NOODLE AND CHICKEN CASSEROLE

*This is a good make-ahead-and-freeze recipe.*

10 oz. pkg. frozen broccoli
10 oz. can cream of chicken soup
1/4 cup milk

1 cup grated cheese
8 oz. noodles, cooked
1 1/2 cups cubed cooked chicken

Cook and drain broccoli. Heat soup, milk, and 3/4 cup cheese until cheese melts. Add broccoli, noodles and chicken; mix well. Bake in a 1 1/2-quart casserole or 13x9 pan. Top with remaining cheese. Bake at 350° for 30 minutes.

*Mrs. Larry Zimmerman, Elkhart, IN*

## OVERNIGHT CHICKEN CASSEROLE

7 oz. dry macaroni (about 2 cups)
2 cups milk
10 oz. can mushroom soup
10 oz. can cream of celery soup
2 cups diced cooked chicken

1 cup diced mushrooms
1 cup whole mushrooms
1 small onion, chopped
1/2 lb. Velveeta cheese, diced
Bread Crumbs, opt

Combine all ingredients. Two cups canned mushrooms may be substituted for fresh mushrooms. Put in a casserole and refrigerate overnight. Top with bread crumbs the next morning. Bake at 350° for 1 hour.

*Elaine Martin, Nappanee, IN*

## TOMATO AND CHICKEN SAUCE OVER RICE

2/3 cup chopped celery
1/2 cup chopped onion
2 T. butter or margarine
2 T. flour
2 cups chopped tomatoes

2 cups diced cooked chicken
1/2 lb. Velveeta cheese cubes
1/2 tsp. basil
4 cups hot rice

Sauté celery and onion in butter. Add remaining ingredients; stir until cheese melts. Serve over rice.

*If any little word of mine may make a life the brighter,*
*If any little song of mine may make a heart the lighter,*
*God help me speak that little word,*
*And take my bit of singing*
*And drop it in some lonely vale,*
*To set the echoes ringing!*

# CHICKEN A LA KING

*Cooked turkey works great too.   A cup or 2 of peas adds color and nutrition.*

| | |
|---|---|
| 1/3 cup butter | 1/2 tsp. poultry seasoning |
| 1/2 cup chopped celery | 1/4 tsp. pepper |
| 1/4 cup chopped onion | 1/3 cup flour |
| 1/4 cup mushrooms | 3 cups milk or broth |
| 1 tsp. salt | 2 cups cubed cooked chicken |

Melt butter; add vegetables; cook several minutes.  Add seasoning.  Blend in flour.  Gradually stir in milk.  Bring to a boil and cook 2 minutes.  Add chicken and heat through.  Serve on rice, noodles, toast or biscuits.

# CHEESY CHICKEN ROLL-UPS

*Your own biscuit dough may be used instead of buying biscuit dough.*

| | |
|---|---|
| 2 T. butter or margarine | 1 cup cubed cooked chicken |
| 2 T. flour | 1/4 cup chopped onion |
| 1 cup milk | 3 T. sliced olives |
| 2 cups shredded cheese, divided | 1 tube Pillsbury biscuits |

Melt butter; blend in flour.  Stir in milk.  Cook and stir over medium heat until thickened.  Add 1 1/2 cups cheese; stir until melted.  Remove from heat; reserve 2/3 cup sauce for topping.  To remaining sauce add chicken, onion and olives.  Separate biscuits into 10 biscuits; press each into 4" circle.  Place 2 tablespoons chicken mixture in center of each biscuit; roll up.  Place seam side down in ungreased 9" square pan.  Bake at 375° for 20 minutes or until golden brown.  Spoon on reserved sauce and 1/2 cup cheese.  Bake 2 minutes longer.

*Laura Kulp, Stratford, WI*

# CHICKEN IN CRUMB BASKETS

*A casserole can be lined with crumbs and baked at 375° for 8 minutes then filled with chicken mixture and baked at 350° another 30 minutes.*

| | |
|---|---|
| 5 to 6 cups soft bread crumbs | 1/3 cup flour |
| 1/4 cup minced onion | 1/2 cup light cream |
| 1 tsp. celery salt | 1 1/2 cups chicken broth |
| 1/8 tsp. pepper | 1/2 tsp. salt |
| 1/4 cup melted butter | 1/2 tsp. pepper |
| 1/2 tsp. poultry seasoning | 1 tsp. Worcestershire sauce |
| 1/3 cup butter or margarine | 3 cups chopped cooked chicken |

Combine first 6 ingredients; press into 6 individual greased casseroles.  Bake at 375° for 15 minutes.  Melt butter; blend in flour.  Add all but chicken.  Cook and stir until thickened.  Add chicken (and a cup of peas if desired); pour into baskets.

*Mrs. Jacob Oberholtzer, Liberty, KY      Mrs. Elmer Sensenig, Quarryville, PA*

# CHICKEN PIE

*A pint of peas from your freezer works just as well as the package of peas and carrots.*

2 cups flour
2 tsp. celery salt
2/3 cup shortening
4 T. water
1/3 cup butter
1/3 cup flour
1 T. dried onion flakes

1 T. soup base or bouillon
1/2 tsp. salt
1/4 tsp. pepper
1 3/4 cups water
2/3 cup milk
2 cups cooked chicken
10 oz. pkg. peas and carrots

Cut shortening into flour and celery salt. Add water a little at a time. Roll out a little over half of dough; line a 10" pie pan. Roll out remaining dough for a top crust. Melt butter; stir in flour, onion, soup base, salt and pepper. Add water and milk, stirring constantly. Boil 1 minute. Stir in chicken and vegetables. Pour into pie plate; top with top crust, crimping to seal. Cut slits in top. Bake at 425° for 30 to 35 minutes.

*Pauline Kulp, Stratford, WI*

# DEEP DISH CHICKEN POT PIE

1/2 cup celery
6 T. butter or margarine
1/3 cup flour
7 chicken bouillon cubes
1/4 tsp. pepper
4 1/2 cups milk
3 cups cubed cooked chicken
1 cup cooked sliced carrots

1 cup cooked diced potatoes
1 cup frozen peas, thawed
3 cups flour
2 T. baking powder
3/4 tsp. salt
5 T. butter
1 cup plus 2 T. milk

Cook celery in butter until tender. Stir in flour, bouillon and pepper. Add milk. Cook and stir till thickened. Stir in chicken, carrots, potatoes and peas; remove from heat. To make biscuits, mix dry ingredients and cut in butter. Using a fork, stir in milk. Knead slightly on floured surface. Put 2/3 of dough into well-greased 13x9 pan. With floured hands, pat evenly all over bottom and sides of pan. Pour in chicken mixture. Cut remaining dough into biscuits and arrange on top of casserole. Bake at 375° for 25 to 30 minutes.

*Mrs. LaVerne (Virginia) Hoover, Goshen, IN*

*Never bear more than one trouble at a time.*
*Some people bear all three kinds:*
*All they have had—*
*All they have now—*
*And all they expect to have.*

# CHICKEN CROQUETTES

*A similar recipe calls for 2 cups chopped cooked chicken, 2 cups bread crumbs, 2 beaten eggs, 1/4 cup chopped onion, and salt and pepper. Shape into balls and deep fry.*

2 T. butter
2 1/2 T. flour
1 cup milk
2 cups minced cooked chicken
1/4 tsp. onion juice or 1/4 cup
  minced onion

1 tsp. salt
1/8 tsp. pepper
2 T. minced parsley or celery
1 cup dried bread crumbs
2 eggs, beaten

Melt butter; blend in flour and stir in milk. Add chicken and seasoning. Cool thoroughly. Shape into balls. Dip into crumbs then into eggs, then into crumbs again. Deep fat fry for 3 to 5 minutes. These freeze well. Put in a tight container. When ready to use place on cookie sheets and cover with aluminum foil. Bake at 350° till hot. These can also be fried like pancakes.

*Mrs. Isaac Brubacker, Versailles, MO    Mrs. Lloyd Troyer, Stella, MO    Mrs. Sam Newswanger, Goshen, IN*

# STUFFING AND GRAVY

## STUFFING I

1 loaf bread, cubed
2 1/2 cups broth or milk
2 eggs
1/4 cup butter
2 T. parsley

1 tsp. onion
1 tsp. poultry seasoning
1 tsp. salt
1/4 tsp. pepper
Accent to taste

Mix all ingredients well. Stuff turkey or chicken or bake in large casserole or roaster. If baked in a casserole, bake at 400° for 25 minutes or until done.

*Esther Martin, Decker, MI*

## STUFFING II

5 eggs
4 cups milk
1/2 cup melted butter
1 tsp. salt
1 tsp. pepper

1/2 tsp. sage
1 cup cooked carrots, opt.
1 cup cooked celery, opt.
1/2 cup cooked onion, opt
1 loaf bread, cubed

Beat eggs well; add remaining ingredients, add bread last. Pour into baking dish. Bake at 350°, covered, until set. When almost done, uncover to brown top.

*Mrs. Elias Martin, Goshen, IN*

233

# CELERY STUFFING

4 cups dry bread crumbs
1 1/2 cups finely chopped celery
3 T. chopped onion
1 tsp salt
1/4 tsp. pepper

1 tsp. sage
1/4 tsp. poultry seasoning
1/3 cup melted butter
1/2 cup milk or broth
1 egg, slightly beaten

Combine bread crumbs, celery, onion and seasonings. Add melted butter and milk. Mix lightly to moisten. Add beaten eggs; toss. Makes 6 1/2 cups, enough to stuff a chicken or small turkey. Omit celery for plain stuffing.

*Mrs. William (Lena) Kilmer, California, MO*

# SAGE STUFFING

1/2 cup butter
Giblets from 1 fowl, chopped
1/2 cup chopped celery
1/4 cup chopped onion
12 cups lightly toasted bread
    cubes

2 quarts milk
4 eggs, slightly beaten
3 T. sage
2 cups hot water

Melt butter in heavy skillet; add giblets and fry slightly. Add celery and onion; fry till tender. Add bread cubes, milk, eggs and sage; mix and heat thoroughly. Stuff fowl which has been salted inside and out. Place remaining stuffing into cloth bag and place beside fowl in roaster. Add hot water. Bake at 325° for 3 hours or until meat thermometer reaches 180° in the thickest part of the thigh.

*Sarah Imhoff, Sheridan, MI*

# NO-EGGS STUFFING

1 cup chopped celery
1 cup chopped onion
1 T. poultry seasoning
1/4 cup butter

1 1/4 cups chicken broth, milk or
    water
10 cups dry, stale or lightly
    toasted bread cubes

Brown first 3 ingredients in butter until tender. Add broth then mix lightly with bread cubes. Bake in 2 quart casserole at 350° for 45 minutes or stuff a 10 pound turkey.

*Mrs. Ray (Elsie) Hoover, Stratford, WI*

**The closer Christians get to Christ the closer they get to one another.**

## DELUXE STUFFING

2 cups diced potatoes
1 cup diced carrots
1 cup diced celery
6 eggs, beaten
6 cups milk
2 cups chicken broth
1/2 cup chopped fresh parsley

1 T. salt
1 T. chicken soup base
1/2 tsp. pepper
2 loaves of bread, toasted and
    cubed
4 cups cubed cooked chicken
1/2 cup butter

Cook vegetables just until tender.  Beat eggs; add milk, broth, parsley, salt, soup base, and pepper.  Combine with drained vegetables, bread and chicken.  Melt butter in a large roaster.  Pour in stuffing.  Bake at 350° for 30 minutes.  Stir, then bake an additional 30 minutes or until set.  Can also be made without chicken

*Katie Troyer, Stone Lake, WI*

## CHICKEN GRAVY

1/4 cup butter
1/4 cup flour

1 1/2 cups chicken broth
1/2 cup milk

Melt butter, blend in flour.  Cook and stir several minutes.  Remove from heat. Stir in broth and milk.  Cook and stir until thickened.  All broth or more or less milk can be used.

## GIBLET GRAVY

Poultry heart, gizzard, neck and
    wing tips
2 1/2 cups water

1 tsp. salt
1/4 cup butter
1/4 cup flour

Simmer meat in water and salt for 1/2 hour.  Remove meat; save broth.  Chop heart and gizzard fine; discard the rest.  Melt butter; add flour.  Slowly stir in 2 cups broth.  Cook until thickened.  Add chopped giblets.  Season to taste.

| WEIGHT | TURKEY ROASTING TIME AT 325° | |
|---|---|---|
| Pounds | Unstuffed | Stuffed |
| 6 to 8 | 2 1/4 to 3 1/4 hours | 3 to 3 1/2 hours |
| 8 to 12 | 3 to 4 hours | 3 1/2 to 4 1/2 hours |
| 12 to16 | 3 1/2 to 4 1/2 hours | 4 1/2 to 5 1/2 hours |
| 16 to 20 | 4 to 5 hours | 5 1/2  to 6 1/2 hours |
| 20 to 24 | 4 1/2 to 5 1/2 hours | 6 1/2 to 7 1/2 hours |

*Meat thermometer should reach 180° to 185° in the thickest part of the thigh.*

# FISH

## PAN-FRIED FISH

2 lb. fish fillets
1 cup cornmeal, cracker crumbs
   or flour
2 tsp. parsley

1/4 tsp. thyme, opt.
1/4 cup milk
Cooking oil
Salt and pepper

Wash and dry fish. Combine crumbs, parsley and thyme; mix well. Dip fish in milk then into crumbs, coating well. Fry in hot oil 2 to 3 minutes per side. Fish should flake easily. Season with salt and pepper. Drain on paper towel.

## FISH AND CHIPS

Cooking oil for deep frying
Potatoes cut in 1/2" strips
1 lb. fish fillets
2/3 cup flour
1/2 tsp. salt

1/2 tsp. soda
1 T. vinegar
2/3 cup water
Vinegar and salt

Fry potatoes at 375° for 5 to 7 minutes. Place on cookie sheet in single layer and keep warm. Pat fish dry. Mix flour and salt. Mix soda and vinegar; add water then add to flour. Beat until smooth. Dip fish into batter and fry till brown, turning once at about 3 minutes. Broil potatoes 6" from heat until crisp, 2 to 3 minutes. Sprinkle with vinegar and salt if desired.

*Mrs. Ray (Elsie) Hoover, Stratford, WI*

## BROILED FISH

3 lb. fish fillets
1/4 cup cooking oil
1/4 cup lemon juice

2 tsp. salt
3/4 tsp. paprika
1/8 tsp. pepper

Place washed and dried fish on a well greased broiler pan. Combine remaining ingredients and brush on both sides of fish. Broil about 4 inches from heat 5 to 8 minutes. Turn fish and brush with remaining oil mixture. Broil 5 to 8 minutes longer or until fish flake easily when tested with a fork.

***Kind actions begin with kind thoughts.***

# BAKED COD

| | |
|---|---|
| 3 T. butter | 3/4 tsp. salt |
| 1/4 cup flour | 1/4 tsp. pepper |
| 1/4 cup cornmeal | 1 lb. cod fillets, fresh or thawed |

Melt butter in an 8x8 pan. Combine flour, cornmeal, salt and pepper. Dredge fish in flour mixture and place in pan. Turn fish to coat with butter. Bake at 450° for 8 to 10 minutes or until fish flakes easily when tested with a fork.

# POACHED ITALIAN COD

| | |
|---|---|
| 1 lb. cod fillets | 1 green pepper, sliced thin |
| 1/4 cup water | 1/4 cup water |
| 2 tsp. cornstarch | 1 tsp. fresh basil |
| 2 T. cooking oil | 1/4 tsp. salt |
| 2 cloves garlic, minced | 1/4 tsp. pepper |
| 2 large tomatoes, chopped | 1/4 cup ripe olives, sliced |
| 1 onion, cut into wedges | 2 cups hot cooked pasta |

Cut cod into 1" pieces. Stir together water and cornstarch. Set aside. Fry garlic in hot oil 15 seconds. Add next 7 ingredients. Cook and stir till onion and green pepper are tender. Add fish; bring to boil, reduce heat. Cover and simmer till fish flakes with a fork, 8 to 12 minutes. Add cornstarch mixture. Cook and stir till thickened and bubbly. Cook and stir 2 minutes more. Stir in olives and serve immediately over hot pasta. Pass parmesan cheese.

# FISH WITH BUTTER SAUCE

| | |
|---|---|
| 3 lb. haddock or white fish fillets | 3 T. flour |
| Boiling salt water to cover | 1/2 tsp. salt |
| 2 T. butter | 1 1/2 cups hot water |
| 1/3 cup butter | 1 tsp. lemon juice |

Cut fish into serving-size pieces. Poach in water and 2 tablespoons butter in skillet for 10 minutes or until fish flakes easily. For sauce, melt 1/3 cup butter; add flour and salt. Stir till well blended. Add water gradually, stirring constantly. Bring to a boil and boil about 2 minutes. Stir in lemon juice and serve with fish.

*Mrs. LaVerne (Virginia) Hoover, Goshen, IN*

*Admitting an error is not a confession of weakness, but a sign of strength.*

# TUNA SKILLET

4 cups water
1 tsp. salt
2 cups dry macaroni

2 cups frozen peas
1/2 lb. Velveeta cheese, cubed
12 oz. tuna, drained

Bring water and salt to a boil. Add macaroni. Reduce heat. Cook 10 to 15 minutes or until tender and most water is gone. Add peas and cheese. Stir until cheese is melted. Gently stir in tuna. Heat through.

# TUNA NOODLE CASSEROLE

8 oz. medium noodles
3 T. butter
1 medium onion, chopped
1/2 cup celery, cut fine
10 oz. can cream of celery soup

1 soup can milk
6 to 12 oz. tuna, drained
2 T. chopped pimento, opt.
1/2 cup shredded cheese

Cook noodles as directed; drain. Melt butter; add onion and celery; simmer till done. Stir in soup and milk; add tuna and pimento; mix in noodles. Put in baking dish. Bake at 350° for 25 minutes. Sprinkle with cheese; bake 5 minutes longer.

*Mrs. Isaac Kulp, Millersburg, IN*

# TUNA BROCCOLI LOAF

5 eggs
1/2 cup milk
1 cup soft bread crumbs
12 oz. tuna, drained
1 T. grated onion
1 tsp. lemon juice

1/2 tsp. salt
1/8 tsp. pepper
Dash of nutmeg
1/2 cup Swiss cheese, grated
10 oz. pkg. frozen chopped
    broccoli, cooked

Beat eggs, milk and crumbs in a large bowl. Let stand 15 minutes. Stir in tuna, onion, lemon juice, salt, pepper, nutmeg and cheese. Process broccoli in blender till smooth. Add to tuna mixture. Turn into a well-greased 8x4 loaf pan. Bake at 375° for 1 hour. Let stand 5 minutes; turn out on a serving dish.

# BAKED TUNA AND CHEESE SWIRLS

3 T. chopped onion
1/3 cup green pepper
3 T. butter
1 tsp. salt
6 T. flour
10 oz. cream of chicken soup

1 1/2 cups milk
7 oz. can tuna
1 T. lemon juice
Favorite biscuit dough
1/2 cup grated American cheese

238

Sauté onion and green pepper in butter. Add salt and flour. Add soup and milk. Cook till thick. Add tuna and lemon juice. Pour into casserole. Roll dough into rectangle. Sprinkle with cheese. Roll up. Slice. Spread on tuna mixture. Bake at 450° for 15 minutes, then at 425° for 15 minutes.

## CHEESE PUFF TUNA PIE

2 T. butter
3 T. flour
13 oz. can evaporated milk or
  1 1/2 cups whole milk
2 cups shredded cheese
12 oz. tuna, drained
1/2 cup chopped celery
1/4 cup chopped green pepper

2 tsp. mustard
1 tsp. Worcestershire sauce
3/4 tsp. basil
1/8 tsp. salt
Dash of pepper
9" unbaked pastry shell
2 eggs, separated
1 cup reserved cheese sauce

Melt butter; blend in flour; stir in milk. Add 1 3/4 cup cheese and stir until melted. Reserve 1 cup sauce. Combine remaining sauce with tuna, vegetables and seasonings; mix well. Spoon into pastry shell. Bake at 425° for 15 minutes. Beat egg whites till stiff peaks form. Blend slightly beaten yolks into cheese sauce. Fold in egg whites. Top pie with cheese puff topping. Decrease heat to 375°. Bake 20 to 25 minutes or until golden brown. Sprinkle with remaining cheese. Serve immediately.

*Berdena Hoover, Elkhart, IN      Sheryl Wenger, Marlette, MI*

## SALMON CAKES WITH WHITE SAUCE AND PEAS

7 1/2 oz. can salmon, drained and
  flaked
1/3 cup cracker crumbs
1 slightly beaten egg
2 T. chopped onion
2 T. milk
1 T. lemon juice

4 T. butter or margarine, divided
1 1/2 T. flour
1/2 tsp. salt
1 cup milk
10 oz. pkg. frozen pea and
  carrots, cooked and drained

Combine ingredients in first column, blending well. Shape into 4 flat patties. Melt 2 tablespoons butter in small skillet; sauté patties on both sides until golden brown and heated through. Add more butter to skillet if necessary. Melt remaining 2 tablespoons butter in saucepan; blend in flour and salt. Add milk; stir and cook until thick and bubbly. Add peas to hot mixture; heat through. Serve with salmon cakes.

*Connie Rodes, Milford, IN*

**Purity in the heart produces power in life.**

# SALMON PATTIES

15 oz. can salmon or mackerel
1 to 2 eggs
1/4 cup milk

1/2 cup cracker crumbs
1/8 tsp. pepper, opt.
Minced onion, opt.

Break fish into small pieces with a fork; add remaining ingredients. Roll into flour and fry in butter or drop by tablespoon into hot butter. Brown on both sides.

*Laura Martin, Ephrata, PA*     *Rita Martin, Nappanee, IN*

# SCALLOPED SALMON OR MACKEREL

2 cups salmon, flaked
2 cups cracker crumbs
2 eggs

2 cups hot milk
1/4 cup melted butter
1 tsp. salt

Place alternate layers of salmon and crushed crackers in a greased casserole. Beat eggs and slowly stir in milk, butter and salt. Pour liquid over contents of casserole. Bake at 375° for 40 minutes.

*Mrs. Isaac Brubaker, Versailles, MO*

# SALMON LOAF

2 cups salmon
2 eggs, beaten
2 T. melted butter
1/2 cup cornmeal

1/4 cup bread or cracker crumbs
1 cup buttermilk
1/2 tsp. salt
1/8 tsp. pepper

Flake and debone salmon. Combine with eggs, butter, cornmeal and crumbs. Add buttermilk, salt and pepper. Pour into greased casserole. Bake at 425° for 20 minutes. Serve with tomato sauce if desired.

# SCALLOPED OYSTERS

1 1/2 cups cracker crumbs
24 oysters
1 tsp. salt
1/4 tsp. pepper

Butter
1/2 cup oyster liquid
1/2 cup milk

Line greased baking dish with crumbs. Add 8 oysters. Sprinkle with 1/3 of salt and pepper. Dot with butter. Make three layers, ending with crumbs. Pour on liquid and milk. Bake at 350° for 30 minutes. Serve with crisp bacon. A layer of macaroni may be added,

# DESSERTS

Elsie Hoover

# PUDDING, CUSTARD, ETC

## VANILLA PUDDING

| | |
|---|---|
| 4 cups milk | 1/8 tsp. salt |
| 5 T. cornstarch | 2 eggs, separated |
| 1 1/4 cups sugar, divided | 1 tsp. vanilla |

Bring milk to a boil in heavy kettle. Combine and add cornstarch, 3/4 cup sugar, and salt. Beat eggs with 1/2 cup sugar. Remove pudding from heat and stir in egg mixture. Stir and cook until thick. Stir in vanilla.

*Mrs. Cyrus Kulp, Auburn, KY*

## CHOCOLATE PUDDING

*This makes great vanilla pudding too. Just delete cocoa and use 1/3 cup cornstarch.*

| | |
|---|---|
| 1 cup sugar | 4 cups milk |
| 1/2 cup cocoa | 2 T. butter |
| 1/4 cup cornstarch | 2 tsp. vanilla |
| 1/4 tsp. salt | |

Combine sugar, cocoa, cornstarch and salt in a heavy saucepan. Stir in milk. Bring to a boil over medium heat, stirring most of the time. Boil and stir two minutes. Remove from heat and add butter and vanilla. Cover with plastic wrap to keep skin from forming.

*Mrs. Ray (Elsie) Hoover, Stratford, WI*

## BUTTERSCOTCH PUDDING

| | |
|---|---|
| 1 cup brown sugar | 6 eggs |
| 6 T. flour | 3 tsp. vanilla |
| 3 T. cornstarch | Graham cracker crumbs |
| 3/4 tsp. salt | Nuts |
| 3 3/4 cups milk | Bananas |
| 3 T. butter or margarine | |

In saucepan combine sugar, flour, cornstarch and salt. Blend in milk; add butter. Cook on low heat, stirring constantly, till mixture thickens and bubbles. Cook 1 minute more. Beat eggs slightly. Stir about half hot mixture into the eggs. Return to saucepan and heat. Cook 1 to 2 minutes more. Do not boil. Remove from heat and add vanilla. Cover surface with wax paper. Cool without stirring. Layer with graham cracker crumbs, nuts and bananas to serve.

*Vera Witmer, Goshen, IN*

# CARAMEL PUDDING

3/4 cup brown sugar
1/4 cup water
1/4 tsp. salt
4 cups milk

1/3 cup cornstarch
2 T. butter
1 tsp. vanilla

Cook sugar, water and salt till slightly brown. Stir together milk and cornstarch and pour into sugar mixture. Cook till thickened. Remove from heat and stir in butter and vanilla. Cool. Good served with sweetened whipped cream or whipped topping, and Corn Flake Crunch.

*Mrs. LaVerne (Virginia) Hoover, Goshen, IN*

# CORNFLAKE CRUNCH

1/2 cup butter, scant
2/3 cup brown sugar

4 cups cornflakes

Melt butter; blend in sugar. Cook until thick and smooth, stirring constantly. Stir in flakes; cook and stir over low heat until cereal is coated. Spread in thin layer on baking sheet to cool. Layer with pudding or sprinkle on top. Do not crush when adding on top of pudding.

*Mrs. Elias Martin, Goshen, IN*

Use a half cup of cornstarch to thicken one quart of liquid. It takes approximately twice as much flour to thicken something as it does cornstarch.

Pudding made with whole or 2% milk tastes better and doesn't burn as quickly as does pudding made with skim milk.

# MAPLE PUDDING

2 cups brown sugar
1 cup flour
6 cups milk
3 eggs, beaten

3 to 4 T. butter
1 tsp. maple flavoring
1 tsp. vanilla

Mix sugar with flour, then mix with 1 cup milk. Add sugar mixture to beaten eggs. Bring the remaining 5 cups of milk to a boil. Add egg mixture. Boil until thick, stirring constantly. Remove from heat and add butter. Stir in flavoring and cool.

*Rachel Newswanger, Barnett, MO*

242

# QUICK CHOCOLATE MOUSSE

| | |
|---|---|
| 1 cup milk | 3/4 cup chocolate chips |
| 3 cups miniature marshmallows | 1/2 cup whipping cream, whipped |

Combine milk, marshmallows, and chocolate chips in a saucepan. Cook over medium heat until hot, but not boiling. Cool, stirring occasionally. Whip cream and add. Chill. Cream may be replaced with a cup of whipped topping.

# CUSTARD

| | |
|---|---|
| 4 to 6 eggs, slightly beaten | 2 tsp. vanilla |
| 1/2 cup sugar | 4 cups hot milk |
| 1/2 tsp. salt | Nutmeg, opt. |

Mix eggs, sugar, salt and vanilla. Add milk very slowly, while stirring egg mixture rapidly. Pour into baking dish, 13x9 pan or individual custard cups and sprinkle liberally with nutmeg. Set dish in a pan of water, as deep as the custard, if possible. Bake at 325° for 40 minutes or until knife inserted in center comes out clean.

*Mrs. Luke Hoover, Goshen, IN*     *Nancy Kilmer, California, MO*

# RICE CUSTARD

| | |
|---|---|
| 4 eggs | 1/8 tsp. salt |
| 1 cup sugar | 1 tsp. vanilla |
| 1 1/2 cups cooked rice | 1/2 cup coconut, opt. |
| 3 1/2 cups milk | |

Beat eggs and sugar. Stir in remaining ingredients. Pour into casserole. Bake at 350° for 1 1/2 hours or until knife inserted in the center comes out clean.

*Mrs. Cyrus Kulp, Auburn, NY*

# RICE PUDDING

| | |
|---|---|
| 1 3/4 cups dry white rice | 1 1/2 cups sugar |
| 2 cups water | 2 T. butter |
| 4 cups milk | |

Combine rice and water in a saucepan; simmer 10 minutes. Add milk and bring to a boil. Reduce heat and simmer, uncovered, for 60 to 70 minutes or until rice is tender. Add sugar and butter; mix well. Good warm or cold.

# GLORIFIED RICE

3 oz. lemon gelatin
1 cup cooked rice
1 cup sugar

1 cup pineapple juice
1/2 cup crushed pineapple
1 cup whipping cream

Mix gelatin as directed. When partially set, whip gelatin. Add rice, sugar, juice and pineapple. Whip cream and add.

*Mrs. Amos Horst, Ephrata, PA*

# TAPIOCA PUDDING

4 cups milk
1/2 cup tapioca (not Minute)
2 eggs, beaten
1 1/2 cups sugar

1 T. cornstarch
Pinch of salt
1 tsp. vanilla
2 cup whipping cream

Heat milk, add tapioca. Keep stirring until it boils, then simmer until soft. Add eggs, beaten with sugar and cornstarch. Cook until thickened; add salt and vanilla. When cool, whip cream and add.

*Mrs. Sam Newswanger, Goshen, IN*

# MINUTE TAPIOCA

1/3 cup sugar
3 T. Minute tapioca
2 3/4 cups milk

1 egg, well beaten
1 tsp. vanilla

Mix first 4 ingredients; let stand 5 minutes. Cook over medium heat, stirring constantly till it comes to a full boil. Remove from heat and stir in vanilla. Cool 20 minutes; stir. Pudding thickens as it cools. For creamier pudding cover surface of pudding with plastic wrap while it is cooling.

# DELUXE TAPIOCA

6 cups water
1/2 tsp. salt
1 cup baby pearl tapioca
3/4 cup brown sugar
2 eggs, beaten
3/4 cup sugar
1 cup evaporated milk

3 T. butter
1 1/2 tsp. vanilla
Chopped candy bars
Chopped peanuts
Sliced bananas
Whipped cream

Simmer water, salt, tapioca and brown sugar till tapioca is clear. Add beaten eggs, sugar and evaporated milk; bring to a boil. Remove from heat. Brown butter; add vanilla, then add to pudding and mix well. Chill. When ready to serve, layer pudding with remaining ingredients.

*Mrs. Laureen Gerber, Fairview, MI*

## ORANGE-PINEAPPLE TAPIOCA

8 oz. (scant 1 1/2 cups) small
    pearl tapioca
7 cups water
1/2 tsp. salt
6 oz. orange gelatin

1 1/4 cups sugar
20 oz. can sweetened crushed
    pineapple
2 cups frozen whipped topping
2 cups miniature marshmallows

Put tapioca, water and salt in saucepan and simmer until most of the tapioca is clear, approximately 25 minutes. Remove from heat. Add dry gelatin and sugar. Stir until dissolved. Cool slightly. Add undrained can of pineapple. When ready to serve add whipped topping and marshmallows. Add a little milk if tapioca is too thick.

*Mrs. Isaac Kulp, Millersburg, IN*

## FRUIT JUICE TAPIOCA

1/3 cup sugar
3 T. Minute tapioca
Pinch of salt

2 cups apple, cranberry, grape,
    orange, or pineapple juice

Mix everything in a medium saucepan. Let stand 5 minutes. Cook on medium heat, stirring constantly until mixture comes to full boil. Remove from heat. Cool 20 minutes; stir. Pudding thickens as it cools. Serve warm or chilled. Whipped topping or drained fruit may be added.

## GRAPE JUICE TAPIOCA

2 1/2 cups water
3/4 cup sugar
2/3 cup Minute tapioca

1 cup grape juice
2 T. lemon juice
Whipped cream or topping

Combine water and sugar; boil till sugar is dissolved. Add tapioca and cook till clear. Add grape and lemon juice; cook another 3 minutes. Cool. Add whipped cream when ready to serve.

*Edna Miller, Snover, MI*

**Take care of your life and the Lord will take care of your death.**

# GRAPE SPONGE

1 1/2 T. unflavored gelatin
2 T. cold water

2 cups grape juice
1/2 cup cream

Soak gelatin in water for 5 minutes. Add some grape juice to gelatin water. Heat till warm or dissolved. Add the rest of the juice. Cool until set enough to whip. Whip and sweeten cream; add.

*Mrs. Phillip Zimmerman, Versailles, MO*

# CHOCOLATE CHIP SPONGE

1 cup milk
8 oz. marshmallows
1 cup cream

1/4 tsp. salt
1 square semisweet chocolate,
   grated

Bring milk and marshmallows to a boil. Remove from heat; chill thoroughly. Whip cream until thick; add salt and grated chocolate. Mix with first mixture.

*Mrs. Elias Martin, Goshen, IN*

# COFFEE SPONGE

2 T. unflavored gelatin
1 cup cold water
2 T. flour
1/2 tsp. salt, scant

4 tsp. instant coffee
1 tsp. vanilla
1 1/2 cups boiling water
2 cups ice cold whipping cream

Dissolve gelatin in cold water. Add flour, then remaining ingredients, except cream. Bring to a boil, stirring constantly. Cool until slightly thickened. Beat cream and fold in.

*Mrs. Elam Hoover, Versailles, MO*

# CAROB SPANISH CREAM

1 T. unflavored gelatin
1/4 tsp. salt
1 T. honey
3 eggs, slightly beaten
2/3 cup powdered milk

1 1/2 cups water
1/4 cup carob powder, sifted
1 tsp. vanilla
3 T. honey

Mix gelatin, salt and honey. Add eggs. Mix powdered milk and water to make 2 cups. Add 1 cup milk and carob to gelatin mixture. Cook over low heat until gelatin is dissolved, about 8 minutes. Chill. Fold in and pour into mold or bowl.

*Hannah Kulp Family, Mt. Hermon, KY*

# CRACKER PUDDING

4 cups milk
2 eggs, separated
3/4 cup sugar
1 cup crushed soda crackers

1 cup shredded coconut
1 tsp. vanilla or coconut flavoring
3 T. sugar

Scald milk. Beat egg yolks and add sugar. Add gradually to milk, stirring constantly. Cook 1 minute. Add cracker crumbs and coconut. Stir till crumbs are soft and mixture is thickened. Remove from heat and add vanilla. Pour into buttered baking dish. Stiffly beat egg whites and 3 tablespoons sugar. Spread on top of pudding. Bake at 350° until meringue is golden brown.

*Ella Horning, Penn Yan, NY*

**An 8 ounce container of frozen whipped topping has approximately three cups of whipped topping.**

# NEAPOLITAN PUDDING

2 2/3 cups sugar
1/2 tsp. salt
1/2 cup flour
4 cups boiling water
2 cups crushed or chunk
    pineapple

1/2 cup maraschino cherries
4 bananas, cut in chunks
1 tsp. vanilla
1 tsp. almond extract
2 cups whipped topping or cream

Mix first 3 ingredients; stir into boiling water and cook till clear and thick. Add pineapple, cherries and bananas. Add vanilla and almond extract. Chill. Fold in whipped topping before serving.

*Edna Miller, Snover, MI*

# TROPICAL PUDDING

3 eggs, beaten
3 T. flour
3/4 cup sugar
1 cup water

20 oz. can pineapple
2 or 3 bananas
2 cups miniature marshmallows
1/2 cup nuts

Cook eggs, flour, sugar, water and juice from pineapple until thick. Let cool and mix in pineapple, bananas, marshmallows and nuts.

*Mrs. Clay Zimmerman, Paltinis, Romania*

# MARSHMALLOW PUDDING

2 cups milk
16 oz. marshmallows
4 cups whipped topping

Graham cracker crust crumbs
Blueberry or cherry pie filling

Melt marshmallows and milk over low heat. Cool and add whipped topping. Line bowl with graham cracker crust. Add marshmallow mixture. Top with pie filling.

*Rachel Newswanger, Barnett, MO*

# VANILLA PEACH PUDDING

2 pkg. (4 serving size) vanilla
   cook pudding
1 pkg. unflavored gelatin
1/4 cup cold water

3 cups whipped topping
4 cups fresh peaches, diced
1 cup sugar
3 T. instant clear jel

Prepare pudding according to directions. Moisten gelatin with 1/4 cup water and add to hot pudding. When it sets add whipped topping. Combine last 3 ingredients and put on pudding. You can make your own pudding.

*Mrs. Lester Weaver, Manheim, PA*

# ICE CREAM PUDDING

*Having friends over? Double the crust ingredients and triple the pudding ingredients to make enough for a 13x9 pan.*

50 Ritz crackers
1/4 cup butter or margarine
1 quart ice cream

1 pkg. (4 serving size) instant
   pudding, any flavor
3/4 cup milk

Line a 9" pie pan with crackers mixed with butter. Save some crumbs to sprinkle on top. Mix rest of ingredients and pour into pan. Sprinkle with crumbs.

*Sheryl Weaver, Goshen, IN*

# COCONUT ICE CREAM DESSERT

4 cups Rice Chex, crushed
1/2 cup butter or margarine
2 quarts vanilla ice cream,
   softened

2 pkg. (4 serving size) coconut
   instant pudding
1 cup milk
8 oz. frozen whipped topping

Mix cereal and butter; line a 13x9 cake pan, saving some crumbs to put on top. Combine ice cream, milk, and dry pudding. Pour into prepared pan. Top with thawed topping and remaining crumbs. Refrigerate, do not freeze.

*Mrs. John (Twila) Kulp, Mosinee, WI*

## OREO COOKIE DESSERT

1 lb. Oreo cookies, crushed
1/2 cup melted butter
16 oz. cream cheese, softened
1/3 cup sugar
1 tsp. vanilla

3 1/2 cups milk
1 pkg. (6 servings) instant vanilla
   pudding
Whipped topping or cream

Combine crumbs and butter. Reserve some to sprinkle on top; press remaining crumbs into a 13x9 pan. Beat cream cheese, sugar and vanilla until creamy. Gradually add milk. Add pudding and beat until smooth. Pour over cookie crust. Top with whipped topping. Sprinkle remaining crumbs on top. Chill.

*Katie Bontrager, Wakarusa, IN        Ina Slabaugh, Nappanee, IN*

## PISTACHIO DESSERT

20 oz. can crushed pineapple
3/4 cup cold water
3 oz. pkg. pistachio instant
   pudding

2 cups miniature marshmallows
8 oz. frozen whipped topping,
   thawed

Pour pineapple in bowl. Rinse can with 3/4 cup cold water; add to pineapple. Sprinkle in dry pudding. Stir lightly. Add marshmallows and whipped topping. Mix well. Chill several hours.

*Gladys Hoover, Sheldon, WI*

Make a quick and easy dessert by dissolving a 4-serving size package of gelatin in a cup of boiling water. Stir in 2 cups vanilla ice cream. Refrigerate until set. Top with whipped topping if you like.

## RAINBOW CAKE GELATIN DESSERT

3 oz. black raspberry gelatin
3 oz. lime gelatin
3 oz. lemon gelatin
3 oz. orange gelatin

3 oz. strawberry gelatin
5 cups boiling water
1 1/4 cups cold water
2 cups whipped topping or cream

Dissolve each kind of gelatin separately in 1 cup boiling water. Add 1/4 cup cold water to each. Chill black raspberry until very thick. Smoothly line sides of angel food cake pan with wax paper. Cut to extend 3" above pan. With mixer, beat black raspberry gelatin till fluffy, doubling volume. Spoon into pan. Chill until set, but not firm. Chill, whip and layer remaining flavors, letting each layer chill until set, but not firm. Refrigerate overnight. Loosen edges and slide out on plate. Frost with whipped topping.

*Mrs. Luke Hoover, Goshen, IN*

# BREAD PUDDING

2 1/2 cups milk
2 beaten eggs
2 cups bread cubes
1/2 cup brown sugar

1/2 tsp. cinnamon
1 tsp. vanilla
1/4 tsp. salt
1/2 cup raisins

Combine milk and eggs. Pour over bread cubes. Stir in remaining ingredients. Bake at 350° for 45 minutes or until knife comes out clean. Delicious with milk.

*Mrs. John (Twila) Kulp, Mosinee, WI*

# DATE PUDDING

1 cup sugar
1 egg, beaten
Pinch of salt
1 T. melted butter
1 tsp. soda

1 cup hot water
1 1/2 cups flour
1 lb. dates, cut fine
1/2 cup nuts
Sweetened whipped cream

Cream sugar, egg, salt and butter. Dissolve soda in water. Add. Stir in flour, dates and nuts. Bake at 350° until done. Cool; cut into bite-sized pieces. Fold in whipped cream.

*Mrs. Christian Weaver, Goshen, IN*

# STEAMED PUDDING

*This can be made without the egg, using only 2 cups wheat flour, 1 cup sorghum molasses instead of sugar, and milk instead of sour cream.*

1 egg
1 cup brown sugar
1 cup sour cream
1 tsp. soda, scant

3 1/2 cups whole wheat flour
1 cup raisins
1 tsp. cinnamon
Nuts, opt.

Mix and put in dish that fits in a kettle of boiling water. Cover with wax paper and steam 2 or 3 hours, or put in pressure cooker for 1 hour.

*Hannah Kulp Family, Mt. Hermon, KY*       *Mrs. Phares Shirk, Liberty, KY*

***Any day is worth the living, if we seek God in prayer,***
***Asking for His gentle guidance, leaving each day in His care.***

# CREAM PUFFS

1/2 cup butter
1 cup boiling water
1 cup flour

1/4 tsp. salt
4 eggs, unbeaten

Melt butter with water over low heat. Sift flour and salt; add all at once to water and butter. Stir vigorously until mixture forms a ball. Remove from heat and add eggs, one at a time, beating thoroughly after each one. Drop by tablespoon onto greased cookie sheet, about 2" apart. Bake at 425° for 30 minutes or until beads of moisture no longer appear on surface. Cool. Remove any sogginess from the center of the cream puffs before filling. Fill with your favorite pudding, ice cream or whipped cream just before serving.

*Mrs. Elias Martin, Goshen, IN*

# CREAM CHEESE DESSERTS

## CLASSIC CHEESECAKE

1 1/4 cups graham cracker
   crumbs
1/4 cup sugar
1 tsp. cinnamon
1/4 cup butter, melted

32 oz. cream cheese, softened
1 cup sugar
2 tsp. lemon juice
1 tsp. vanilla
4 eggs

Spray a 9" springform pan with nonstick cooking spray. Combine crumbs, sugar, cinnamon and butter. Press firmly into the bottom of the pan. Beat cream cheese just until smooth. Add sugar; beat 30 strokes. Scrape bowl and add lemon juice, vanilla and 1 egg. Add remaining eggs one at a time, beating until just blended. Scrape the bowl after each addition. Pour over crust. Bake at 300° for 75 to 80 minutes; until firm except the very center. Refrigerate at least 4 hours. Eat plain or top with fruit pie filling.

## LIGHT CHEESECAKE

1 pkg. unflavored gelatin
1/2 cup sugar
1 cup boiling water

16 oz. cream cheese, softened
1 tsp. vanilla or lemon extract
9-inch graham cracker crust

Mix gelatin with sugar. Add boiling water and stir until gelatin is completely dissolved. With mixer, beat in cream cheese and vanilla until smooth. Pour into crust. Chill until firm. Top with fresh or canned fruit or marble with 1/3 cup ice cream topping before chilling.

An envelope of unflavored gelatin contains a little over 2 teaspoons. As a rule, a tablespoon of bulk gelatin may be substituted when recipes call for a package or envelope of unflavored gelatin.

## CHOCOLATE CHEESECAKE

1 1/2 cups crushed crisp
  chocolate cookies
2 T. butter, melted
24 oz. cream cheese, softened
1 cup sugar

1 tsp. vanilla
8 squares semi-sweet baking
  chocolate, melted
3 eggs

Mix crushed cookies and butter; press firmly into a sprayed or greased 9-inch springform pan. Bake at 325° for 10 minutes. Beat cream cheese, sugar and vanilla until well blended. Add slightly cooled chocolate; mix well. Add eggs, 1 at a time, mixing on low after each addition, just until blended. Pour over crust. Bake at 325° for 45 to 55 minutes or until center is almost set. Cool before removing rim of pan. Refrigerate 4 hours or overnight. Eat plain or top with whipped topping and fruit.

If you don't have a springform pan just serve cheesecake from the pan. If you want to remove cheesecake, smoothly line a cake pan with foil, leaving enough foil on two sides to crunch up and use as handles. Cool cheesecake before removing from pan.

## LEMONY CHEESECAKE

*If two 13x9 pans of cheesecake is greater than your expectations, cut the recipe in half, using a small can of pineapple or some other garnish. For a more lemony taste add a tablespoon of lemon juice with the hot water.*

6 oz. lemon gelatin
2 cups hot water
4 cups graham cracker crumbs
1 cup butter or margarine, melted
16 oz. cream cheese

1 1/2 cups sugar
1/4 cup vanilla
2-12 oz. cans evaporated milk,
  chilled
20 oz. can crushed pineapple

Mix gelatin with hot water; set aside cool. Mix crumbs and butter; press into two 13x9 pans. Beat cream cheese, sugar and vanilla. Add to gelatin and beat. Whip cold milk (like whipped cream). Add to cheese mixture. Fold together and pour into pans. Garnish with crushed pineapple. Chill until set.

*Lizzie Hoover, Goshen, IN*

# ORANGE CHEESECAKE

*Any flavor gelatin may be used.*

14 graham crackers, crushed
1/4 cup butter
6 oz. orange gelatin
2 cups hot water

16 oz. cream cheese
1 cup sugar
1 tsp. vanilla
12 oz. can evaporated milk

Mix cracker crumbs and butter; press into a 13x9 pan. Bake at 350° for 15 minutes; cool. Dissolve gelatin in hot water; set aside to cool. Beat cream cheese, sugar and vanilla. Whip evaporated milk. Add cooled gelatin and cream cheese mixture. Pour over crust and chill.

# BLUEBERRY CHEESECAKE

2 pkg. graham crackers
3/4 cup butter, softened
3 small eggs
1/2 cup honey
2 T. lemon juice
8 oz. cream cheese
3 cups cottage cheese
2 tsp. vanilla

4 cups fresh or frozen blueberries
2 cups water
1 cup sugar
1/2 cup honey
1/2 cup clear jel
2 T. lemon juice
2 cups blueberries

Crush crackers; mix with butter and press firmly and evenly into a 13x9 pan. Combine eggs, honey, lemon juice, cream cheese, cottage cheese and vanilla in blender. Blend. Pour this over crumbs. Bake at 300° for 35 to 40 minutes. When done sprinkle with cinnamon. In a saucepan combine 4 cups blueberries, water, sugar and honey; cook 5 minutes. Add enough water to clear jel to make a paste; add to blueberry mixture. Cook until thick enough for bubbles to "pouff". Stir in remaining blueberries; cool. Pour over cheese mixture. Serve with sweetened whipped cream.

*Mrs. William Kilmer, California, MO*

# BLUEBERRY DELIGHT

2 cups graham cracker crumbs
1/2 cup butter or margarine,
   melted
2 cups powdered sugar

8 oz. cream cheese, softened
3 cups whipped cream or topping
Blueberry pie filling

Mix cracker crumbs with butter and press into a serving dish or a 13x9 pan. Mix powdered sugar with cream cheese; fold in whipped cream or whipped topping. Top with blueberry pie filling. Any kind of pie filling may be used.

*Mary Ann Newswanger, Fortuna, MO*

# CHERRY CHEESECAKE

*For raspberry cheesecake, dissolve 6 ounces raspberry gelatin in 2 cups of boiling water. Stir in two to four cups raspberries. When mixture starts to set, spoon it over cream cheese filling. Chill until set. Any fruit may be used.*

| | |
|---|---|
| 24 graham cracker squares | 1 cup powdered sugar |
| 1/2 cup butter, melted | 4 cups whipped cream or topping |
| 1/2 cup sugar | 1 tsp. vanilla |
| 1 tsp. cinnamon | 1 T. lemon juice, opt. |
| 8 to 16 oz. cream cheese | 1 to 2 cans cherry pie filling |

Crush crackers; add butter, sugar and cinnamon. Press into a 13x9 pan. Mix softened cream cheese, powdered sugar and vanilla together. Fold in whipped cream and pour onto crust. Top with pie filling. Chill.

**If you don't have graham crackers you can make a crust by combining 1 1/2 cups flour, 1/2 cup powdered sugar, and 3/4 cup soft butter. Press into a 13x9 pan and bake at 350° for 15 minutes.**

# BAKED CHERRY CHEESECAKE

*For a different crust, combine 1 /14 cups flour, 1 cup chopped walnuts, 1/2 cup brown sugar, 1/2 cup coconut and butter. Bake at 350° for 15 minutes. Add filling and bake.*

| | |
|---|---|
| 2 cups graham cracker crumbs | 1 cup sugar |
| 3/4 cup butter, melted | 2 eggs |
| 1/4 cup sugar | 2 cans cherry pie filling |
| 16 oz. cream cheese | |

Combine crumbs, butter and 1/4 cup sugar. Press into a 13x9 pan. Beat together cream cheese, 1 cup sugar and eggs. Pour onto crust. Bake at 375° for 15 minutes. Cool. Spread pie filling on top.

*Laura Kulp, Stratford, WI*

# PETITE CHERRY CHEESECAKES

| | |
|---|---|
| 16 oz. cream cheese, softened | 1 tsp. vanilla |
| 3/4 cup sugar | 24 vanilla wafers |
| 2 eggs | 21 oz. can cherry pie filling |
| 1 T. lemon juice | |

Beat first 5 ingredients until light and fluffy. Line small muffin tins with paper baking cups. Place a wafer in the bottom of each one. Fill the cups 2/3 full with cream cheese mixture. Bake at 375° for 15 to 20 minutes or until set. Remove from oven and top each with approximately one tablespoon of pie filling. Chill.

*Mrs. Isaac Newswanger, Jr., Carson City, MI*

# FOUR LAYER DESSERT

*Try using chocolate pudding and adding 3/4 cup peanut butter with the cream cheese.*

1 1/2 cups flour
3/4 cup butter
1/2 to 1 cup chopped pecans
8 oz. cream cheese, softened
8 oz. tub frozen whipped topping
   or 3 cups whipped cream

1 cup powdered sugar
2 pkg. (3.4 oz.) butterscotch,
   chocolate or lemon pudding
3 cups cold milk
Whipped topping or cream
Chopped nuts, opt.

Combine flour, butter and chopped pecans; press into a 13x9 pan. Bake at 350° for 15 minutes. Combine cream cheese, topping, and powdered sugar; spread on cooled crust. Prepare pudding with milk and spread on second layer. Top with more whipped topping. Sprinkle with chopped nuts.

*Mrs. Vernon Kurtz, Ewing, IL   Mrs. Elias Martin, Goshen, IN   Alice Moser, Tyrone, NM*
*Ruth Ramer Strumland, Harrizon, AR   Rachel Weirich, Stone Lake, WI*

# BERRY PIZZA

2 cups flour
1/2 cup powdered sugar
3/4 cup butter
8 oz. cream cheese, softened
14 oz. sweetened condensed milk
1/2 cup sugar

2 T. cornstarch
1/2 cup water
3 oz. raspberry gelatin
4 cups raspberries, blueberries,
   or blackberries

Combine flour, powdered sugar and butter; press into a 14" pizza pan. Bake at 350° for 10 minutes. Mix cream cheese and sweetened condensed milk and spread on cooled crust. Combine sugar and cornstarch; add water. Mix well then cook until thickened. Stir in dry gelatin. Cool slightly; add berries. Carefully spread on filling. Garnish with whipped topping, if desired. Chill.

# FRUIT PIZZA I

1/4 cup butter
1/4 shortening
3/4 cup sugar
1/8 tsp. salt
1 egg
1 tsp. cream of tartar
1 1/3 cups flour

1/2 tsp. soda
8 oz. cream cheese
1/2 cup powdered sugar
1/4 cup whipping cream
1 T. cornstarch
15 oz. can pineapple, reserve
   juice

Cream shortenings and sugar. Add next 5 ingredients. Press into pizza pan. Bake 8 to 10 minutes. Mix cream cheese and powdered sugar. Whip cream and fold in; spread over crust. Cook pineapple juice and cornstarch. Arrange pineapple chunks over cream cheese mixture. Top with glaze and chill.

*Elaine Zimmerman, Versailles, MO*

# FRUIT PIZZA II

*Use any combination of fresh fruit or canned pineapple.*

| | |
|---|---|
| 1/2 cup sugar | 1/3 cup sugar |
| 1/2 cup powdered sugar | 1 tsp. vanilla |
| 1/2 cup butter | 3 cups fresh blueberries, washed |
| 1/2 cup cooking oil | and drained |
| 1 egg | 2 kiwi fruit, peeled and sliced thin |
| 2 cups plus 2 T. flour | 1/2 cup water |
| 1/2 tsp. cream of tartar | 1/2 cup orange juice |
| 1/2 tsp. soda | 2 T. lemon juice |
| 1/2 tsp. vanilla | 1/4 cup sugar |
| 8 oz. cream cheese | 1 to 2 T. cornstarch |

Mix first 9 ingredients together to make crust. Press into two greased 12" pizza pans. Build up a slight rim around the edge. Bake at 350° for 10 to 12 minutes. Cool. Carefully remove one crust to a round platter. (Freeze the other crust for later use.) Mix cream cheese, 1/3 cup sugar and vanilla; spread on crust. Spread fruit on in decorative pattern. Refrigerate. Combine last 5 ingredients and bring to a boil; boil 1 minute. Cool. Spread over fruit layer. Refrigerate.

*Kathleen Ramer, New Paris, IN        Connie Rodes, Milford, IN*

# FRUIT DESSERTS

## QUICK BAKED APPLES

| | |
|---|---|
| 2 large baking apples | 4 T. corn syrup |
| 2 T. butter | Cinnamon |

Cut apples in half and core. Don't peel. Put halves in a glass dish. Place 1/2 tablespoon of butter in the center of each apple half. Spoon 1 tablespoon of corn syrup into each half. Sprinkle with cinnamon. Cover with plastic wrap. Microwave on high for 4 minutes. Spoon syrup over them after 2 minutes. Let stand 2 minutes before serving. Little red cinnamon candies give added flavor.

## APPLE COBBLER

| | |
|---|---|
| 8 large baking apples | 1/2 cup sugar |
| 1 cup sugar | 2 tsp. baking powder |
| 2 T. flour | 1/2 tsp. salt |
| 1 1/2 tsp. cinnamon | 1/2 tsp. cinnamon |
| 1/4 tsp. nutmeg | 6 T. soft butter |
| 2 cups flour | 1 cup milk |

Peel and slice apples. Mix next 4 ingredients and toss with apples. Put into a 13x9 pan. Combine dry ingredients; work in butter. Stir in milk. Drop by spoonfuls onto apples. Bake at 375° approximately 45 minutes.

## APPLE CRISP

8 large baking apples
1/4 cup water
1 1/2 cups brown sugar
1 1/2 cups oatmeal

1/2 cup flour
1 tsp. cinnamon
1/2 cup butter, melted

Peel apples. Slice into a 13x9 pan; add water. Combine dry ingredients and add butter. Spread crumbs evenly over apples. Bake at 375° for 40 to 45 minutes.

*Mrs. Ray (Elsie) Hoover, Stratford, WI*

## OLD-FASHIONED APPLE DUMPLINGS

6 medium baking apples
2 cups flour
2 1/2 tsp. baking powder
1/2 tsp. salt
2/3 cup butter or margarine

1/2 cup milk
2 cups brown sugar
2 cups water
1/4 tsp. cinnamon
1/4 cup butter

Pare and core apples. Leave whole. Mix flour, baking powder and salt. Cut in butter until crumbly. Add milk and mix lightly, working dough together. Roll dough into 6 squares. Place an apple on each. Fill cavity in apple with sugar and cinnamon. Wrap dough around apple. Place dumplings in baking pan. Combine remaining ingredients, except butter. Cook 5 minutes. Add butter. Pour sauce over dumplings. Bake at 375° for 35 to 40 minutes. Serve hot with milk. Dough can also be rolled out in one piece; sprinkled with chopped apples, and rolled up like a jelly roll. Cut slices 1 1/4 inch thick; place in pan and cover with sauce.

*Mrs. James Kulp, Unity, WI*

## DUMPLINGS IN APPLE SAUCE

1 1/2 cups corn syrup
1 cup water
2 T. butter
3 medium apples, sliced
1/2 tsp. cinnamon
1 cup flour

2 tsp. baking powder
1/4 tsp. salt
2 tsp. sugar
1/4 tsp. nutmeg
2 T. milk
1 egg

Bring first 5 ingredients to a boil. Mix remaining ingredients and drop spoonfuls into boiling sauce. Cover tightly and cook 20 minutes without removing cover.

*Edna Miller, Snover, MI*

# APPLE FRITTERS

Apples
1 cup flour
1 1/2 tsp. baking powder
1/2 tsp. salt

2 T. sugar
1 egg, beaten
1/2 cup plus 1 T. milk

Peel and core apples; slice into 1/4-inch thick rings. Make batter of remaining ingredients. Dip apples in batter and deep-fry in hot oil. Drain and roll in sugar and cinnamon or in powdered sugar. Best if eaten soon after frying.

*Edna Miller, Snover, MI*

# APPLE PIZZA

2 cups flour
1 tsp. salt
3/4 cup shortening
4 to 5 T. cold water
6 to 7 apples, peeled and sliced
1/2 cup sugar

1 tsp. cinnamon
1/4 tsp. nutmeg
3/4 cup flour
1/2 cup brown sugar
1/2 cup butter

Mix flour and salt; work in shortening; gradually add water. Press dough into a pizza pan. Arrange apple slices in circles on crust, overlapping edges. Sprinkle with sugar, cinnamon and nutmeg. Mix remaining ingredients; sprinkle over apples. Bake at 450° for 35 minutes. Apple pie filling can also be used.

# BLUEBERRY COBBLER

*For peach cobbler, substitute sliced peaches for blueberries. Add a little cinnamon with cornstarch.*

3/4 cup sugar
2 T. cornstarch
6 cups fresh blueberries
1 T. lemon juice
1 1/2 cups flour

1/2 cup sugar
2 tsp. baking powder
1/2 tsp. salt
1/3 cup butter
3/4 cup milk

Cook first 4 ingredients, stirring constantly, until mixture thickens and boils. Boil and stir 1 minute. Pour into a 13x9 pan. Combine dry ingredients; work in butter until crumbly. Stir in milk. Drop by spoonfuls onto blueberries. Sprinkle dough with sugar. Bake at 400° approximately 30 minutes.

*The secret of peace is the constant referral of all our anxieties to God.*

# CHERRY COBBLER I

6 cups frozen tart cherries
1/2 cup sugar
1 cup sugar
1/4 cup shortening
1 egg

2 cups flour
2 tsp. baking powder
1 cup milk
1 tsp. vanilla

Preheat oven to 350°. Put cherries in a 13x9 or 8x8 pan; sprinkle with 1/2 cup sugar. Put in oven to thaw. Cream sugar and shortening; beat in egg. (If using cooking oil just mix everything.) Add flour and baking powder, then milk and vanilla. Beat until smooth and pour over cherries. Bake at 350° approximately 30 minutes. Peaches can also be used.

*Mrs. Norman Burkholder, Mertztown, PA*

# CHERRY COBBLER II

4 cups tart cherries (frozen with
    1/2 sugar)
2 cups water
1 cup sugar
3 T. tapioca
2 T. lemon juice
2 T. butter or margarine
1/3 cup butter or margarine

1 cup sugar
2 eggs
1 1/2 cups flour
2 tsp. baking powder
1/4 tsp. salt
1/2 cup milk
1 tsp. vanilla

Mix first 6 ingredients in a 13x9 pan. Cream 1/3 cup butter and sugar; add unbeaten eggs and beat thoroughly. Combine dry ingredients; add alternately with milk and vanilla. Stir just enough to blend ingredients. Pour over cherry mixture. Bake at 375° for 30 minutes.

*Mrs. William (Lena) Kilmer, California, MO*

# CHERRY PIZZA

*To make rhubarb pizza, use 3 to 4 cups chopped rhubarb and strawberry gelatin instead of cherries and cherry gelatin.*

1 cup flour
1/4 cup sugar
1 tsp. baking powder
1/4 tsp. salt
2 T. cooking oil
1 egg

2 T. milk
3 cup cherries
3 oz. cherry gelatin
1/2 cup sugar
1/2 cup flour
1/2 cup butter

Mix first 4 ingredients; add oil and egg beaten in milk. Press into pan. Put cherries on crust and sprinkle with gelatin. Combine remaining ingredients and crumble over cherries. Bake at 350° for 45 minutes. Good with ice cream.

*Mrs. Levon Martin, Goshen, IN*     *Mrs. Clarence Martin, Snover, MI*

# CHERRY CRUNCH TOPPINGS

*Choose one of the following toppings. Sprinkle over a can or two of cherry pie filling—or thickened canned cherries. Any pie filling can be used.*

**TOPPING ONE**
1 cup flour
1 cup brown sugar

1/8 tsp. salt
1 cup oatmeal
1/2 cup butter

**TOPPING TWO**
2 1/2 cups Rice Chex, crushed
1/2 cup flour

1/2 cup brown sugar
1/4 tsp. cinnamon
1/4 cup butter

**TOPPING THREE**
3/4 cup flour
3/4 cup oatmeal
3/4 cup brown sugar
1/2 cup chopped nuts

1 tsp. cinnamon
1/2 tsp. soda
1/4 tsp. salt
1/2 cup butter

Combine dry ingredients; cut in butter. Pat half of crumbs into a greased 8x8 pan. Pour thickened fruit over crumbs. Spread remaining crumbs on top. Or put cherries in a 13x9 and top with crumbs. Bake at 350° for 25 to 30.

*Anna Mae Hoover, Reinholds, PA     Mrs. Isaac Kulp, Millersburg, IN     Mrs. Lester Weaver, Manheim, PA*

# STEAMED CHERRY PUDDING

1 egg
1 cup sugar
1 T. melted butter
1/2 tsp. salt
1 1/2 cups flour

1 1/2 tsp. baking powder
1/4 tsp. soda
1/2 cup milk
1 cup tart cherries, drained

Combine all the ingredients and steam for 45 minutes.

*Mrs. Ernest Newswanger, Kutztown, PA*

# GROUND CHERRY DESSERT

1 quart canned ground cherries
2 T. Clearjel, rounded
1/2 cup sugar
1 T. butter

1 box butter pecan cake mix
1 cup oatmeal
1/2 cup butter

Drain ground cherries. Combine Clearjel and sugar with a little juice to make a runny paste. Heat juice and add thickening; cook and stir until it thickens; add butter and ground cherries. Pour into 13x9 pan. Combine cake mix, oatmeal and butter. Sprinkle over ground cherries. Bake at 350° until lightly browned.

*Alta Martin, Goshen, IN*

# EASY FRUIT SALAD DESSERT

1/2 cup sugar
2 T. cornstarch
20 oz. can pineapple chunks,
    reserve juice
1 T. lemon juice

1 T. grated orange peel
1/3 cup orange juice
11 oz. can mandarin oranges
2 medium apples, diced
2 bananas, sliced

Combine sugar and cornstarch in saucepan. Blend in 3/4 cup pineapple juice, lemon juice, orange juice and peel. Cook over medium heat, stirring constantly, until mixture thickens and boils. Boil and stir one minute. While hot pour over combined fruit. Refrigerate, uncovered, several hours or overnight.

*Rita Martin, Nappanee, IN*

# FRUITY KOOL-AID DESSERT

*Adding one part cottage cheese to two parts fruit can turn this into a salad.*

1 pkg. orange Kool-Aid
1 cup sugar
2 quarts water or fruit juice
5 heaping T. Clearjel

6 oz. orange gelatin
1 to 2 quarts fresh, canned or
    frozen fruit
Whipped cream or topping, opt.

Cook first four ingredients until clear; add dry gelatin. Cool; add any combination of fruit. Any flavor Kool-Aid or gelatin may be used. This will seem runny until it is completely cold. Top with cream if desired.

*Sarah Imhoff, Sheridan, MI   Mary Ann Martin, Sauk Centre, MN   Charlene Ramer, Goshen, IN*
*Kathleen Ramer, New Paris, IN   Linda Hoover Shaum, Roann, IN   Mrs. Carlton Zimmerman, Brooten, MN*

# LEMON CRUMBLE

3/4 cup butter or margarine
1/2 cup sugar
1 3/4 cups crushed soda crackers
3/4 cup flour
1 tsp. baking powder
1/2 cup coconut
1 T. milk

1 egg
1 T. butter
1 cup sugar
2 1/2 T. cornstarch
1/2 cup lemon juice or to taste
2 cups water

Mix butter and sugar; add crackers. Combine flour and baking powder. Add to first mixture. Add coconut and milk; mix well. Press 3/4 of crumbs into a 13x9 pan. Cook remaining ingredients; cool slightly. Pour or spread on crumbs. Top with reserved crumbs. Bake at 350° until golden brown.

*Ethel Hoover, Goshen, IN*

# BAKED PEARS

**4 or 5 very ripe pears, sliced thick**  
**Cinnamon**  
**1/4 cup brown sugar**

**1 cup cream**  
**1 T. flour**

Place pears in a 9x9 pan. Sprinkle lightly with cinnamon. Mix sugar, cream and flour. Pour over pears. Bake at 350° for 30 minutes.

*Donna Herr, Nappanee, IN*

# PEAR CRISP

*To make peach crisp use 6 cups fresh or canned, drained peaches. Delete raisins.*

**5 ripe pears**  
**2 T. lemon juice**  
**3/4 cup raisins**  
**3/4 cup oatmeal**  
**2/3 cup flour**  
**2/3 cup brown sugar**

**6 T. soft butter**  
**1/2 cup chopped pecans or**  
**walnuts, opt.**  
**1 tsp. cinnamon**  
**1/4 tsp. nutmeg**

Peel and core pears. Slice 1/2-inch thick. Toss with lemon juice. Place pears and raisins in a 13x9 pan. Mix remaining ingredients until crumbly. Sprinkle evenly over pears. Bake at 375° for 25 to 30 minutes or until pears are tender.

# PUMPKIN DESSERT

*Spice this up with applesauce or spice cake mixes.*

**1 tsp. cinnamon**  
**1/2 tsp. ginger**  
**1/4 tsp. cloves**  
**1/4 tsp. nutmeg**  
**16 oz. can pumpkin**

**1 1/2 cups sugar**  
**4 eggs**  
**12 oz. can evaporated milk**  
**1 yellow cake mix**  
**1/2 cup butter or margarine**

Mix first 8 ingredients; pour into a 13x9 pan. Sprinkle dry cake mix on top. Melt butter and drizzle over cake mix. Bake at 350° for 30 to 40 minutes. Top with whipped cream or ice cream, if desired.

*Lizzie Hoover, Goshen, IN     Mrs. Luke Hoover, Goshen, IN     Esther Martin, Decker, MI*

***When we get to the place where there is nothing left but God, we find that God is enough.***

## PUMPKIN PIE SQUARES

1 cup flour
1/2 cup quick oatmeal
1/2 cup brown sugar
1/2 cup butter
2 cups pumpkin
3/4 cup buttermilk or milk
2 eggs
3/4 cup sugar

1/2 tsp salt
1 tsp. cinnamon
1/2 tsp. ginger
1/4 tsp. cloves
1/2 cup brown sugar
2 T. butter
1/2 cup chopped nuts

Mix flour, oatmeal, 1/2 cup brown sugar and 1/2 cup butter until crumbly. Press into 13x9 pan. Bake at 350° for 15 minutes. Combine pumpkin, milk, eggs, sugar, salt and spices; beat well. Pour into crust. Bake 20 minutes. Mix remaining ingredients; sprinkle over bars. Bake another 20 minutes or until set.

*Cretora Hilty, Elida, OH     Mrs. James Kulp, Unity, WI*

**Pumpkins, like other orange vegetables, are a great source of beta carotene. They are also a good source of vitamin C and fiber and have only 40 calories in a half cup serving.**

## PUMPKIN NUT ROLL

*For a fluffier filling cook together 1 cup flour and 1 3/4 cups milk until thickened. Cool, then beat in 8 ounces of cream cheese, 1/2 cup of shortening, 1 cup powdered sugar, 1 teaspoon vanilla and 1/2 teaspoon of salt.*

3 eggs, beaten 5 minutes
1 cup sugar
2/3 cup pumpkin
1 tsp. lemon juice
3/4 cup flour
1 tsp. baking powder
1/2 tsp. salt
2 tsp. cinnamon

1 tsp. ginger
1/2 tsp. nutmeg
1 cup chopped walnuts
6 oz. cream cheese
1/4 cup butter
1 cup powdered sugar
1/2 tsp. vanilla

Add sugar to beaten eggs; stir in pumpkin and lemon juice. Combine flour, baking powder, salt and spices. Fold into egg mixture. Pour into greased 15x10 jelly roll pan. Sprinkle nuts on top. Bake at 375° for 15 minutes. Turn onto clean tea towel sprinkled generously with powdered sugar. Roll towel and cake together from widest side; cool. Beat remaining ingredients well. Unroll pumpkin cake and spread with filling. Roll back up, minus the towel, of course. Cool before slicing.

*Mrs. Lavon Martin, Goshen, IN     Velma Martin, Nappanee, IN     Rachel Ramer, Cazenovia, WI*
*Sheryl Weaver, Goshen IN*

# PUMPKIN TORTE

24 graham cracker squares
1/3 cup sugar
1/2 cup butter
2 eggs, beaten
3/4 cup sugar
8 oz. cream cheese

2 cups mashed pumpkin
2 pkg. (4-serving size) instant
  vanilla pudding
3/4 cup milk
8 oz. tub frozen whipped topping,
  thawed

Crush crackers; mix with 1/3 cup sugar and butter. Press into a 13x9 pan. Mix beaten eggs, sugar, and cream cheese. Pour over crust. Bake at 350° for 20 minutes. Cool. Combine pumpkin, pudding, and milk; mix well. Fold in one cup whipped topping. Spread over cream cheese layer. Top with remaining whipped topping, about two cups.

*Mrs. Levon Martin, Goshen, IN*

# RASPBERRY DELIGHT

2-10 oz. pkg. frozen red
  raspberries
8 oz. miniature marshmallows

1/2 cup sugar
1 cup chopped nuts
2 cups whipping cream

Thaw berries; drain juice. Add marshmallows, sugar and nuts. Refrigerate 30 minutes; stir. Whip cream and fold in.

*Elizabeth B. Hoover, Fort Wayne, IN*

Though rhubarb is included with the fruit desserts, it is actually a vegetable. Because the leaves are poisonous, only rhubarb stalks are used in cooking. Rhubarb should not be prepared in aluminum pot because acid in the rhubarb causes both the pot and the rhubarb to darken.

# RHUBARB CRUNCH

1 cup flour
3/4 cup oatmeal
1 cup brown sugar
1/2 cup butter, melted
1 tsp. cinnamon

4 cups diced rhubarb
1 cup sugar
1 cup water
2 T. cornstarch
1 tsp. vanilla

Mix first 5 ingredients until crumbly. Press half of the crumbs in a 9-inch cake pan. Spread rhubarb over crumbs. Cook remaining ingredients until clear. Pour over rhubarb. Top with remaining crumbs. Bake at 350° for 1 hour.

*Nancy Kilmer, California, MO*    *Pauline Kulp, Stratford, WI*

# RHUBARB DESSERT

4 cups diced rhubarb
1 cup sugar
3 oz. strawberry gelatin

1 box yellow cake mix
2 cups water

Layer ingredients in a 13x9 pan in order given. DO NOT STIR. Bake at 350° for 50 minutes. Serve warm with ice cream or milk.

*Esther Burkholder, New Providence, PA*     *Mrs. Isaac Martin, Martinsburg. PA*

# RHUBARB MERINGUE SQUARES

1 cup flour
1 1/2 tsp. sugar
1/2 cup butter
1 1/2 cups sugar
2 T. cornstarch
3 cups diced rhubarb

1/2 cup milk
1/4 cup orange juice
3 egg yolks, beaten
3 egg whites
1/4 tsp. cream of tartar
3 T. sugar

Mix flour, 1 1/2 tsp. sugar and butter; press into a 10x7 pan. Bake at 350° for 15 minutes or till brown. Cook and stir 1 1/2 cup sugar, cornstarch, rhubarb, milk, and juice over medium heat until it thickens and rhubarb is tender. Remove from heat. Stir small amount of hot mixture into egg yolks, then add to cooked rhubarb. Return to heat until filling just begins to boil. Cool then put into crust. To make meringue beat together egg whites, cream of tartar and sugar until foamy and stiff. Spread on rhubarb. Brown in a 350° oven for 12 to 15 minutes.

*Miriam Hoover, Goshen, IN*

# RHUBARB TAPIOCA

4 1/2 cups water
4 cups diced rhubarb
2 cups sugar

1/2 cup Minute tapioca
3 oz. red gelatin

Bring all but gelatin to a boil. Stir in gelatin. Cook until rhubarb falls apart. Cool. Eat plain or swirl with whipped cream or whipped topping.

*The one concern of the devil is to keep Christians from praying.*
*He fears nothing from prayerless studies, prayerless work,*
*and prayerless religion. He laughs at our toil, mocks at our wisdom,*
*but trembles when we pray.*
*Samuel Chadwick*

# RHUBARB TORTE

1 cup graham cracker crumbs
2 T. sugar
1/4 cup butter, melted
1 cup sugar
3 T. cornstarch
4 cups diced rhubarb

1/2 cup water
Several drops food coloring
1/2 cup whipping cream
1 1/2 cups miniature
marshmallows
3 3/4 oz. instant vanilla pudding

Mix first 3 ingredients; press into a serving dish or pan, reserving some crumbs for the top. Mix sugar and cornstarch. Stir in rhubarb and water. Cook and stir until thickened; reduce heat and cook 2 to 3 minutes. Add food coloring. Spread on crust. Cool. Whip cream; fold in marshmallows. Spoon on rhubarb. Prepare pudding as directed; spread on top. Sprinkle with reserved crumbs.

*Mrs. Isaac Newswanger, Jr., Carson City, MI*

# STRAWBERRY CHIFFON SQUARES

*If you don't have wafers make a crust using 1 1/2 cups flour, 1/2 cup powdered sugar and 3/4 cup butter. Bake at 350° for 15 minutes before adding filling. Cool.*

1/2 cup butter, melted
2 cups crushed vanilla wafers
3 oz. strawberry gelatin
3/4 cup boiling water
14 oz. sweetened condensed milk

1 1/2 cups frozen strawberries in
syrup, thawed
3 to 4 cups miniature
marshmallows
1 cup whipping cream

Mix butter and wafer crumbs; press into a 13x9 pan. In a large bowl dissolve gelatin in boiling water; stir in sweetened condensed milk and undrained strawberries. Fold in marshmallows. Whip cream and fold in. Pour on top of crumbs; chill 2 hours. Garnish with whipped cream and strawberries, if desired.

# STRAWBERRY PRETZEL DESSERT

2 cups crushed pretzels
3 T. sugar
3/4 cups butter, melted
8 oz. cream cheese, softened
1/2 cup powdered sugar

8 oz. tub thawed whipped topping
2 cups miniature marshmallows
6 oz. strawberry gelatin
2 1/2 cups boiling water
10 oz. pkg. frozen strawberries

Mix finely crushed pretzel crumbs, sugar and butter; press into a 13x9 pan. Bake at 350° for 15 minutes. Cool. Mix cream cheese and powdered sugar. Fold in whipped topping. Add marshmallows; spread on cooled crust. Dissolve gelatin in warm water; stir in strawberries. Chill until slightly thickened. Spread over cream cheese layer. Chill several hours or overnight.

# STRAWBERRY TORTE

2 cups flour
1/2 cup brown sugar
1 cup chopped nuts
1 cup butter, melted
8 oz. cream cheese

1 cup powdered sugar
1 tsp. vanilla
2 cups whipped cream or topping
1 box strawberry Danish dessert

Combine first 4 ingredients; press into a 13x9 pan. Bake at 400° for 15 minutes. Cool slightly, then crumble crust and repress lightly into pan. Combine cream cheese, powdered sugar, vanilla, and whipped cream. Pour over cooled crust. Make Danish dessert as directed on the box; pour over cream cheese layer. Chill 12 hours. Serve in squares.

*Esther Martin, Decker, MI*

# STRAWBERRY LONG CAKE

3/4 cup sugar
4 cups fresh strawberries, sliced
2 cups flour
4 tsp. baking powder
6 T. sugar
3/4 tsp. salt

1/3 cup butter or margarine
2/3 cup milk
1 large egg
1/2 cup butter, melted
1/2 cup brown sugar
5 T. flour

Sprinkle 3/4 cup sugar over strawberries. Let set at room temperature. Mix next 4 ingredients. Cut in 1/3 cup butter. Add milk and egg. Spread into a greased 13x9 pan. Pour berries and juice evenly over top. Mix melted butter with brown sugar and flour; dribble over berries. Bake at 375° for 35 minutes. Serve warm with milk and additionally strawberries. Good cold too.

*Vera Fox, Memphis, MO*

# STRAWBERRY SHORTCAKE

2 eggs
1 cup sugar
1 cup milk
1 tsp. vanilla

2 1/2 cups flour
2 tsp. baking powder
1/2 tsp. salt
2 T. melted butter

Beat eggs; add sugar, milk and vanilla. Combine and add dry ingredients; add butter. Bake at 375°for 25 to 30 minutes. Serve with strawberries and milk.

*Mrs. James Kulp, Unity, WI*

# SHORTCAKE

*To make individual shortcakes, bake batter in muffin tins.*

| | |
|---|---|
| 1 1/2 cups sugar | 1 tsp. cream of tartar |
| 1/2 cup butter | 1 tsp. soda |
| 2 eggs | 1 tsp. salt |
| 3 cups flour | 1 1/2 cups milk |

Mix sugar and butter; add eggs.  Mix dry ingredients with flour; add milk and flour alternately to egg mixture.  Bake at 350° till done.  Serve warm with milk and fruit.

*Mrs. Isaac Kulp, Millersburg, IN*

# CORN WHEAT SHORTCAKE

| | |
|---|---|
| 2 eggs | 2 tsp. soda |
| 1 cup brown sugar | 1 tsp. cream of tartar |
| 1/2 cup shortening | 3 cups whole wheat flour |
| 3 cups milk or sour milk | 3 cups cornmeal |

Cream eggs and sugar.  Melt shortening and add along with milk.  Combine dry ingredients and mix with first mixture.  Bake in a greased pan at 350° for 45 minutes or until done.  A 3/4 cup of sour cream can be substituted for shortening.

*Mrs. Phares Shirk, Liberty, KY*

**God judges what we give by what we keep.**

# FROZEN
# DESSERTS

Elsie
Hoover

# FRUITY AND CREAMY FROZEN DESSERTS

## FRUIT SLUSH

*For a bigger batch use 20 ounces of pineapple and 12 ounces orange juice. Adding a cup of lemon-lime soda gives it a different twist.*

3 cups water
2 cups sugar
6 bananas, sliced or cubed

8 oz. can crushed pineapple
6 oz. can orange juice
   concentrate

Boil water and sugar. Cool. Add remaining ingredients. Freeze, then serve partially thawed. This can be frozen in plastic thermos bottles for school lunches.

*Anna Zimmerman, Decker, MI*

## FROZEN PINEAPPLE DELIGHT

10 oz. pkg. marshmallows
1 cup milk
15 oz. can crushed pineapple

2 cups whipped topping
1 cup pecans
1/3 lb. graham crackers

Melt marshmallows with milk over low heat; cool. Add pineapple, whipped topping and pecans. Crush crackers; put half of crumbs into a 13x9 pan. Pour on pineapple mixture. Sprinkle with remaining crumbs. Freeze.

## LEMON FREEZE DESSERT

3 cups graham cracker crumbs
2/3 cup butter, melted
1/3 cup sugar
21 oz. can lemon pie filling

14 oz. sweetened condensed milk
1/2 cup lemon juice
1 can fruit cocktail
8 oz. tub thawed whipped topping

Mix cracker crumbs, butter and sugar. Reserve 1/3 cup for top. Press remaining crumbs into a 13x9 pan. Mix next 4 ingredients. Pour into crumb lined pan. Top with whipped topping and sprinkle with reserved crumbs. Freeze. Cut into squares to serve.

*Mrs. Elam Hoover, Versailles, MO*

***God hears the heart without words—but never the words without heart.***

# BANANA SPLIT DESSERT

5 cups graham cracker crumbs
2/3 cup butter, melted
2 to 3 bananas
1/2 gallon Neapolitan ice cream
1 cup chopped nuts
1 cup chocolate chips

1/2 cup butter
2 cups powdered sugar
12 oz. can evaporated milk or
    1 1/2 cups whole milk
1 tsp. vanilla
2 cups whipping cream

Mix crumbs and 2/3 cup butter; reserve 1 cup. Press the rest into a 15x11 pan. Slice bananas crosswise and layer over crust. Cut ice cream 1/2-inch thick and place over bananas. Sprinkle nuts over ice cream. Freeze until firm. Melt chocolate chips and 1/2 cup butter; add powdered sugar and milk. Cook until thick and smooth, stirring constantly. Remove from heat; add vanilla. Cool, then pour over ice cream. Freeze until firm. Whip cream until stiff. Spread over chocolate layer. Top with reserved crumbs. Freeze. Remove from freezer about 10 minutes before serving. Half of this recipe makes a 13x9 pan.

*Mrs. Cleon (Carol) Bauman, Elmira, Ont. Canada*

# FROZEN PUMPKIN DESSERT

3 cups crushed graham crackers
2/3 cup butter, melted
1/2 cup sugar
2 cups mashed cooked pumpkin
1 cup brown sugar

1/2 tsp. salt
1/2 tsp. nutmeg
2 tsp. cinnamon
1/2 gallon soft vanilla ice cream

Mix first 3 ingredients; press into a 13x9 pan. Blend remaining ingredients, except ice cream. Stir in ice cream and pour onto crust. Freeze. Cut into squares and serve plain or with whipped topping.

*Karen Weaver, Milford, IN*

# PISTACHIO ICE CREAM DESSERT

50 Ritz crackers, crushed
1/2 cup powdered sugar
1/4 cup butter or margarine
3 oz. pkg. pistachio instant
    pudding

2 cups milk
5 cups soft vanilla ice cream
1 cup whipped topping

Combine first 3 ingredients. Save 1/2 cup of crumbs; press remaining crumbs into a 13x9 pan. Mix pudding and milk. Stir in very soft ice cream. Pour on top of crumbs and freeze. Take out of freezer a little while before serving. Top with whipped topping and sprinkle with reserved crumbs.

*Mrs. Cyrus Kulp, Auburn, NY*

## EASY COOKIES AND CREAM DESSERT

1/2 gallon soft vanilla ice cream
8 oz. frozen whipped topping

1 1/4 lb. crisp chocolate sandwich
   cookies, crushed

Mix soft ice cream and thawed topping. Stir in cookie crumbs. Pour in a 13x9 pan. Freeze. Thaw 10 minutes before serving. Cut in squares to serve.

## NUTTY CHOCOLATE DESSERT

16 oz. Oreo cookies, crushed
1/2 cup butter, melted
1/2 gallon ice cream
2 cups powdered sugar
12 oz. can evaporated milk

2/3 cup chocolate chips
1/2 cup butter
1 tsp. vanilla
1 1/2 cups peanuts
Whipped topping, opt.

Combine cookie crumbs and melted butter; press into a 13x9 pan. Freeze 15 minutes. Spread ice cream on frozen crust. Freeze several hours. Boil powdered sugar, evaporated milk, chocolate chips and butter for 8 minutes, stirring constantly. Remove from heat and add vanilla. Cool. Sprinkle peanuts on firm ice cream. Top with cooled chocolate mixture and topping. Freeze 3 to 4 hours or overnight. Thaw 10 minutes before serving. Cut in squares to serve.

## CHOCOLATE PEANUT LOAF

1 cup vanilla wafer crumbs, about
   33 wafers
1/2 cup chopped salted peanuts
2 T. powdered sugar
3 T. melted butter
6 cups chocolate ice cream

3 oz. cream cheese, softened
3/4 cup powdered sugar
1/3 cup peanut butter
1/3 cup milk
1/2 cup whipping cream, whipped
Chocolate syrup

Combine first 4 ingredients; reserve half for topping. Press remaining crumbs into the bottom of a foil-lined 9x5x3 pan; place in freezer 15 minutes. Soften 3 cups of ice cream; spread over frozen crust; return to freezer. Beat cream cheese, sugar and peanut butter until fluffy. Add milk gradually, beating until fluffy; fold in whipped cream. Spread over ice cream; return to freezer. Freeze until firm. Spread 3 more cups ice cream over filling. Sprinkle with reserved crumbs, patting lightly into ice cream. Cover with foil; freeze. Unmold just before serving, peeling off foil. Slice to serve. Drizzle with chocolate syrup.

*Kathleen Ramer, New Paris, IN*

# FROZEN PIES

## ICE CREAM PIE

1/2 cup crunchy peanut butter
1/2 cup light corn syrup
3 cups Rice Krispies

4 cups ice cream
Whipped topping
Nuts, opt.

Warm peanut butter and corn syrup just till melted; add Rice Krispies. Press into a 9-inch pie plate. Freeze. Then fill with ice cream that has been melted enough to handle. Top with whipped topping and garnish with Danish Dessert, strawberries, nuts or chocolate, if desired.

*Charlene Ramer, Goshen, IN      Sheryl Weaver, Goshen, IN*

## FROSTY PEANUT BUTTER PIE

3 oz. soft cream cheese
1/2 cup creamy peanut butter
1/2 to 1 cup powdered sugar

1/2 cup milk
8 oz. frozen whipped topping
1 graham cracker crust

Beat together cream cheese, peanut butter, sugar and milk until smooth. Fold in whipped topping. Pour into pie shell. Freeze at least 4 hours. Thaw 10 minutes before serving.

*Martha Schrock, Colby, WI*

## PEANUT BUTTER ICE CREAM PIE

18 squares graham crackers
3/4 cup salted peanuts
1/4 cup sugar

1/4 cup butter, melted
4 cups soft vanilla ice cream
1/2 cup chunky peanut butter

Crush crackers and peanuts. Combine crumbs, nuts, sugar and butter. Pat in a 9-inch pie plate. Bake at 375° for 8 minutes. Chill. Put ice cream and peanut butter in a large mixing bowl and mix on medium-low speed. Pour into pie crust. Sprinkle with chopped peanuts. Freeze 6 hours or until firm.

*Rachel Ramer, Cazenovia, WI*

**While you prepare a place for us, Lord, prepare us for that place.**

## FROZEN PUMPKIN PIE

1 1/2 cups crushed gingersnaps
1 T. sugar
1/4 cup butter, melted
1 cup mashed cooked pumpkin
1 cup sugar
1/2 tsp. salt

1/2 tsp. ginger
1/2 tsp. cinnamon
1/4 tsp. nutmeg
1 cup whipping cream
2 cups ice cream

Combine cookie crumbs, sugar and butter; press into a 9-inch pie pan. Bake at 300° for 15 minutes. Cool. Mix pumpkin, sugar, salt and spices. Whip cream and fold in. Place scoops of ice cream in cooled pie shell; pour pumpkin mixture over ice cream. Freeze at least 2 hours.

# ICE CREAM, SHERBET, AND POPSICLES

For smooth textured ice cream use 8 to 10 parts ice to 1 part rock salt. Adding too much salt freezes ice cream too fast and makes it coarser. If ice cubes are used they should be crushed first - the finer the ice, the smoother the texture of the ice cream.

## BASIC VANILLA ICE CREAM

*To make strawberry ice cream, add 3 cups mashed strawberries. To make cinnamon walnut ice cream, add 2 cups chopped walnuts and a teaspoon of cinnamon.*

6 cups cream
6 cups milk
2 1/2 cups sugar

3 T. vanilla
1/2 tsp. salt

Combine all ingredients. Chill for 30 minutes if you have time. Freeze in a six quart freezer. If you have only a one gallon freezer use 4 cups cream, 4 milk and 2 cups sugar.

## ICE CREAM I

3 pkg. unflavored gelatin
1 cup water
8 cups light cream
1 cup sugar
2 cups brown sugar

1/2 tsp. salt
14 oz. sweetened condensed milk
12 oz. can evaporated milk
2 1/2 tsp. vanilla
Milk

Dissolve gelatin in water; let stand. Heat cream to dissolve sugar and salt; add gelatin. Put in 6-quart freezer; add remaining ingredients. Fill to about 4 inches from top with milk. Freeze.

*Mrs. Luke Hoover, Goshen, IN*

## ICE CREAM II

3/4 cup instant Clearjel
2 cups sugar
2 cups brown sugar

2 cups cream
Vanilla or fruit to taste
Milk

Mix all ingredients and add enough milk to fill a 6-quart freezer.

*Mrs. Edwin Nolt, Liberty, KY*

## CHOCOLATE CHIP ICE CREAM

2 1/2 quarts milk and cream
2 cups sugar
1 tsp. salt
2 T. unflavored gelatin
2 to 4 egg whites

2 T. vanilla
1 1/2 squares baking chocolate
1 T. butter
Sugar to taste

Heat milk on low; add sugar and salt. Stir well. Sprinkle gelatin on top. Heat slowly till hot; add beaten egg whites. Heat, but do not boil. Remove from heat; add vanilla. Cool till thickened; beat with beater till bubbly. Freeze in 1-gallon freezer. Melt together chocolate, butter and sugar. When ice cream is ready, pour in warm chocolate. Replace lid quickly and crank fast for several minutes.

*Lydia Ann Ramer, Elkhart, IN*

## COOKIES AND CREAM ICE CREAM

*This makes great vanilla ice cream too. Just delete the cookies.*

3 pkg. unflavored gelatin or 3 T.
  bulk gelatin
1/2 cup water
6 cups scalded milk
3 cups sugar

1/2 tsp. salt
6 cups cream
3 T. vanilla
Crisp chocolate sandwich
  cookies, crushed

Soften gelatin in water; add to hot milk. Stir in sugar and salt. Cool, but do not let it congeal before adding cream and vanilla. Freeze in a 6-quart freezer. When it's done add as many cookies as you want. Freeze any leftovers in a cake pan. Thaw 10 minutes before serving. Cut into squares to serve.

*Mrs. Ray (Elsie) Hoover, Stratford, WI*

## MAPLE ICE CREAM

2 pkg. unflavored gelatin
1 cup cold water
4 cups milk
1 cup brown sugar
1/2 cup sugar

2 tsp. vanilla
1 to 2 tsp. maple flavoring
1 tsp. salt
3 cups cream

Soak gelatin in cold water. Scald milk; add sugars and gelatin. Add vanilla, maple flavoring and salt. Cool; add cream. Chill until thickened. Freeze in a 1-gallon ice cream freezer.

*Sarah Imhoff, Sheridan, MI*

## PEACH ICE CREAM

4 cups fresh peaches
1 1/2 cups sugar
2 cups whipping cream
4 cups milk

1 T. vanilla
1 T. lemon juice
1/2 tsp. salt

Mix peaches and sugar and let stand 30 minutes. Add remaining ingredients and freeze in a 1-gallon ice cream freezer.

## PEPPERMINT ICE CREAM

2 cups milk
1 cup sugar
1/4 tsp. salt
4 cups whipping cream

2 T. vanilla
1 1/2 cups crushed peppermint
candy

Scald milk; add sugar and salt; stir to dissolve. Add cream and stir in vanilla. Cool. Freeze in an ice cream freezer. Add candy after ice cream is mushy. Candy can be crushed in the blended; add half at a time.

*Mrs. Ray (Elsie) Hoover, Stratford, WI*

## FROZEN STRAWBERRY YOGURT

8 cups plain yogurt
3 cups sliced strawberry in syrup

1 1/2 cups sugar
2 cups whipping cream

Combine ingredients in bowl. Cover and refrigerate 30 minutes. Freeze in a 1 gallon ice cream freezer. Thawed, frozen strawberries may be used.

## SHERBET

1 cup water
1/2 cup sugar
3 oz. any flavor gelatin

1 T. lemon juice
2 1/2 cups milk

Boil water and sugar one minute. Add gelatin. Cool. Stir in lemon juice and milk. Freeze one hour. Beat well and enjoy!

# POPSICLES

*If you don't have popsicle molds, pour liquid into ice cube trays and cover trays with plastic wrap. Poke toothpicks through plastic wrap for sticks. Freeze.*

2 cups hot water
1 cup sugar
3 oz. any flavor gelatin

1 pkg. unsweetened Kool-Aid
2 cups cold water

Add sugar, gelatin and Kool-Aid to hot water; stir to dissolve. Add cold water and fill popsicle molds. Freeze.

*Mrs. James Kulp, Unity, WI*

# PUDDING POPSICLES

*For richer popsicles use only two cups milk, or use 3 cups milk and 1 cup ice cream.*

3 3/4 oz. pkg. any flavor instant
 pudding

4 cups milk
1/4 cup sugar, opt.

Mix in blender. Freeze in popsicle molds or in 5 ounce cups with wooden sticks or plastic spoon inserted. Flavor possibilities include chocolate pudding with a few drops of peppermint, or banana pudding with a ripe banana mashed in.

*Mrs. Mervin (Lucille) Martin, Wallenstein, Ont. Canada     Edna Miller, Snover, MI*
*Stephanie Ramer, Nappanee, IN     Vera Witmer, Goshen, IN*

# MAKE-YOUR-OWN-PUDDING POPS

1/4 cup cornstarch
1/8 tsp. salt
2 1/2 cups milk
1 cup semi-sweet chocolate chips

1/3 cup light corn syrup
2 T. margarine
1 tsp. vanilla

In a 2-quart saucepan, stir together cornstarch and salt. Add milk, stir till smooth. Add chocolate chips and corn syrup then, stirring constantly, bring to a boil. Boil 1 minute. Remove from heat and add margarine and vanilla. Cool slightly and pour into plastic molds or paper cups. Insert sticks or plastic spoons.

*Mrs. Ray (Elsie) Hoover, Stratford, WI*

# PUDDING WICHES

1 1/2 cups cold milk
1/2 cup peanut butter

3 oz. instant chocolate pudding
24 graham crackers

Gradually add milk to peanut butter; beat until smooth. Add dry pudding; let set 5 minutes. Spread 1/2" thick on crackers, top with another cracker. Freeze.

*Anna Mae Hoover, Reinholds, PA*

# PIES

# PIE CRUSTS AND TOPPINGS

Overhandling pie dough develops gluten and results in tougher pie crusts. Chilling dough makes flakier crusts. Pie dough may be refrigerated at least a week before using. Remove dough from the refrigerator an hour before using to avoid overhandling. Roll out 1/8 inch thick or less. Bake pies in a preheated oven—cold pies baked in hot ovens have flakier crusts.

## PIE CRUST I

1 1/3 cups flour
1/2 tsp. salt

1/2 cup butter flavored shortening
3 T. ice water

Combine flour and salt. Cut in shortening. Add water, a little at a time, with a fork. Roll out. Makes a nice flaky pie crust. Regular shortening can be used.

*Kathleen Ramer, New Paris, IN*

## PIE CRUST II

1 1/2 cups pastry flour
1 tsp. baking powder
1/2 tsp. salt

1/2 cup shortening
4 T. milk, approximately

Combine dry ingredients. Cut in shortening. Add milk. Makes one 2-crust pie.

*Mrs. Elverne Martin, Nappanee, IN*

## PIE CRUST III

3 cups flour
1 cup shortening
2 tsp. vinegar plus enough water
    to make 1/4 cup

1/4 cup milk
1/4 cup cooking oil
1/8 tsp. salt

Cut shortening into flour. Use about a fourth cup less of shortening if using lard. Mix together liquids and salt; blend into flour. Makes 3 crusts.

*Mrs. LaVerne (Virginia) Hoover, Goshen IN*

## PIE CRUST IV

1/2 cup water
1 cup cooking oil
3 cups flour

2 tsp. baking powder
1 tsp. salt

Combine water and oil. Add flour, baking powder and salt. Mix and roll out. Make 3 crusts.

*Mrs. Elias Martin, Goshen, IN*

# EASY PIE CRUST

| | |
|---|---|
| 1 1/2 cups flour | 1/2 cup cooking oil |
| 1/2 tsp. salt | 2 T. milk |
| 1 1/2 T. sugar | |

Mix all ingredients together in a pie pan. Pat around the sides and bottom. Bake at 375° for about 15 minutes. Do not let get brown.

*Mrs. John (Twila) Kulp, Mosinee, WI*

# GRAHAM PIE CRUST

| | |
|---|---|
| 1 1/2 cups graham cracker crumbs | 1/4 cup sugar |
| | 1/4 cup butter, melted |

Mix well; press into a 9-inch pie plate. Chill or bake at 300° for 15 minutes.

**For a smoother crumb crust, pat crumbs into place then press another 9-inch pie plate firmly over the crumbs. Trim edge if necessary.**

# OATMEAL PIE CRUST

| | |
|---|---|
| 1 cup quick oatmeal | 1/2 tsp. salt |
| 1/3 cup flour | 1/3 cup butter or margarine |
| 1/3 cup sugar | |

Mix first 4 ingredients. Cut in butter until crumbly. Press firmly on bottom and sides of a 9-inch pie plate. Bake at 375° approximately 15 minutes. Pie shell may need reshaping after baking—do so while still warm. Cool. Use in place of graham cracker crust for cream fillings.

*Edna Miller, Snover, MI*

# RICE KRISPIE PIE CRUST

*Another ice cream crust possibility is melting 2 cups semi-sweet chocolate chips and 3 tablespoons of butter, and then mixing with 2 cups Rice Krispies. Press into a pie plate. Chill. Fill with mint or other ice cream.*

| | |
|---|---|
| 1/3 cup corn syrup | 2 cups Rice Krispies |
| 1/3 cup peanut butter | |

Mix and press into pie pan. Good filled with chocolate or vanilla ice cream.

*Sarah Imhoff, Sheridan, MI*

# SHORTBREAD PIE CRUST

1/2 cup butter
3 T. powdered sugar

1 1/4 cups flour

Cream butter and sugar. Add flour and mix well. Press firmly and evenly into pie plate. Bake at 350° for 15 minutes or until lightly browned.

# WHOLE WHEAT PIE CRUST

2 cups whole wheat flour
1 cup flour
1 tsp. salt
1 cup lard, soft but not runny

1 egg
1/2 cup water
1 T. vinegar

Combine flours and salt. For a nuttier flavor all whole wheat flour can be used. Cut in lard. Beat egg, water and vinegar; add all at once to flour mixture. Mix only till moistened. Makes four 9-inch pie crusts.

*Nancy Kilmer, California, MO*

# MERINGUE

2 egg whites
1/4 tsp. cream of tartar
1/4 cup sugar

1/2 tsp. cornstarch
1 tsp. vanilla

Beat egg whites and cream of tartar to a soft peak. Mix sugar and cornstarch and add to egg whites. Add vanilla. Beat mixture till stiff. Spread on pie. Bake at 325° until golden brown, approximately 20 minutes.

*Suetta Hoover, Tipton, MO*

# NEVER FAIL MERINGUE

1 T. cornstarch
2 T. cold water
1/2 cup water

3 egg whites
6 T. sugar
1 tsp. vanilla

Blend cornstarch and cold water. Boil water in a saucepan; add cornstarch mixture and cook, stirring constantly, until clear and thickened. Cool in sink with cold water. Beat egg whites at high speed till foamy. Gradually add sugar, from 2 to 6 tablespoons; beat until stiff, but not dry. On low speed add vanilla, then cornstarch mixture. Beat thoroughly on high speed. Spread on pie and bake at 325° until golden brown, about 20 minutes.

*Mrs. William (Lena) Kilmer, California, MO    Esther Martin, Decker, MI*

## TOPPING FOR FRUIT PIES I

1/2 cup sugar
3/4 cup flour

1/3 cup butter

Combine ingredients. Blend with pastry blender. Sprinkle over fruit pie.

*Edna Miller, Snover, MI*

## TOPPING FOR FRUIT PIES II

1/2 cup oatmeal
1/2 cup brown sugar
1/2 cup flour

1/2 cup butter or margarine
1/4 cup chopped nuts, opt.

Combine ingredients. Sprinkle over fruit pie.

*Doreen Zimmerman, Elkhart, IN*

# FRUIT PIES

## APPLE PIE

3 cups sliced apples
1 cup sugar
2 T. flour
Dash of cinnamon

1 unbaked pie shell
1/2 cup brown sugar
1/2 cup flour
3 T. butter or margarine

Mix first four ingredients; put into pie shell. Mix remaining ingredients; sprinkle over apples. Bake at 400° for 15 minutes, reduce heat to 350° and bake until apples are soft in center of the pie.

*Mrs. Luke Hoover, Goshen, IN*

## THE MOST UNUSUAL APPLE PIE

1 cup flour
1 tsp. baking powder
3/4 cup sugar
1/8 tsp. salt

1/2 cup butter or margarine
1 egg, beaten
4 to 5 apples, peeled and sliced
Sugar and cinnamon

Mix together dry ingredients. Add butter and stir in egg. Mix everything with a fork. Put apple slices into a heavy Pyrex pan. Pour batter over apples and sprinkle with sugar and cinnamon. Bake at 350° for 30 or 40 minutes.

*Rebecca Ringler, Fleetwood, PA*

# APPLE-LEMON PIE

3 egg whites
2 cups applesauce
1/2 cup sugar
3 egg yolks

1/4 cup butter, melted
1 tsp. lemon flavoring
1 unbaked pie shell

Beat egg whites until stiff. Combine remaining ingredients; fold in egg whites. Bake at 350° until set.

*Mrs. Ivan Zimmerman, Scottsville, KY*

# APPLE-PECAN PIE

3 T. soft butter
3 eggs
1 cup sugar
3/4 cup corn syrup
1/4 tsp. salt

1 tsp. vanilla
1 1/2 cups peeled chopped apples
1 cup chopped pecans
1 unbaked pie shell

Blend butter, eggs, sugar, syrup, salt and vanilla until smooth. Stir in apples and pecans. Pour into pie shell. Bake at 375° for 40 to 45 minutes or until done.

*Donna Hoover, Goshen, IN*

# NORWEGIAN APPLE PIE

9-inch unbaked pie shell
1 cup dried apples
3/4 cup sugar
1/2 cup flour

1 egg
1/2 tsp. vanilla
1/4 tsp. salt
1/2 cup nuts

Arrange apples in crust. Mix remaining ingredients and pour over apples. Bake at 350° until done. This is like a rich cake, moist and chewy.

*Mrs. Elam Hoover, Versailles, MO*

# SHOESTRING APPLE PIE

4 cups shredded apples
2 1/2 cups sugar
2 T. cornstarch or flour
3 well beaten eggs

1/4 cup water
1/8 tsp. salt
2 unbaked pie shell
Cinnamon

Combine first 6 ingredients. Put in pie shells. Sprinkle with cinnamon. Bake at 350° until done.

*Sarah Imhoff, Sheridan, MI*

# SOUR CREAM APPLE PIE

3/4 cup sugar
2 T. flour
1/8 tsp. salt
1/4 tsp. nutmeg
1 egg, beaten
1 cup sour cream
1 tsp. vanilla

2 cups peeled chopped apples
1 unbaked pie shell
1/3 cup sugar
1/3 cup flour
1 tsp. cinnamon
1/4 cup hard butter

Combine dry ingredients; stir in egg, sour cream, vanilla and apples. Pour into pie shell. Bake at 400° for 12 minutes. Reduce heat to 350° for 15 to 17 minutes. Combine remaining ingredients until the size of large peas. After pie baked 15 to 17 minutes at 350°, sprinkle crumbs on pie. Bake another 10 minutes.

*Mrs. Cleon (Carol) Bauman, Elmira, Ont. Canada*

# BANANA CREAM PIE

3/4 cup sugar
1/4 cup cornstarch
1/2 tsp. salt
2 1/2 cups milk
2 eggs, well beaten

2 T. butter
1 tsp. vanilla
2 to 3 bananas
9-inch unbaked pie shell
1/2 cup whipping cream, whipped

Combine dry ingredients in a heavy saucepan; stir in milk. Stir until pudding thickens. Stir small amount of pudding into eggs. Blend well and beat into pudding in saucepan. Cook and stir 2 minutes. Add butter and vanilla; cover and chill. Slice bananas into pie shell; cover with pudding. Top with sweetened whipped cream or whipped topping.

# BLUEBERRY PIE

2 1/2 cups fresh or frozen
   blueberries
1 cup sugar
2 T. flour
2 T. minute tapioca

1/8 tsp. salt
9-inch unbaked 2-crust pie shell
1 T. lemon juice
2 T. butter

Combine first 5 ingredients. Pour into pie shell. Dribble lemon juice over pie and dot with butter. Wet pastry edge with fingertips and cover with top pastry. Cut several slits in top crust to allow steam to escape. Sprinkle with sugar. Bake at 350° until done.

*Charlotte Martin, Goshen, IN*

# FRESH BLUEBERRY PIE I

3/4 cup sugar
3 T. cornstarch
1 1/2 cups water
3 oz. blueberry gelatin

3 cups fresh blueberries
1 baked graham cracker or
   regular pie shell
Whipped topping, opt.

Mix sugar and cornstarch; stir in water until smooth. Bring to a boil, stirring constantly. Boil 1 minute. Remove from heat; stir in gelatin until completely dissolved. Cool to room temperature. Stir in blueberries. Pour into pie shell. Refrigerate 3 hours or until firm. Eat plain or top with whipped topping.

# FRESH BLUEBERRY PIE II

4 cups fresh blueberries
9-inch baked pie shell
1 cup sugar
3 T. cornstarch
1/4 tsp. salt

1/4 cup water
1 T. butter
1 T. lemon juice, opt.
Whipped cream or topping

Line cooled pie shell with 2 cups blueberries. Cook remaining blueberries, sugar, cornstarch, salt and water until thickened. Remove from heat. Add butter and lemon juice; cool. Pour over blueberries in pie shell. Top with sweetened whipped cream or topping.

*Mrs. Cyrus Kulp, Auburn, NY*

**To thicken pies with tapioca, mix four cups fresh blueberries, cherries or peaches with 1/4 cup minute tapioca (3T. for cherries). Add needed sugar and flavoring; let stand 15 minutes. Fill crust and bake.**

# CHERRY PIE

4 cups cherries
1 1/4 cups sugar
1/4 cup cherry juice or water

3 T. cornstarch
Cinnamon
Unbaked 2-crust pie shell

Combine all but crust and cook until thick, stirring constantly. Pour into pie shell. Moisten edge with water; put top crust on, sealing edges. Prick top to allow steam to escape. Bake at 400° for 30 minutes or until done.

*Laura Kulp, Stratford, WI*

*If any little word of mine may make a life the brighter,*
*If any little song of mine may make a heart the lighter,*
*God help me speak the little word, and take my bit of singing*
*And drop it in some lonely vale, to set the echoes ringing!*

## CHERRY CHEESE PIE

*To make this without sweetened condensed milk delete the milk and add 2 tablespoons of sugar along with the cream cheese.*

1 pkg. graham crackers
1/2 cup butter, melted
8 oz. cream cheese, softened
14 oz. sweetened condensed milk
1/3 to 1/2 cup lemon juice
1 tsp. vanilla
21 oz. can cherry filling

Make a crust with crackers and butter. Press into a 9-inch pie pan. Beat cream cheese till fluffy. Add sweetened condensed milk; blend well. Add lemon juice and vanilla; beat till blended. Pour into pie crust as soon as possible as the mixture sets up fast after lemon juice is added. Pour pie filling over cream cheese mixture. Chill. Any fruit pie fillings may be used.

*Mrs. Isaac Brubacker, Versailles, MO    Mrs. Lloyd E. Troyer, Stella, MO*

## CRAN-APPLE PIE

2 1/2 cups fresh cranberries
1/3 cup water
1/4 cup minute tapioca
1 1/2 cups sugar
1/4 tsp. salt
2 1/2 cups shredded apples
1 unbaked pie shell
1/2 cup flour
1/4 cup sugar
1/4 cup butter

Cook cranberries in water until skins pop, about 6 minutes. Add tapioca, sugar, salt and apples. Mix well and cool. Pour into pie shell. Combine remaining ingredients and sprinkle on top. Bake at 425° for 15 minutes. Reduce heat to 350° and bake another 30 minutes.

## GRAPE PIE

2 1/2 cups grape juice
3/4 cup sugar
2 T. cornstarch
1 unbaked pie shell
1/2 cups sugar
3/4 cup flour
1/3 cup butter

Add sugar to juice and bring to a boil. Moisten cornstarch with water and add to boiling juice. Boil a few minutes then pour into an unbaked pie shell. Combine remaining ingredients to make fine crumbs; sprinkle on top. Bake at 425° for 10 minutes then reduce heat and bake at 350° for 30 minutes.

*Mrs. William (Lena) Killmer, California, MO*

*The cost of obedience is nothing compared to the cost of disobedience.*

# GOOSEBERRY PIE

3 T. cornstarch
1 1/3 cups sugar
1/2 cup water

2 cups fresh or frozen
    gooseberries
1 unbaked 2-crust pie shell

Mix cornstarch and sugar. Stir in water; add gooseberries. Cook until berries are tender. Pour into an unbaked pie shell. Cover with top crust. Brush top crust with cream or milk and sprinkle with sugar. Bake at 350° for 50 minutes.

*Cretora Bear Hilty, Elida, OH*

When putting a top crust on, moisten the edges of the crust with a little water before putting on the top crust. Press the edges of the crust together to seal. Trim if necessary. Cut several slits in the top to let steam escape.

# GROUND CHERRY PIE I

1/3 cup sugar
1/3 cup flour
1 unbaked pie crust
3 to 4 cups ground cherries

2/3 cup brown sugar
1 T. lemon juice
1/2 tsp. cinnamon
2 T. butter

Mix sugar and flour; sprinkle in the bottom of crust. Fill with ground cherries. Put brown sugar on top and sprinkle with lemon juice and cinnamon. Dot with butter. Moisten edges and put on top crust, sealing the edges. Bake at 400° for 15 minutes. Reduce heat to 350° and bake until done.

*Miriam Hoover, Goshen, IN*

# GROUND CHERRY PIE II

4 cups canned ground cherries
2 rounded T. Clearjel
1/2 cup sugar

1 T. butter
1 unbaked 2-crust pie shell

Drain juice from cherries; put in saucepan. Mix Clearjel and sugar with a little juice to make a runny paste. Add to juice before it boils. Stir and cook till it thickens. Add butter. Add ground cherries and remove from heat. Sprinkle bottom of pie shell with flour to prevent sogginess. Add hot mixture. Put top crust on. Bake at 475° for 10 minutes, then at 350° for 10 to 15 minutes or until brown.

*Alta Martin, Goshen, IN*

285

# GROUND CHERRY APPLE PIE

| | |
|---|---|
| 1 cup cold water | 2 T. butter |
| 1 cup Clearjel or cornstarch | 6 cups ground cherries |
| 3 cups water | 4 big apples, chopped |
| 3 1/2 cups sugar | 4 unbaked 2-crust pie shells |
| 1 tsp. salt | |

Mix one cup water with clear jel; set aside. Mix 3 cups water, sugar and salt in a saucepan; add Clearjel mixture. Boil 1 minute or till thick. Add butter. Pour over ground cherries and apples; mix. Pour into pie shells; put top crust on. Bake. You can cook apples with filling first-the flavor goes through better.

*Edna Miller, Snover, MI*

# LEMON CAKE PIE

| | |
|---|---|
| 1 cup sugar | 3 large egg yolks |
| 2 1/2 T. melted butter | 1 1/4 cups milk |
| 1/4 cup cake and pastry flour | 3 egg whites |
| 5 T. lemon juice | |

Beat sugar and butter. With beater on low, add flour, lemon juice, egg yolks and milk; scrape sides of bowl occasionally. In another bowl, beat egg whites until stiff. Carefully fold into lemon mixture with a whisk. Pour into a deep 9-inch pie plate. If too full, save out 1/2 cup for 5 minutes then carefully add at the center. Bake at 425° for 8 minutes. Reduce heat to 325° for 25 minutes longer until barely set. During the last 10 minutes you may want to cover top with foil to prevent browning too much.

*Mrs. Cleon (Carol) Bauman, Elmira, Ont. Canada*

# LEMON CHEESE PIE

| | |
|---|---|
| 1 1/2 cups sugar · | 2/3 cup lemon juice |
| 6 T. cornstarch | 11 oz. cream cheese |
| 1/2 tsp. salt | 3/4 cup powdered sugar |
| 1 1/4 cups water | 1 1/2 cups whipped topping |
| 2 T. butter | 1 T. lemon juice |
| 2 T. grated lemon peel | 1 baked 9-inch deep dish pie shell |

Bring sugar, cornstarch, salt and water to a boil over medium-high. Reduce heat. Cook and stir 2 minutes or until thick and bubbly. Remove from heat; stir in butter and lemon peel. Stir in lemon juice without overmixing. Cool to room temperature, about 1 hour. Beat cream cheese and powdered sugar until smooth. Fold in topping and lemon juice. Spread in pie shell and top with lemon filling. Chill thoroughly before serving.

## LEMON CUSTARD PIE

*For Lemon Meringue pie, mix 1/4 cup cornstarch, 1 cup sugar, and 1/4 cup lemon juice; add 3 beaten egg yolks and 1 1/2 cups water. Bring to a boil; simmer 5 minutes, stirring constantly. Add 1 T. butter. Pour into pie shell. Use the meringue from this recipe.*

1/4 cup butter or margarine
1 cup sugar
1 cup milk
1/2 cup water
3 T. flour
Juice and rind of 1 lemon

3 egg yolks
1 baked pie shell
3 egg whites
1/3 cup sugar
1/4 tsp. cream of tartar

Cream butter with sugar. Add milk, water, flour, rind, juice and egg yolks. Cook in a double boiler or heavy pan until thick, stirring constantly. Pour into baked pie shell. Beat remaining ingredients to make meringue. Spread on pie and brown in a hot oven.

*Mary Ann Newswanger, Fortuna, MO*

**Cornstarch and Clearjel may be used interchangeably; however cornstarch is more often used with milk. Cornstarch thickens slightly after cooling, Clearjel does not. It takes approximately 1/2 cup of thickening to thicken one quart of liquid. Flour is another option, but it takes twice as much. For best results always make a runny paste of thickening and cold water before stirring into boiling liquid. Instant Clearjel should be added to sugar before mixing with liquid. Instant Clearjel thickens without heat.**

## PINK LEMONADE PIE

14 oz. sweetened condensed milk
8 oz. frozen whipped topping

6 oz. pink lemonade concentrate
9-inch baked pie shell

Combine milk, thawed topping and thawed concentrate. Pour into pie shell. Chill.

*Lucinda Zimmerman, Rutledge, MO*

## PEACH PIE

6 to 8 peaches
1 cup sugar
3 T. flour
1/4 tsp. salt

1/8 tsp. cinnamon
2 T. butter
1 unbaked 2-crust pie shell

Peel and slice peaches. Mix dry ingredients and sprinkle 1/4 of the mixture into the pie shell. Fill with peaches and add remaining crumbs. Dot with butter. Put top crust on. Brush with milk and sprinkle with sugar. Bake at 400° for 15 minutes, reduce heat to 350° and bake for 45 minutes.

*Mrs. Ray (Elsie) Hoover, Stratford, WI*

## FRESH PEACH PIE

3/4 cup sugar
1/4 tsp. salt
1 rounded T. Clearjel
1 cup water

1/3 cup peach or orange gelatin
Fresh sliced peaches
9-inch baked pie shell
Whipped cream

Mix together sugar, salt, and Clearjel. Stir in water. Cook until thickened and clear. Remove from heat; stir in gelatin. Cool. Mix in desired amount of peaches. Spread into crust. Top with sweetened whipped cream. Chill.

*Mrs. Allen Garman, Roaring Spring, PA*

## CARAMEL CRUNCH PEACH PIE

1/2 cup flour
1 1/2 cups oatmeal
2/3 cup brown sugar
1 tsp. cinnamon

1/2 tsp. salt
1/2 cup butter, melted
1 to 2 quarts drained peaches

Combine first 5 ingredients. Mix in butter. Press into a 9-inch pie pan, reserving 1/2 cup. Arrange well drained peaches on top. Sprinkle with reserved crumbs. Bake at 375° for 30 minutes.

*Mrs. LaVerne (Virginia) Hoover, Goshen, IN*

## PINEAPPLE CREAM PIE

*If you wish, you can delete the eggs and increase cornstarch to 1/4 cup.*

3/4 cups sugar
3 T. cornstarch
1/4 tsp. salt
2 cups milk
2 eggs, well beaten

2 T. butter or margarine
1 tsp. vanilla
1 cup crushed pineapple, drained
1 baked pie shell
Sweetened whipped cream

Combine sugar, cornstarch, and salt; blend in milk. Cook and stir until thickened. Mix eggs with a small amount of hot mixture before stirring into hot mixture; cook 2 more minutes. Remove from heat; stir in butter and vanilla. Add well-drained pineapple. Cool; pour into pie shell. Top with cream. Chill.

## PUMPKIN PIE

2 cups mashed cooked pumpkin
1 1/2 cups sugar
2 1/2 cups milk
2 egg yolks
2 T. flour
3/4 tsp. cinnamon

1/2 tsp. nutmeg
1/3 tsp. cloves
1/2 tsp. salt
2 egg whites
2 unbaked pie shells

Mix all but the last two ingredients. Beat egg whites and stir in last. Pour into pie shells. Bake at 425° for 15 minutes, reduce heat to 325° and bake another 35 minutes or until done.

*Grace Shirk, Goshen, IN*

## BLENDER PUMPKIN PIE

1 cup milk
1/2 cup cream
1 cup brown sugar
1 1/4 cups cooked pumpkin or
    squash
1 T. flour
1 tsp. vanilla

1/2 tsp. salt
1/2 tsp. ginger
1/2 tsp. allspice
1 tsp. cinnamon
2 eggs
9-inch unbaked pie shell

Put filling ingredients into blender in order given. Blend until smooth. Pour into pie shell. Bake at 350° for 45 minutes or until done. Top with whipped cream or ice cream.

*Mrs. Lloyd (Sharon) Martin, McConnellsburg, PA*

## CHEESY PUMPKIN PIE

8 oz. cream cheese
1 cup canned or cooked pumpkin
1/2 cup sugar

1/2 tsp. pumpkin pie spice
8 oz. tub frozen whipped topping
1 graham cracker pie crust

Beat together first 4 ingredients until smooth. Gently stir in thawed whipped topping. Spoon into crust. Chill at least 3 hours.

## RAISIN PIE

2 cups water
1 1/2 cups raisins
3/4 cup sugar
1/8 tsp. salt
3 T. cornstarch

1/4 cup water
1 T. lemon juice
1 baked pie shell
Sweetened whipped cream or
    whipped topping

Bring water, raisins and sugar to a boil; simmer 5 minutes. Dissolve cornstarch in 1/4 cup water and stir into raisin mixture. Boil 1 minute. Remove from heat and add lemon juice. Pour into pie shell. Cool. Top with cream or topping.

*Mrs. Ray (Elsie) Hoover, Stratford, WI*

*We stumble over pebbles, not mountains.*

# RASPBERRY CREAM PIE

*For a slightly different taste, mix sugar, flour and cream. Stir in a beaten egg and pour over raspberries.*

2 cups raspberries
1 unbaked 8-inch pie shell
3/4 to 1 cup sugar

3 T. flour
1 cup cream
1 tsp. vanilla

Sprinkle raspberries in pie shell, covering the bottom well. Combine sugar and flour; sprinkle over raspberries. Combine cream and vanilla; pour on top. Bake at 425° for 10 minutes; reduce heat to 350° and 45 minutes longer or until done.

*Karen Meador, Rossville, IN     Vera Witmer, Goshen, IN*

# RHUBARB PIE

*Fresh blueberries or peaches work great in this recipe. Add a little cinnamon if using peaches.*

1/2 cup sugar
1/2 cup brown sugar
1/2 cup flour
1/4 tsp salt

3 cups diced rhubarb
1 cup creamy milk or evaporated
   milk
1 unbaked 9-inch pie shell

Make crumbs with sugars and flour. Put half of crumbs into pie shell; add rhubarb. Top with remaining crumbs. Pour milk over everything. Bake at 350° until rhubarb is soft, approximately 50 minutes.

*Mary Ann Martin, Sauk Centre, MN*

# RHUBARB MERINGUE PIE

1 1/2 cups sugar
2 T. flour
1/2 tsp. salt
2 eggs, separated

3 cups diced rhubarb
1 unbaked 9-inch pie shell
6 T. sugar

Mix sugar, flour and salt; add beaten yokes and rhubarb. Place mixture in pie shell and bake. To make meringue; stiffly beat egg whites and add 6 tablespoons sugar. Place on baked pie; brown in oven.

*Lizzie Hoover, Goshen, IN*

**When you pray for God's guidance, don't complain when it is different from your preference.**

# FRENCH RHUBARB PIE

1 egg, beaten
3/4 cup sugar
1 tsp. vanilla
2 heaping cups chopped rhubarb
2 T. flour

3/4 cup oatmeal
3/4 cup brown sugar
1/4 cup melted butter
1 8-inch unbaked pie shell

Combine first 5 ingredients; pour into pie shell. Combine remaining ingredients. Sprinkle on top of filling. Bake at 350° for 40 to 45 minutes.

*Mrs. James Horst, East Earl, PA*

# STRAWBERRY PIE I

*Putting strawberries in the freezer an hour before mixing into glaze will help the pie set up sooner. The filling can also be heaped higher in the pie shell.*

1 1/2 cups sugar
2 cups water
3 T. cornstarch
3 oz. box strawberry gelatin

4 cups whole or halved fresh
  strawberries
1 baked pie shell
Frozen whipped topping, thawed

Bring sugar, water and cornstarch to a boil. Stir in gelatin until dissolved. Cool. Mix strawberries and glaze; fill pie shell. Top with whipped topping. Chill.

*Mrs. John (Twila) Kulp, Mosinee, WI*     *Mrs. Isaac Kulp, Millersburg, IN*

# STRAWBERRY PIE II

1 cup butter
1/4 cup sugar
2 cups flour
6 cups fresh strawberries
2 cups sugar
5 T. Clearjel or cornstarch

1/4 tsp. salt
2 cups cold water
1/3 cup light corn syrup
3 oz. strawberry gelatin
Sweetened whipped cream

Combine butter, sugar and flour until crumbly; press into 2 pie pans. Bake at 350° until lightly browned. Cool. Fill pie shells with berries. In a saucepan, mix 2 cups sugar, Clearjel, and salt. Add water and syrup. Bring to a boil; cook and stir until clear. Add gelatin; stir until dissolved. Boil another minute. Cool slightly. Pour over strawberries in pie shell using just enough syrup to fill pies. Refrigerate overnight. Top with cream or whipped topping.

*Mrs. James Kulp, Unity, WI*

***Never look down on your fellowmen, only God sits that high.***

## STRAWBERRY PIE III

1 3/4 cups sugar
1/3 cup instant Clearjel
4 cups mashed berries (part water)

2 baked pie shells
Fresh strawberry halves
Sweetened whipped cream

Mix sugar and instant Clear jel well; add to mashed berries to make glaze. Fill each crust with 1/4 of the glaze. Cover with a layer of strawberry halves, then the remaining glaze. Top with cream. Chill.

*Anna Mae Hoover, Reinholds, PA*

## STRAWBERRY CREAM CHEESE PIE

2 cups Rice Krispies, crushed
1 cup flour
1 cup butter
2 T. milk
6 oz. cream cheese
3 T. sugar

6 cups fresh strawberries
1/2 cup sugar
1 T. cornstarch
1/4 cup water
1 T. lemon juice

Combine Rice Krispies, flour and butter; gradually stir in milk. Press into a 9-inch pie plate. Prick bottom and sides with fork. Bake at 400° for 12 minutes or until lightly browned. Cool. Beat cream cheese and 3 tablespoons sugar. Spread in crust. Mash enough strawberries to make 1/2 cup. Combine with 1/2 cup sugar, cornstarch and water in a saucepan; boil 2 minutes, stirring constantly. Remove from heat; stir in lemon juice. Cool slightly. Stir in remaining strawberries. Spoon over cream cheese. Chill.

# NUT AND CREAM PIES

## NUTTY CHOCOLATE PIE

3 eggs
1 cup light or dark corn syrup
1 cup coarsely chopped walnuts
1 cup chocolate chips

2 T. butter
1 tsp. vanilla
1/2 tsp. salt
1 unbaked pie shell

Beat eggs. Mix in syrup, nuts, chocolate chips, butter, vanilla and salt. Pour into pie shell. Bake at 350° for 50 to 60 minutes.

*Edith Hoover Martin, Sauk Centre, MN*

## ELEGANT PEANUT PIE

*This can be made without adding peanut butter.*

3 eggs
1 cup corn syrup
1/2 cup sugar
1/2 cup peanut butter

1 tsp. vanilla
1 cup salted peanuts
1 unbaked 9-inch pie shell
Sweetened whipped cream

Beat eggs with corn syrup, sugar, peanut butter and vanilla until smooth. Stir in peanuts; pour into pie shell. Bake at 400° for 15 minutes; reduce heat to 350° and bake 30 minutes longer. Cool. Top with cream.

*Diane Bauman, Listowel, Ont. Canada*

## PECAN PIE

*Chocolate lovers can delete 1/2 cup sugar and add 1 cup semisweet chocolate chips. To make maple pecan pie, use maple syrup instead of corn syrup.*

1 cup light corn syrup
1 cup brown sugar
1/8 tsp. salt
1/3 cup butter, melted
1 tsp. vanilla

3 eggs
1 heaping cup pecan halves or
  pieces
1 unbaked pie shell

Stir together first 6 ingredients until well blended; add nuts. (For less weepy pie add a tablespoon or two of flour with sugar.) Pour into pie shell. Bake at 350° for 50 to 55 minutes or until knife inserted halfway between center and edge comes out clean. For less calories use only 1/4 cup sugar and 2 tablespoons butter.

*Pauline Kulp, Stratford, WI      Mrs. Levon Martin, Goshen, IN*

## CHEESY CARAMEL PECAN PIE

16 oz. cream cheese, softened
1/2 cup sugar
1 tsp. vanilla
2 eggs

20 caramels
2 T. milk
1/2 cup chopped pecans
1 graham cracker crust

Mix cream cheese, sugar and vanilla until well blended. Beat in eggs. Melt caramels in milk on low heat, stirring until smooth. Stir in pecans. Pour caramel mixture into crust. Top with cream cheese mixture. Bake at 350° for 40 minutes or until center is almost set. Refrigerate at least 3 hours.

*Kelsie LaRaye Hoover, Stratford, WI*

**A loose tongue can get you into tight places.**

## CHEESY PECAN PIE

8 oz. cream cheese
1/3 cup sugar
1 egg
1 unbaked 9-inch pie shell
1 1/4 cups chopped pecans
1/2 cup Grape-Nuts

1/2 cup warm water
3 eggs
1/4 cup sugar
1 tsp. vanilla
1 cup corn syrup

Beat cream cheese, sugar and egg until thick and creamy. Spread mixture in bottom of pie shell. Sprinkle with nuts. Soak Grape-Nuts in water. Beat 3 eggs, 1/4 cup sugar, vanilla and corn syrup. Add Grape-Nuts and pour gently over cream cheese mixture. Bake at 350° for 35 to 40 minutes or until center is firm.

*Margaret Zimmerman, Ephrata, PA*

## OATMEAL PECAN PIE

1 cup brown sugar
1 cup corn syrup
3 eggs
1 tsp. vanilla
1/4 cup butter, melted

1/2 cup milk
1/2 cup coconut
1/2 cup pecans
3/4 cup oatmeal
1 unbaked pie shell

Combine first 8 ingredients and mix well. Stir in oatmeal. Pour into pie shell. Bake at 350° until set.

*Mrs. Phillip Zimmerman, Versailles, MO*

To make sweetened whipped cream, whip 1 cup whipping cream until soft peaks form. Add 2 to 3 tablespoons powdered sugar, and 1/2 teaspoon vanilla. This makes approximately two cups of whipped cream.

## WALNUT CREAM PIE

3/4 cup butter
1 1/2 cups sugar
2 eggs
1/4 cup light cream
1 1/2 tsp. cloves, opt
1/2 cup raisins, opt.

1 1/2 cups walnut pieces
2 T. flour
2 tsp. vanilla
1 unbaked 9-inch pie shell
1 cup whipping cream

Cream butter and sugar; beat in eggs one at a time. Slowly blend in cream. Add cloves. Dredge raisins and nuts in flour. Add to mixture along with vanilla. Spoon into pie shell. Bake at 450° for 10 minutes, reduce heat to 350° and bake 40 minutes longer. Cool. Top with whipped, sweetened cream.

*Mrs. Jacob Oberholtzer, Liberty, KY*

# CREAM PIE

3 cups cream
1 1/2 cups sugar
3/4 cup brown sugar
3 T. flour

5 eggs, separated
1 T. vanilla
1/8 tsp. salt
2 unbaked 9-inch pie shells

Mix cream, sugars, flour, egg yolks, vanilla and salt.  Beat egg whites; add to cream mixture.  Pour into pie shells.  Bake at 300° for 45 minutes or until set.

*Rhoda Martin, Nappanee, IN*

# OLD-FASHIONED CREAM PIE

2 cups white sugar
1 1/2 cups brown sugar
1 cup flour
1/4 tsp. salt

2 cups boiling water
2 cups whipping cream
2 unbaked pie shells

Mix dry ingredients then add boiling water and whipping cream.  Pour into pie shells.  Bake at 350° for 45 minutes or until done.

*Mrs. Ray (Elsie) Hoover, Stratford, WI*

# CHOCOLATE CREAM PIE I

2/3 cup cocoa
2 1/2 cups sugar
2/3 cup cornstarch
1/2 tsp. salt

6 cups milk
6 T. butter
1 T. vanilla
2 baked pie shells

Mix cocoa, sugar, cornstarch and salt.  Blend in milk.  Cook and stir; boil 3 minutes.  Remove from heat; add butter and vanilla.  Pour into shells.  Put plastic wrap on surface and cool.  Top with whipped cream or whipped topping.

*Edna Miller, Snover, MI*

# CHOCOLATE CREAM PIE II

2 cups milk, separated
3/4 cup sugar
1/3 cup flour
1/4 tsp. salt
2 small eggs, beaten

1/2 cup chocolate chips
1 T. butter or margarine
1 tsp. vanilla
1 baked pie shell
Sweetened whipped cream

Heat 1 1/2 cups milk, sugar, flour and salt.  Stir eggs into remaining milk and add.  Stir and cook until mixture thickens.  Remove from heat; add chocolate chips, butter and vanilla; stir till dissolved.  Cool.  Pour into pie shell.  Top with cream.

*Mrs. William (Lena) Kilmer, California, MO*

## COCONUT CREAM PIE WITH MERINGUE

*If you don't want meringue, use whole eggs in pudding. Eat pie plain or top with cream.*

| | |
|---|---|
| 1 cup sugar | 2 T. butter |
| 1/4 cup flour | 1 tsp. vanilla |
| 1/4 tsp. salt | 1 1/4 cups coconut |
| 2 cups milk | 1 baked pie shell |
| 2 eggs, separated | 1/4 cup sugar |

Combine dry ingredients; stir in milk. Cook on low heat, stirring constantly, until mixture thickens. Beat egg yolks and mix with small amount hot mixture; add to hot mixture while stirring. Cook and stir 2 minutes longer. Remove from heat; add butter, vanilla and 1 cup coconut. Cool. Pour into pie shell. Make meringue by adding sugar to stiffly beaten egg whites. Sprinkle remaining coconut on top. Bake at 350° until meringue is golden brown.

## CREAMY FRENCH SILK PIE

| | |
|---|---|
| 1/4 cup sugar | 1 tsp. vanilla |
| 3 T. cornstarch | 2 cups whipping cream |
| 1 1/2 cups milk | 2 T. powdered sugar |
| 1 cup semisweet chocolate chips | 1 baked pie shell |

Combine sugar and cornstarch in a saucepan. Add milk while stirring. Bring to a boil over medium heat, stirring constantly. Remove from heat; mix in chocolate chips and vanilla. Stir until smooth. Pour into a bowl and cover with plastic wrap. Cool completely. Whip cream and powdered sugar till soft peaks form. Reserve 2 1/2 cups for topping. Beat cold chocolate mixture until light and fluffy, about 1 minute. Fold chocolate mixture into whipped cream. Spoon into pie shell. Top with reserved cream. Garnish with chocolate curls if desired. Chill 2 to 3 hours.

*Katrina Lauren Hoover, Stratford, WI*

## PEANUT BUTTER PIE

| | |
|---|---|
| 1/2 cup peanut butter | 3.4 oz. instant vanilla or |
| 1 cup powdered sugar | chocolate pudding |
| 1 baked regular or graham | 2 cups cold milk |
| cracker pie shell | Frozen whipped topping, thawed |

Mix peanut butter and powdered sugar; sprinkle in pie shell, reserving a little for the top. Combine pudding and milk; mix until well blended. Pour pudding over crumbs. Refrigerate until set. Top with whipped topping. Sprinkle with reserved crumbs.

*Mrs. James Kulp, Unity, WI*

## DELUXE PEANUT BUTTER PIE

1 1/4 cups chocolate cookie
   crumbs
1/4 cup butter, melted
8 oz. cream cheese, softened

1 cup creamy peanut butter
1 cup sugar
1 tsp. vanilla
1 cup whipping cream

Combine crumbs and butter; press into a 9-inch pie plate. Bake at 375° for ten minutes. Cool. Combine all but cream; beat until smooth. Whip cream and fold into peanut butter mixture. Pour into crust. Chill. Sprinkle cookie crumbs on top if desired.

# MISCELLANEOUS PIES

## CHOCOLATE CHESS PIE

1 cup sugar
3 T. cornmeal
3 T. cocoa
3 eggs, beaten

1/2 cup butter, melted
1/2 cup light corn syrup
1 tsp. vanilla
1 unbaked 9-inch pie shell

Mix sugar, cornmeal and cocoa in a bowl. Add eggs, butter, corn syrup and vanilla; mix well. Pour into pie crust. Bake at 350° for 45 minutes.
*Mrs. James (Margaret) Ramer, Dallas, TX*

## IMPOSSIBLE PIE

*For a 9-inch pie plate, use only one egg, 1/4 cup butter and 1/4 cup flour, along with remaining ingredients.*

4 eggs
1 cup coconut
6 T. butter
1/2 cup flour
1/2 tsp. salt

1/4 tsp. baking powder
1 cup sugar
2 cups milk
1 tsp. vanilla

Put all ingredients in blender. Blend 10 seconds at a time, 3 or 4 times. Pour into a buttered and floured 10-inch pie plate. Bake at 350° for 50 to 60 minutes. Pie is done when top is golden. This pie makes its own crust.
*Mrs. Isaac Brubacker, Versailles, MO    Laura Kulp, Stratford, WI*

**It's wiser to choose what you say, than to say what you choose.**

## MYSTERY PIE

3 egg whites
1 cup sugar
1 tsp. vanilla

21 Ritz crackers
1 cup nutmeats
Frozen whipped topping

Beat egg whites. Add sugar and vanilla. Crush the crackers and fold into egg whites. Fold in nutmeats and pour into well-buttered pie pan. Bake at 300° for 25 to 30 minutes. Do not let it get brown.

*Mrs. John (Twila) Kulp, Mosinee, WI*

## OATMEAL PIE

1/4 cup butter
1/2 cup sugar
1/2 tsp. cinnamon
1/2 tsp. cloves
1/4 tsp. salt

1 cup dark corn syrup
3 eggs
1 cup quick oatmeal
1 unbaked pie shell

Cream butter and sugar. Add cinnamon, cloves and salt. Stir in syrup. Add eggs, one at a time, stirring after each addition until blended. Stir in oatmeal (any amount from 1/2 to 1 cup). Pour into pie shell. Bake at 350° approximately 1 hour or until knife comes out clean.

*Ada Mae Miller, Nappanee, IN*

## SHOO-FLY PIE

1 cup flour
2/3 cup brown sugar
1 T. butter
1 cup molasses or dark corn
   syrup

3/4 cup boiling water
1 tsp. soda
1 egg, beaten
1 unbaked 8 or 9-inch pie shell

Mix the first 3 ingredients into crumbs. Set aside half of this mixture. Combine molasses and water. Add soda, then egg. Fold half of the crumbs into this mixture, but do not beat. Pour into pie shell and cover with remaining crumbs. Bake at 375° for 11 minutes, then at 350° for 30 minutes.

*Elizabeth B. Hoover, Fort Wayne, IN*

*You don't need to know where you are going provided you know who you are following.*

## WET BOTTOM SHOO-FLY PIE

6 cups flour
2 cups brown sugar
1 cup shortening
1 tsp. soda
3 cups light molasses

3 cups hot water
2 tsp. soda
1 cup brown sugar
6 eggs, beaten
5 or 6 unbaked pie shells

Combine first 4 ingredients; mix well. Reserve 3 cups crumbs. Combine molasses, water, soda, brown sugar and beaten eggs. Add 3 cups crumbs; mix well. Pour into 5 or 6 pie shells, depending on size. Top with remaining crumbs. Bake at 425° for 10 minutes, then at 350° for 45 minutes.

*Mrs. James Horst, East Earl, PA*

## SWEET POTATO PIE

1 1/4 cup cooked mashed sweet
    potatoes
3/4 cup sugar
1/2 cup brown sugar
1/2 cup French vanilla instant
    pudding mix

3/4 cup evaporated milk
2 eggs
6 T. butter or margarine, softened
1 1/2 T. vanilla
9-inch unbaked pie shell

Combine all but pie shell and beat at medium speed until well blended. Spread evenly in unbaked pie shell. Bake at 450° for 10 minutes. Reduce heat to 350° and bake 40 minutes more, or until set.

*Mary Bontrager, Taylorsville, MS*

## LITTLE FRIED PIES

2 eggs
12 oz. can evaporated milk
5 cups flour
1 tsp. salt

2 T. sugar
1 cup shortening
Pie filling

Beat eggs and milk. Combine flour, salt and sugar. Add egg mixture to flour, a little at a time, as you do ordinary pie dough. Cut in shortening. Roll out dough and cut approximately thirty 4-inch circles. Place 1 to 2 tablespoons of your favorite pie filling on one side of each circle. Fold dough over pie filling; pinch edges together. Deep fry in hot oil or shortening until golden brown. Add 1/4 cup vinegar to fat to reduce splattering. May be glazed if desired.

*Mrs. Elmer Sensenig, Quarryville, PA*

# BLENDER ZUCCHINI PIE

1 cup peeled, cooked zucchini,
   well drained
1 cup sugar
1 egg
2 T. flour
1 cup evaporated milk

1 tsp. vanilla
1/2 tsp. cinnamon
1/4 tsp. nutmeg
1/4 tsp. salt
1 unbaked pie shell

Blend all but pie shell in blender. Pour into unbaked pie shell. Bake at 425° for 10 minutes, then at 350° until set.

*The fellow who is pulling on the oars usually doesn't have time to rock the boat.*

# CAKES
## and
# CUPCAKES

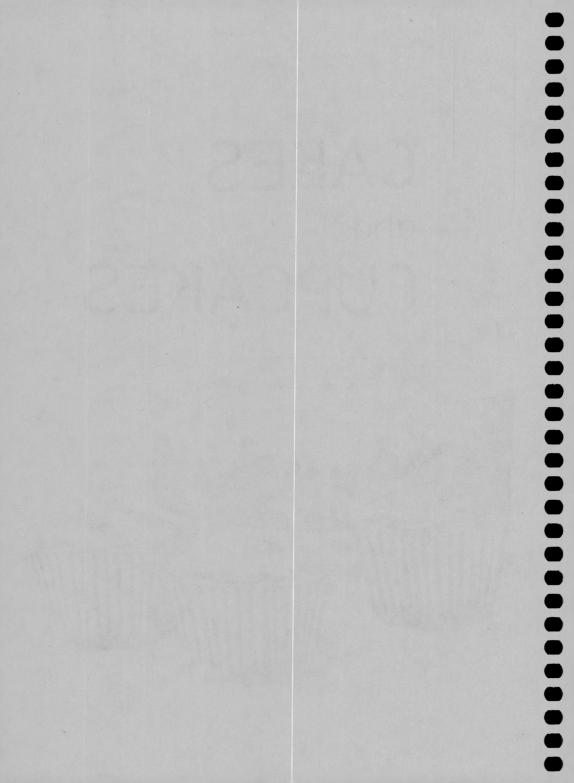

# SHEET CAKES

Use room temperature ingredients to make cakes. If a recipe calls for shortening, butter, margarine or solid white shortening can be used – or use a combination. Butter tastes best, but shortening makes a lighter cake. Stop frequently to scrape the bowl while mixing a cake. Pack brown sugar when measuring; don't pack flour. Do not beat longer than two minutes after adding flour. Grease the bottom but not the sides of cake pans then spread batter well into corners with a slight depression in the center.

Baking times given in this book assume the oven is preheated. Cakes are done if the center springs back when touched lightly or when a wooden pick inserted in the center comes out clean. Because ovens vary it is better to set the timer for less time so you can check if the cake is done.

## APPLE CAKE I

*Crumbs for the top can be made by mixing 1/4 cup sugar, 1/2 cup brown sugar, 1/2 teaspoon cinnamon and 1/2 cup chopped nuts. Sprinkle on top before baking.*

4 cups diced apples
1/2 cup cooking oil
2 cups sugar
2 eggs, well beaten
2 cups flour

1/2 tsp. salt
1 1/2 tsp. soda
1 to 2 tsp. cinnamon
1 tsp. vanilla
1 cup chopped nuts or raisins

Combine apples, oil and sugar. Add eggs. Combine and add dry ingredients. Stir in vanilla and nuts. Spread into a greased 13x9 pan. Bake at 350° for 45 minutes or until done. This recipe can be cut in half and baked in an 8x8 pan at 350° for 30 to 35 minutes, or until done.

*Mrs. Cyrus Kulp, Auburn, NY      Laura Kulp, Stratford, WI      Edna Miller, Snover, MI*
*Rebecca Ringler, Fleetwood, PA*

## APPLE CAKE II

4 cups diced peeled apples
2 cups sugar
2 eggs
2 cups flour
3 tsp. cinnamon
2 tsp. soda
1 cup chopped nuts

1 cup sugar
1 cup brown sugar
1/4 cup flour
2 cups water
1/2 cup butter or margarine
2 tsp. vanilla

Mix apples and sugar; set aside until sugar dissolves. Add eggs; beat well. Mix and add flour, cinnamon and soda. Add nuts. Pour into a greased 13x9 pan. Bake at 375° for 40 minutes. This can be cut in half for an 8x8 pan. Bring last six ingredients to a boil; cook and stir until thickened. Serve sauce with cake.

*Lizzie Hoover, Goshen, IN      Mrs. James Kulp, Unity, WI*

# APPLE CAKE III

| | |
|---|---|
| 1 1/2 cups flour | 1 T. melted butter |
| 1/2 cup sugar | 1/2 cup milk |
| 2 tsp. baking powder | 8 cups sliced apples |

Combine first 3 ingredients; add butter and milk. Mix like pie dough. Place apples in bottom of 13x9 pan. Sprinkle liberally with sugar and cinnamon. Drop dough on top of apples by tablespoon. Bake at 350° for 45 minutes.

*Esther Horst, East Earl. PA*

# BUTTERSCOTCH APPLE CAKE

| | |
|---|---|
| 1 cup cooking oil | 1 tsp. soda |
| 2 cups sugar | 1 tsp. baking powder |
| 2 eggs | 1/2 tsp. salt |
| 3 cups grated apples | 2 1/2 cups flour |
| 1 tsp. cinnamon | 1 cup butterscotch chips |

Beat oil, sugar, and eggs; add apples. Mix and add dry ingredients. Pour into a greased 13x9 pan; top with butterscotch chips. Bake at 325° for 15 minutes; then at 350° for 45 minutes. Good without frosting.

*Anna Mae Hoover, Reinholds, PA*

# APPLE PUDDING CAKE

*This cake makes its own sauce.*

| | |
|---|---|
| 2 1/2 cups peeled chopped apples | 1/2 cup butter, melted |
| 1 1/2 cups flour | 3/4 cup milk |
| 1 cup sugar | 3/4 cup raisins |
| 1 tsp. soda | 3/4 cup pecans or walnuts, opt. |
| 1 tsp. cinnamon | 1 1/2 cups brown sugar |
| 1/4 tsp. nutmeg | 2 T. butter |
| 1/2 tsp. salt | 1 1/2 cups water |

Combine all but the last 3 ingredients. Pour into a 13x9 pan. Bring brown sugar, butter and water to a boil. Carefully pour over batter. Bake at 350° for approximately 40 minutes. Good plain or with whipped cream, milk or ice cream.

*Mrs. Ray (Elsie) Hoover, Stratford, WI*

***It doesn't take much power to toot your horn, but it does to
let your light shine.***

## SPICY APPLESAUCE CAKE

2 3/4 cups flour
2 cups sugar
1 1/2 tsp. soda
1 1/2 tsp. salt
1/4 tsp. baking powder
1 tsp. cinnamon
1/2 tsp. cloves

1/2 tsp. allspice
1/2 cup soft shortening
2 eggs
2 cups unsweetened applesauce
1 cup walnut halves
20 large marshmallows

Combine dry ingredients; add shortening, eggs and applesauce. Beat until smooth. Stir in walnuts. Pour into a greased and floured 13x9 pan. Press whole marshmallows into batter to bottom of pan in 4 rows with 5 in a row. Bake at 350° approximately 50 minutes.

*Lizzie Hoover, Goshen, IN*

## BANANA CAKE I

2 1/2 cups flour
2 1/2 tsp. baking powder
1/2 tsp. salt
1/2 cup shortening
1 cup sugar

2 eggs, separated
1 tsp. vanilla
1/2 cup sour cream
1/2 tsp. soda
1 cup ripe mashed bananas

Mix flour, baking powder and salt. Cream shortening and sugar until fluffy. Add egg yolks and vanilla; beat again. Add dry ingredients alternately with sour cream and soda. Add mashed banana. Fold beaten egg whites. Spread in a greased 13x9 pan. Bake at 350° for 30 to 40 minutes.

*Mrs. Isaac Brubaker, Versailles, MO*

**Cut ripe bananas into fourths, leaving the peeling on, and freeze until ready to bake. Peelings turn black but bananas stay white.**

## BANANA CAKE II

1 1/2 cups sugar
1/2 cup butter
2 eggs
2 cups flour
2 tsp. baking powder
1/8 tsp. salt

1/2 cup milk
1 cup nuts
1/2 tsp. vanilla
1 tsp. soda
3 ripe bananas, mashed

Beat sugar and butter; add eggs. Add dry ingredients alternately with milk. Add nuts and vanilla. Mix soda with mashed bananas and add. Pour into a greased 13x9 pan. Bake at 350° for 35 to 40 minutes.

*Susan Hilty Hoover, Elida, OH*

# BLUEBERRY CAKE I

2/3 cup butter
2 eggs
1 1/2 cups sugar
1 cup milk
2 cups flour

2 tsp. baking powder
1 tsp. salt
3/4 cup blueberries
1/4 cup sugar
1 T. cinnamon

Beat butter, eggs, sugar and milk. Add dry ingredients. Beat on medium speed until smooth. Pour into a greased 13x9 pan. Drop blueberries on batter. Mix sugar and cinnamon; sprinkle on top. Bake at 350° for 30 minutes. Good drizzled with a thin powdered sugar frosting while cake is still warm.

*Mrs. James Kulp, Unity, WI*

# BLUEBERRY CAKE II

2 cups flour
1 1/2 cups sugar
1/2 tsp. salt
1/2 cup cold butter or margarine

1 cup milk
2 eggs, separated
1 tsp. baking powder
2 cups fresh or frozen blueberries

Mix flour, sugar, salt and butter until crumbly. Set aside 3/4 cup for topping. Add milk, egg yolks and baking powder to remaining mixture; mix well. Beat egg whites until soft peaks form; fold into batter. Pour into a 13x9 pan. Sprinkle with fresh or unthawed blueberries and reserved crumb mixture. Bake at 350° for 30 to 35 minutes or until golden brown.

*Julia Kulp, Unity, WI*

# BLUEBERRY TOPPING CAKE

1/4 cup sugar
2 T. cornstarch
1/8 tsp. nutmeg
1/2 cup water
2 tsp. lemon juice
2 cups fresh or frozen blueberries
1 1/2 cups flour
2 1/2 tsp. baking powder
1/2 tsp. salt

1/2 cup butter
3/4 cup sugar
1 tsp. vanilla
1 large egg
1/2 cup milk
1/2 cup sugar
1/4 cup flour
1 tsp. cinnamon
1/4 cup butter

Stir first 3 ingredients together in saucepan; add water, lemon juice and blueberries. Cook and stir until thickened. Cool. Combine flour, baking powder and salt. Cream butter, sugar and vanilla. Beat in egg. Add flour mixture alternately with milk. Beat until smooth. Pour into a greased 10x6 pan. Spread sauce on top. Combine remaining ingredients to make crumbs; sprinkle on top. Bake at 375° for 40 to 45 minutes or until golden brown.

*Rachel Ramer, Cazenovia, WI*

# BUTTER CAKE

1 3/4 cups sugar
2/3 cup butter, softened
2 eggs
1 1/2 tsp. vanilla

3 cups flour
2 1/2 tsp. baking powder
1 tsp. salt
1 1/4 cups milk

Beat first 4 ingredients until smooth. Combine dry ingredients; add alternately with milk. Spread in a greased 13x9 pan. Bake at 350° for 35 minutes.

*Barbara Zimmerman, Nappanee, IN*

# CAROB CAKE

3 1/2 cups flour
3 cups sugar
2/3 cup carob powder
2 1/2 tsp. soda
2 tsp. salt

1 cup lard
2 cups milk
4 eggs
2 tsp. vanilla

Combine dry ingredients. Add lard and 1 1/3 cups milk. Beat 2 minutes. Add remaining ingredients and beat 2 more minutes. Spread in a greased 15x11 pan. Bake at 350° for 30 minutes. Cool and frost with favorite frosting.

*Wayne Kilmer, California, MO*

**Cake batters with sour milk or sour cream, as well as those with acidic ingredients like molasses and spice, usually contain baking soda.**

# CARROT CAKE

4 eggs
2 cups sugar
1 1/4 cups cooking oil
3 cups grated raw carrots
1 cup nuts, chopped fine

2 cups flour
2 tsp. cinnamon
2 tsp. baking powder
1 tsp. soda

Combine eggs, sugar and oil; mix in carrots and nuts. Add dry ingredients. Spread in a greased 13x9 pan. Bake at 350° for 45 to 60 minutes. Good with cream cheese frosting.

*Mrs. Isaac Kulp, Millersburg, IN*

***Life's greatest tragedy is to lose the sense of God's presence and not miss it.***

# PINEAPPLE-CARROT CAKE

1 cup cooking oil
1 1/2 cups sugar
3 eggs
2 1/2 cups flour
1 tsp. salt
1 tsp. soda

1 tsp. cinnamon
2 cups grated raw carrots
1 1/2 cups crushed pineapple
1 cup nuts, chopped
1 cup raisins
2 tsp. vanilla

Beat oil, sugar and eggs. Mix and add dry ingredients. Add carrots, drained pineapple, nuts, raisins and vanilla. Spread in a greased 13x9 pan. Bake at 350° for 45 minutes. A very moist cake that is good with cream cheese frosting.

*Ethel Hoover, Goshen, IN*

# ZUCCHINI-CARROT CAKE

4 eggs
2 cups sugar
1 1/3 cups cooking oil
1 tsp. salt
2 tsp. cinnamon
2 tsp. baking powder

2 tsp. soda
2 1/2 cups flour
2 cups grated carrots
2 cups grated zucchini
1 cup nuts

Cream eggs, sugar and oil. Mix and add dry ingredients. Stir in carrots, zucchini, and nuts. Spread in a greased 13x9 pan. Bake at 350° until center springs back when touched.

*Mrs. Elam Hoover, Versailles, MO*

# CHOCOLATE CAKE

*To make peppermint chocolate cake, add a half cup of crushed peppermint candy after cake is mixed.*

3/4 cup butter
1 3/4 cups sugar
2 tsp. vanilla
2 eggs
2 cups flour

2/3 cup cocoa
1 tsp. baking powder
1 tsp. soda
1/2 tsp. salt
1 cup water

Beat butter, sugar and vanilla until creamy. Beat in eggs one at a time. Combine dry ingredients; add alternately with water. Spread in a greased 13x9 pan or two 9-inch round pans. Bake at 350° approximately 30 minutes.

**As long as revenge would seem sweet there is still bitterness in your heart.**

## CHOCOLATE CAKE WITH COFFEE

2 cups flour
2 cups sugar
3/4 cup cocoa
2 tsp. soda
1 tsp. baking powder
1/2 tsp. salt

2 eggs
1/2 cup cooking oil
1 1/2 tsp. instant coffee crystals
1 1/2 cups hot water
1/2 cup milk

Mix ingredients in order given, dissolving coffee in hot water. (This can also be made using 1 cup oil and only 1 cup hot water.) Beat until smooth. Batter will be thin. Pour into a greased 13x9 pan. Bake at 350° for 35 to 40 minutes. Frost with your favorite frosting. This moist cake freezes well.

*Mrs. Isaac Kulp, Millersburg, IN        Karen Riffey, Bernville, IN*

## CHOCOLATE CAKE WITH BUTTERMILK

3 cups flour
2 cups sugar
1 cup cocoa
2 tsp. soda
2 tsp. baking powder

1 cup buttermilk or sour milk
1 cup shortening
2 eggs
1 tsp. vanilla
1 cup boiling water

Mix dry ingredients. Beat in the rest; add boiling water last. Spread into a large greased cake pan. Bake at 350° for 30 to 40 minutes.

*Mrs. Harvey Mazelin, Cincinnati, IA*

## CHOCOLATE CAKE WITH SALAD DRESSING

1 cup sugar
3 T. cocoa
2 cups flour
1 cup warm water

2 tsp. soda
1 tsp. vanilla
1 cup Miracle Whip salad
   dressing

Mix first 3 ingredients. Mix and add remaining ingredients. Pour into a 13x9 greased pan. Bake at 375° approximately 30 minutes.

*Mrs. John (Twila) Kulp, Mosinee, WI        Mrs. Carlton Zimmerman, Brooten, MN*

## CRAZY CHOCOLATE CAKE

3 cups flour
2 cups sugar
6 T. cocoa
1 T. soda

1 tsp. salt
2 cups water
3/4 cup cooking oil
1/4 cup vinegar

Mix ingredients well. Pour into a greased 13x9 pan. Bake at 350° until done.

*Laura Kulp, Stratford, WI*

# RIBBON CHOCOLATE CAKE

*No baking chocolate?  Just layer cream cheese filling with any chocolate cake batter.*

2 cups flour
2 cups sugar
1 tsp. salt
1 tsp. baking powder
1/2 tsp. soda
1 1/3 cups milk
1/2 cup butter
1 tsp. vanilla

4 squares (4 oz.) unsweetened
   chocolate, melted
2 eggs
8 oz. cream cheese
1/4 cup sugar
1 T. cornstarch
1/2 tsp. vanilla
1 egg

Combine dry ingredients.  Add milk, butter, vanilla, melted chocolate and eggs. Beat well.  Beat remaining ingredients for 2 minutes or until smooth and creamy. Layer half of batter in a greased 13x9 pan.  Spoon cream cheese over batter and spread.  Spoon on remaining batter.  Bake at 350° for 50 to 60 minutes.  Frost.

# MISSISSIPPI FUDGE CAKE WITH FROSTING

1 cup butter or margarine
1/3 cup cocoa
2 cups sugar
4 eggs
1 1/2 cups flour
Miniature marshmallows

1/2 cup butter or margarine
1/4 cup cocoa
3 1/2 cups powdered sugar
1/4 cup milk
1 tsp. vanilla
Chopped walnuts

Melt together 1 cup butter and cocoa.  Beat in sugar, eggs and flour.  Spread in an ungreased 13x9 pan.  Bake at 350° for 30 minutes.  Cover with marshmallows and let in oven to melt.  Cool.  To make frosting, melt 1/2 cup butter and cocoa. Beat in powdered sugar, milk and vanilla.  Sprinkle with nuts.

*Mrs. Luke Hoover, Goshen, IN*

# TEXAS SHEET CAKE

1 cup butter or margarine
1/4 cup cocoa
1 cup water
2 cups flour
2 cups sugar

1 1/2 tsp. soda
1/2 tsp. salt
1/2 cup buttermilk or sour cream
2 eggs
1 tsp. vanilla

Bring butter, cocoa and water to a boil.  Combine dry ingredients. Pour cocoa mixture over dry ingredients; beat well.  Add buttermilk, eggs and vanilla.  Spread in a greased 15 1/2 x 10 1/2 pan.  Bake at 350° for 20 to 25 minutes.  While cake is still slightly warm, frost with Fudge Frosting found in frosting section.

*Donna Herr, Nappanee, IN*   *Mrs. Clay Zimmerman, Paltinis, Romania*

# CHOCOLATE PUDDING CAKE

*This cake makes its own sauce.*

1 cup flour
2 tsp. baking powder
1/4 tsp. salt
3/4 cup sugar
2 T. cocoa
1/2 cup milk

2 T. cooking oil
1 cup chopped nuts
1 cup brown sugar
1/4 cup cocoa
1 3/4 cups hot water

Combine dry ingredients. Stir in milk, oil, and nuts. Spread in a 9x9 pan. Mix brown sugar, cocoa and; sprinkle on batter. Carefully pour water over all. Bake at 350° for 45 minutes. Serve with milk, cream or ice cream.

*Roma Jo ( Martin) Miller, Goshen, IN*

# CREAM FILLED CHOCOLATE CAKE

Chocolate cake batter
5 T. flour
1 1/4 cups milk
1 cup solid white shortening
1/2 cup butter or margarine
1 cup sugar

1/2 cup butter
3 T. milk
2 T. cocoa
1 tsp. vanilla
2 cups powdered sugar

Bake chocolate cake in a greased 15x10 pan. Cool. Cook and stir flour and milk until thick. Cool. Cream shortening, butter and sugar; add cooled flour mixture. Beat well. Spread over cake. To make frosting, bring butter, milk and cocoa to a boil. Remove from heat; beat in vanilla and powdered sugar. Frost.

*Edna Miller, Snover, MI*

# CHOCOLATE CHIP CAKE

3 cups flour
2 tsp. baking powder
1/2 tsp. salt
1 cup butter, softened
1 cup sugar
1 cup brown sugar

2 tsp. vanilla
3 eggs
1 cup milk
1 1/2 cups small semisweet
    chocolate chips

Combine flour, baking powder and salt. Beat butter, sugars, and vanilla until light and fluffy. Add eggs and beat well. Add flour mixture alternately with milk. Mix well. Fold in chocolate chips. Pour into a greased 13x9 pan. Bake at 350° for 45 to 50 minutes. This can also be baked in a greased tube pan, at 350° for 55 to 60 minutes. Cool. Frost, or glaze with glaze made by dissolving 2 tablespoons of sugar in 2 tablespoons of boiling water. Add 1/2 cup of small chocolate chips and stir until dissolved.

## CINNAMON PUDDING CAKE

2 cups brown sugar
1 1/2 cups cold water
2 T. butter
2 cups sugar
2 cups flour

2 tsp. baking powder
1 tsp. cinnamon
1 cup milk
1/4 cup butter
Nuts, opt.

Bring first 3 ingredients to a boil. Combine remaining ingredients and spread in a 13x9 pan. Carefully pour syrup over everything; sprinkle with nuts. Bake at 350° until cake rises to the top and is done. Good with whipped cream or ice cream.

*Danette Schrock Martin, Waterloo, Ont. Canada*

## GINGERBREAD CAKE

6 eggs
2 cups sugar
2 cups cooking oil
1 1/2 cups molasses
2 tsp. cloves
2 tsp. ginger

2 tsp. cinnamon
4 tsp. soda
1/4 cup hot water
4 1/2 cups flour
2 cups boiling water

Cream first 7 ingredients. Dissolve soda in water. Add to creamed mixture. Add flour; beat well. Stir in boiling water. Pour into a greased 13x9 pan. Bake at 350° for 45 minutes, or until done. This makes a very moist cake.

*Mrs. Edwin Nolt, Liberty, KY*

## SOFT GINGERBREAD CAKE

1 cup sugar
1/2 cup shortening
2 eggs, well beaten
1 cup black molasses
3 cups flour
2 tsp. ginger

2 tsp. cinnamon
1 tsp. cloves
1/4 tsp. nutmeg
1 cup buttermilk or sour milk
1 tsp. soda
1/4 cup boiling water

Cream sugar and shortening. Add eggs and molasses; mix well. Combine flour and spices. Add alternately with milk to first mixture. Dissolve soda in water and stir in. Pour into a greased 13x9 pan. Bake at 350° for 30 minutes.

*Mrs. Isaac Kulp, Millersburg, IN*

***The best way to bring people to God is first to bring them to God in prayer.***

## OATMEAL CAKE

| | |
|---|---|
| 1 cup quick oatmeal | 1 tsp. cinnamon |
| 1 1/3 cups boiling water | 1 tsp. salt |
| 1/2 cup butter | 1 cup brown sugar |
| 1 cup sugar | 1 cup coconut |
| 1 cup brown sugar | 1 cup nuts or raisins |
| 2 eggs, beaten | 1/4 cup cream or milk |
| 1 1/2 cups flour | 6 T. melted butter |
| 1 tsp. soda | |

Pour boiling water over oatmeal; stir and let cool. Cream butter and sugars; add beaten eggs. Combine flour, soda, cinnamon and salt; add alternately with the oatmeal. Pour into a greased 13x9 pan. Bake at 350° for 35 minutes. While cake is baking mix remaining ingredients. Spread topping on hot cake. Broil 4 inches from heat until melted and bubbly. Watch carefully so it doesn't burn.

*Mrs. Marvin (Lydia) Sensenig, Penn Yan, NY*     *Rachel Wierich, Stone Lake, WI*

## CHOCOLATE OATMEAL CAKE

| | |
|---|---|
| 1 cup oatmeal | 1 T. hot water |
| 2 cups boiling water | 2 cups flour |
| 2 2/3 cups brown sugar | 6 1/2 T. cocoa |
| 1 cup butter | 2 tsp. baking powder |
| 4 eggs, beaten | 1 tsp. salt |
| 2 tsp. soda | 2 tsp. vanilla |

Pour water over oatmeal; cover and cool. Cream sugar and butter. Add beaten eggs. Dissolve soda in hot water; add. Add oatmeal mixture. Mix and add dry ingredients. Add vanilla. Spread in a greased and floured 13x9 pan. Bake at 350° for 40 to 45 minutes. Makes a moist chocolate cake.

*Diane Bauman, Listowel, Ont. Canada*

## HONEY OATMEAL CAKE

| | |
|---|---|
| 1 cup oatmeal | 1 3/4 cups sifted whole wheat |
| 1/2 cup butter |   flour |
| 1 1/4 cups boiling water | 1 tsp. soda |
| 1 1/2 cups honey | 3/4 tsp. salt |
| 1 1/2 tsp. vanilla | 1 1/2 tsp. cinnamon |
| 2 eggs, beaten | 1/4 tsp. nutmeg |

Mix first 3 ingredients; let stand 20 minutes. Add honey, vanilla and eggs. Add remaining ingredients. Pour into a greased and floured 13x9 pan. Bake at 350° for 35 minutes. Frost if desired.

*Mary Ann Martin, Sauk Centre, MN*

## UNFROSTED OATMEAL CAKE

| | |
|---|---|
| 1 cup oatmeal | 1 tsp. soda |
| 1 1/2 cups boiling water | 1/2 tsp. salt |
| 1 cup sugar | 1 T. cocoa |
| 1 cup brown sugar | 1 1/2 cups flour |
| 1/2 cup butter | 1 cup chocolate chips |
| 2 eggs | 1 cup nuts |

Pour boiling water over oatmeal; let stand 10 minutes. Add sugars and butter; beat well. Add eggs; beat again. Add dry ingredients, 1/2 cup chocolate chips and 1/2 cup nuts. Pour into a greased 13x9 pan. Top with remaining chips and nuts. Bake at 350° for 30 to 35 minutes.

*Sarah Imhoff, Sheridan, MI*

## PEACH CUSTARD CAKE

*Another option for the custard part is to combine a cup of peach syrup, a 12 ounce can evaporated milk and one third cup flour. Pour over peaches.*

| | |
|---|---|
| 1 1/2 cups flour | 1 cup sugar |
| 1/2 cup butter, softened | 1 tsp. cinnamon |
| 1/2 tsp. salt | 2 eggs |
| 2 quarts peaches, drained | 2 cups evaporated milk or cream |
| 1 cup peach syrup | |

Mix flour, butter and salt; press into an13x9 pan. Arrange peach slices on top. Sprinkle sugar and cinnamon on peaches. Bake at 375° for 20 minutes. Mix peach syrup, eggs and milk. Pour over peaches. Bake another 30 minutes.

*Sheryl Weaver, Goshen, IN*

## PINEAPPLE CAKE

| | |
|---|---|
| 2 cups flour | 20 oz. can crushed pineapple |
| 2 cups sugar | 1/4 cup butter |
| 2 tsp. soda | 8 oz. cream cheese |
| 1/2 tsp. salt | 2 cups powdered sugar |
| 2 eggs | 1 tsp. vanilla |

Mix dry ingredients. Add undrained pineapple. Add eggs. Bake at 350° for 35 to 40 minutes. Combine remaining ingredients to make frosting. Frost.

*Miriam Hoover, Goshen, IN    Susan Hilty Hoover, Elida, OH    Sheryl Weaver, Goshen, IN*
*Rachel Wierich, Stone Lake, WI*

**There are no losers with Christ and no winners with the devil.**

## STOVE TOP PINEAPPLE UPSIDE DOWN CAKE
*Peaches may be substituted for pineapple.*

| | |
|---|---|
| 1/2 cup butter | 1 T. melted butter |
| 1 cup brown sugar | 1 cup sugar |
| 20 oz. can pineapple slices | 1 tsp. vanilla |
| 8 maraschino cherries, opt. | 1 cup flour |
| 2 eggs | 1 tsp. baking powder |
| 1/2 cup milk | 1/8 tsp. salt |

Melt butter and sugar together in a large skillet. Arrange pineapple slices and cherries in skillet. Beat together remaining ingredients. Pour over pineapples. Cover and bake over low heat until done, approximately 35 minutes. During the last 5 minutes remove lid to dry out cake top. Turn upside down on a large platter. Serve plain, with whipped cream or with milk.

*Mrs. Eugene Weaver, Fleetwood, PA*

## POPPY SEED CAKE

| | |
|---|---|
| 1 1/2 cups sugar | 2 tsp. baking powder |
| 2/3 cup butter, softened | 1 tsp. salt |
| 2 eggs | 1 cup milk |
| 1 T. lemon extract | 1/3 cup poppy seed |
| 2 1/2 cups flour | |

Cream sugar and butter. Beat in eggs and extract. Combine dry ingredients and add alternately with milk; mix well. Mix in poppy seeds. Spread in a greased 13x9 pan. Bake at 350° for 35 to 40 minutes. Bake 40 to 45 minutes in a tube pan.

## SPICY PUMPKIN CHIP CAKE

| | |
|---|---|
| 4 eggs | 2 tsp. baking powder |
| 2 cups mashed cooked pumpkin | 1 tsp. soda |
| 1 cup cooking oil | 1/2 tsp. salt |
| 1 1/2 cups bran flakes | 1 1/2 tsp. cinnamon |
| 1 cup chocolate or butterscotch chips | 1/2 tsp. cloves |
| | 1/4 tsp. allspice |
| 2 cups flour | 2 cups sugar |

In a large bowl beat eggs until foamy. Add pumpkin, oil, flakes and chips. Combine dry ingredients; add to egg mixture, mixing only until combined. Bake at 350° until done.

*Mrs. Isaac Z. Newswanger, Kutztown, PA*

# PUMPKIN SHEET CAKE

2 cups mashed cooked pumpkin
2 cups sugar
1 cup oil
4 eggs, beaten

2 cups flour
2 tsp. soda
1 tsp. cinnamon
1/2 tsp. salt

Combine pumpkin, sugar and oil; beat in eggs. Mix well. Combine and add dry ingredients; mix well. Pour into a greased 15x10 pan. Bake at 350° for 25 to 30 minutes, or until done. Cool. Good with cream cheese frosting.


A substitute for sour milk or buttermilk can be made by putting a tablespoon of vinegar or lemon juice in a cup then filling it up with milk-preferably room temperature milk. Let it stand 5 or 10 minutes.

# SPICE CAKE

3/4 cup butter
3/4 cup sugar
1 cup brown sugar
3 eggs
2 1/4 cups flour
2 tsp. baking powder

1 tsp. salt
1 tsp. cinnamon
1/2 tsp. nutmeg
1/2 tsp. allspice
1/4 tsp. cloves
1 cup milk

Cream shortening and sugars; beat in eggs. Combine dry ingredients and add alternately with milk. Beat well. Pour into a greased 13x9 pan. Bake at 350° for 35 to 40 minutes or until done.

# RHUBARB CAKE

1 1/2 cups brown sugar
1/2 cup butter or margarine
1/2 tsp. salt
1 egg
1 cup buttermilk
1 tsp. soda

1 tsp. vanilla
2 cups flour
1 1/2 cups diced raw rhubarb
1/4 cup sugar
1 tsp. cinnamon

Cream brown sugar and butter; add salt and egg. Stir in buttermilk, soda, vanilla and flour. Add rhubarb. Spread in a 13x9 pan. Combine sugar and cinnamon; sprinkle on top. Bake at 350° for 30 to 35 minutes.

## WHITE BUTTERMILK CAKE

2 cups sugar
1 cup shortening
3 cups cake flour
1 tsp. soda
1 tsp. cream of tartar

1 cup buttermilk
1 tsp. vanilla
1/4 tsp. almond extract
1/4 tsp. lemon extract
6 stiffly beaten egg whites

Cream sugar and shortening. Sift dry ingredients; add alternately with buttermilk and flavorings. Fold in egg whites. Spread in a greased 13x9 pan. Bake at 350° approximately one hour. To make flavored cakes, add a 3 ounce box of flavored gelatin. Delete an equal amount of sugar.

*Alta Martin, Goshen, IN*

## WHITE TEXAS SHEET CAKE

1 cup butter
1 cup water
2 cups sugar
1/2 tsp. salt
2 1/4 cups flour

2 eggs, beaten
1 tsp. vanilla
1/2 cup sour milk or sour cream
1 tsp. soda

Heat butter and water until butter melts. Add sugar, salt and flour. Mix well. Add remaining ingredients; mix well. Pour into a greased 15x10 pan. Bake at 350 for 20 minutes. Frost with Butter Cream Frosting.

*Verna Overholt, Due West, S.C.*

# LAYER AND TUBE CAKES

## APPLE RAISIN CAKE

3 cups flour
2 cups sugar
1 cup mayonnaise
1/3 cup milk
2 eggs
2 tsp. soda
1 1/2 tsp. cinnamon
1/2 tsp. nutmeg

1/2 tsp. salt
1/4 tsp. cloves
3 cups chopped, peeled apples
1 cup raisins
1/2 cup coarsely chopped
   walnuts
Whipped cream

Beat first 10 ingredients on low speed for 2 minutes, or 30 vigorous strokes by hand, scraping bowl occasionally. Batter will be thick. Stir in apples, raisins and nuts. Bake at 350° approximately 45 minutes. Remove from pans. Fill and frost with whipped cream.

*Sarah Nolt, Fortuna, MO*

# BOSTON CREAM PIE

| | |
|---|---|
| 2 eggs | 1 3/4 cups milk |
| 1 cup sugar | 1 oz. unsweetened chocolate |
| 1 cup flour | 1 T. butter |
| 1 tsp. baking powder | 1 1/2 T. hot milk |
| 1/2 cup boiling water | 3/4 cup powdered sugar |
| 3.4 oz. instant vanilla pudding | 1/8 tsp. salt |

Beat eggs lightly; beat in sugar. Add flour and baking powder. Gradually add boiling water. The batter is thin. Pour into two greased round cake pans. Bake at 350° for 15 to 20 minutes. Cool. Mix pudding with milk. Spread between cake layers. Melt chocolate and butter together. Combine hot milk, sugar and salt in a bowl. Gradually add chocolate mixture; blend well. Quickly spread over the top of the cake.

*Mrs. Larry Zimmerman, Elkhart, IN*

# ITALIAN CREAM CAKE

| | |
|---|---|
| 5 eggs, separated | 1 cup buttermilk |
| 1/2 cup butter or margarine | 3 oz. coconut, about 1 1/4 cups |
| 1/2 cup white shortening | 1 cup chopped nuts,opt. |
| 2 cups sugar | 1 tsp. vanilla |
| 2 cups flour | 1 tsp. coconut flavoring |
| 1 tsp. soda | |

Beat egg whites until stiff; set aside. Cream butter, shortening and sugar. Add egg yolks one at a time, beating well after each. Dissolve soda in buttermilk; add alternately with flour. Beat well. Add remaining ingredients. Fold in egg whites. Pour into 3 greased and floured 9-inch cake pans, using 2 cups batter for each. Bake at 350° for 25 minutes. Cool. Fill and frost with Cream Cheese Frosting II.

*Edna Miller, Snover, MI*

# COCONUT CAKE

| | |
|---|---|
| 1 3/4 cups cake flour | 2 eggs |
| 2 1/4 tsp. baking powder | 2/3 cup milk |
| 3/4 tsp. salt | 1 tsp. vanilla |
| 1/2 cup butter | 2/3 cup coconut |
| 1 cup plus 2 T. sugar | |

Combine first 3 ingredients. Cream butter and sugar until fluffy. Add eggs one at a time, beating well after each addition. Alternately add flour mixture and milk, beating after each addition. Stir in vanilla and coconut. Spread in two greased 8-inch round cake pans. Bake at 350° for 25 to 30 minutes. Frost.

# RAW COCONUT CAKE

*When buying coconuts, shake to make sure the milk is still inside. Punch out the three holes. Drain and save the milk. Bake coconut at 350° for 20 minutes or until it cracks. Cool. Pop open the rest of the way with a hammer if necessary. Remove shell; peel brown skin with a potato peeler. Rinse and dry coconut. Grate; freeze extra coconut.*

| | |
|---|---|
| 2 cups sugar | 1 cup water from coconut |
| 1/2 cup white shortening | 1 1/2 tsp. coconut flavoring |
| 1/2 cup butter or margarine | 5 eggs whites, stiffly beaten |
| 2 1/2 cups flour | 1 cup white shortening |
| 1 T. baking powder | 4 to 5 cups powdered sugar |
| 1 tsp. salt | 1 tsp. coconut flavoring |
| 3/4 cup raw grated coconut | Several T. hot water |

Cream sugar, shortening and butter. Combine dry ingredients; add alternately with coconut water and flavoring. Fold in egg whites. Pour into two 9-inch round cake pans. Bake at 350° for 25 to 30 minutes. Combine remaining ingredients to make frosting, adding hot water until spreading consistency. Frost. Coat with raw grated coconut. Store in refrigerator in a tight container for 2 days to age.

*Mrs. Lloyd E. Troyer, Stella, MO*

# KENTUCKY STACK CAKE

| | |
|---|---|
| 1 cup sorghum molasses | 2 tsp. baking powder |
| 1 cup sugar | 1/2 tsp. soda |
| 1 cup butter | 1/2 tsp. salt |
| 1/4 cup milk | 1/2 tsp. cloves |
| 4 large eggs, well beaten | Applesauce |
| 4 cups flour | Whipping cream |

Cream molasses, sugar and butter. Stir together milk and eggs. Combine dry ingredients. Alternately add molasses mixture and egg mixture to dry ingredients. Stir just until smooth. Divide batter in six well-greased 9-inch round pans; approximately 1 cup in each. Bake at 350° for 12 to 15 minutes. Spread layers with sweetened applesauce; stack layers. Refrigerate in an airtight container 2 days before using. Serve plain or with whipped cream. Dried apples, cooked and sweetened, can also be used.

*Mrs. Jacob Oberholtzer, Liberty, KY*

*The colored sunsets and the starry heavens, the beautiful mountains and the painted flowers, are not half so beautiful as a soul that is serving Jesus out of love, in the wear and tear of life. Faber*

# ORANGE FILLED PARTY CAKE

2/3 cup butter or margarine
2 cups sugar
3 eggs
1 1/2 tsp. vanilla
2 3/4 cups flour
2 1/2 tsp. baking powder
1/2 tsp. salt
1 1/2 cups milk

1 1/4 cups sugar
5 T. cornstarch
1/8 tsp. salt
2/3 cup water
1/2 cup orange juice
1 tsp. vanilla
Red and yellow food coloring

Cream butter, sugar, eggs and vanilla till fluffy. Stir in flour, baking powder, salt and milk. Beat 2 minutes on medium. Pour into two greased and floured 9-inch pans. Bake at 350° for 35 to 40 minutes. Cool 5 minutes before removing from pans. To make filling, combine sugar, cornstarch, and salt. Stir in water and orange juice. Cook and stir until thick and clear. Stir in vanilla and a few drops of food coloring, if desired. Cool. Spread half of filling between cakes, put the rest on the top. Frost the sides with Butter Cream Frosting I.

# PEANUT BUTTER CAKE

1/2 cup butter or margarine
1 1/3 cups sugar
1/4 cup peanut butter
1 tsp. vanilla
2 eggs

2 cups flour
2 tsp. baking powder
1/2 tsp. soda
1 tsp. salt
1 cup milk

Cream butter and sugar till fluffy. Add peanut butter, vanilla and eggs; beat well. Mix dry ingredients and add alternately with milk, mixing well after each addition. Spread in greased and floured 8 or 9-inch round cake pans. Bake at 350° for 35 to 40 minutes. Cool 10 minutes; remove from pans. Frost with peanut butter frosting.

*Mrs. Ray (Elsie) Hoover, Stratford, WI*

# VELVET CAKE

2 cups sugar
1 cup shortening
4 eggs
3 cups cake flour

2 tsp. baking powder
1/2 tsp. salt
1 cup milk
1 tsp. vanilla

Cream sugar and shortening. Beat in eggs, one at a time. Add dry ingredients alternately with milk and vanilla. Pour into two greased and floured 9-inch round pans. Bake at 375° for 35 minutes. A nice cake for decorating since it is firm.

*Mrs. Lloyd E. Troyer, Stella, MO*

# BROWN SUGAR ANGEL CAKE

1 1/2 cups (12) egg whites
1 1/2 tsp. cream of tartar
1 tsp. salt

2 tsp. vanilla
2 cups brown sugar, divided
1 1/4 cups flour

Beat egg whites with cream of tartar, salt and vanilla. Beat till soft peaks form, but still moist and glossy. Gradually sift 1 cup brown sugar over egg whites. Beat till stiff peaks form. Sift remaining cup brown sugar and flour. Fold into egg whites. Pour into tube pan. Bake at 350° for 45 to 50 minutes or until done.

*Sarah Imhoff, Sheridan, MI*

# GOLDEN ANGEL FOOD CAKE

5 egg yolks
1/2 cups cold water
1 1/2 cups sugar, sifted before
     measuring
1 1/2 cups flour

1 1/2 tsp baking powder
1/4 tsp. salt
1 tsp. vanilla
5 egg whites
3/4 tsp. cream of tartar

Beat yolks well. Add water and beat till yolks look like egg whites. Add sugar and beat mixture again. Sift together flour, baking powder and salt; fold into yolk mixture. Fold beaten egg whites into batter and pour into angel food cake pan. Bake at 325° approximately 1 hour.

*Mrs. Harvey (Ruth) Brubaker, Tylertown, MS*

# BURNT SUGAR CHIFFON CAKE

1 cup brown sugar
1/2 cup boiling water
2 cups flour
1 1/2 cups sugar
1 T. baking powder
1 tsp. salt

1/2 cup cooking oil
7 unbeaten egg yolks
1 tsp. vanilla
1/4 cup cold water
1 cup egg whites
1/2 tsp. cream of tartar

Melt brown sugar over low heat till medium brown, stirring constantly. Remove from heat and add boiling water; set aside. Sift together several times flour, sugar, baking powder and salt. Make a well in flour mixture and add oil, yolks, vanilla, burnt sugar and cold water in order given. Beat with spoon till smooth. In a large bowl whip egg whites and cream of tartar till stiff peaks form. Gradually pour first mixture over whites, folding in gently. Pour into tube pan. Bake at 325° for 65 to 70 minutes.

*Mrs. LaVerne (Virginia) Hoover, Goshen, IN*

## MARBLE CHIFFON CAKE

1/3 cup cocoa
2 T. sugar
1/4 cup water
2 T. cooking oil
2 cups flour
1 1/2 cups sugar
1 T. baking powder

1 tsp. salt
1/2 cup cooking oil
7 eggs, separated
3/4 cup cold water
2 tsp. vanilla
1/2 tsp. cream of tartar

Mix cocoa, sugar, water and oil; stir until smooth; set aside. Combine flour, sugar, baking powder and salt in a large bowl; add oil, egg yolks, cold water and vanilla. Beat on low until combined, then on high for 5 minutes. Beat egg whites and cream of tartar in large mixer bowl until stiff. Pour batter in slowly; fold in lightly by hand. Remove 1/3 of batter to a separate bowl; fold in chocolate mixture. Pour half of light mixture in a 10-inch tube pan. Top with half of dark mixture. Repeat layers. With a narrow spatula, swirl gently through batters to marble. Bake at 325° for 65 to 70 minutes or until done. Invert cake.

*Linda Hoover Shaum, Roann, IN*

## FRUIT CAKE

1 1/2 lb. dates
1 lb. candied pineapple chunks
1/2 lb. green candied cherries
1/2 lb. red candied cherries
1 lb. pecan halves
1 lb. English walnuts
2 cups flour

2 tsp. baking powder
1/2 tsp. salt
4 eggs, beaten
1/2 cup light corn syrup
1/4 cup brown sugar
1/4 cup cooking oil

Mix fruits and nuts; set aside. Mix dry ingredients. Stir in remaining ingredients; mix with fruit mixture. Pack firmly into a greased 10x4 tube pan lined with brown paper, (optional). Bake at 275° for 2 hours and 15 minutes or until top appears dry. Cool in pan. The quality of this cake is unsurpassed!

*Mrs. Lloyd E. Troyer, Stella, MO*

## CHRISTMAS PUMPKIN FRUITCAKE

2 cups flour
1/2 tsp. salt
2 tsp. baking powder
1/4 tsp. soda
1 1/2 tsp. pumpkin pie spice
3/4 cup butter, softened
1 1/2 cups sugar

3 eggs
1 cup mashed canned pumpkin
3/4 cup milk
1/2 cup chopped pecans
1/2 cup dates
1/2 cup raisins
10 glazed cherries

Combine flour, salt, baking powder, soda and pumpkin pie spice. In a large bowl, cream butter and sugar until light and fluffy. Add eggs, 1 at a time, beating well after each addition. Add pumpkin; mix well. Add dry ingredients alternately with milk, mix well. Fold in pecans, dates and raisins. Spoon batter in greased and floured 9-inch tube pan. Put cherries on top. Bake at 350° for 1 hour or until done. Let cool in pan.

*Mrs. James (Margaret)Ramer, Dallas, TX*

## UNBAKED FRUIT CAKE I

1 lb. graham crackers
1 lb. raisins
1 lb. dates
1/2 cup candied cherries

1 cup nuts
1 lb. marshmallows
2 cups whipping cream

Roll crackers fine. Chop fruits, nuts and marshmallows. Add cracker crumbs; mix well. Whip cream and fold in. Press into a 9x5x4 pan. Pat mixture with a spoon to smooth top. Refrigerate several weeks before serving.

*Mrs. Cyrus Kulp, Auburn, NY*

## UNBAKED FRUIT CAKE II

1 lb. marshmallows
12 oz. can evaporated milk
1 lb. graham crackers, crushed
1 lb. white raisins
1 lb. pecans

1 lb. walnuts
1/2 lb. red candied cherries, halved
1/2 lb. green candied cherries, halved

Melt marshmallows in milk over low heat. Add cracker crumbs. Add remaining ingredients and pack into pans. Refrigerate or freeze.

*Mrs. Laureen Gerber, Fairview, MI*

## HUMMINGBIRD CAKE

3 cups flour
2 cups sugar
1 tsp. salt
1 tsp. soda
1 tsp. cinnamon
1 1/2 tsp. vanilla

1 cup cooking oil
3 eggs, beaten
1 cup undrained crushed pineapple
2 cups bananas
1 cup chopped pecans

Combine dry ingredients. Add remaining ingredients, stirring only until well mixed. Pour into a bundt pan. Bake at 350° for 1 1/2 hours. A moist cake.

*Mrs. Leonard Weaver, Orrville, AL*

## POUND CAKE

1 1/2 cups sugar
1 cup butter
4 eggs

1 tsp. vanilla
1/2 cup milk
2 cups self-rising flour

Combine ingredients and beat 20 minutes. Pour into a greased tube or loaf pan. Start in cold oven. Bake 350° until toothpick comes out clean.

*Mrs. Lloyd E. Troyer, Stella, MO*

**Self-rising flour has approximately 1 teaspoon baking powder and 1/4 teaspoon salt per cup of flour. Not all recipes turn out well when substitutions are used.**

## YOGURT POUND CAKE

2 cups plus 2 T. whole wheat
    flour
1 tsp. soda
1 tsp. baking powder
1/2 tsp. cinnamon
1/8 tsp. ground cardamom, opt.

1/4 tsp. salt
1/2 cup butter
3/4 cup honey
3 eggs
1 tsp. almond extract
1 cup yogurt

Mix dry ingredients. Cream butter and honey in a large bowl. Beat in eggs, 1 at a time. Beat in extract. Add dry ingredients to egg mixture alternately with yogurt, stirring smooth after each addition. Pour batter into an oiled, floured 9x5 loaf pan. Bake at 350° for 50 to 60 minutes until top is golden. Cool 10 minutes before removing from pan.

*Hannah Kulp Family, Mt Hermon, KY*

Cakes made from
# CAKE MIXES

## CARROT CAKE

1 spice cake mix
2 cups shredded carrots

8 oz. can crushed pineapple
3/4 cup chopped pecans, opt.

Make cake mix as directed; stir in carrots, drained pineapple and nuts. Pour into a 13x9 greased pan. Bake at 350° for 30 to 35 minutes. This can also be put in layer cake pans. Bake layer cakes 25 to 30 minutes. Frost with cream cheese frosting.

# CHERRY POKE CAKE

*For a bit of variety, spread cherry pie filling on cooled cake before adding topping.*

1 white cake mix
2 cups boiling water

6 oz. cherry gelatin
8 oz. frozen whipped topping

Bake cake as directed. Using a fork, poke holes in the cake at 2 inch intervals. Mix water and gelatin, stirring until dissolved, at least 2 minutes. Slowly pour gelatin over hot cake. Refrigerate 3 hours. Top with thawed whipped topping. Any flavor gelatin may be used.

# COOKIES AND CREAM CAKE

1 box white cake mix
16 Oreo cookies

8 oz. frozen whipped topping
Additional cookie crumbs

Prepare cake mix according to instructions. Crush cookies; fold into batter. Spoon into a greased 13x9 pan. Bake at 350° as long as directed on package. Cool. Frost with thawed topping. Sprinkle with additional cookie crumbs.

*Mrs. Isaac Kulp, Millersburg, IN*

# LEMON POKE CAKE

1 box yellow cake mix
3 oz. instant lemon pudding
3/4 cup cooking oil
3/4 cup water
4 eggs

2 cups powdered sugar
2 T. melted butter
2 T. water
1/2 cup lemon juice

Beat cake mix, pudding, oil, water and eggs. Bake in a greased 13x9 pan at 350° for 30 to 35 minutes. To make glaze, combine remaining ingredients. When cake is baked poke holes in it with a fork. Pour glaze over hot cake.

# CREAMY PINEAPPLE CAKE

1 yellow cake mix
20 oz. can crushed pineapple
1 cup powdered sugar
3 oz. instant vanilla pudding

1 cup coconut
8 oz. frozen whipped topping
1 cup chopped pecans, opt.

Bake cake mix as directed on the box in a greased 13x9 pan. Meanwhile simmer pineapple and powdered sugar. Remove cake from oven; poke holes in it; cover with pineapple and chill. Mix pudding as directed on the box. Add coconut and spread over pineapple. Cover with thaweded topping; sprinkle with nuts.

*Irene Peachey, East Flat Rock, NC*

# EASY PINEAPPLE CAKE

20 oz. can crushed pineapple          1/2 cup butter
1 yellow cake mix

Pour undrained pineapple in a 13x9 pan. Sprinkle dry cake mix on top. Melt butter and drizzle over cake mix. Bake at 350° for 35 minutes.

# 4 DAY MAKE AHEAD SOUR CREAM TORTE

1 chocolate cake mix               2 cups sour cream
3 eggs                             1 cup sugar
1 cup water                        3 cups coconut
1/3 cup cooking oil                3 cups frozen whipped topping

Blend cake mix, eggs, water and oil. Beat 2 minutes on high. Bake at 350° for 30 to 35 minutes. Cool 15 minutes. Remove from pans; cool completely. Split each layer in half. Combine sour cream, sugar and coconut; fold in thawed topping. Spread between layers.

*June L. Hartman, Elida, OH*

# TURTLE CAKE

1 box German chocolate cake mix    1/2 cup evaporated milk
14 oz. pkg. caramels               1 cup chocolate chips
1/2 cup butter or margarine        1 cup chopped pecans

Mix cake according to package directions. Pour 1/2 the batter in a 13x9 pan. Bake at 350° for 15 minutes. Melt caramels, butter and milk over low heat, stirring constantly. Pour over baked cake; sprinkle with chips and nuts. Pour the rest of the batter on top. Bake another 15 minutes, or until done. Frost if desired.

*Sheryl Weaver, Goshen, IN*

# TWINKIE CAKE

1 box yellow cake mix              1 cup milk
1/2 cup white shortening           1/2 cup butter or margarine
4 eggs                             1/2 cup white shortening
3 oz. instant vanilla pudding      1 cup sugar
1 cup water                        1 tsp. vanilla
3 T. flour

Combine cake mix, shortening, eggs, pudding and water; mix well. Divide batter on 2 greased cookie sheets. Bake at 350° for 15 to 20 minutes. Cook flour and milk until thick. Cool. Add remaining ingredients. Beat till thick; spread on one cake. Place second cake on top. Chocolate cake mix can be used as well.

*Anna Zimmerman, Decker, MI*

# UGLY DUCKLING CAKE

1 yellow cake mix
16 oz. can fruit cocktail in syrup
2 1/2 cups coconut
2 eggs

1/2 cup brown sugar
1/2 cup butter or margarine
1/2 cup sugar
1/2 cup evaporated milk

Combine cake mix, undrained fruit cocktail, 1 cup of coconut and eggs; beat for 2 minutes on medium speed. Pour into a greased 13x9 pan. Sprinkle with brown sugar. Bake at 325° for 45 minutes. Meanwhile bring butter, sugar and milk to a boil; boil 2 minutes. Remove from heat and stir in remaining coconut. Spoon over hot cake in pan. Serve warm or cold.

*Mrs. Lloyd E. Troyer, Stella, MO*

# COFFEE CAKES

## BLUEBERRY COFFEECAKE

2 cups flour
3/4 cup sugar
2 tsp. baking powder
1/4 tsp. salt
1 egg, beaten

1/2 cup milk
1/2 cup butter, melted
1 cup blueberries
1/2 cup sugar
1/3 cup flour

Combine dry ingredients. Beat in egg, milk and butter. Fold in blueberries. Spread in a greased 9x9 pan. Mix sugar and flour and sprinkle on top. Bake at 375° for 35 minutes.

## CINNAMON CRUNCH COFFEECAKE

2 cups whole wheat flour
2 1/2 tsp. baking powder
1 tsp. cinnamon
1/2 tsp. salt
1/4 tsp. nutmeg
3/4 cup honey
1/3 cup butter

1 cup milk
2 eggs
2/3 cup brown sugar
2 T. flour
2 T. butter
1 cup chopped pecans

In a large bowl mix first 5 ingredients. Blend in honey, butter and milk; beat 1 1/2 minutes. Add eggs and beat 1 minute. Spread 1/3 of batter into a greased and floured 13x9 pan. Mix brown sugar and flour; cut in butter. Add nuts. Sprinkle half of crumbs on batter. Carefully spread remaining batter over crumbs; sprinkle with remaining crumbs. Bake at 350° for 30 to 35 minutes. Serve warm.

## PEACHES AND CREAM COFFEECAKE

1/2 cup butter, softened
3/4 cup sugar
1 tsp. vanilla
2 eggs
2 cups flour
2 tsp. baking powder

1/2 tsp. salt
1 cup milk
16 oz. cream cheese, softened
1 cup sugar
5 cups sliced peaches
Sugar and cinnamon

Cream butter, sugar and vanilla. Beat in eggs. Mix flour, baking powder and salt; add alternately with milk. Pour into a greased 15x10 pan. Combine cream cheese with sugar. Mix in sliced peaches. Spoon over batter. Sprinkle with sugar and cinnamon. Bake at 350° approximately 40 minutes.

## QUICK FRENCH COFFEE CAKES

1/3 cup cooking oil
1/2 cup sugar
1 egg
1 1/2 cups flour
1 1/2 tsp. baking powder
1/2 tsp. salt

1/4 tsp. nutmeg
1/2 cup milk
3/4 cup sugar
1 1/4 tsp. cinnamon
1/2 cup butter or margarine

Mix oil, sugar and egg. Combine flour, baking powder, salt and nutmeg; add alternately with milk. Divide batter evenly in greased muffin tin. Bake at 350° for 15 to 20 minutes. Mix remaining sugar and cinnamon. Melt butter. Roll baked cakes in melted butter, and then dip into sugar mixture. Serve warm.

*Mrs. Larry Zimmerman, Elkhart, IN*

## SOUR CREAM COFFEECAKE

1/2 cup butter
1/2 cup sugar
1 tsp. vanilla
3 eggs
2 cups flour
1 tsp. baking powder
1 tsp. soda
1 cup sour cream
1 3/4 cups mashed pumpkin

1 egg, beaten
1/3 cup sugar
1 tsp. pumpkin pie spice
1 cup brown sugar
1/3 cup butter
1/3 cup flour
2 tsp. cinnamon
1 cup chopped nuts

Cream butter, sugar and vanilla. Beat in eggs. Add flour, baking powder, and soda alternately with sour cream. Combine pumpkin, egg, sugar and spice. Spoon half of batter into a13x9 pan. Combine remaining ingredients; sprinkle half in pan. Spread pumpkin over crumbs. Carefully spread remaining batter over pumpkin. Top with remaining crumbs. Bake at 325° for 50 to 60 minutes.

*Margaret Zimmerman, Ephrata, PA*

# CUPCAKES

## BANANA CUPCAKES

1/2 cup butter
1/2 cup sugar
1 egg
1 large ripe banana, mashed

2 T. sour cream or milk
1 cup flour
1/2 tsp. soda
1/4 cup chopped nuts, opt.

Cream butter and sugar; add egg, mashed banana and sour cream. Add flour and soda. Divide batter into 12 greased or lined muffin cups. Bake at 375° for 20 minutes. Frost and top with nuts.

## CHOCOLATE CUPCAKES

2 cups flour
2 cups sugar
1 tsp. salt
1 tsp. baking powder
2 tsp. soda

3/4 cup cocoa
1 cup cooking oil
1 cup milk
2 eggs
1 cup hot coffee

Mix ingredients in order given. Batter will be thin. Spoon into greased or lined muffin tins. Bake at 350° approximately 35 minutes. Frost.

*Mrs. Elias Martin, Goshen, IN*

## CHOCOLATE CUPCAKES WITH FILLING

2 cups sugar
1/2 cup cooking oil
1 egg
3 cups flour
6 T. cocoa
2 tsp. soda
1 tsp. baking powder
1 tsp salt

2 cups cold water
2 tsp. vanilla
1 cup milk
1/4 cup flour
1/8 tsp. salt
1 cup powdered sugar
1 cup shortening
1 tsp. vanilla

Beat sugar, oil and egg until fluffy. Add flour, cocoa, soda, baking powder and salt alternately with water. Add vanilla. Fill greased or lined muffin tins. Bake at 350° for 20 minutes. To make filling combine milk, flour and salt. Stir and cook until thick; cool. Beat until fluffy. Add powdered sugar, shortening and vanilla. Beat until thick and fluffy. Cut center out of cooled cupcakes with a sharp knife. Fill; set centers back on filling.

*Mrs. Isaac Brubacker, Versailles, MO*

## CHOCOLATE CUPCAKES WITH COCONUT FILLING
*Chocolate lovers can substitute chocolate chips for coconut.*

8 oz. cream cheese, softened
1/3 cup sugar
1 egg
1 cup coconut
1 1/2 cups flour
1 cup sugar
1/4 cup cocoa

1 tsp. soda
1/2 tsp. salt
1 cup water
1/3 cup cooking oil
1 T. vinegar
1 tsp. vanilla

Beat cream cheese and sugar until smooth. Beat in egg. Add coconut. Set aside. Combine flour, sugar, cocoa, soda and salt; stir in liquids. Mix well. Fill 18 cupcake papers 1/2 full of batter. Add a spoonful of filling. Top with a spoonful of batter. Bake at 350° for 30 minutes or till done. Eat plain, or frost with chocolate or white frosting.

*Kristie LaVonne Hoover, Stratford, WI*

## EASY FILLED CHOCOLATE CUPCAKES

1 chocolate cake mix
8 oz. cream cheese, softened
1/3 cup sugar

1 egg
1/8 tsp. salt
1 to 2 cup chocolate chips

Mix cake mix as directed; fill cupcake papers 2/3 full of batter. Beat cream cheese with sugar; add egg and salt. Stir in desired amount of chocolate chips. Divide filling evenly over cupcakes. Bake at 350° approximately 20 minutes, or until done.

*Anna Zimmerman, Decker, MI*      *Mrs. Larry Zimmerman, Elkhart, IN*

## CHOCOLATE CHIP CUPCAKES
*Try this recipe using butterscotch chips and caramel frosting.*

1 1/4 cups sugar
2/3 cup cooking oil
2 eggs, beaten
1 tsp. vanilla
2 cups flour

2 tsp. baking powder
1/2 tsp. salt
3/4 cup milk
1 1/2 cups chocolate chips

Beat sugar, oil, eggs and vanilla. Add dry ingredients alternately with milk; mix well. Stir in chocolate chips. Fill greased or lined muffin tins. Makes 24 cupcakes. Bake at 350° approximately 25 minutes. Eat plain or frost with chocolate or white frosting.

*William Paul Hoover II, Stratford, WI*

## EASY CUPCAKES

*Add Kool-Aid powder of your choice for flavored cupcakes.*

1 1/2 cups sugar
1/2 cup shortening
2 eggs
1 tsp. vanilla

2 1/4 cups flour
1 T. baking powder
1 tsp. salt
1 cup milk

Cream sugar and shortening; beat in eggs and vanilla. Add dry ingredients alternately with milk. Fill cupcake papers 1/2 to 3/4 full. Bake at 350° approximately 25 minutes.

*Edna Miller, Snover, MI*

## LEMON FILLED CUPCAKES

4 eggs
2 cups sugar
1 cup hot milk
1 tsp. orange flavoring
1/2 tsp. lemon flavoring
2 cups flour
1/2 tsp. salt

2 tsp. baking powder
3/4 cup white shortening
1/3 cup milk
1 tsp lemon flavoring or to taste
3 cups powdered sugar
1 to 2 cups whipped topping

Beat eggs till thick and lemon-colored. Slowly add sugar; beat well. Add hot milk gradually, stirring vigorously. Add flavorings. Sift dry ingredients. Slowly sift into egg mixture, folding in with a whisk until well blended. Bake in greased or lined muffin tins at 350° until done. Cool completely. To make filling, cream shortening, milk, and flavoring. Beat in powdered sugar. Fold in whipped topping. Cut out middle of cupcake at the top. Fill. Replace top.

*Mrs. Elias Martin, Goshen, IN*

## PEANUT BUTTER CUPCAKES

1/3 cup butter or margarine
1 1/2 cups brown sugar
1/2 cup peanut butter
2 eggs, beaten
1 tsp. vanilla

2 cups flour
1/2 tsp. salt
1 1/2 tsp. baking powder
1/2 tsp. soda
3/4 cup milk

Cream butter and sugar; mix in peanut butter. Add eggs and vanilla; beat. Combine dry ingredients and add alternately with milk, beating after each addition. Divide batter into 24 greased or lined muffin cups. Bake at 350° approximately 25 minutes. Eat plain or frost with white, chocolate or peanut butter frosting.

329

## SHOO-FLY CUPCAKES

| | |
|---|---|
| 2 1/2 cups flour | 1 cup brown sugar |
| 1 1/2 cups brown sugar | 1 1/2 cups boiling water |
| 1/2 cup butter | 1 tsp. soda |
| 1 tsp. baking powder | |

Make crumbs with the first 4 ingredients. Reserve one cup. To remaining crumbs, add brown sugar, boiling water and soda. Mix well. Fill cupcake liners 2/3 full. Put approximately 1 teaspoon on top of each cupcake. Bake at 350° for 20 minutes or until done.

*Esther Martin, Decker, MI*

**Even if you are on the right track, you won't get anywhere if you just sit there.**

# FROSTING

Pure
POWDERED
SUGAR

Elsie
Hoxer

## BROWNED BUTTER FROSTING

1/2 cup butter
4 cups powdered sugar

1/4 cup milk
1 tsp. vanilla

Heat butter over medium heat until golden. Remove from heat and add remaining ingredients. Beat until smooth.

## BUTTER CREAM FROSTING I

1/2 cup butter
1/4 cup milk

1 tsp. vanilla
1 lb. (about 4 c.) powdered sugar

Beat butter, milk and vanilla until fluffy. Beat in powdered sugar.

*Verna Overholt, Due West, SC*

## BUTTER CREAM FROSTING II

1 1/4 lb. powdered sugar
1.5 oz. powdered milk
1 cup butter or margarine

1/4 cup water
Vanilla

Mix sugar, milk and butter. Add water and vanilla till right consistency. Beat well.

*Suetta Hoover, Tipton, MO*

## CARAMEL FROSTING

*For caramel nut frosting add 3/4 cup nuts.*

1/2 cup butter or margarine
1 cup brown sugar
1/4 cup milk

2 cups powdered sugar
1 tsp. vanilla

Melt butter. Stir in brown sugar and milk. Heat just enough to dissolve sugar. Remove from heat; cool. Beat in powdered sugar and vanilla.

*Mrs. James Kulp, Unity, WI*

## CHOCOLATE BUTTER CREAM FROSTING

1/2 cup butter, softened
1/4 to 1/3 cup cocoa
3 cups powdered sugar

1/3 cup milk
1 tsp. vanilla

Cream butter; add cocoa and powdered sugar alternately with milk. Beat to spreading consistency, adding more milk if needed. Add vanilla.

*Mrs. Ray (Elsie) Hoover, Stratford, WI*

# DARK CHOCOLATE FROSTING

1/2 cup butter
1/2 to 2/3 cup cocoa
3 cups powdered sugar

1/3 cup milk
1 tsp. vanilla

Melt butter; stir in cocoa. Alternately add powdered sugar and milk. Add vanilla. Beat until smooth. Add more milk if needed.

One pound of powdered sugar contains 3 1/2 to 4 cups powdered sugar.

# FLUFFY CHOCOLATE FROSTING

*To use this for white frosting, delete cocoa and use less milk.*

4 cups powdered sugar
1/4 cup cocoa
1/2 cup butter or margarine

1 tsp. vanilla
1/2 cup evaporated milk

Cream powdered sugar, cocoa and butter. Blend in vanilla and half of milk. Add remaining milk; beat to desired consistency. Enough for two 9-inch layers.

*Mrs. Norman Burkholder, Mertztown, PA*

# CHOCOLATE CHIP FROSTING

1/4 cup butter
1/4 cup milk
1 cup semisweet chocolate chips

1 tsp. vanilla
2 cups powdered sugar

Bring butter and milk to a boil. Remove from heat; stir in chips and vanilla. Stir until smooth. Blend in powdered sugar until smooth. If necessary thin with milk.

# COCOA GLAZE

2 T. butter or margarine
2 T. cocoa
2 T. milk

1/8 tsp. salt
1 cup powdered sugar
1 tsp. vanilla

Bring first 4 ingredients to a boil. Remove from heat; add powdered sugar. Beat until smooth then stir in vanilla.

*The best proof of love for God is love for one another.*

## COCONUT CREAM CHEESE FROSTING

*For chocolate coconut cream cheese frosting, add 1/4 cup cocoa. Thin with milk if necessary.*

8 oz. cream cheese, softened
1/4 cup butter, softened
1 T. milk

1 tsp. vanilla
3 1/2 cups powdered sugar
2 cups coconut

Beat cream cheese, butter, milk and vanilla. Add powdered sugar; beat until smooth. Stir in coconut. Enough frosting for a 13x9 cake.

## GOLDEN COCONUT FROSTING

1/2 cup butter
1 1/3 cups coconut
1 cup brown sugar

1/4 cup milk
2 cups powdered sugar

Melt 2 tablespoons butter in skillet. Add coconut and stir until golden. Remove about 1/2 of coconut; set aside. Melt remaining butter in skillet with coconut; add brown sugar. Cook and stir over low heat 2 minutes. Add milk; bring to a boil. Remove from heat. Cool. Gradually add powdered sugar, beating well after each addition. Spread on cake and sprinkle with reserved coconut.

*Mrs. Ray (Elsie) Hoover, Stratford, WI*

## COCONUT TOPPING

1 1/3 cups coconut
1 cup brown sugar
6 T. melted butter

1/3 cup light cream
1 cup chopped nuts, opt

Combine all ingredients; mix well. Spread on cake and place under broiler. Broil till topping is bubbly and lightly browned. Good on chocolate, spice or oatmeal cakes. Enough for a 13x9 cake.

## COFFEE FROSTING

1 lb. powdered sugar
1/2 cup butter or margarine
1/4 cup boiling water

1 tsp. instant coffee crystals
1 tsp. vanilla

Beat everything together until fluffy. Enough for a 13x9 cake.

*Vera Fox, Memphis, MO*

# COLORFUL FROSTING

4 cups powdered sugar
1 tsp. unsweetened Kool-Aid
   powder

1/2 cup butter, softened
4 to 5 T. hot water

Mix sugar and powder; add butter and hot water. Beat until smooth. Enough for a 13x9 cake or 30 cupcakes.

# CREAM CHEESE FROSTING I

1/4 cup butter or margarine
3 oz. cream cheese

1 tsp. vanilla
2 cups powdered sugar

Cream butter, cream cheese and vanilla. Add powdered sugar; beat till smooth.

*Mrs. Phillip Zimmerman, Versailles, MO*

# CREAM CHEESE FROSTING II

*To make lemon cream cheese frosting, delete vanilla and nuts and add 2 tablespoons of lemon juice.*

1/2 cup butter, softened
8 oz. cream cheese, softened
4 cups powdered sugar

2 tsp. vanilla
1 cup chopped nuts, opt.

Beat butter, cream cheese and sugar until creamy; add vanilla and nuts. This makes enough to frost tops and sides of a layer cake.

*Mrs. Ray (Elsie) Hoover, Stratford, WI*

# FLUFFY CREAM CHEESE FROSTING OR FILLING

16 oz. cream cheese, softened
2 cups powdered sugar

8 oz. frozen whipped topping
   (about 3 cups)

Beat cream cheese and sugar until well blended. Fold in thawed whipped topping. Mix well.

# CREAMY VANILLA FROSTING

*Add several tablespoons of cocoa for creamy chocolate frosting. Increase milk if necessary.*

1/2 cup white shortening
1 lb. (about 4 c.) powdered sugar

1/3 cup milk
1 tsp. vanilla

Combine everything and mix well. Makes 2 cups.

*Mrs. Ray (Elsie) Hoover, Stratford, WI*

# DECORATING FROSTING I

1 lb. powdered sugar, sift if lumpy
2/3 cup white shortening
1/8 tsp. salt

1/2 tsp. vanilla
1/2 tsp. clear butter flavoring
2 to 3 T. water

Beat at medium speed until creamy, 5 to 10 minutes.

*Mrs. Larry Zimmerman, Elkhart, IN*

# DECORATING FROSTING II

1/2 cup butter
1/2 cup white shortening
1 tsp. vanilla

1/8 tsp. salt
1 lb. (about 4 c.) powdered sugar
3 T. cold milk or cream

Cream butter and shortening. Add vanilla and salt. Beat in sugar, 1 cup at a time, blending well after each addition. Scrape sides and bottom of bowl often. Add milk and beat at high speed until light and fluffy. This can be stored in the refrigerator in an airtight container for a week, and then whipped up again before using. Makes 3 cups.

# EASY FROSTING

*Add 2 to 3 tablespoons of cocoa for chocolate frosting or filling.*

1/2 cup white shortening
1/2 cup butter
3/4 cup sugar

7 T. flour
1 tsp. vanilla
1/2 cup milk

Put all ingredients in a bowl and let set for at least 30 minutes, then beat for 5 minutes. Do not cook. This is also good filling for filled doughnuts.

*Susan Miller, Nappanee, IN*

# FUDGE FROSTING

1/2 cup butter or margarine
6 T. milk
2 T. cocoa

1 tsp. vanilla
1 lb. (about 4 c.) powdered sugar
1 cup chopped nut, opt.

Boil butter, milk and cocoa for several minutes. Remove from heat. Add vanilla and powdered sugar. Beat well. Good on Texas Sheet Cake.

*Donna Herr, Nappanee, IN    Mrs. Clay Zimmerman, Paltinis, Romania*

## EASY FUDGE FROSTING

2 cups chocolate chips                    2 tsp. vanilla
14 oz. sweetened condensed milk

Combine everything and melt over low heat; stir until smooth.  Frost immediately.

## GLAZE

1 cup powdered sugar                      1 T. milk
2 T. melted butter

Combine all the ingredients and mix well.  If too thin add more powdered sugar.

## LEMON BUTTER FROSTING

1/4 cup butter, softened                  2 T. milk or water
3 cups powdered sugar                     1 tsp. vanilla
2 T. lemon juice                          1/8 tsp. salt

Combine all the ingredients and beat until smooth.  Makes approximately 2 cups.

## LEMON FILLING

3/4 cup sugar                             6 T. lemon juice
3 T. cornstarch                           2 T. butter
1/4 tsp. salt                             3/4 cup water
1 1/2 T. grated lemon rind

Combine dry ingredients.  Add remaining ingredients; mix well and bring to a boil, stirring constantly.  Boil one minute.  Chill.

## MAPLE BUTTER FROSTING

3 cups powdered sugar                     1/2 cup maple syrup
6 T. soft butter

Blend sugar and butter.  Add maple syrup and mix until fluffy.

*The best way to know God's will, is to say "I will" to God.*

# MARSHMALLOW FROSTING OR FILLING

1 cup butter
2 cups powdered sugar

2 cups marshmallow crème
1 tsp. vanilla

Cream butter and sugar; add crème and vanilla. Add a little milk if too thick.

# NO-POWDERED-SUGAR FROSTING I

4 to 5 T. flour
1 cup milk
1/2 cup butter, softened

1/2 cup white shortening
1 cup sugar or brown sugar
1 tsp. vanilla

Bring flour and milk to a boil. Set aside to cool. Cream butter and shortening; add sugar and vanilla. Beat in flour mixture. Beat until light and creamy.

*Charlotte Martin, Goshen, IN     Verna Overholt, Due West, SC*

# NO-POWDERED-SUGAR FROSTING II

1 cup sugar
6 T. cocoa
3 T. cooking oil

1/2 cup dry milk
1/3 cup water
1/8 tsp. salt

Put sugar in blender; blend 1 minute on high. Add rest of ingredients. Blend 3 minutes or till thick. If too thin, chill awhile.

*Edna Miller, Snover, MI*

# ORANGE FROSTING

*If you don't have orange juice use milk, and add a teaspoon of orange extract.*

2 2/3 cups powdered sugar
2 T. melted butter

1/4 cup orange juice
1/2 tsp. orange or lemon extract

Mix ingredients. Enough for a 10-inch angel food or sponge cake.

# PEANUT BUTTER FROSTING

1/4 cup peanut butter
1/4 cup butter
1 tsp. vanilla

1/4 tsp. salt
3 cups powdered sugar
3 T. milk

Cream peanut butter, butter, vanilla and salt. Add sugar alternately with milk. Beat until light and fluffy.

*Mrs. Ray (Elsie) Hoover, Stratford, WI*

# PEANUT BUTTER FROSTING OR FILLING

2/3 cup peanut butter
1/4 cup white shortening

4 cups powdered sugar
1/2 cup milk

Cream peanut butter and shortening. Add sugar and milk. Beat until fluffy.

# PINEAPPLE FROSTING

4 cups powdered sugar
1/2 cup butter, softened
1 tsp. lemon flavoring

1 tsp. vanilla
1/8 tsp. salt
1 cup crushed pineapple, drained

Combine all but pineapple and mix well. Stir in drained pineapple.

# ROCKY ROAD FROSTING

*For a rockier road add 3/4 cup chopped walnuts.*

1 cup chocolate chips
2 cups miniature marshmallows
1/4 cup water

1/4 cup butter
2 1/2 cups powdered sugar
1 tsp. vanilla

Heat chocolate chips, half of the marshmallows, water and butter until blended, stirring constantly. Cool slightly. Add powdered sugar and vanilla. Beat until thick. Stir in remaining marshmallows. Enough frosting to frost a 13x9 cake.

# SANDWICH COOKIE FILLING

4 cups powdered sugar, divided
2 cups white shortening, divided

1/4 cup flour
1/4 cup milk

Mix 2 cups powdered sugar, 1 cup shortening, flour and milk until creamy. Beat in remaining 2 cups powdered sugar and 1 cup shortening.

*Melinda Weaver, Spencer, WI*

# STRAWBERRY FROSTING

1/4 cup butter
1/8 tsp. salt
3 cups powdered sugar

1/3 cup fresh strawberries,
   crushed
1 tsp. vanilla

Mix all the ingredients together. Beat until smooth and creamy.

# COOKIES

# DROP COOKIES AND SHAPED COOKIES

Baking times given are for preheated ovens. These times are only guidelines. Bigger cookies take longer while smaller cookies may get done sooner. Pack brown sugar into measuring cups, but fill flour lightly. Generally butter, margarine, solid white shortening or lard can be used in recipes calling for shortening. A combination works great – butter for flavor and shortening to keep the cookies from spreading out as much.

## APPLESAUCE COOKIES

1 1/2 cups sugar
3/4 cup shortening
1 egg
2 1/2 cups flour
1 tsp. soda
1/2 tsp. baking powder

1/2 tsp. salt
1 tsp. cinnamon
1/2 tsp. nutmeg
1/4 tsp. cloves
1 cup applesauce
3/4 cup raisins or nuts

Cream sugar and shortening; add egg. Add dry ingredients alternately with apple sauce. Add raisins. Bake on a greased cookie sheet at 375° about 10 minutes.

## BLACK WALNUT TEA COOKIES

1 lb. black walnuts
1 lb. brown sugar

3 eggs
1 cup flour

Grind nuts fine. Combine all ingredients; dough will be sticky. Roll dough in balls the size of a small nut and place on ungreased cookie sheets. Pat flat. Bake at 375° for 8 to 10 minutes. This is an old recipe made at Christmas time.

*Cretora Bear Hilty, Elida, OH*

## BROWN SUGAR COOKIES

2 cups brown sugar
1/2 cup shortening
2 eggs
3 1/2 cups flour

1/2 tsp. salt
2 tsp. baking powder
1 tsp. soda
1 cup milk

Cream sugar and shortening; add eggs and beat well. Mix dry ingredients; add alternately with milk. Bake at 350° until done. Coconut, chocolate chips or nuts can be added.

*Esther Horst, East Earl, PA*

## BUTTERMILK COOKIES I

1 cup shortening
2 cups sugar
3 eggs
2 tsp. vanilla
4 cups flour

1T. baking powder
1 tsp. soda
1 tsp. salt
1 cup buttermilk

Cream shortening and sugar; add eggs and vanilla. Mix dry ingredients and add alternately with buttermilk. Drop by teaspoon on ungreased sheet. Bake at 375° approximately 10 minutes. Frost with cream cheese frosting, or other frosting.

*Edna Miller, Snover, MI*

## BUTTERMILK COOKIES II

6 3/4 cups brown sugar
2 cups butter or other shortening
2 tsp. vanilla
2 T. soda
4 cups buttermilk

10 cups flour
1 T. cream of tartar
1 tsp. cinnamon or cloves
1 tsp. salt

Cream sugar, butter and vanilla. Mix soda with buttermilk and add alternately with dry ingredients. Bake at 350° approximately 15 minutes. When cool, dust with powdered sugar or frost. Using less sugar and adding a little blackstrap molasses adds flavor. An egg or two may also be added.

*Mrs. Elam Hoover, Versailles, MO        Mrs. Susan Martin, Romulus, NY*
*Mrs. Ivan Zimmerman, Scottsville, KY*

## BUTTER PECAN COOKIES

1 cup butter
1/2 cup brown sugar
1 egg
1 tsp. vanilla
1 3/4 cups flour

3/4 cup powdered sugar
1/4 tsp. soda
1/4 tsp. salt
1 cup chopped pecans

Cream butter and brown sugar. Add egg and vanilla; beat well. Stir in flour, powdered sugar, soda and salt. Mix in pecans. Drop onto cookie sheets 2 inches apart. Bake at 375° for 10 to 12 minutes, until lightly browned.

*Salvation is not something we achieve – it is something we receive.*

# CARROT COOKIES

1 cup whole wheat flour
1 tsp. baking powder
1/8 tsp. salt
1 cup oatmeal
1/4 cup sunflower seeds
1/4 cup chopped walnuts

1/4 cup raisins
1 cup shredded carrots
1/2 cup honey
1/2 cup cooking oil
1/4 tsp. vanilla

Combine flour, baking powder, salt and oatmeal; mix well. Stir in seeds, nuts, raisins and carrots. Beat together honey, oil and vanilla and stir in until well moistened. Drop by rounded teaspoon onto greased cookie sheet. Flatten with fingers, compressing dough so cookies stay together. Bake at 375° for 10 to 12 minutes. Wait 1 minute before removing cookies from cookie sheet.

*Hannah Kulp Family, Mt. Herman, KY*

# CHOCOLATE ALMOND COOKIES

1 1/2 cups brown sugar
2/3 cup butter or margarine
1 T. water
1 tsp. almond extract
2 eggs
1 1/2 cups flour

1/3 cup cocoa
1/2 tsp. salt
1/4 tsp. soda
2 cups chocolate chips
1 cup finely chopped almonds

Mix sugar, butter, water and flavoring; add eggs and beat until well blended. Combine flour, cocoa, salt and soda; add, mixing well. Stir in chocolate chips and almonds. Drop by rounded tablespoonfuls. Bake at 375° for 7 to 9 minutes, or until cookies are set. Do not overbake.

# CHOCOLATE CHIP COOKIES.

1 cup butter
1 cup sugar
1 cup brown sugar
2 eggs
1 tsp. vanilla
1 tsp. salt

1 tsp. soda
2 T. hot water
3 cups flour
12 oz. (2 cups) chocolate chips
1 cup nuts, opt.

Cream butter, sugars, eggs and vanilla. Add salt, soda and hot water. Mix in flour (if you don't use Gold Medal it will take more flour, dough should be stiff, but not dry). Add chips and nuts. Bake at 350° approximately 10 minutes. Do not overbake.

*Mrs. Luke Hoover, Goshen, IN*      *Doreen Zimmerman, Claypool, IN*

341

# CHOCOLATE CHIP CEREAL COOKIES

| | |
|---|---|
| 3 1/2 cups flour | 1 cup butter or margarine |
| 1 T. soda | 1 egg |
| 1 tsp. salt | 1 T. milk |
| 1 cup sugar | 2 tsp. vanilla |
| 1 cup brown sugar | 1 cup cooking oil |
| 1 cup crushed cornflakes | 2 cups chocolate chips |
| 1 cup oatmeal | |

Combine dry ingredients. Add flakes and oatmeal. Beat together remaining ingredients except oil and chips. Add alternately with oil to dry ingredients. Add chips. Bake at 350° for 12 minutes on ungreased cookie sheets.

*Karen Weaver, Milford, IN*

A 12 ounce package of chocolate, butterscotch or peanut butter chips contains approximately two cups chips.

# CHOCOLATE AND PEANUT BUTTER CHIP COOKIES

| | |
|---|---|
| 3/4 cup butter or margarine | 2 cups flour |
| 1 cup sugar | 1 tsp. soda |
| 1/2 cup brown sugar | 1/4 tsp. salt |
| 1 tsp. vanilla | 1 cup chocolate chips |
| 2 eggs | 1 cup peanut butter chips |

Cream butter and sugar, brown sugar and vanilla until fluffy. Add eggs; beat well. Combine and add flour, soda and salt. Stir in chocolate and peanut butter chips. Drop by rounded teaspoonfuls onto greased cookies sheets. Bake at 350° for 10 to 12 minutes or until lightly browned. Cool slightly before removing from cookie sheets. Do not overbake.

*Pauline Kulp, Stratford, WI*

# CHOCOLATE COOKIES WITH PEANUT BUTTER CHIPS

| | |
|---|---|
| 1 cup butter or margarine | 2/3 cup cocoa |
| 1 1/2 cups sugar | 3/4 tsp. soda |
| 2 eggs | 1/2 tsp. salt |
| 2 tsp. vanilla | 2 cups peanut butter chips |
| 2 cups flour | |

Cream butter and sugar; add eggs and vanilla; blend well. Combine flour, cocoa, soda and salt; blend into creamed mixture. Stir in peanut butter chips. Drop by teaspoonfuls onto ungreased cookie sheets. Bake at 350° for 8 to 9 minutes. Do not overbake.

*Pauline Kulp, Stratford, WI*     *Mrs. Sam Newswanger, Goshen, IN*

## CHOCOLATE COVERED PEANUT COOKIES

1 cup butter or margarine
3/4 cup sugar
3/4 cup brown sugar
2 eggs
1 tsp. vanilla

1 tsp. soda
1/4 tsp. salt
2 1/4 cups flour
2 cups chocolate covered
    peanuts

Cream butter and sugars. Add eggs and vanilla; beat until fluffy. Beat in soda and salt. Stir in flour. Add chocolate covered peanuts. Drop by rounded teaspoonfuls onto ungreased cookie sheets. Bake at 350° for 9 to 11 minutes or until just barely golden. Do not overbake.

## CHOCOLATE PRETZEL COOKIES

1/2 cup butter or margarine
2/3 cup sugar
1 egg
2 oz. unsweetened chocolate,
    melted

2 tsp. vanilla
1 3/4 cups flour
1/2 tsp. salt
Chocolate for dipping

Cream butter and sugar; beat in egg, cooled chocolate and vanilla. Mix well. Gradually add flour and salt; mix well. Chill dough 1 hour or until firm. Divide dough into four 6-inch logs. Cut each log into 12 pieces; roll each piece into a 9-inch rope. Place ropes on a greased cookie sheet. Form into pretzels. Bake at 400° approximately 6 minutes. Cool 1 minute before removing from sheet. Melt chocolate and dip pretzels. Place on wax paper. Drizzle with melted white chocolate if desired.

*Katrina Lauren Hoover, Stratford, WI*

## CRANBERRY NUT DROP COOKIES

1/2 cup butter
1 cup sugar
3/4 cup brown sugar
1/4 cup milk
2 T. orange or lemon juice
1 egg

3 cups flour
1 tsp. baking powder
1/2 tsp. salt
1/4 tsp. soda
1 cup chopped nuts
2 1/2 cups chopped cranberries

Cream butter and sugars. Beat in milk, juice and egg. Combine and add dry ingredients; mix well. Stir in nuts and coarsely chopped cranberries. Drop dough by teaspoonfuls on greased cookie sheets. Bake at 375° for 10 to 12 minutes.

# CREAM CHEESE COOKIES

2/3 cup butter or margarine
8 oz. cream cheese
2 1/2 cups brown sugar
2 1/2 cups flour
4 tsp. baking powder

3/4 tsp. salt
1/3 tsp. soda
1 1/2 cups coconut
1/4 cup milk
Cornflake crumbs

Blend butter, cream cheese and sugar. Combine and add dry ingredients, coconut and milk; mix well. Chill several hours. Form into small balls and roll into cornflake crumbs. Bake at 350° for 8 to 10.

*Berdena Hoover, Elkhart, IN     Sheryl Wenger, Marlette, MI*

# FARMER COOKIES

1 cup shortening
2 cups sugar
2 eggs
1/4 cup milk
1/2 tsp. salt

4 tsp. baking powder
2 cups flour
1 cup whole wheat flour
1/2 cup cornmeal
1/2 cup oatmeal

Cream shortening and sugar; add eggs and milk; beat well. Add dry ingredients. Drop by teaspoonfuls on greased cookie sheets or chill and roll thin on a well floured surface. Bake at 350° for 10 to 15 minutes.

*Mrs. Harvey Mazelin, Cincinnati, IA*

# FOUR WAY EASY COOKIES

2 cups sugar or brown sugar
1/2 cup shortening
2 eggs
1 cup milk

1 tsp. soda
1/4 tsp. salt
2 tsp. baking powder
Approximately 4 cups flour

Cream sugar, shortening and eggs. Add remaining ingredients just until mixed. Dough should not be too stiff. Bake one cookie to check amount of flour. Adjust if necessary. For raisin cookies add 1 cup raisins. For nut cookies add 1 cup chopped nuts. For chocolate chip cookies add 1 cup chocolate chips. For chocolate cookies add 1/2 cup cocoa and decrease flour. Bake at 350° till light brown. Frost if desired.

*Mrs. Amos Horst, Ephrata, PA*

***The smallest deed is better than the grandest intention.***

# FROSTY HERMIT COOKIES

1 cup Bran Buds
1/2 cup milk
1 cup flour
1/2 tsp. soda
1/2 tsp. cinnamon
1/4 tsp. nutmeg
1/4 tsp. ginger
1 cup brown sugar
1/2 cup butter, softened

2 eggs
1 tsp. vanilla
1 cup raisins
Chopped nuts
1 1/2 cups powdered sugar
2 T. melted butter
2 T. milk
1 tsp. vanilla

Combine Bran Buds and milk; let stand until moisture is taken up. Combine flour, soda and spices; set aside. Beat sugar and butter until fluffy. Add eggs, vanilla and bran mixture. Beat well. Add dry ingredients. Stir until mixed. Stir in raisins and nuts. Drop by level tablespoons onto lightly greased cookie sheet. Combine last 4 ingredients to make icing and ice.

*Susie St. John, Alvordton, OH*

# HERMIT COOKIES

2 cups raisins
1 cup water
1 tsp. baking soda
1 cup shortening
2 cups sugar
1 1/2 tsp. cinnamon
1/4 tsp. nutmeg

1/4 tsp. allspice
3 eggs
1 tsp. vanilla
4 cups flour
1 tsp. baking powder
1 tsp. salt

Boil raisins in water; drain and save 1/3 cup liquid. Cool raisins; add soda to them. Combine shortening, sugar and spices. Add eggs, 1 at a time, beating after each addition. Add vanilla and reserved liquid. Stir in flour, baking powder and salt. Add raisins. Chill. Drop by tablespoon on greased cookie sheets. Bake at 375° for 12 to 15 minutes. Don't allow to brown or will be crisp. To store, place wax paper between layers.

*Edna Miller, Snover, MI*

*Some one started the day aright, was it you?*
*Some one made it happy and bright, was it you?*
*Early this morning, we are told,*
*Some one smiled, and all through the day*
*This smile encouraged young and old, was it you?* S. I. Long

## HONEY COOKIES

1/2 cup shortening
1/2 cup sugar
1/2 cup honey
1 egg
1/2 cup nuts

2 1/2 cups flour
1 tsp. baking powder
1/4 tsp. soda
1/4 tsp. salt

Cream shortening, sugar and honey; stir in egg and nuts. Add dry ingredients; mix well. Shape dough into 2 rolls. Chill 2 hours. Slice 1/8-inch thick. Bake on ungreased cookie sheet at 400° for 8 to 10 minutes.

## LEMON COOKIES

1 cup butter
1 cup sugar
2 eggs

3 cups flour
1 tsp. soda
6 oz. lemonade concentrate

Cream butter and sugar; add eggs; beat till fluffy. Add flour and soda alternately with 1/2 cup thawed concentrate. Drop on ungreased cookie sheet. Bake at 375°. Brush hot cookies with remaining concentrate. Sprinkle with sugar.

*Mrs. Larry Zimmerman, Elkhart, IN*

## LEMON SUGAR COOKIES

3 1/2 cups sugar
2 cups butter
6 eggs
2 tsp. soda
2 cups sour milk

2 tsp. lemon flavoring
2 tsp. salt
4 tsp. baking powder
8 cups flour

Mix sugar, butter and eggs. Add soda to sour milk, then add to egg mixture. Add all but flour. Mix gradually, adding flour. Bake and ice. A soft cake-like cookie.

*Suetta Hoover, Tipton, MO*

## M & M COOKIES

15 oz. plain or peanut M & M's
1 cup butter or margarine
3/4 cup sugar
3/4 cup brown sugar
2 eggs

1 tsp. vanilla
2 1/2 cups flour
1/2 tsp. soda
1/2 tsp. salt
1 cup chopped nuts, opt.

Coarsely chop 1 1/2 cups candies; reserve remaining candy for decoration. Cream butter and sugars; add eggs and vanilla. Add combined flour, soda and salt; mix well. Stir in chopped candy and nuts. Drop on greased cookie sheet. Bake at 350° for 9 to 11 minutes. Remove from oven and immediately press 3 candies on each cookie.

## MACADAMIA CHUNK COOKIES

1 cup butter
3/4 cup sugar
1 cup brown sugar
2 eggs
1 tsp. vanilla

2 1/2 cups flour
1/2 tsp. soda
1/2 tsp. salt
2 cups white baking chips
1 cup macadamia nuts, chopped

Cream butter, sugar and brown sugar. Beat in eggs and vanilla. Mix well. Add flour, soda and salt. Mix well; add baking chips and nuts. Drop by rounded teaspoonfuls onto ungreased cookie sheets. Bake at 375° for 8 to 10 minutes.

## MARASCHINO KRISPIE COOKIES

1 cup butter
1 cup sugar
1 cup brown sugar
2 eggs
1 tsp. vanilla
2 cups flour
1 tsp. soda

1/2 tsp. baking powder
1/2 tsp. salt
2 cups quick oatmeal
2 cups chocolate chips
1/4 cup coconut
16 maraschino cherries, cut fine

Cream butter and sugars. Add eggs and vanilla; beat well. Mix dry ingredients and add. Stir in chocolate chips, coconut and cherries. Drop by teaspoon onto greased cookie sheet. Bake at 400° for 10 to 12 minutes.

*Lizzie Hoover, Goshen, IN*

## MELTING MOMENTS COOKIES

1 cup flour
1/2 cup cornstarch
1/2 cup powdered sugar

3/4 cup butter or margarine
1 tsp. vanilla

Combine first 3 ingredients. Beat butter until smooth; add flour mixture and vanilla. Refrigerate 1 hour. Shape into balls. Press lightly with a floured fork. Bake at 375° until edges are lightly browned. Cool. Roll into powdered sugar.

*Mrs. Sam Newswanger, Goshen, IN*

## MEXICAN WEDDING CAKE COOKIES

1 cup butter or margarine
1/2 cup powdered sugar
2 cups flour

2 cups chopped nuts
1/2 tsp. vanilla

Blend butter and powdered sugar together by hand. Add other ingredients. Form into 3/4-inch balls. Bake at 350° for 15 to 20 minutes. Cool. When lukewarm roll each ball into powdered sugar.

*Laura Kulp, Stratford, WI*

## MOLASSES COOKIES

1 cup butter or margarine
2 cups brown sugar
2 eggs
1/2 cup baking or black strap
    molasses

1/4 tsp. salt
4 tsp. cinnamon
4 tsp. ginger
4 tsp. soda
4 cups Gold Medal flour

Mix butter, sugar and eggs. Add molasses, salt, spices and soda. Mix well and stir in flour. Form into small balls and roll in sugar. Bake at 350°, 8 to 10 minutes or until tops are cracked and centers begin to fall. If not using Gold Medal flour you may have to add 1/2 to 3/4 cup more flour. Store in an airtight container.

*LaVerne Hoover, Goshen, IN*

## RUSSIAN MOLASSES COOKIES

1 cup butter or margarine
1 1/2 cups sugar
2 T. molasses
2 eggs, beaten
3 3/4 cups flour

2 tsp. soda
1 tsp. cinnamon
1 tsp. cloves
1 tsp. ginger
1/2 to 1 tsp. anise oil

Cream butter and sugar. Add molasses and eggs. Combine and add dry ingredients. Add anise oil and mix well. Form into 1-inch diameter rolls. Refrigerate overnight. Slice 1/4-inch thick. Bake at 375° for 15 minutes.

*Ruth Weaver, Nappanee, IN*

*Children are like wet cement. Whatever falls on them*
*makes an impression.*

# MONSTER COOKIES

| | |
|---|---|
| 2 cups sugar | 8 tsp. soda |
| 4 1/2 cups brown sugar | 3 lb. peanut butter |
| 2 cups butter | 18 cups oatmeal |
| 12 eggs, beaten | 16 oz. chocolate chips |
| 1/4 cup vanilla | 16 oz. M & M's |
| 1 T. molasses | |

Cream sugars and butter; add eggs and vanilla. Beat well. Stir in molasses, soda and peanut butter. Add oatmeal, chocolate chips, and M & M's. Drop onto cookie sheets and flatten. Bake at 350° till done. Do not overbake. Yields 124 large cookies. These cookies freeze well. Six cups of brown sugar and 1/2 cup corn syrup may be substituted for the sugars and molasses.

*Mrs. Allan Garman, Roaring Spring, PA        Alta Martin, Goshen, IN*

# CLASSIC OATMEAL COOKIES

*In a hurry? Spread batter in a lightly greased 13x9 pan and bake at 350° for 20 to 30 minutes. Cut into bars.*

| | |
|---|---|
| 1 cup butter or margarine | 2 cups flour |
| 1 cup sugar | 2 1/2 cups oatmeal |
| 1 cup brown sugar | 1 tsp. salt |
| 2 eggs | 1 tsp. soda |
| 1 tsp. vanilla | 1 tsp. cinnamon, opt. |

Cream butter and sugars. Beat in eggs and vanilla. Combine remaining ingredients and add. Drop by rounded tablespoonfuls onto an ungreased cookie sheet. Bake at 350° approximately 10 minutes. A cup and a half to two cups of chocolate chips, butterscotch chips, peanut butter chips, cinnamon chips, coconut, raisins or nuts may be added.

# BUTTERSCOTCH OATMEAL COOKIES

| | |
|---|---|
| 2 cups brown sugar | 1 1/2 tsp. salt |
| 1 7/8 cups (3 3/4 sticks) butter or margarine | 1/2 cup evaporated or whole milk |
| | 1 1/2 tsp. vanilla |
| 5 eggs | 2 cups coconut |
| 4 1/2 cups flour | 2 cups butterscotch chips |
| 1 1/2 tsp. baking powder | 1 cup chopped nuts |
| 1 1/2 tsp. soda | 4 cups oatmeal |

Cream sugar and butter; add eggs. Add dry ingredients with milk and vanilla. Add coconut, chips, nuts and oatmeal last. Bake at 375° for 10 minutes.

*Laura Kulp, Stratford, WI*

# DATE OATMEAL COOKIES

**3/4 cup butter or margarine**
**1 cup brown sugar**
**2 eggs**
**3 T. milk**
**1 tsp. vanilla**
**2 cups flour**

**3/4 tsp. soda**
**1 tsp. salt**
**2 cups oatmeal**
**1 1/2 cups cut-up dates**
**3/4 cup chopped nuts**

Cream butter, sugar, eggs, milk and vanilla. Combine flour, soda and salt; stir in. Mix in oatmeal, dates and nuts. Chill. Roll into balls using a rounded teaspoon of dough for each. Place 3 inches apart on a lightly greased cookie sheet. Flatten to 1/4-inch thick with bottom of glass dipped in flour. Bake at 350° for 10 to 12 minutes. Makes about 4 dozen cookies.

*Carol Hoover, Plymouth, IN*

# OVERNIGHT OATMEAL COOKIES

**4 cups brown sugar**
**2 cups shortening**
**4 eggs**
**1 tsp. salt**
**2 tsp. baking powder**

**2 tsp. soda**
**2 tsp. vanilla**
**3 cups flour**
**6 cups oatmeal**

Cream sugar, shortening and eggs. Add salt, baking powder, soda and vanilla. Stir in flour and oatmeal. Cover and refrigerate overnight. Roll into balls. Flatten on greased cookies sheet with a glass dipped in powdered sugar. Bake at 375° for 8 to 10 minutes.

*Mrs. Orie Martin, Etna Green, IN*

# PEANUT BUTTER OATMEAL COOKIES

*That's right! There's no flour in this recipe.*

**1 1/2 cups sugar**
**1 1/2 cups brown sugar**
**1/2 cup butter or margarine**
**4 eggs**
**1 tsp. vanilla**

**2 cups chunky peanut butter**
**6 cups quick or old-fashioned**
  **oatmeal**
**2 cups chocolate chips**
**2 1/2 tsp. soda**

Mix first 6 ingredients thoroughly. Add remaining ingredients and mix well. Drop on greased cookie sheet. Bake at 350° for 8 to 10 minutes.

*Ruth (Ramer) Strumland, Harrison, AR*

***Correction does much, but encouragement does more.***

350

# PECAN OATMEAL COOKIES

1 cup butter or margarine
1 1/3 cups sugar
1 1/3 cups brown sugar
2 eggs
1 tsp. vanilla
1 1/2 cups flour

1 tsp. salt
1 tsp. soda
3 cups quick oatmeal
1 1/2 cups chopped pecans
1 cup chocolate chips, opt.

Cream butter and sugars. Add eggs and vanilla. Beat until fluffy. Combine and add dry ingredients. Stir in oatmeal, pecans, and chocolate chips. Bake at 375° for 10 to 12 minutes. These can also be made using 2/3 cup less sugar; formed into 1 1/2-inch diameter rolls; chilled, cut into 1/4-inch slices and baked 10 minutes or until lightly browned.

*Frances Hoover, Elkhart, IN     Rosemary Kauffman, Virginia Beach, VA*

# RAISIN OATMEAL COOKIES

1 cup shortening
1 cup sugar
1 cup brown sugar
2 eggs
2 tsp. vanilla
2 cups flour

1 tsp. baking powder
1 tsp. salt
1 tsp. soda
2 cups oatmeal
1 cup coconut
1 cup raisins

Cream shortening and sugars. Beat in eggs and vanilla. Add dry ingredients. Drop on ungreased cookie sheets. Bake at 375° for 9 to 12 minutes.

*Sarah Imhoff, Sheridan, MI*

# WHOLE WHEAT PEANUT BUTTER OATMEAL COOKIES

1 1/2 cups peanut butter
3/4 cup butter, softened
3/4 cup shortening
3 3/4 cups brown sugar
3 eggs
3 tsp. vanilla

3 cups whole wheat flour
3 tsp. baking powder
1 1/2 tsp. salt
3 cups oatmeal
2 cups chocolate chips or
    coconut

Cream peanut butter, butter, shortening, brown sugar, eggs and vanilla. Mix in dry ingredients. Bake at 350° until done. Don't overbake.

*Miriam Hoover, Goshen, IN     Janice Weaver, Unity, WI*

***Do what you can, with what you have, where you are.***

## ORANGE COOKIES

1 cup butter
2 cups sugar
2 eggs
Juice and rind of 1 orange
3 1/2 to 4 cups flour

1/2 tsp. salt
1 tsp. soda
1 tsp. baking powder
1 cup buttermilk or sour milk

Cream butter and sugar; add eggs and beat till fluffy. Add orange juice and rind. Combine dry ingredients and add alternately with milk to creamed mixture. Mix thoroughly. Drop by teaspoonfuls onto greased cookie sheets. Bake at 375° for 10 to 12 minutes. Frost with butter cream or orange frosting.

*Naomi M. Zimmerman, Goshen, IN*

## OVERNIGHT COOKIES

2 cups brown sugar
1/2 cup butter, softened
1/2 cup lard, softened
2 eggs
1 tsp. vanilla

4 cups flour
1 tsp. soda
1 tsp. baking powder
1 cup nuts and/or chocolate chips

Mix in order given. Form into a long roll. Refrigerate overnight or till firm. Slice. Bake at 350° till brown.

*Ellen Newswanger, Kutztown, PA*

## PEANUT BUTTER COOKIES

1 1/2 cups sugar
1 1/2 cups brown sugar
1 1/2 cups peanut butter
1 1/2 cups butter or margarine
1 T. vanilla

3 eggs
3 cups flour
1 T. soda
1/2 tsp. salt

Cream sugars, peanut butter and butter. Add vanilla and eggs; beat well. Add remaining ingredients. Shape into balls and flatten twice with a fork, to make a crisscross design. Bake at 350° for 10 minutes or until done.

*Mrs. Isaac Kulp, Millersburg, IN*

## 1-2-3 PEANUT BUTTER COOKIES

1 cup peanut butter
1 cup sugar

1 egg

Mix all 3 ingredients. Shape into balls and roll into sugar. Flatten with a fork, making a crisscross design on top. Bake at 350° for 10 minutes.

*Laura Hoover Martin, Ephrata, PA*

## APPLE CRUNCHY PEANUT BUTTER COOKIES

3/4 cup peanut butter
1/4 cup butter
2 cups brown sugar
1 tsp. vanilla
2 eggs
2 tsp. soda, scant

3/4 tsp. salt
1/4 cup wheat germ
1 1/2 cups flour
1 cup oatmeal
1 cup finely chopped apples

Combine peanut butter, butter and sugar. Beat in vanilla and eggs. Add dry ingredients. Bake at 350° till done. Extra oatmeal may be used if you don't have wheat germ on hand.

*Mrs. Isaac Brubacker, Versailles, MO*

## PEANUT BUTTER CHIP COOKIES

2 cups flour
1 tsp. baking powder
1/4 tsp. salt
1 cup butter

3/4 cup brown sugar
1/2 cup vanilla
1 egg
2 cups peanuts butter chips

Combine first 3 ingredients; set aside. Beat butter, sugar and vanilla on medium speed until creamy. Add egg; beat well. With beater on low, gradually add flour mixture. Stir in peanut butter chips. Drop by teaspoonfuls onto ungreased cookie sheets. Bake at 375° for 7 to 9 minutes. Cool on cookie sheets 2 minutes before removing.

*Laura Kulp, Stratford, WI*

## PINEAPPLE COOKIES

*Stir in one cup coconut for coconut pineapple cookies.*

1 cup sugar
1 cup brown sugar
1 cup shortening
2 eggs
1 cup crushed pineapple, drained

1 tsp. pineapple or lemon flavor
4 cups flour
1 1/2 tsp. soda
1/2 tsp. baking powder
1/2 tsp. salt

Cream sugars and shortening. Beat in eggs. Add pineapple and flavoring. Gradually beat in remaining ingredients. Drop on cookie sheets. Bake at 350° for 20 minutes. Frost if desired.

*When you are tempted to lose patience with your fellowmen, stop and think how patient God has been with you.*

# PUMPKIN COOKIES

1 cup brown sugar
1 1/4 cups shortening
1 egg
1 cup mashed cooked pumpkin
2 cups flour
1 tsp. cinnamon
1/2 tsp. salt

1 tsp. baking powder
1 tsp. soda
1 T. butter
1 T. milk
1/4 cup pumpkin
Powdered sugar

Cream sugar and shortening; beat in egg. Add pumpkin; mix well. Combine dry ingredients and gradually stir into mixture; mix well. Drop on cookie sheet. Bake at 350° until done. Cool slightly then frost. To make frosting beat butter, milk and pumpkin. Add powdered sugar to desired consistency.

*Charlotte Martin, Goshen, IN*

# PUMPKIN CHOCOLATE CHIP COOKIES

1 cup mashed cooked pumpkin
1 cup sugar
1/2 cup cooking oil
1 egg
2 cups flour
1 tsp. cinnamon
2 tsp. baking powder

1/2 tsp. salt
1 tsp. soda dissolved in 1 tsp.
  milk
1 tsp. vanilla
1 cup chocolate chips
1/2 cup nuts, opt.

Combine first 4 ingredients; mix. Add dry ingredients and vanilla; mix well. Fold in chips and nuts. Bake at 350° for 10 minutes on lightly greased cookie sheets.

*Mrs. Susan Martin, Romulus, NY*

# PUMPKIN GRANOLA COOKIES

2 1/2 cups flour
1 1/2 cups quick oatmeal
1 cup coconut
1/4 cup wheat germ
1 tsp. soda
1 tsp. cinnamon
1/2 tsp. salt
1 cup butter or margarine

1 cup sugar
1 cup brown sugar
1 egg
1 tsp. vanilla
1 cup mashed cooked pumpkin
1 cup raisins
1 cup chopped nuts

Combine first 7 ingredients. Cream butter and sugars in a large bowl. Add egg and vanilla; beat till fluffy. Add dry ingredients alternately with pumpkin, beating well after each addition. Stir in raisins and nuts. Drop by rounded tablespoonfuls onto greased cookie sheets. Spread 3/8 inch thick. Bake at 350° for 15 to 20 minutes. Do not stack while cookies are warm.

*Vera Witmer, Goshen, IN*

## SOUR CREAM RAISIN COOKIES

1 cup butter or margarine
3 cups brown sugar
4 eggs
5 cups flour
2 tsp. soda
1/2 tsp. cinnamon

1/2 tsp. nutmeg
2 cups sour cream
2 tsp. vanilla
2 tsp. burnt sugar flavoring
1 tsp. butter rum flavoring
2 cups raisins

Cream butter and sugar. Add eggs and beat. Combine dry ingredients; add alternately with sour cream to egg mixture. Add flavoring and raisins. Drop on cookie sheets. Bake at 350° for 10 minutes.

*Nancy Kilmer, California, MO*

## SOUR CREAM COOKIES

1/2 cup shortening
2 cups sugar
2 eggs
1 tsp. vanilla
4 cups flour

1 tsp. soda
1/2 tsp. salt
1 cup sour cream
1/4 cup sugar-cinnamon mixture

Cream shortening and sugar. Add eggs and vanilla; beat until fluffy. Combine dry ingredients; add alternately with sour cream. Mix thoroughly. Drop by teaspoonfuls onto greased cookie sheets 2 to 3 inches apart. Sprinkle with sugar-cinnamon mixture. Bake at 375° for 12 minutes.

*Anna Mary Kilmer Evans, MO*

## SUGAR COOKIES

1 cup sugar
1 cup brown sugar
1 cup butter or margarine
2 eggs, well beaten
2 tsp. vanilla

4 cups flour
1 tsp. soda
1 tsp. baking powder
1/2 tsp. salt
3/4 cup milk

Cream sugars and butter. Beat in eggs and vanilla. Combine dry ingredients and add alternately with milk. Drop by spoonfuls and sprinkle with sugar, or roll into balls and flatten with a glass dipped in sugar. Bake at 350° for 12 to 15 minutes.

*We must adjust ourselves to the Bible, not the Bible to ourselves*

# SUGAR AND SPICE COOKIES

3/4 cups shortening
1 cup sugar
1 egg
1/4 cup molasses or sorghum
2 cups flour

2 tsp. soda
1/4 tsp. salt
1 tsp. cinnamon
3/4 tsp. cloves
3/4 tsp. ginger

Blend together first 4 ingredients. Mix remaining ingredients and add to first mixture; mix well. Form into balls. Bake on a greased cookie sheet at 375° for 10 to 12 minutes. Dip into powdered sugar while still warm.

*Susan Miller, Nappanee, IN*

# WHOLE WHEAT COOKIES

1 cup dates
1/2 cup raisins
1/2 cup black walnuts
1/2 cup butter
1/2 cup olive oil
4 egg yolks

5 T. sour cream
1/2 tsp. salt
2 cups brown sugar
1 T. soda
3 cups whole wheat flour

Grind dates, raisins and nuts together. Melt butter. Mix all ingredients, adding flour last. Shape into two 3-inch in diameter rolls. Chill. Slice off thin. Bake.

*Mrs. Phares Shirk, Liberty, KY*

**Because many nutrients are contained in the germ and outer covering, whole grains have more complex carbohydrates, fiber, vitamins and minerals than do refined grains. Whole grains are also low in fat.**

# WHOLE WHEAT BUTTERSCOTCH COOKIES

1 cup butter
2 cups brown sugar
1 egg
4 cups whole wheat flour
2 tsp. baking powder

1/2 tsp. salt
1/4 tsp. soda
1 cup sour cream
1 cup chopped dates, opt.
1 cup chopped nuts

Cream butter and sugar; beat in egg. Combine dry ingredients; add alternately with sour cream. Stir in dates and nuts. Drop by teaspoon on cookie sheets. Bake at 375° for 12 to 15 minutes.

*Mrs. James Kulp, Unity, WI*

# CUTOUT COOKIES

## CUTOUT COOKIES I

1 cup sugar
1/2 cup butter or margarine
1 T. milk
2 eggs

1/2 tsp. vanilla
3 cups flour, scant
1/8 tsp. salt
2 tsp. baking powder

Cream sugar and butter; beat in milk, eggs and vanilla. Combine and add remaining ingredients. Roll out on a lightly floured surface. Cut with cookie cutters. Bake at 375° for 7 to 8 minutes.

*Joan Weaver, Elkhart, IN*

## CUTOUT COOKIES II

*To make chocolate cutout cookies add 2/3 cup cocoa. Decrease flour to 4 cups.*

1 cup butter
2 cups sugar
3 eggs
2 tsp. vanilla

4 1/2 cups flour
1 T. baking powder
1/2 tsp. salt

Cream butter and sugar. Beat in eggs and vanilla. Combine and add dry ingredients. Roll out 1/4 inch thick on a floured or powdered sugar surface. Cut with cookie cutters. Bake at 375° for 7 to 8 minutes. Do not bake small thinner cookies as long. Cool cookies. Frost.

*Mrs. James Kulp, Unity, WI*

## BUTTERY CUTOUT COOKIES

2 cups butter or margarine
1 cup sugar
1 cup brown sugar
3 eggs
2 tsp. vanilla

5 1/2 cups flour
1 tsp. soda
1 tsp. cream of tartar
1/4 tsp. salt

Cream butter and sugars well. Add eggs and beat well. Add vanilla. Combine dry ingredients and add 1 cup at a time, mixing well. Chill several hours. Take about 1/3 of mixture at a time and roll out on well floured surface to desired thickness. Cut with cookie cutters. Bake at 350° until done. Cool and frost. Freezes well and easy to make.

*Ruth Zehr, Goshen, IN*

## FROSTED OATMEAL CUTOUT COOKIES

1 cup shortening
1 cup sugar
2 eggs
1 cup ground raisins
1/2 cup chopped nut, opt.

2 cups flour
1 tsp. soda
1/8 tsp. salt
2 tsp. vanilla
2 cups oatmeal

Cream sugar and shortening; beat in eggs. Stir in raisins and nuts. Combine and add dry ingredients. Mix in vanilla, then oatmeal. Chill. Roll out on a floured surface; cut into 1x4-inch strips. Bake at 375° for 10 - 15 minutes. Frost.

*Rachel Weirich, Stone Lake, WI*

## GINGERSNAP CUTOUT COOKIES

1 1/2 cups blackstrap molasses
3/4 cup brown sugar
1/2 cup water
1 cup butter or margarine

1 T. ginger
2 tsp. soda
1/2 tsp. salt
6 cups flour, approximately

Cook molasses, sugar and water slowly for 15 minutes. Just before removing from heat add butter and ginger; stir until butter is melted. Cool. Add soda, salt and flour. Mix thoroughly. Dough will be very stiff. Chill dough for several hours. Turn out dough on a lightly floured cookie sheets. Roll out 1/3 inch thick. Cut with round cookie cutter. Place 1/2-inch apart. Bake at 375° till they turn a slightly lighter color. These cookies improve if allowed to ripen in a stone jar for several weeks.

*Nancy Kilmer, California, MO*

## MORAVIAN SPICE CUTOUT COOKIES

*This dough can be used for gingerbread houses. Be sure to cut out pieces before baking.*

4 cups flour
3/4 tsp. soda
1/2 tsp. salt
1 tsp. ginger
1 tsp. nutmeg
1 tsp. cinnamon

1/2 tsp. allspice
1/2 tsp. cloves
1/2 cup brown sugar
1/2 cup butter or margarine
1 cup sorghum or molasses

Combine first 8 ingredients; set aside. In a large bowl, beat sugar, butter and molasses until well combined. With wooden spoon stir in flour mixture, then mix by hand until well combined. Dough will be stiff and dry, almost crumbly. Wrap in plastic wrap; refrigerate overnight. Divide dough into 4 parts. Refrigerate until ready to roll out. On lightly floured surface, roll out dough 1/8-inch thick. Cut with cookie cutters. Bake at 375° for 6-8 minutes. Cool; glaze or frost if desired.

*Vera Witmer, Goshen, IN*

## SPICED CHERRY CUTOUT BELL COOKIES

3 cups flour
1/2 tsp. soda
1/2 tsp. salt
1 tsp. ginger
1/2 tsp. instant coffee cream
1 cup butter
1 1/4 cups brown sugar
1/4 cup dark corn syrup

1 unbeaten egg
1 T. cream
1/3 cup brown sugar
1 T. butter
3 T. maraschino cherry juice
1 1/2 cups pecans, chopped fine
Maraschino cherries

Combine first 5 ingredients. Add butter and sugar, creaming well. Blend in corn syrup, egg and cream. Mix thoroughly. To make filling bring sugar, butter and cherry juice to a boil; cool and add pecans. Roll out dough a third at a time on floured surface to 1/8-inch thick. Cut 2 1/2-inch circles with a cutter. Place on ungreased cookie sheet. Place 1/2 teaspoon of filling in the center of each circle. With a spatula pull sides over filling making top of bell narrow. Place a piece of maraschino cherry at open end of each bell for clapper. Bake at 350° for 12 to 15 minutes.

*Mrs. Dale (Margaret) Love, Goshen, IN*

# FILLED COOKIES

## BONBONS

1/2 cup butter, softened
3/4 cup powdered sugar
1 tsp. vanilla
1 1/2 cups flour
1/8 tsp. salt
Food coloring, opt.

Hershey's Kisses or maraschino
  cherries
1 cup powdered sugar
2 T. cream
1 tsp. vanilla
Food coloring, opt.

Mix first 6 ingredients. Add 1 to 2 tablespoons cream if batter is dry. Make small balls with batter placing Kisses or cherries inside, covering completely. Place 1 to 2 inches apart on ungreased cookie sheet. Bake at 350° for 10 to 12 minutes. To make icing combine remaining ingredients. Dip tops into icing.

*Berdena Hoover, Elkhart, IN*

***Nothing lies beyond the reach of prayer except that which lies
outside the will of God.***

## CHOCOLATE MARSHMALLOW COOKIES

1 cup brown sugar
1/2 cup butter or margarine
1 egg
1 tsp. vanilla
1/2 tsp. soda

1/2 cup cocoa
1 1/2 cups flour
1/2 cup milk
16 oz. bag large marshmallows,
    halved crosswise

Cream sugar and butter; beat in egg, vanilla, and soda. Stir in cocoa and flour. Add milk; beat until smooth. Drop by teaspoonfuls onto lightly greased cookie sheet. Bake at 350° for 10 to12 minutes. Immediately place marshmallow halves cut side down on each cookie. Return to oven 1 minute, or until marshmallow is warm enough to stick to cookie. Frost with chocolate frosting.

## DATE FILLED JUMBO COOKIES

1 cup butter or margarine
2 cups brown sugar
3 eggs
1/2 cup water
1 tsp. vanilla
1/2 tsp. salt
1 tsp. soda

1/8 tsp. cinnamon
3 1/2 cups flour
2 cups dates, finely chopped
3/4 cup sugar
3/4 cup water
1/2 cup nuts, chopped

Thoroughly mix butter, brown sugar and eggs. Stir in water and vanilla. Combine and add dry ingredients; mix well. To make filling, cook dates, sugar and water until well blended; stirring constantly. Add nuts; cool slightly. Drop dough by teaspoons onto ungreased baking sheet. Place 1/2 teaspoon filling on dough; cover with 1/2 teaspoon dough. Bake at 375° for 10 to 12 minutes.

*Miriam Hoover, Goshen, IN*

## DATE PINWHEEL COOKIES

1 cup shortening
3/4 cup sugar
3/4 cup brown sugar
2 eggs
2 tsp. vanilla
3 cups flour
2 tsp. baking powder

1/2 tsp. salt
1 cup dates
1/2 cup sugar
1 T. orange rind
1/2 cup water
Chopped nuts

Cream shortening and sugars; add eggs and vanilla. Combine flour, baking powder and salt; add to mixture. Chill. To make filling, cook dates, sugar, rind and water until blended and thick. Add nuts. Chill. Roll out dough; spread filling on top. Roll up like a jelly roll. Chill. Slice and bake at 350° until done.

*Rachel Weirich, Stone Lake, WI*

# FRUIT FILLED COOKIES

1 cup shortening
1 cup butter
3 cups brown sugar
4 eggs
4 cups flour
4 tsp. soda

1 tsp. salt
2 tsp. baking powder
1/2 cup milk
4 tsp. vanilla
2 cups oatmeal
Favorite fruit filling

Cream shortening, butter, sugar and eggs.  Add dry ingredients alternately with milk and vanilla.  Mix in oatmeal.  Drop on cookie sheets; make an indentation in cookies and fill with fruit filling.  Bake at 350° until done.

*Mrs. Allen Garman, Roaring Spring, PA*

# RAISIN FILLED COOKIES

1 cup butter or margarine
2 cups brown sugar
2 eggs
1/4 cup milk
1 tsp. vanilla
4 cups flour

1 tsp. salt
1 tsp. soda
1 cup raisins
1/2 cup sugar
1 T. cornstarch
1 cup water

Cream butter and sugar.  Add eggs; beat well.  Stir in milk and vanilla.  Gradually add dry ingredients.  Mix well.  To make filling cook raisins, sugar, cornstarch and water until mixture thickens.  Cool slightly.  Drop cookie dough on cookie sheets.  Make an indentation in the center and fill with filling.  Bake at 350° until done.

*Mrs. James Martin, New Paris, IN      Verna M. Ramer, Goshen, IN*

# CHOCOLATE SANDWICH COOKIES

1 cup butter or margarine
2 cups sugar
2 eggs
1 cup cocoa
1 tsp. salt
4 cups flour
1 cup sour milk
2 tsp. vanilla

1 cup hot water
2 tsp. soda
1/3 cup milk
1 T. vanilla
1/4 cup flour
4 cups powdered sugar
1 1/2 cups white shortening

Cream butter and sugar; beat in eggs.  Combine cocoa, salt and flour; add alternately with sour milk and vanilla.  Mix soda in hot water and add.  Bake at 350° until done.  To make filling, stir together milk, vanilla and flour until smooth.  Add 2 cups powdered sugar; beat until creamy.  Add remaining sugar and shortening.  Mix well.  Spread thickly between two cookies.

*Mrs. James Kulp, Unity, WI*

## OATMEAL SANDWICH COOKIES

1 cup shortening
3 cups brown sugar
4 eggs
2 tsp. cinnamon
1 tsp. nutmeg
1 tsp. soda

3 cups flour
3 cups oatmeal
4 cups powdered sugar
2 tsp. vanilla
1/4 cup milk
1 cup white shortening

Cream shortening, sugar and eggs. Add next 5 ingredients. Roll into small balls and flatten on cookie sheet. Bake at 350° until done. To make filling, beat remaining 4 ingredients until fluffy. Spread filling between two cooled cookies.

*Mrs. Elverne Martin, Nappanee, IN     Mrs. Isaac Martin, Martinsburg, PA*

## SPICE SANDWICH COOKIES

4 cups brown sugar
2 cups butter or margarine
4 eggs
1 T. vanilla
1/2 tsp. salt
2 tsp. cinnamon
2 tsp. nutmeg
6 cups flour

2 cups buttermilk
2 tsp. soda
1/2 cup milk
1/4 cup flour
1 T. vanilla
4 cups powdered sugar
1 1/2 cups white shortening

Beat sugar, butter and eggs. Add vanilla, salt and spices. Add flour alternately with buttermilk and soda mixture. Mix well. Drop on cookie sheets. Bake at 350° until done. To make filling, combine milk, flour and vanilla; add powdered sugar and shortening. Beat until fluffy. Spread filling thickly between cooled cookies.

*Mrs. James Kulp, Unity, WI*

## STRAWBERRY SANDWICH COOKIES

1 pkg. strawberry cake mix
1 cup flour
3 1/2 cups sugar
2 cups butter
6 eggs
2 tsp. soda

2 cups sour milk
2 tsp. vanilla
2 tsp. salt
4 tsp. baking powder
1 env. Strawberry Kool-Aid
8 cups flour

Mix cake mix according to directions; add one cup flour and set aside. Beat together sugar, butter and eggs. Add soda to sour milk; add to egg mixture. Add vanilla, salt, baking powder and 1/2 of Kool-Aid powder. Stir in cake mix. Gradually add flour. Bake at 350° until done. Mix remaining Kool-Aid with your favorite frosting or filling. Spread frosting between cooled cookies.

*Linda Shirk, Barnett, MO*

# STARLIGHT MINT SURPRISE COOKIES

3 cups flour
1 tsp. soda
1/2 tsp. salt
1 cup sugar
1/2 cup brown sugar
1/2 cup shortening

1/2 cup butter
2 eggs
1 tsp. vanilla
12 oz. solid chocolate mint wafers
  or Andes mints
Walnut halves

Combine first 3 ingredients. Cream sugars, shortening, butter, eggs and vanilla. Gradually add dry ingredients. Cover and refrigerate 2 hours. Enclose each wafer in 1 tablespoon of dough. Top each with a walnut half. Bake at 350° for 10 to 12 minutes.

*Mrs. Vernon Kurtz, Ewing, IL*

# CHOCOLATE FILLED THUMBPRINT COOKIES

*If you don't have chocolate chips on hand just fill the indentations with your favorite jam or jelly.*

1 1/2 cups flour
1/2 tsp. salt
1/2 cup margarine, not butter
1/2 cup brown sugar
1 tsp. vanilla
2 T. milk
1/4 cup semisweet chocolate
  chips, chopped

Powdered sugar
3/4 cup semisweet chocolate
  chips
1 T. shortening
2 T. light corn syrup
1 tsp. vanilla
1 T. water

Mix flour and salt; work in margarine then sugar. Add vanilla, milk and chopped chips. Shape into walnut-sized balls and place 2-inches apart on greased cookie sheet. Press thumb in center to make a depression. Bake at 375° for 10 to 12 minutes. Remove from oven and sprinkle with powdered sugar. While cookies are cooling melt remaining chocolate chips with shortening, stirring frequently. Remove from heat; stir in corn syrup, water and vanilla until smooth. Fill cookies.

*Mary Ellen Hission, Plymouth, IN*

*They are slaves*
*Who fear to speak for the fallen and the weak;*
*They are slaves who will not choose hatred, scoffing and abuse*
*Rather than in silence shrink from the truth they needs must think;*
*They are slaves who dare not be*
*In the right with two or three.*
*James Russell Lowell*

## PEANUT BUTTER AND JELLY THUMBPRINT COOKIES

| | |
|---|---|
| 3 cups flour | 1 1/2 cups peanut butter |
| 2 cups sugar | 1/2 cup butter or margarine |
| 1 tsp. soda | 2 T. milk |
| 1/2 tsp. salt | 1/2 cup jam or jelly |

Combine dry ingredients. Add peanut butter and softened butter. Mix until crumbly. Add milk. Form dough into 1-inch ball. Place on an ungreased cookie sheet 2 inches apart. Press thumb into center of each. Place approximately 1/2 teaspoon of jam into indentations. Bake at 375° for 8 to 10 minutes.

## VANILLA FILLED CHOCOLATE THUMBPRINT COOKIES

*For chocolate covered cherry cookies place a whole maraschino cherry in the indentation before baking. Drizzle with melted chocolate chips while still warm.*

| | |
|---|---|
| 1 cup butter or margarine | 1/2 cup cocoa |
| 1 1/3 cups sugar | 1/2 tsp. salt |
| 1 egg | 2 cups powdered sugar |
| 1/4 cup milk | 2 T. milk |
| 1 tsp. vanilla | 1 tsp. vanilla |
| 2 cups flour | 1/4 cup butter or margarine |

Cream butter, sugar and egg. Mix in milk and vanilla, then flour, cocoa and salt. Roll dough into little balls; place on cookie sheet. Press thumb in center to make a depression. Bake at 350° until done. Don't overbake. To make frosting, beat last 4 ingredients until creamy. Fill cooled cookies with frosting. Half of a walnut or maraschino cherry can be placed on frosting. The balls of dough may also be rolled in finely chopped nuts before baking.

*Mrs. Allan Garman, Roaring Spring, PA     Mrs. Marvin Sensenig, Penn Yan, NY*

## WALNUT FROSTIES

| | |
|---|---|
| 2 cups flour | 1 egg |
| 1/2 tsp. soda | 1 tsp. vanilla |
| 1/4 tsp. salt | 1 cup chopped walnuts |
| 1 cup brown sugar | 1/2 cup brown sugar |
| 1/2 cup butter | 1/4 cup sour cream |

Mix flour, soda and salt. Cream sugar and butter until fluffy. Add egg and vanilla; beat well. Stir in dry ingredients. Shape into 1-inch balls. Place 2 inches apart on ungreased cookie sheets. To make filling combine nuts, sugar and sour cream. Make a depression in the center of each cookie. Place 1 teaspoon filling in each depression. Bake at 350° for 12 to 14 minutes.

*Sheryl Weaver, Goshen, IN*

# BARS

# APPLE BARS

1 cup flour
1/2 tsp. salt
1/2 tsp. soda
1/2 cup brown sugar
1 cup oatmeal

1/2 cup shortening
2 1/2 cups sliced apples
2 T. butter
1/2 cup sugar

Stir together first 5 ingredients; cut in shortening and mix until crumbly. Spread half of mixture into a greased 10x7 pan. Slice apples over crumbs. Dot with butter and sprinkle with sugar. Cover with remaining crumbs. Bake at 350° for 40 minutes. Good drizzled with powdered sugar glaze. Cut bars while warm.

*Mrs. Larry Zimmerman, Elkhart, IN*

# DANISH APPLE BARS

3 cups flour
1 tsp. salt
1 cup shortening
1 egg
Milk
1 cup crushed cornflakes

8 cups sliced peeled apples
1 cup sugar
1 tsp. cinnamon
1 cup powdered sugar
2 T. milk
1/2 tsp. vanilla

Mix flour and salt; cut in shortening until crumbly. Add enough milk to egg to make 1/2 cup. Add to flour mixture. Divide dough in half. Roll out half. Place in 15x10 pan. Arrange apple slices over cornflakes. Combine sugar and cinnamon. Sprinkle over apples. Roll out other half of dough to fit, and put on top. Make vents in top. Bake at 375° for 45 minutes. Combine powdered sugar, milk and vanilla. Spread on warm bars. May be sprinkled with nuts.

*Mrs. James Kulp, Unity, WI*

# GOLDEN APPLE BARS

3/4 cup butter or margarine
3/4 cup powdered sugar
1 1/2 cups flour
1/4 cup butter or margarine
3/4 cup brown sugar
2 cups chopped apples
1 tsp. grated lemon peel
1 beaten egg

1 tsp. vanilla
1 3/4 cups flour
1 tsp. baking powder
1/2 tsp. salt
1 1/2 cups powdered sugar
1/4 tsp. cinnamon
2 to 3 T. milk

Cream butter and sugar; blend in flour. Press into a greased 15x10 pan. Bake at 350° for 10 to 12 minutes. Melt butter; blend in brown sugar, apples, lemon, egg and vanilla. Combine flour, baking powder and salt; add to apple mixture. Spread on crust; bake 25 minutes. Mix last 3 ingredients; drizzle on warm bars.

*Vera Witmer, Goshen, IN*

365

# SOUR CREAM APPLE BARS

2 cups flour
2 cups brown sugar
1/2 cup butter or margarine
2 tsp. cinnamon
1 tsp. soda

1/2 tsp. salt
1 cup sour cream
1 tsp. vanilla
1 egg
2 cups chopped peeled apples

Combine flour, sugar and butter. Press 2 3/4 cups of mixture into an ungreased 13x9 pan. To remaining mixture add cinnamon, soda, salt, sour cream, vanilla and egg; blend well. Stir in apples. Spoon evenly over crust. Bake at 350° approximately 30 minutes.

# APPLESAUCE BARS

1/2 cup shortening
1 cup applesauce
1 cup sugar
2 cups flour
1 tsp. soda
1/2 tsp. salt

1 tsp. cinnamon
1 tsp. nutmeg
1/2 tsp. cloves
1 cup raisins
1/2 tsp. vanilla
1/2 cup chopped nuts

Mix first 3 ingredients. Mix flour, soda, salt and spices; add to first mixture. Stir in remaining ingredients. Spread butter in greased 13x9 pan. Bake at 350° for 35 minutes. Glaze while bars are warm.

*Lizzie Hoover, Goshen, IN*

# BANANA BARS

1/2 cup butter or margarine
2 cups sugar
3 eggs
1 1/2 cups mashed ripe bananas

1 tsp. vanilla
2 cups flour
1 tsp. soda
1/4 tsp. salt

Cream butter and sugar; beat in eggs, bananas and vanilla. Combine flour, soda, and salt and add. Pour into a greased 15x10 pan. Bake at 350° approximately 25 minutes. Cool. Frost with plain or cream cheese frosting.

*When you go out in the morning, to begin the work of the day,*
*Don't neglect the little chances you will find along the way;*
*For in lifting another's burden, and speaking a word of cheer,*
*You will find you own cares lighter, and easier far to bear.* F. S. Lovejoy

# BASIC BROWNIES

*These brownies are very versatile. Eat them plain, sprinkled with powdered sugar, frosted, or embellished with any of the following toppings. For more elaborate brownies add a cup or two of chocolate chips or a cup of chopped maraschino cherries.*

| | |
|---|---|
| 1 cup butter or margarine | 1/4 cup cocoa, rounded |
| 2 cups sugar | 1 1/2 cups flour |
| 3 eggs | 1/4 tsp. salt |
| 1 tsp. vanilla | 3/4 cup chopped nuts, opt. |

Cream butter and sugar; beat in eggs and vanilla. Add cocoa, then flour, salt and nuts. Mix well. Spread into a greased 13x9 pan, pushing plenty of batter into the corners so brownies bake even. Bake at 350° approximately 30 minutes.

*Mrs. Ray (Elsie) Hoover, Stratford, WI*

# MINT TOPPING FOR BROWNIES

| | |
|---|---|
| 1/4 cup butter, softened | 1/2 tsp. peppermint extract |
| 2 cups powdered sugar | 1/2 cup chocolate chips |
| 2 T. milk | 2 T. margarine |

Beat first 4 ingredients until creamy. Frost baked brownies; let stand until firm. Melt chocolate chips with margarine; drizzle over frosting. Chill until firm.

# PEANUT BUTTER TOPPING FOR BROWNIES

| | |
|---|---|
| 1 1/2 cups powdered sugar | 2 T. milk |
| 1/2 cup creamy peanut butter | 1/4 cup chocolate chips |
| 1/4 cup butter, softened | 1 T. butter |

Beat first 4 ingredients until well mixed. Frost baked brownies. Melt chocolate chips and butter; stir until smooth. Drizzle over frosting. Chill until firm.

# ROCKY ROAD TOPPING FOR BROWNIES

| | |
|---|---|
| 2 cups miniature marshmallows | 1 cup coarsely chopped walnuts |
| 2 cups chocolate chips | or pecans |

Sprinkle all 3 ingredients on hot brownies. Return to oven 3 to 5 minutes or just until topping is warmed enough to stick together. Cool before cutting. Nuts may be deleted.

# BUN BARS

1/2 cup butter or margarine
1/2 cup brown sugar
1 1/3 cups flour
1/3 cup sugar

2/3 cup light corn syrup
1 cup chocolate chips
1/2 cup chunky peanut butter
2 cup cornflakes

Cream butter and sugar; stir in flour until crumbly. Press into an ungreased 13x9 pan. Bake at 350° for 15 minutes. Cool. Bring sugar and syrup to a boil. Remove from heat; add chocolate chips and peanut butter. Stir until melted. Stir in cornflakes. Spread mixture on top of crust. Cool before cutting.

*Ellen Stoesz, Indianapolis, IN*

# BUTTERSCOTCH BARS I

*If you don't have butterscotch chips you can make these bars by increasing butter to one cup and brown sugar to two cups.*

2 cups butterscotch chips
1/2 cup butter or margarine
1 1/2 cups brown sugar
3 eggs
1 tsp. vanilla

1 3/4 cups flour
1 tsp. baking powder
1/4 tsp. salt
1 cup walnuts, opt.

Melt butterscotch chips and butter over low heat. Stir in sugar; cool slightly. Add eggs and vanilla, beat well. Beat in flour, baking powder, salt and nuts. Spread into a greased 13x9 pan. Bake at 350° approximately 30 minutes. Eat plain, sprinkle with powdered sugar, or frost. These bars freeze well.

*Scott Patrick Hoover, Stratford, WI*

# BUTTERSCOTCH BARS II

1/4 cup butter
1 cup brown sugar
1 egg
1 cup flour

1 tsp. baking powder
1/4 tsp. salt
1/2 cup chopped nuts
1 tsp. vanilla

Melt butter; blend in sugar. Beat in egg. Combine dry ingredients. Add to egg mixture and mix well. Add nuts and vanilla. Spread into a greased 8x8 pan. Bake at 350° for 30 minutes. Cut into squares or bars while still warm.

*Alta Newswanger, Versailles, MO*

**Christ's blood makes us safe; God's Word makes us sure.**

# CARAMEL BARS

1 cup butter
1/2 cup sugar
2 1/4 cups flour
1 cup butter

1 cup brown sugar
1/4 cup corn syrup
14 oz. sweetened condensed milk
2 cups chocolate chips

Combine first 3 ingredients; press into an ungreased 15 x 10 pan with sides. Bake at 350° for 20 minutes. Boil next 4 ingredients for 5 minutes. Pour on baked crust. Sprinkle with chocolate chips while hot. Cool before cutting.

*William Paul Hoover II, Stratford, WI*

# CHEESECAKE BARS

6 T. butter, melted
2 cups graham cracker crumbs
16 oz. cream cheese, softened
3/4 cup sugar

2 eggs
1 tsp. vanilla
2 cups fruit pie filling

Combine butter and crumbs. Mix well then press firmly and evenly into a 13x9 pan. Beat cream cheese until smooth. Add sugar, eggs and vanilla, beating until well blended. Spread pie filling evenly over crust. Top with cream cheese mixture. Bake at 350° for 30 minutes or until slightly puffed. Cool completely in pan before cutting into bars. Refrigerate leftovers.

*Mrs. Ray (Elsie) Hoover, Stratford, WI*

# CHEESY CHOCOLATE ALMOND BARS

12 oz. (2 cups) chocolate chips
8 oz. cream cheese, softened
2/3 cup cream or evaporated milk
1 cup chopped almonds
1/2 tsp. vanilla
1 cup butter or margarine

1 1/2 cups sugar
1 egg
1/2 tsp. vanilla
3 cups flour
1 tsp. baking powder
1/4 tsp. salt

Stir chocolate chips, cream cheese and cream over low heat until melted and smooth. Remove from heat; stir in nuts and vanilla. Set aside. Cream butter and sugar; beat in egg and vanilla. Add remaining ingredients, mixing well. Press half of butter mixture into a lightly greased 13x9 pan. Spread chocolate mixture on top. Sprinkle remaining butter mixture over chocolate. Bake at 375° approximately 35 minutes. Cool before cutting.

# CHERRY SQUARES

1 cup butter or margarine
1 1/2 cups sugar
4 eggs
2 cups flour

1 1/2 tsp. vanilla
1/2 tsp. lemon extract or use 2
    tsp. vanilla
2 cups cherry pie filling

Cream butter and sugar. Add eggs; beat until fluffy. Beat in flour and extract. Spread in a greased 15x10 jellyroll pan. Mark 24 or 28 squares on surface of batter. Spoon pie filling into the center of each square. Batter will puff around filling while baking. Bake at 350° for 30 minutes or until bars are firm and golden. Cool before removing from pan. Sprinkle with powdered sugar; cut into squares.

*Mrs. James Kulp, Unity, WI*

# CHEWY CHINESE BARS

1 cup flour
1/2 cup butter or margarine
2 T. sugar
2 eggs
1 1/2 cups brown sugar

2 T. flour
1/4 cup coconut
1/2 tsp. vanilla
1 cup chopped nuts

Combine first 3 ingredients; press into a 9x9 pan. Bake at 350° for 15 minutes. Beat eggs. Add remaining ingredients and mix well. Bake another 30 minutes.

*Dawn High, Unity, WI*

# CHOCOLATE CHEESE LAYER BARS

1/2 cup butter
1 cup sugar
2 eggs
1 tsp. vanilla
1 oz. baking chocolate, melted
1 cup flour
1 tsp. baking powder
1/2 cup chopped nuts
1/4 cup butter
6 oz. cream cheese, softened
1/2 tsp. vanilla
1/2 cup sugar

1 egg
2 T. flour
1/4 cup chopped nuts
1 cup chocolate chips, opt.
3 cups miniature marshmallows
1/4 cup butter
2 oz. cream cheese, softened
1 oz. baking chocolate
2 T. milk
3 cups powdered sugar
1 tsp. vanilla

Cream butter, sugar, eggs, vanilla and chocolate. Beat in flour, baking powder, and nuts; spread in a greased 13x9 pan. Beat together butter, cream cheese, vanilla, sugar, egg, flour, and nuts. Blend well; spread over chocolate layer. Sprinkle with chocolate chips if desired. Bake at 350° for 20 to 25 minutes. Remove from oven and sprinkle with marshmallows. Return to oven for 2 minutes then swirl melted marshmallows. Cool. Over low heat melt butter, cream cheese, chocolate and milk. Remove from heat and beat in powdered sugar and vanilla. Frost bars. These bars freeze well.

*Elaine Martin, Nappanee, IN*

## CHOCOLATE COCONUT BARS

*Delete chocolate chips for great tasting coconut bars. A cup of chopped nuts may be added.*

| | |
|---|---|
| 1 1/2 cups flour | 1 cup brown sugar |
| 1/2 cup brown sugar | 1 tsp. vanilla |
| 1/2 cup butter or margarine | 2 T. flour |
| 1/4 tsp. salt | 1/2 tsp. baking powder |
| 1 cup semisweet chocolate chips | 1/4 tsp. salt |
| 2 eggs | 1 1/2 cups coconut |

Combine first 4 ingredients. Mix until crumbly. Press into an ungreased 13x9 pan. Bake at 375° for 10 minutes. Sprinkle chocolate chips over hot crust and return to over 1 minute to soften. Remove from oven and spread chocolate chips evenly. Beat eggs until thick and light colored. Beat in sugar and vanilla. Stir in flour mixed with baking powder and salt, then add coconut. Spread over chocolate. Bake at 375° for 14 minutes or until set. Cool before cutting.

*Mrs. Levon Martin, Goshen, IN     Mrs. Phillip Zimmerman, Versailles, MO*

## CHOCOLATE DATE BARS

*To make date bars delete chocolate chips and add 1/2 cup sugar and 2 T. butter to dates.*

| | |
|---|---|
| 1 cup flour | 7 oz. dates, cut fine |
| 1 tsp. soda | 1 T. flour |
| 2 cups quick oats | 1 cup water |
| 1 cup brown sugar | 1 cup chocolate chips |
| 3/4 cup butter, melted | 1 tsp. vanilla |

Mix first 5 ingredients; press half of crumbs into a greased 13x9 pan. Cook next 4 ingredients until thick and well blended; remove from heat; stir in vanilla. Spread over crust. Sprinkle with remaining crumbs; press in lightly. Bake at 375° for 20 minutes.

***The strength that comes from confidence can quickly be lost in conceit.***

# CHOCOLATE PEANUT BUTTER BARS

1 cup sugar
1/2 cup butter or margarine
2 eggs
2 tsp. baking powder
1/2 tsp. salt
3/4 cup flour

1 oz. unsweetened chocolate
3 cups miniature marshmallows
1 cup chocolate chips
3/4 cup peanut butter
1 cup Rice Krispies

Cream sugar and butter; add eggs; beat well. Add dry ingredients. Melt chocolate; add to mixture. Mix well. Pour in greased 13x9 pan. Bake at 350° for 15 to 20 minutes. Sprinkle marshmallows on while hot. Cool. Melt chocolate chips; stir in peanut butter. Stir in Rice Krispies. Spread on marshmallows.

*Mrs. Larry Zimmerman, Elkhart, IN*

# CHOCOLATE REVEL BARS

1 cup butter
2 cups brown sugar
2 eggs
2 tsp. vanilla
2 1/2 cups flour
1 tsp. soda
1 tsp. salt

3 cups oatmeal
12 oz. (2 cups) chocolate chips
14 oz. sweetened condensed milk
2 T. butter
1/4 tsp. salt
1 cup chopped nuts
2 tsp. vanilla

Cream butter and sugar; add eggs and vanilla. Beat till fluffy. Stir in flour, soda, salt and oatmeal. Press 2/3 of crumbs in a greased 15x10 pan. Melt chocolate chips, milk, butter and salt. Stir in nuts and vanilla. Spread chocolate filling evenly over crust. Dot with remaining crumbs. Bake at 350° approximately 25 minutes. Do not overbake.

*Mrs. James (Arlene) Martin, Nappanee, IN    Mrs. Levon Martin, Goshen, IN*

# COCONUT BLONDIES

1 cup butter or margarine
2 cups brown sugar
2 eggs
2 tsp. vanilla
2 1/4 cups flour

1 tsp. baking powder
1/4 tsp. salt
1 cup chopped pecans
1 cup coconut

Cream butter and sugar; add eggs and vanilla. Add flour, baking powder and salt. Mix in pecans and coconut. Spread in a greased 13x9 pan. Bake at 350° for 35 minutes.

*Mrs. Clay Zimmerman, Paltinis, Romania*

# COOKIE DOUGH BROWNIES

| | |
|---|---|
| 2 cups sugar | 1/2 cup brown sugar |
| 1 1/2 cups flour | 1/4 cup sugar |
| 1/2 cup cocoa | 2 T. milk |
| 1/2 tsp. salt | 1 tsp. vanilla |
| 1 cup cooking oil | 1 cup flour |
| 4 eggs | 1 cup semisweet chocolate chips |
| 2 tsp. vanilla | 1 T. shortening |
| 1/2 cup butter | |

Combine first 4 ingredients. Beat together oil, eggs and vanilla. Add to dry ingredients and beat well. Spread in greased 13x9 pan and bake at 350° for 30 minutes. Combine butter and sugars; add milk and vanilla. Mix well then add flour. Spread on baked brownies. Melt chips; stir in shortening. Drizzle on bars.

*Jennifer Kulp, Unity, WI*

# CREAM CHEESE BROWNIES

*For a special treat mix one cup chocolate chips into cream cheese mixture.*

| | |
|---|---|
| 1 cup butter or margarine | 1 1/2 cups flour |
| 2 cups sugar | 1/4 tsp. salt |
| 3 eggs | 8 oz. cream cheese, softened |
| 1 tsp. vanilla | 1/3 cup sugar |
| 1/4 cup cocoa | 1 tsp. vanilla |

Cream butter and sugar; beat in eggs and vanilla. Add cocoa, then flour and salt. Mix well. Pour into a greased 13x9 pan. Combine remaining ingredients; mix well. Make 3 lengthwise trenches in batter. Fill trenches with cream cheese mixture. Using a knife, cut crosswise through batter 7 to 8 times and lengthwise 4 to 5 times. Don't swirl too much, just enough to make a nice design. Cream cheese mixture can also be dropped by spoonfuls on batter and then swirled. Bake at 350° approximately 30 minutes.

*Kelsie LaRaye Hoover, Stratford, WI*

# CREAM CHEESE JAM BARS

| | |
|---|---|
| 2 cups flour | 1/2 cup butter |
| 1 cup sugar | 1 egg, beaten |
| 2 tsp. baking powder | 8 oz. cream cheese, softened |
| 1/2 tsp. salt | 1/2 cup jam |

Combine all but cream cheese and jam; mix well. Press 2 cups of crumbs in a greased 13x9 pan. Blend cream cheese and jam until smooth. Spread evenly on crust. Sprinkle with reserved crumbs. Press down lightly. Bake at 350° for 25 to 30 minutes. Cool.

# DAVY CROCKETT BARS

1 cup butter or margarine
1 cup sugar
1 cup brown sugar
3 eggs
2 cups oatmeal
2 cups flour

1 tsp. salt
1 tsp. soda
1 tsp. baking powder
1 tsp. vanilla
1 cup chopped nuts
1 cup chocolate chips

Cream butter, sugars and eggs. Add dry ingredients and mix. Stir in vanilla, nuts and chocolate chips. Spread in shallow layers on two cookie sheets. Bake at 350° for 10 to15 minutes. Do not overbake. Glaze bars while hot.

*Esther Shirk, Union Co., PA*     *Naomi M. Zimmerman, Goshen, IN*

# DOUBLE CHOCOLATE BROWNIES

2 cups flour
3/4 cup cocoa
1 tsp. soda
1/2 tsp. salt
1 cup butter, softened
2/3 cup sugar

2/3 cup brown sugar
1 tsp. vanilla
2 large eggs
1 3/4 cups regular or swirled
   chocolate chips

Combine flour, cocoa, soda and salt. Beat butter, sugars, and vanilla until creamy. Beat eggs in one at a time. Gradually beat in flour mixture. Stir in chips. Spread in a 13x9 pan. Bake at 350° for 25 to 30 minutes.

*Bethany Kulp, Unity, WI*

# FIG BARS

8 oz. dried figs
1/2 cup water
1/3 cup sugar
1/8 tsp. salt
2 tsp. butter
1 T. lemon juice
1/2 cup shortening
3/4 cup brown sugar

1 egg
1 T. milk
1/2 tsp. vanilla
1 1/3 cups flour
2 tsp. baking powder
1/2 tsp. salt
1/2 cup oatmeal
1/8 tsp. soda

Combine first 4 ingredients; simmer and stir till thick. Remove from heat; stir in butter and lemon juice. Cream shortening, sugar and egg. Add milk and vanilla; stir in dry ingredients. Turn onto floured surface. Divide into 4 parts; roll out 1 at a time into a 9x4 rectangle. Spread 2-inch strip of filling, 1/4-inch thick, lengthwise on dough. Fold sides of dough up over filling. Seal sides and ends. Place on cookie sheet, seam side down. Bake at 350° for 15 to 20 minutes. Cut each roll crosswise into bars. Raisins may be used instead of figs.

*Mrs. Jacob Oberholtzer, Liberty, KY*

# FRUIT BARS

1 cup butter or margarine
1 1/2 cups sugar
3 eggs, well beaten
2 cups flour

1/2 tsp. salt
1 tsp. baking powder
1 tsp. vanilla
Thickened fruit or pie filling

Cream butter and sugar; add eggs. Add dry ingredients and vanilla; mix well. Put half of batter in bottom of a 13x9 cake pan. Spread filling on batter; top with remaining batter. Bake at 350° until done.

*Sarah Imhoff, Sheridan, MI*

# FUDGE NUT ORANGE BARS

1 butter cake mix
1 cup oatmeal
1/3 cup butter or margarine
1 egg
1 cup chocolate chips
1/2 cup sugar
1/2 cup butter or margarine

2 eggs
1 cup chopped pecans
2 tsp. grated orange peel
1/4 cup orange juice
1/2 cup chocolate chips
2 T. butter or margarine
1 tsp. orange juice

Mix dry cake mix, oatmeal, and butter until crumbly. Reserve 1 cup crumbs. To remaining crumbs, blend in 1 egg until well mixed. Press into a greased 13x9 pan. Heat chocolate chips, sugar and butter over low heat stirring constantly, until chips are melted. Remove from heat. Add 2 eggs; mix well. Stir in pecans, orange peel and juice. Pour over base. Sprinkle with reserved crumbs. Bake at 350° for 30 to 40 minutes, until center is set. Cool completely. To make glaze, melt chocolate chips; stir in butter and orange juice. Drizzle glaze over bars.

*Ellen Stoesz, Indianapolis, IN*

# LEMON BARS

2 cups flour
1/2 cup powdered sugar
1 cup butter, softened
4 eggs
2 cups sugar

1/2 cup flour
1/2 tsp. salt
6 T. lemon juice
1 1/2 cups coconut, opt.

Mix flour, powdered sugar and butter; press into a 13x9 pan. Bake at 350° for 15 to 20 minutes. Mix remaining ingredients and pour over baked crust. Bake 25 to 30 minutes longer. Cool. Sprinkle with powdered sugar. Best if made a day before serving.

*Mrs. Ray (Elsie) Hoover, Stratford, WI*

## LEMON CREAM CHEESE BARS

14 oz. sweetened condensed milk
1/2 cup lemon juice
1 1/2 cups flour
1 cup oatmeal

1 cup brown sugar
1 tsp. baking powder
3/4 cup butter or margarine

Combine sweetened condensed milk and juice. Set aside. Combine remaining ingredients; press half of crumbs into a greased 13x9 pan. Spread with lemon mixture. Sprinkle with remaining crumbs. Bake at 350° for 25 to 30 minutes. Cool before cutting.

## MARSHMALLOW FUDGE BARS

3/4 cups flour
1/2 tsp. baking powder
1/2 tsp. salt
2 oz. baking chocolate
1/3 cup butter or margarine

2 eggs
1 cup sugar
1/2 cup chopped nuts
1 tsp. vanilla
2 cups miniature marshmallows

Combine dry ingredients; set aside. Melt chocolate and butter over low heat. Beat eggs and sugar. Add chocolate mixture. Stir in dry ingredients, nuts and vanilla. Spread in well greased 9x9 pan. Bake at 350° for 25 to 30 minutes. Spread marshmallows on top of hot bars; return to oven until marshmallows are soft and spread evenly. Cool. Frost with chocolate frosting.

*Erla (Horst) Horning, Penn Yan, NY*

## OATMEAL TOFFEE BARS

8 cups oatmeal
1 cup sugar
1 1/3 cups butter
2 cups brown sugar

1 tsp. vanilla
12 oz. (2 cups) chocolate chips
1 cup peanut butter

Mix first 5 ingredients; press into two 15x10 pans. Bake at 375° for 10 minutes. Melt chocolate chips and peanut butter over low heat; spread on top of hot bars. Cut while warm.

*Janice Weaver, Unity, WI*

## PEANUT BUTTER BROWNIES

1/4 cup shortening
1/2 cup peanut butter
1 1/2 cups sugar
3/4 cup brown sugar
3 eggs

1 1/2 tsp. vanilla
2 cups flour
2 tsp. baking powder
3/4 tsp. salt
1/4 cup chopped peanuts

Cream shortening and peanut butter. Add sugars; beat well. Add eggs and vanilla. Beat until creamy; add dry ingredients. Add peanuts. Spread in a greased 13x9 pan. Bake at 350° for 30 to 35 minutes.

*Mrs. Clay Zimmerman, Paltinis, Romania*

## PEANUT BUTTER CHIP BROWNIES

1 1/4 cups butter or margarine
2 cups sugar
4 eggs
2 tsp. vanilla
2 cups flour

3/4 cup cocoa
1 tsp. soda
1/2 tsp. salt
2 cups peanut butter chips

Beat butter and sugar till fluffy. Beat in eggs and vanilla. Combine flour, cocoa, soda, and salt; add. Mix well. Add peanut butter chips. Spread into greased 15x10 pan. Bake at 350° for 20 to 25 minutes, or till set. Cool before cutting.

## PEANUT BUTTER FINGERS

1/2 cup butter
1/3 cup peanut butter
1/2 cup sugar
1/2 cup brown sugar
1 egg
1/2 tsp. soda
1/4 tsp. salt

1/2 tsp. vanilla
1 cup flour
1 cup oatmeal
1 cup chocolate chips
1/2 cup powdered sugar
1/4 cup peanut butter
2 to 4 T. milk

Cream butter, peanut butter and sugars; add egg, soda, salt and vanilla. Beat well; add flour and oatmeal. Spread in a greased 13x9 pan. Bake at 350° for 20 to 25 minutes. Remove from oven; sprinkle hot bars with chocolate chips. To make frosting combine powdered sugar, peanut butter and milk till proper consistency to drizzle. Cool before cutting.

*Mrs. Luke Hoover, Goshen, IN      Mrs. Levon Martin, Goshen, IN*

## PECAN PIE BARS

2 cups flour
2/3 cup sugar
3/4 cup butter, softened
1/2 tsp. salt
4 eggs, slightly beaten

1 1/2 cups sugar
1 1/2 cups dark corn syrup
3 T. melted butter
1 1/2 tsp. vanilla
2 1/2 cups chopped pecans

Mix flour, sugar, butter and salt; press firmly into a 15x10 pan. Bake at 350° until golden brown, 15 to 20 minutes. Combine remaining ingredients, adding nuts last. Pour over crust. Bake 25 minutes longer, or until filling is set.

*Mrs. LaVerne (Virginia) Hoover, Goshen, IN*

# PECAN TURTLE BARS

2 cups flour
1 cup brown sugar
1/2 cup soft butter or margarine
1 cup pecan halves

2/3 cup butter or margarine
1/2 cup brown sugar
1 cup milk chocolate chips

Mix flour, brown sugar and butter; press firmly into an ungreased 13x9 pan. Sprinkle with nuts. Bring butter and brown sugar to a boil, stirring constantly. Pour over nuts. Bake at 350° for 20 minutes or until caramel is bubbly. Remove from oven; sprinkle with chocolate chips. Allow chips to melt slightly, then swirl.

*Kathleen Ramer, New Paris, IN*

# PUMPKIN BARS

3/4 cup butter or margarine
2 cups sugar
2 cups mashed cooked pumpkin
4 eggs
2 cups flour
2 tsp. baking powder
1 tsp. cinnamon
1/2 tsp. soda

1/2 tsp. salt
1/4 tsp. nutmeg
1 cup chopped nuts
3 oz. cream cheese, softened
1/3 cup soft butter or margarine
1 tsp. vanilla
3 cups powdered sugar

Cream butter and sugar until fluffy. Beat in pumpkin and eggs. Add combined dry ingredients; mix well. Stir in nuts. Spread into a greased and floured 15x10 jellyroll pan. Bake at 350° for 30 to 35 minutes or until done. To make frosting, beat cream cheese, butter and vanilla until creamy. Gradually beat in powdered sugar. Frost cooled bars. These bars can be frozen; thaw at room temperature.

*Cindy (Lee) Hilty, Brooksville, MS*

# RAISIN BARS

3/4 cup soft butter or margarine
1 cup brown sugar
1 3/4 cups flour
1/2 tsp. salt
1/2 tsp. soda
1 1/2 cups oatmeal
2 1/2 cups raisins

1/2 cup sugar
2 T. cornstarch
3/4 to 1 cup water
3 T. lemon juice
1 cup powdered sugar
1/4 tsp. cinnamon
1 T. milk

Combine first 6 ingredients; mix well. Press half of crumbs into a greased 13x9 pan. Cook and stir raisins, sugar, cornstarch, water and lemon juice over low heat until thickened. Spread on unbaked crust. Sprinkle with remaining crumbs, pressing lightly. Bake at 350° for 35 minutes, or until lightly browned. To make icing, combine powdered sugar, cinnamon and milk; drizzle on bars.

*Vera Fox, Memphis, MO*     *Verna M. Ramer, Goshen, IN*     *Mrs. Ivan Zimmerman, Scottsville, KY*

# RAISIN TOFFEE BARS

1 cup flour
1/2 tsp. baking powder
1/2 tsp. salt
1/2 cup butter or margarine
1 cup brown sugar

2 eggs
1 tsp. vanilla
2 cups 40% bran flakes
1 cup raisins

Combine first 3 ingredients; set aside. Beat butter and brown sugar until fluffy. Add eggs and vanilla; beat well. Stir in bran flakes and raisins. Add flour mixture and stir well. Spread evenly in a greased 9x9 pan. Bake at 350° approximately 35 minutes. Cool. Frost, and sprinkle with nuts if desired.

*Miriam Hoover, Goshen, IN*

# TOFFEE BRAN BARS

3/4 cups flour
1/2 cup 100% bran
1/2 cup brown sugar
1/2 cup butter or margarine
2 eggs, beaten
3/4 cup chopped pecans

1 tsp. baking powder
1 tsp. vanilla
1/4 tsp. salt
1/4 cup 100% bran
3/4 cup brown sugar

Combine first 4 ingredients. Press into a 13x9 pan. Bake at 350° for 10 minutes. Combine remaining ingredients; spread over baked crust. Bake 25 minutes longer.

*Ray Hoover, Stratford, WI*

# WHOLE GRAIN JAM BARS

2 cups oatmeal
1 3/4 cups flour
1 cup butter or margarine
1 cup brown sugar
1/2 cup chopped nuts

1 tsp. cinnamon
1/4 tsp. nutmeg
3/4 tsp. salt
1/2 tsp. soda
3/4 cup jam

Beat all ingredients except jam at low speed until crumbly. Reserve 2 cups crumbs; press remaining crumbs into a greased 13x9 pan. Spread jam on crust. Sprinkle with reserved crumbs. Bake at 400° for 25 to 30 minutes. Cool. A cup of applesauce mixed with 3/4 cup of raisins can be used instead of jam.

*Rachel Newswanger, Barnett, MO*     *Janice Weaver, Unity, WI*

***Character is much easier kept than recovered.***

## WHOLE WHEAT BROWNIES

1 cup flour
1 cup whole wheat flour
1 tsp. soda
1/2 tsp. salt
1 cup butter or margarine
2/3 cup sugar

2/3 cup brown sugar
2 eggs
1 tsp. vanilla
1 cup chopped nuts
1 cup chocolate chips

Combine dry ingredients. Cream butter, sugars and eggs. Add dry ingredients. Beat. Add vanilla, nuts and chips. Spread on a greased cookie sheet. Bake at 375° for 15 minutes. Cool and frost with powdered sugar glaze.

*Donna Hoover, Goshen, IN*

## WHOLE WHEAT CHIP AND COFFEE BARS

2 cups flour
1 cup whole wheat flour
1 tsp. soda
1 tsp. salt
2 eggs
2 cups brown sugar
1 cup cooking oil
2 tsp. vanilla

2 tsp. instant coffee granules
1 cup cold water
1 cup chocolate chips
1 cup chopped walnuts
1/2 tsp. instant coffee granules
4 tsp. water
1 cup powdered sugar
1 T. soft butter

Combine flours, soda, and salt; set aside. In a large bowl beat eggs till fluffy. Gradually add brown sugar, oil and vanilla; beat well. Dissolve coffee granules in cold water; gradually stir in egg mixture. Add dry ingredients; beat well. Pour into a greased 15x10 pan. Sprinkle chocolate chips and nuts evenly on top. Bake at 350° for 25 to 30 minutes. Cool slightly. To make glaze dissolve coffee in water; mix in powdered sugar and butter; drizzle over bars.

*Janice Weaver, Unity, WI*

## ZUCCHINI BARS

1 cup cooking oil
2 cups sugar
4 eggs
2/3 cup water
2 cups grated zucchini
2 1/2 cups flour
1 cup whole wheat flour

2 tsp. soda
1 1/2 tsp. salt
2 tsp. cinnamon
1 1/2 tsp. nutmeg
12 oz. (2 cups) chocolate chips
12 oz. (2 cups) butterscotch chips
1 cup nuts

Combine oil, sugar, and eggs; stir in water and zucchini. Add dry ingredients; mix well. Spread into two 13x9 pans. Bake at 350° for 5 minutes. Sprinkle with chips and nuts; bake 30 minutes longer, or until done. Less chips may be used.

*Janice Weaver, Unity, WI*

# NO
# BAKE
# TREATS

# ALMOND BARK TREATS

2 1/2 lb. almond bark (white
   chocolate)
1 cup peanut butter

3 cups Rice Krispies
3 cups miniature marshmallows
3 cups salted peanuts

Melt bark and peanut butter together. Cool slightly; add cereal, marshmallows and peanuts. Stir together then drop by spoonfuls onto wax paper.

# BASIC RICE KRISPIE SQUARES

*For color and added flavor stir 3 ounces of flavored gelatin into melted marshmallows before adding cereal.*

2 to 4 T. butter
6 cups miniature marshmallows

6 cups Rice Krispies

Melt butter and marshmallows over low heat. Remove from heat. Add Rice Krispies. Press into a buttered 13x9 pan. To make in a microwave, place butter in a microwave safe bowl; microwave for 45 seconds or until butter melts. Stir in marshmallows and coat well. Microwave on high for 1 1/2 minutes, stirring after 45 seconds. Immediately stir in cereal; press in a buttered 13x9 pan.

# CARAMEL NO-BAKE COOKIES

*Brown sugar and vanilla pudding will also give cookies a caramel flavor. Try different kinds of instant pudding for different flavors.*

2 cups sugar
3/4 cup butter
3/4 cup evaporated milk or cream

4-serving size butterscotch
   instant pudding
3 1/2 cups quick oatmeal

Bring sugar, butter and milk to a full rolling boil. Remove from heat; add pudding and oatmeal. Stir thoroughly. Drop by rounded teaspoonfuls onto wax paper when cool enough to handle.

# CHEERIOS SQUARES

2 cups sugar
2 cups corn syrup
1 1/2 cups butter or margarine
2 cups peanut butter

8 cups Cheerios
4 cups cornflakes
1 to 2 cups chopped peanuts

Bring sugar, syrup and butter to a boil. Remove from heat; add peanut butter, stir until smooth. Pour mixture over combined cereals and nuts; mix well. Press into a buttered pan. Cool before cutting.

*Mrs. John (Twila) Kulp, Mosinee, WI*

381

## CHEWY NO-BAKE OATMEAL COOKIES

1 cup chocolate chips
1/3 cup butter or margarine
16 large marshmallows or 1 1/2
    cups miniature marshmallows

1 tsp. vanilla
2 cups quick oatmeal
1 cup coconut, raisins or nuts

Melt chocolate chips, butter and marshmallows over low heat, stirring until smooth. Remove from heat; cool slightly. Stir in remaining ingredients. Drop by rounded tablespoons onto wax paper.

## CHINESE NOODLE TREAT I

1 cup chocolate chips
2 cups butterscotch chips

5 oz. chow mein noodles
1/2 cup nuts

Melt chips over low heat. Cool slightly; add noodles. Stir in nuts. Drop by teaspoon onto wax paper. Let set until firm.

*Mrs. James Kulp, Unity, WI*

## CHINESE NOODLE TREAT II

1 cup sugar
1/2 cup molasses

1 cup peanut butter
3 oz. Chinese noodles

Bring sugar and molasses to a boil. Remove from heat; add peanut butter and noodles. Stir until well mixed. Drop by teaspoon onto wax paper.

*Edna Miller, Snover, MI*

## CHOCOLATE PEANUT BUTTER RICE KRISPIE SQUARES

1 cup sugar
1 cup light corn syrup
1 cup peanut butter

6 cups Rice Krispies
6 oz. (1 cup) chocolate chips
6 oz. (1 cup) butterscotch chips

Bring sugar and corn syrup to a boil. Remove from heat and stir in peanut butter. Pour over cereal and mix. Press in a buttered 13x9 pan. Melt the chips together; spread over top.

*Mrs. James Kulp, Unity, WI*    *Naoma Zimmerman, Goshen, IN*

***Going to church doesn't make you a Christian any more than going to a garage makes you a mechanic.***

## CHOCOLATE PEANUT BUTTER SNACK

1/2 cup butter or margarine
16 oz. chocolate or butterscotch
   chips
1/2 cup peanut butter

12 cups Chex, Cheerios, oatmeal
   or any combination
2 cups powdered sugar

Melt butter and chips together; stir in peanut butter and pour over cereal. Mix well. Put powdered sugar in a brown bag or large container with a lid; pour cereal mixture into it. Shake well until powdered sugar is used up.

*Janice Weaver, Unity, WI*

## COCONUT NESTS

1/2 cup butter or margarine
3 cups coconut
2 cups powdered sugar

3/4 cup chocolate or butterscotch
   chips, melted

Melt butter; stir in coconut and powdered sugar. Mix by hand if necessary. Roll into walnut size balls. Make a dent in each and fill with melted chocolate.

## CRISPY CLUSTERS

4 1/2 cups miniature
   marshmallows
1/2 cup butter or margarine
5 cups Rice Krispies

1 cup coconut
1/2 cup chopped nuts
1 cup chocolate chips, melted

Melt marshmallows and butter over low heat; stir until smooth. Remove from heat; add cereal, coconut and nuts. Mix well. Drop by tablespoonfuls onto wax paper. Top clusters with melted chocolate; chill.

## CRUNCH AND CHEW TREAT

1/2 cup peanut butter
1 cup rice cereal
1/4 cup raisins, opt.

1/4 cup powdered sugar
1/4 cup honey

Put everything in a bowl. Mix well. Drop by teaspoon onto wax paper. Chill.

*Anna Zimmerman, Decker, MI*

*Contentment comes not so much from greater wealth as from fewer wants.*

## FAIL-PROOF MARSHMALLOW TREAT

1 cup butterscotch chips
1 cup chocolate chips
1 cup crunchy peanut butter

1/2 cup butter or margarine
1 tsp. vanilla
1 pkg. miniature marshmallows

Melt chips, peanut butter and butter over low heat. Add vanilla; stir well. Put marshmallows in a greased 13x9 pan. Pour chocolate mixture on top. Chill until firm before cutting.

*Ruth (Ramer) Stromlund, Harrison, AR*

## FRUIT CHEWS

1 cup dried apricots, cut up
1 cup dates, cut up
1 1/2 cups raisins

1 cup coconut
1/2 cup chopped nuts
1/4 cup sesame seeds

Grind first 3 ingredients in a food grinder or blender. Mix with coconut and nuts. Form into 1-inch balls. Roll into sesame seeds, pressing seeds firmly into chews.

## GOLDEN GRAHAM SMORES

1/3 cup light corn syrup
1 T. butter or margarine
1 cup milk chocolate chips
1/2 tsp. vanilla

4 cups Golden Graham cereal
1 1/2 cups miniature
   marshmallows

Bring syrup and butter to a boil; remove from heat. Stir in chocolate chips and vanilla; stirring until chips are melted. Fold in cereal and marshmallows. Press into a 9x9 pan.

*Miriam Hoover, Goshen, IN*

## GRANOLA BARS

20 oz. miniature marshmallows
1/4 cup honey
1/4 cup peanut butter
1/4 cup cooking oil
3/4 cup butter

5 cups quick oats
4 1/2 cups Rice Krispies
1/3 of a box of graham crackers
1 1/2 cups coconut
1 cup chocolate chips

Melt first 5 ingredients just until barely melted. Combine remaining ingredients in a large bowl; pour melted mixture on top. Stir together; press into a greased jelly roll pan.

*Christina Yutzy, Unity, WI*

# HONEY BALLS

1 cup honey
1 cup dry milk
1 cup peanut butter

Crushed peanuts, wheat germ or
chocolate sprinkles

Mix honey, milk and peanut butter; shape into small balls.  Roll into peanuts.
Can also be shaped into logs and sliced after firm.

*Edna Miller, Snover, MI*

# NO-BAKE COOKIES

*Coconut, nuts or chocolate chips may be added or used instead of peanut butter.*

2 cups sugar
3 T. cocoa
1/4 cup butter
1/2 cup milk

3 to 4 cups quick oatmeal
1 tsp. vanilla
3/4 cup peanut butter

Boil first 4 ingredients 1 minute.  Remove from heat; stir in remaining ingredients.
Drop quickly by teaspoon onto wax paper.  Increase butter by 1/4 cup if deleting
peanut butter.

*Mrs. Allen Garman, Roaring Spring, PA     Sylvan Horning, Penn Yan, NY*

# PEANUT BUTTER CRACKER TREATS

56 Ritz crackers
Peanut butter

12 oz. almond bark or chocolate
coating, melted

Spread peanut butter between crackers.  Dip cracker sandwiches into melted
chocolate; place on wax paper.

# PEANUT BUTTER RICE KRISPIE TREATS

1/4 cup butter or margarine
40 large marshmallows or 4 cups
miniature marshmallows

1/2 cup peanut butter
5 cups Rice Krispies

Melt butter and marshmallows over low heat, stirring constantly.  Remove from
heat; stir in peanut butter.  Add Rice Krispies, stirring until well coated.  Spread
into a buttered 13x9 pan; press firmly with a buttered spatula or wax paper. Cool.

*Rebecca Ringler, Fleetwood, PA*

# PEANUT CHEWS

1/2 cup peanut butter
1/2 cup corn syrup
1/2 cup sugar

3 cups cornflakes or Rice
  Krispies

Mix peanut butter, syrup and sugar; bring to a full boil. Remove from heat; add cereal. Mold into balls. These can also be pressed into a buttered pan.

*Arlene Hoover, Fortuna, MO*

# RICE KRISPIE COOKIES

*A cup of peanuts, coconut or raisins may be added.*

12 oz. (2 cups) chocolate or
  butterscotch chips

1/2 cup chunky peanut butter
5 cups Rice Krispies

Melt chips and peanut butter together over low heat. Remove from heat; add Rice Krispies. Drop by spoonfuls on wax paper or press firmly into a butter 13x9 pan.

*Ruth (Ramer) Strumland, Harrison, AR*

# SHOESTRING COOKIES

6 oz. (1 cup) chocolate chips
12 oz. (2 cups) butterscotch chips

7 oz. shoestring potatoes
1/4 cup chopped nuts

Melt chocolate and butterscotch chips. Add shoestring potatoes and nuts. Drop by teaspoonfuls onto wax paper. Let stand overnight or until firm. Chow mein noodles may be used instead of potatoes.

*Mary Ellen Hission, Plymouth, IN*

**To toast nuts in the microwave, place on a plate in a single layer and microwave on high for two minutes. Stir, then microwave another minute or two until nuts are fragrant and toasted to taste.**

# SNACK MIX

1 cup pecans
4 cups popped popcorn
1 cup pretzels

6 oz. almond bark (white
  chocolate)

Toast pecans over low heat in a greased skillet; salt lightly. Mix nuts with popcorn and pretzels. Pour melted almond bark over the mixture.

*Mrs. Dale (Margaret) Love, Goshen, IN*

# CANDY

| CANDY | | |
|---|---|---|
| Fudge | 238° | Soft Ball |
| Caramels | 245° | Firm Ball |
| Taffy | 265° | Hard Ball |
| Butter-Scotch | 275°-280° | Soft Crack |
| Peanut Brittle | 290°-310° | Hard Crack |

Sugar

Elsie Hoover

## BUTTERMILK CANDY

| | |
|---|---|
| 1 cup buttermilk | 1 tsp. soda |
| 1/2 cup butter or margarine | 2 cups sugar |

Mix all ingredients and boil to soft ball stage (235°). Beat with a mixer until light brown. Pour into a greased 9x9 pan.

*Mrs. Carlton Zimmerman, Brooten, MN*

## BUTTERSCOTCH PATTIES

| | |
|---|---|
| 1 cup sugar | 1/2 cup milk |
| 1/2 cup brown sugar | 3 T. butter |
| 1/3 cup corn syrup | 3/4 to 1 cup nuts |
| 1/8 tsp. salt | 1/2 tsp. vanilla |

Combine first 5 ingredients and stir until sugar is dissolved. Cook to firm ball stage (244° to 248°). Remove from heat; add butter, nuts and vanilla. Beat until thick and creamy. Drop by spoonfuls onto wax paper.

*Mrs. Harvey (Ruth) Brubaker, Tylertown, MS*

## CARAMEL FUDGE CANDY

| | |
|---|---|
| 3 cups brown sugar | 1/4 cup butter |
| 3 T. corn syrup | 1 tsp. vanilla |
| 2/3 cup cream or milk | |

Bring all ingredients to a boil; boil until it forms a ball when dropped in cold water, (238°). Beat till creamy; pour into a buttered pan. Add nuts or cocoa before beating, if desired.

*Mrs. Harvey (Ruth) Brubaker, Tylertown, MS*

## CARAMEL NUT CANDY

| | |
|---|---|
| 1 1/2 cups sugar | 1 2/3 cups evaporated milk or |
| 1/2 cup brown sugar | 1 3/4 cup cream |
| 2 cups light corn syrup | 1 tsp. vanilla |
| 1/4 tsp. salt | 1 cup chopped nuts |
| 1/2 cup butter | |

Cook sugars, syrup and salt rapidly over medium-high heat to 244°, or firm ball stage. Add butter and milk gradually so mixture doesn't stop boiling. Cook over medium heat back up to 244°, stirring frequently at first, then constantly, about 25 minutes. Remove from heat; add vanilla and nuts; mix well. Pour into a buttered 13x9 or 9x9 pan. Cut hardened caramel into squares using a knife heated with hot water and wiped dry before making each cut.

*Mrs. Ray (Elsie) Hoover, Stratford, WI     Alta Martin, Goshen, IN*

## CARAMEL PECAN PATTIES

2 3/4 cups brown sugar
1 cup butter or margarine
1 cup light corn syrup
1/8 tsp. salt
14 oz. sweetened condensed milk

1 tsp. vanilla
1 1/2 cups pecan halves
2 cups chocolate chips
2 T. cooking oil

Cook sugar, butter, syrup, and salt over medium heat until sugar is dissolved. Gradually add milk; mix well. Cook to 244° or firm ball stage. Remove from heat; stir in vanilla. Fold in pecans. Drop by tablespoonfuls onto wax paper. Chill until firm. Melt chocolate chips and shortening together. Drizzle chocolate on top of each cluster.

## CASHEW CRUNCH

1 cup sugar
1 cup butter
2 T. corn syrup

1 1/2 to 2 cups raw or salted
    cashew pieces

In a 2-quart saucepan combine sugar, butter and syrup. Bring to a boil over medium-high heat. Stir constantly, to 290° or until syrup forms brittle strands when dropped into cold water. Stir in nuts. Spread 1/4 inch thick on a wax paper lined 15x10 pan. Cool completely. Break into pieces to serve.

*Mrs. Wesley (Donna) Weaver, Conrath, WI*     *Joanna Weaver, Unity, WI*

## CHIP-NUT TOFFEE

1 cup chopped nuts
1 1/2 cups brown sugar

1 cup butter
2 cups milk chocolate chips

Spread nuts in a buttered 13x9 pan. Bring sugar and butter to a rolling boil, stirring constantly. Boil to 270°. Pour evenly over nuts. Sprinkle with chocolate chips. Cover pan until chips soften; spread evenly. Cool and break into pieces.

## CHOCOLATE COVERED CHERRIES I

1/2 cup butter or cooking oil
6 T. corn syrup
14 oz. sweetened condensed milk
1 tsp. vanilla

3 lb. powdered sugar
Maraschino cherries
12 oz. (2 cups) chocolate chips
1 square paraffin

Mix first 5 ingredients. Form into balls with cherries in the center. Freeze 1 hour. Melt chocolate chips and paraffin. Dip into chocolate and place on wax paper.

*Edna Miller, Snover, MI*

# CHOCOLATE COVERED CHERRIES II

60 maraschino cherries with
   stems
3 T. butter

3 T. corn syrup
2 cups powdered sugar
1 1/2 lb. chocolate coating

Drain cherries well. Combine butter and corn syrup. Stir in sugar and knead until smooth. Chill if too soft. Shape a marble sized piece around each cherry. Chill. Melt chocolate and dip cherries. Store in a covered container for a week or two till fondant begins to liquefy.

# CHRISTMAS COOKIE CANDY

6 oz. (1 cup) chocolate chips
2 T. light corn syrup
1/2 cup orange juice

2 1/2 cups vanilla wafer crumbs
1/2 cup powdered sugar
1 cup pecans, chopped fine

Melt chocolate chips. Mix in syrup and orange juice. Mix wafer crumbs, sugar and nuts in a bowl; add chocolate mixture. Mix well. Cool 1 hour then form into balls and roll in powdered sugar.

*Mrs. Dale (Margaret) Love, Goshen, IN*

To melt chocolate chips in the microwave, place chips in a microwave-safe bowl on medium-high or 70% power for 1 minute. Stir. Microwave at 15 second intervals stirring each time. Heat just until melted.

# CLARK BAR TASTE ALIKES

1 cup butter or margarine
1 lb. crunchy peanut butter
2 1/2 cups powdered sugar

1 T. vanilla
1 lb. graham crackers, crushed
Chocolate for dipping

Mix first 5 ingredients with hands. Roll into bonbon-size balls; dip into chocolate.

*Edna Miller, Snover, MI*

# COCONUT BONBONS

1 lb. powdered sugar
2 cups coconut
1/2 tsp. vanilla

1/2 cup butter
1 cup sweetened condensed milk
Dipping chocolate

Combine first 5 ingredients and shape into balls. Dip into chocolate.

*Connie Rodes, Milford, IN*

## COCONUT CREMES

3 T. soft butter
3 T. light corn syrup
1 tsp. vanilla
1/4 tsp. salt

2 1/2 cups powdered sugar
1 1/4 cups coconut
2 cups milk chocolate chips
1 T. cooking oil

Combine butter, syrup, vanilla and salt. Gradually add sugar; mix well. Mixture will be crumbly. Add coconut and knead until smooth. Shape into 1-inch balls; freeze 10 minutes. Melt chocolate chips and oil till smooth. Dip balls into chocolate. Shake excess chocolate off; place on wax paper-lined cookie sheets.

*Mrs. Ray (Elsie) Hoover, Stratford, WI*

## CRACKER DELIGHT

Soda crackers
1 cup brown sugar

1 cup butter
12 oz. (2 cups) chocolate chips

Cover jellyroll pan with soda crackers. Melt sugar and butter; pour over crackers. Bake at 350° for 3 to 4 minutes. Remove from oven; sprinkle with chocolate chips. Put in oven for 1 minute or until chips soften. Spread chocolate. Cool.

*Edna Miller, Snover, MI*

## FUDGE

2/3 cup evaporated milk
1/4 cup butter
1 1/2 cups sugar
1/4 tsp. salt

2 cups miniature marshmallows
1 1/2 to 2 cups chocolate chips
1 tsp. vanilla
1/2 to 3/4 cup chopped nuts

Bring evaporated milk, butter, sugar and salt to a boil over medium heat in a heavy saucepan and boil 4 to 5 minutes; stirring constantly. Remove from heat; stir in marshmallows, and then chocolate chips. Beat until chips melt. Mix in vanilla and nuts. Pour into a buttered or foil-lined 8 or 9-inch pan. Chill until firm.

## CHOCOLATE PEANUT BUTTER FUDGE

36 oz. (6 cups) chocolate chips
1 cup butter
2 cups marshmallow crème
2 cups peanut butter

2 T. vanilla
4 1/2 cups sugar
12 oz. evaporated milk

Combine first 5 ingredients in a bowl. Cook sugar and milk over low heat for 10 minutes, stirring often. Pour over ingredients in bowl; stir until smooth. Pour into buttered pans.

*Ella Horning, Penn Yan, NY*

## COCOA FUDGE

3 cups sugar
2/3 cup cocoa
1/8 tsp. salt

1 1/2 cups milk
1/4 cup butter or margarine
1 tsp. vanilla

Butter an 8 or 9-inch square pan. Combine sugar, cocoa, salt and milk in a heavy saucepan; bring to a boil over medium heat, stirring constantly until mixture comes to a boil. Boil without stirring to 234° (or until syrup forms a soft ball when dropped into very cold water). Remove from heat. Add butter and vanilla but do not stir. Cool to 110°, or lukewarm. Beat with a spoon until fudge thickens and loses some of its gloss. Quickly spread into pan.

## EASY FUDGE

*If you like mint, delete 1/2 teaspoon of vanilla and add 1/2 teaspoon mint extract. To make mocha fudge, delete nuts and stir in a tablespoon of instant coffee granules when adding vanilla.*

18 oz. (3 cups) semisweet
   chocolate chips
14 oz. sweetened condensed milk

1/8 tsp. salt
3/4 cup nuts
1 1/2 tsp. vanilla

Melt chips and milk in a heavy saucepan over low heat. Remove from heat; stir in salt, nuts and vanilla. Spread evenly into a wax paper-lined 8 or 9-inch square pan. Chill till firm. Turn out fudge; peel off paper and cut into 1-inch squares.

*Mary Ann Martin, Sauk Centre, MN*

**Be creative when making fudge. Use butterscotch chips to make butterscotch fudge or white baking chips for white fudge. Add chopped and patted dry maraschino cherries or dried cranberries to white or chocolate fudge for a bit of color, or make two toned fudge by layering two different kinds of fudge.**

## EASY CREAM CHEESE FUDGE

12 oz. (2 cups) semisweet
   chocolate chips
8 oz. cream cheese, softened

1/2 cup chopped nuts
1 tsp. vanilla

Melt chocolate chips in a heavy saucepan over low heat, or in microwave. Beat cream cheese with a mixer just until smooth. Beat in melted chocolate. Stir in nuts and vanilla. Scrape into a buttered 8 or 9-inch square pan. Refrigerate until firm. Refrigerate leftovers.

# EASY ROCKY ROAD FUDGE

12 oz. (2 cups) semisweet
   chocolate chips
14 oz. sweetened condensed milk

1 tsp. vanilla
3 cups marshmallows
1 cup coarsely chopped walnuts

Stir and melt chocolate chips and sweetened condensed milk over low heat just until melted. Remove from heat; stir in vanilla. Fold in marshmallows and nuts. Press into a buttered 13x9 pan.

# PEANUT BUTTER FUDGE

2/3 cup evaporated or whole milk
2 cups sugar
1 cup crunchy peanut butter

2 cups marshmallow crème
1 tsp. vanilla

Cook milk and sugar to 234°, or just boil 4 to 5 minutes. Remove from heat; add peanut butter, marshmallow crème, and vanilla. Beat until smooth. Pour into a buttered 8 or 9-inch square pan.

*Esther Horst, East Earl, PA*     *Mrs. Aaron Weaver, Penn Yan, NY*

# QUICK FUDGE

1/2 cup butter, cut up
1/2 cup milk
12 oz. (2 cups) semisweet
   chocolate chips

4 cups powdered sugar
1 tsp. vanilla
1/2 cup chopped walnuts, opt.

Cook and stir butter, milk and chocolate chips over low heat until melted. Pour into a large bowl. Add powdered sugar and vanilla; beat at medium speed, scraping bowl often, until smooth. Add walnuts. Spread in buttered 8-inch square pan. Cover and refrigerate until firm. Refrigerate leftovers.

# VELVEETA CHEESE FUDGE

1 lb. Velveeta cheese
1 lb. butter
1 tsp. vanilla

4 lb. powdered sugar
1 cup cocoa
1 cup coconut or nuts, opt.

On low heat in a large pan, melt cheese, butter and vanilla. Add powdered sugar and cocoa. Add coconut or nuts. Pour in a buttered 13x9 pan. Cut and serve.

*Edna Miller, Snover, MI*

# HARD CANDY

2/3 cup light corn syrup
3/4 cup water
2 cups sugar

1/2 tsp. cinnamon oil
Food coloring

Bring water and syrup to a boil; add sugar and stir until sugar dissolves. Boil without stirring to 300°, or until drops of syrup form hard, brittle threads in cold water. Remove from heat. After boiling action has stopped, add flavoring and coloring. Pour onto lightly greased cookie sheet. Cool and break into pieces. Dust with powdered sugar to keep from sticking.

**When making candy do not let the thermometer touch the bottom of the saucepan. On humid days many candies need to boil longer and temperatures need to be two degrees higher than on dry days.**

# LAYERED CHOCOLATE CARAMEL CANDY

2 cups milk chocolate chips
1/2 cup butterscotch chips
1/2 cup peanut butter
1/4 cup butter or margarine
1 cup sugar
1/4 cup evaporated milk

1 1/2 cups marshmallow crème
1/4 cup peanut butter
1 tsp. vanilla
1 1/2 cups salted peanuts
14 oz. bag caramels
1/4 cup evaporated milk

Stir chips and peanut butter over low heat until melted. Spread half of the mixture into a lightly greased 13x9 pan. Refrigerate till set. Melt butter in a heavy saucepan over medium heat; add sugar and milk. Bring to a boil; boil and stir for 5 minutes. Remove from heat; stir in marshmallow crème, peanut butter and vanilla. Add peanuts. Spread over first layer. Refrigerate until set. Stir caramels and milk over low heat until melted and smooth. Spread over second layer. Refrigerate until set. Top with remaining chocolate, reheating if necessary.

# MILK CHOCOLATE PRALINES

3 cups sugar
3/4 cup water
1/4 cup light corn syrup
1 tsp. vinegar

1/2 tsp. salt
11.5 oz. (2 cups) milk chocolate
   chips
1 cup broken pecans

Bring all but chocolate and nuts to a boil, stirring constantly. Boil on high for 3 minutes without stirring. Cool 5 minutes. Add chips; stir quickly till melted. Stir in nuts. Drop by tablespoon onto foil, working fast. Garnish with pecan halves if desired. Refrigerate 20 minutes; peel off foil.

*Mrs. Ray (Elsie) Hoover, Stratford, WI*

# CHOCOLATE MINTS

4 cups chocolate chips,
1/2 cup cooking oil
5 T. butter
1/2 cup light corn syrup

4 1/2 cups powdered sugar
5 drops peppermint oil or 1 tsp.
   peppermint extract
Green or red food coloring

Heat 2 cups chocolate chips and 1/4 cup oil over low heat until melted. Spread on bottom of a 13x9 pan. Bring butter, corn syrup and 2 cups powdered sugar to a boil. Remove from heat; add peppermint oil and several drops food coloring. Add remaining powdered sugar. Mix well. Shape dough to fit pan and lay on top of chocolate while still a little warm. Melt remaining chips and oil. Spread on top.

*Mrs. James (Arlene) Martin, Nappanee, IN*

# DINNER MINTS

3 oz. cream cheese
4 cups powdered sugar

1/2 tsp. peppermint flavoring
Food coloring

Mix everything together. Spearmint or other flavoring may be used. Roll into a rope; cut into pieces. If liquid coloring is used more sugar may be needed.

*Lucinda Zimmerman, Rutledge, MO*

# PASTEL BUTTER MINTS

2 lb. powdered sugar
1/2 cup butter, melted
5 to 6 T. cold water

Red and green food coloring
3 tsp. peppermint extract

Combine sugar, butter and water; knead until smooth. Divide in half. Add red food coloring and 1 1/2 teaspoons extract to half and green food coloring and remaining extract to the other half. Mix well; shape into thin round patties on a cookie sheet. Press with a fork. These can also be dipped in chocolate.

*Mrs. Ray (Elsie) Hoover, Stratford, WI*

# NAPOLEON CRÈMES

1/2 cup butter
1/4 cup sugar
1/4 cup cocoa
1 tsp. vanilla
1 egg, slightly beaten
2 cups finely crushed graham
   crackers

1 cup coconut
1/2 cup butter
3 T. milk
3.75 oz. vanilla instant pudding
2 cups powdered sugar
1 cup semisweet chocolate chips
2 T. butter

Combine first 4 ingredients in a double boiler or heavy saucepan; cook till butter melts. Stir in egg; cook until thick, about 3 minutes. Stir in cracker crumbs and coconut. Press into buttered 9-inch pan. Cream butter; stir in milk, dry pudding and powdered sugar. Beat until fluffy. Spread evenly over crust; chill till firm. Melt chocolate chips with butter; pour on top.

*Verna Martin, Goshen, IN*

## OPERA CREAMS

2 cups sugar
3/4 cup whipping cream
1 cup milk

2 T. light corn syrup
1/8 tsp. salt
1 tsp. vanilla

Bring first 5 ingredients to a boil in a large heavy pan, stirring until sugar is dissolved. Cover and cook about 3 minutes until steam has washed sugar crystals off sides of pan. Uncover; cook over low heat to 238°. Remove from heat. Cool to lukewarm, 110°. Add vanilla; beat until creamy. Pour into buttered molds or a buttered pan. Cool; cut into squares. If desired dip room-temperature candy into melted chocolate coating. Best if dipped the day after it's made.

## PEANUT BRITTLE

2 cups sugar
1 cup light corn syrup
1/2 cup water

1 lb. raw peanuts
3 T. butter
1 T. soda

Boil sugar, syrup, and water 2 to 3 minutes. Add peanuts (or pecans or cashews). Stir and cook to 310°. Remove from heat; stir in butter and soda. Beat well. Spread quickly and thinly onto a buttered cookie sheet. Do not stir after pouring. Cool. Break into pieces. This can also be made using only 2 teaspoons soda, and then pouring, without stirring, onto a greased jellyroll pan. As soon as it is cool enough to handle put on wax paper and pull to stretch.

*Lizzie Hoover, Goshen, IN*    *Mrs. Cyrus Kulp, Auburn, NY*    *Thelma Martin, Osceola, IN*

## MICROWAVE PEANUT BRITTLE

1 cup sugar
1/2 cup light corn syrup
1 cup roasted salted peanuts

1 tsp. butter
1 tsp. vanilla
1 tsp. soda

Combine sugar and syrup in a 1 1/2 quart casserole. Microwave on high 4 minutes; stir in nuts. Microwave on high 3 to 5 minutes, until light brown. Add butter and vanilla; mix well. Microwave on high 1 to 2 minutes longer. Peanuts will be lightly browned and syrup very hot. Add soda and gently stir until light and foamy. Pour onto lightly greased cookie sheet. Cool. Break into pieces.

*Susie Ramer, Bonham, Texas*

## PEANUT BUTTER BALLS

*These are also good without Rice Krispies.*

2 cups butter or margarine
4 cups crunchy peanut butter
2 1/2 lb. powdered sugar
6 cups Rice Krispies

3 cups chocolate chips
1/4 slab paraffin or 1/3 cup
   shortening

Mix first 4 ingredients well with hands. Form into 1-inch balls. Chill. Melt chocolate and paraffin. Dip balls into chocolate and place on wax paper.

*Mrs. Cyrus Kulp, Auburn, NY*

## PEANUT BUTTER CANDY SQUARES

3 cups powdered sugar
1 1/2 cups fine graham cracker
   crumbs

1 cup crunchy peanut butter
1 cup butter, melted
2 cups chocolate chips, melted

Mix first 4 ingredients well; press into a buttered 13x9 pan. Melt chocolate chips and spread on top. Chill until firm. Cut into small squares. These squares can be frozen.

*Florence Kulp, Millersburg, IN*

## PECAN LOGS

7 oz. jar marshmallow crème
3 1/2 cups powdered sugar
1 tsp. vanilla

1/4 tsp. almond extract
16 oz. bag caramels, melted
2 1/2 cups chopped pecans

Knead together all but caramels and nuts. Shape into 8x1-inch rolls. Wrap into plastic and freeze hard. Dip logs into melted caramel. Roll logs in nuts.

## PEPPERMINT ICE

1 cup peppermint candy

1 lb. white chocolate

Put peppermint candy in blender and grind almost to powder. Melt chocolate; add candy and mix well. Spread thinly on foil. When set, peel off foil.

*Mrs. Larry Zimmerman, Elkhart, IN*

**People are born with two eyes, but only one tongue, that they may see twice as much as they say.**

# RICE KRISPIE DATE BALLS I

1/3 cup water
1 cup sugar
1 cup chopped dates
1 egg, well beaten

1 tsp. vanilla
2 to 4 cups Rice Krispies
Coconut

Cook first 5 ingredients slowly for 15 minutes. Cool slightly. Stir in Rice Krispies. With buttered hands, shape into 1-inch balls, and then roll into coconut.

*Sarah Imhoff, Sheridan, MI*

# RICE KRISPIE DATE BALLS II

3/4 cup brown sugar
1/2 cup butter or margarine
1 lb. dates

1 tsp. vanilla
3 cups Rice Krispies
Sugar

Cook and stir first 4 ingredients until soft and pasty. Stir in Rice Krispies. With buttered hands, shape into 1-inch balls. Roll balls into sugar.

# SUCKERS

1 cup sugar
3/4 cup corn syrup
1/4 cup butter

1/4 tsp. food coloring
1/4 tsp. mint extract

In heavy pan bring first 3 ingredients to a boil, stirring. Stir in coloring. Cook to 265°, stirring occasionally. Remove from heat; stir in extract. Place sticks on cookie sheet. Drop by tablespoon onto sticks.

*Edna Miller, Snover, MI*

# TAFFY

1 pkg. unflavored gelatin
1/4 cup water
2 cups sugar

2 cups cream or evaporated milk
2 cups light corn syrup
Paraffin size of a walnut

Soften gelatin in cold water. Put all other ingredients in a kettle and boil 15 minutes. Add gelatin; continue boiling until a hard ball forms when dropped into cold water. Pour into well-greased pans. When cool enough to handle, grease hands and pull until light in color. Pull into a long rope; cut into pieces.

*Rebecca Glick, Spencer, WI*

# SALT WATER TAFFY

2 cups sugar
2 T. cornstarch
1 cup light corn syrup
3/4 cup water

2 T. butter or margarine
1 tsp. salt
1/4 tsp. flavoring oil, opt.
Food coloring, opt.

Mix sugar and cornstarch in a heavy saucepan. Stir in corn syrup, water, butter and salt. Stir over medium heat until sugar dissolves; cook to 266°. Remove from heat; add flavoring and coloring if desired. Stir gently. Pour into a greased pan to cool. When cool enough to handle, grease hands and pull until light in color and has a satiny gloss. Pull into a long rope: cut with scissors and wrap in wax paper squares twisting ends.

*If none but you in the world today*
*Had tried to live in a Christ-like way,*
*Could the rest of the world look close at you,*
*And find a path that is straight and true?*
*F.M. Morton*

# CANNING
## and
# FREEZING

# FREEZING CHART

| | DIRECTIONS | SCALDING TIME |
|---|---|---|
| ASPARAGUS | Cut tips into lengths to fit containers, or 1" pieces | Small stalks, 3 minutes<br>Larger stalks, 4 minutes |
| GREEN BEANS | Cut into 1 to 1 1/2" lengths or cut lengthwise | 3 minutes |
| LIMA BEANS | Shell and scald according to size | 1 1/2 to 3 1/2 minutes |
| BROCCOLI | Soak in brine (1/4 cup salt to 1 qt. water) for 1/2 hour. Split lengthwise so heads are about 1" in diameter | 4 minutes |
| CARROTS | Wash and scrape. Cut into 1/4" pieces. Very small carrots may be left whole if scalded 5 minutes | 3 minutes |
| CAULIFLOWER | Trim leaves and break into flowerets no larger than 1" across. Soak in brine (1/4 cup salt to 1 quart water for 1/2 hour) | 3 minutes |
| CORN | Scald on cob, then cut | 4 1/2 minutes |
| PEAS | Shell, sort and wash | 2 minutes |
| SPINACH | Wash thoroughly, discard thick stems. Scald and drain thoroughly. | |

Bring 1 gallon of water to a boil for each 1 to 1 1/2 pounds of vegetables. Add vegetables and start timing immediately, keeping heat on high. Remove promptly at end of scalding time. Change water every third or fourth batch. If you live over 4000 feet above sea level, add 1 minute to times given.

## SYRUP
### for canning

| | SUGAR | WATER | USED FOR |
|---|---|---|---|
| THIN | 1 cup | 3 cups | Small, soft fruits |
| MEDIUM | 1 cup | 2 cups | Peaches, apples, pears & sour berries |
| HEAVY | 1 cup | 1 cup | Sour fruits or those to be extra sweet |

Boil sugar and water together until sugar is dissolved. Keep syrup hot, but do not let it boil down.

# GENERAL CANNING INFORMATION

Thoroughly wash and rinse jars. After filling jars, remove air bubbles to help avoid discoloration. Wipe the jar rims to clean off any food particles. Tighten the band firmly over the lid, but do not overtighten. Place jars into a canner of hot water, making sure at least an inch of water is covering the tops of the jars. (Pressure canners should have only 2 to 3 inches of water.) Start counting processing time when water begins to boil, or, if using a pressure canner, when correct pressure is reached. If living in high altitudes, contact a local county Extension agent for adjusted cooking times.

# VEGETABLES

## PICKLED GREEN BEANS

4 quarts green or wax beans
1/4 to 1 tsp. cayenne pepper or 1
   small dried hot pepper
1/2 to 1 head dill or 1 tsp. dill
   seed or weed

1 to 4 cloves garlic or 1 tsp.
   minced garlic
5 cups vinegar
5 cups water
1/2 cup salt

Wash beans; cut into lengths to fit pint jars, if necessary. Place pepper, dill and garlic into 7 or 8 pint jars. Pack beans vertically into jars. Combine remaining ingredients; heat to a boil. Pour over beans filling to 1/2 inch of the top. Put lids on and process in boiling water canner for 10 minutes.

*Mrs. Lloyd E. Troyer, Stella, MO*

## PICKLED BEETS

4 quarts small beets, cooked and
   peeled
8 cups vinegar
2 cups water
6 cups sugar

3 sticks cinnamon
2 tsp. cloves
2 tsp. allspice
2 T. salt

Wash beets, leaving on 1 inch of stem and the roots. Cook, unpeeled, until skins slip off easily. Bring remaining ingredients to a boil. Pack skinned beets into 7 or 8 pint jars. Pour liquid over beats. Put lids on and process in boiling water canner for 30 minutes.

*Nancy Kilmer, California, MO*

## COLE SLAW FOR THE FREEZER

| | |
|---|---|
| 1 medium cabbage, chopped | 1 cup vinegar |
| 1 pepper, chopped | 1 to 3 tsp. celery seed |
| 1 carrot, grated | 2 cups sugar |
| 1 small onion, chopped, opt. | 1/4 cup water |
| 1 to 2 tsp. salt | 1 tsp. mustard seed, opt |

Mix first 5 ingredients. Let set 1 hour; drain well. Bring remaining ingredients to a boil; boil 1 minute. Cool. Stir into cabbage mixture. Put in containers; freeze.

*Mrs. Elam Hoover, Versailles, MO     Hannah Kulp Family, Mt. Hermon, KY*
*Elaine Zimmerman, Versailles, MO*

## CHILI SAUCE

| | |
|---|---|
| 15 lb. tomatoes | 1/2 tsp. cloves |
| 3 cups sugar | 1 tsp. cinnamon |
| 1/2 cup chopped onion | 1 T. celery seed |
| 1/2 tsp. red pepper | 1/2 tsp. allspice |
| 4 1/4 cups vinegar | 2 T. salt |

Chop tomatoes in blender. Mix with sugar, onion and red pepper. Bring to boil and simmer an hour and 20 minutes. Bring vinegar, cloves, cinnamon, celery seed and allspice to a boil; strain. Add vinegar mixture to tomatoes along with salt. Cook 30 minutes or until desired thickness. Fill and close pint jars; process 15 minutes in boiling water canner.

*Laura Kulp, Stratford, WI*

## CORN RELISH

| | |
|---|---|
| 2 1/2 quarts cut-off sweet corn | 2 cups sugar |
| 2 cups chopped onions | 2 T. salt |
| 1 bunch celery | 1 T. mustard seed |
| 4 red sweet peppers | 4 cups vinegar |

Bring everything to a boil. Cover and simmer 20 minutes, stirring occasionally. Pack into pint jars. Process in boiling water canner for 20 minutes.

*He who is too big to help an individual is too small to serve the masses.*

# HOT DOG RELISH

2 quarts finely chopped green
   tomatoes
2 quarts chopped or ground
   cucumbers
2 quarts finely chopped onions
3 carrots, pared and chopped fine

3 red peppers, finely chopped
1/2 cup pickling salt
2 T. mixed pickling spices
1/2 tsp. cayenne pepper
1 1/2 cups vinegar
3 cups sugar

Combine vegetables in a large bowl. Sprinkle with salt and refrigerate overnight or for 6 to 8 hours. Drain off brine. Tie spices in a cheesecloth bag. Place vinegar and sugar in a large kettle; add spice bag. Bring to a boil and then add vegetables. Simmer 30 to 45 minutes. Pack immediately into hot pint jars, leaving 1/2 inch head space. Top with boiled lids and jar rings. Process in boiling water canner for 15 minutes. This can be mixed with sour cream and mayonnaise to make tartar sauce.

*Irene Breneman, Elida, OH*

# KETCHUP I

2 gallons tomato pulp
2 onions, chopped
7 to 8 T. salt
2 1/2 cups apple cider vinegar

10 drops cinnamon oil
10 drops clove oil
4 cups sugar
6 T. Clearjel

Cook tomatoes and onions together; run through a sieve. Tomatoes can also be put in blender without peeling, along with onions. Boil tomato pulp, onions, salt, vinegar and oils until only 1/3 of mixture remains. Mix sugar and Clearjel; add to tomato mixture. Cook several minutes more; pour into pint jars. Process 20 minutes in a boiling water canner. Ketchup can also be frozen.

*Mrs. William (Lena) Kilmer, California, MO    Mrs. Elias Martin, Goshen, IN*
*Mrs. Sam Newswanger, Goshen, IN*

# KETCHUP II

1 peck or 13 lb. tomatoes
3 large onions, chopped
4 cups sugar
1 T. salt
1/2 tsp. cloves

1/2 tsp. cinnamon
1/2 tsp. dry mustard
1/2 tsp. red pepper
2 cups vinegar

Cook quartered tomatoes and chopped onions until soft. Drain in a bag for 2 hours. Pour juice away and run pulp through sieve or strainer. Add remaining ingredients to pulp and boil 20 minutes. Pour into pint jars and process in boiling water canner for 20 minutes.

*Vera Witmer, Goshen, IN*

# BANANA PICKLES

| | |
|---|---|
| Cucumbers | 1 tsp. mustard |
| 2 cups vinegar | 1 tsp. celery seed |
| 1 cup water | 1 tsp. turmeric |
| 5 cups sugar | 1 tsp. salt |

Choose cucumbers as long as a quart jar; peel. Slice in quarters lengthwise. Place in wide-mouth quart jars. Mix remaining ingredients. Fill jars. Process in boiling water canner for 10 minutes.

*Janet Fox, Memphis, MO*

**Pickle recipes with an unspecified amount of cucumbers generally make just enough brine for 2 or 3 quarts. Make as many batches of brine as needed to fill cucumber-filled jars.**

# BREAD AND BUTTER PICKLES

| | |
|---|---|
| 6 cups sliced cucumbers | 1/2 tsp. turmeric |
| 1 lb. onions, sliced thin | 1/4 tsp. cloves |
| 1 green pepper, chopped | 1 T. mustard seed |
| 1/4 cup salt | 2 cups vinegar |
| 2 cups sugar | |

Mix vegetables with salt. Let set 3 hours. Drain. Make syrup with remaining ingredients. Bring to a boil; add to vegetable mixture. Put in jars. Process in boiling water canner for 10 minutes.

*Mrs. Ivan Zimmerman, Scottsville, KY*

**If dill ripens before cucumbers, store washed and dried dill in the freezer in closed plastic bags or put washed dill heads in a large jar and cover with vinegar. Cover the jar and keep it in a cool place. The vinegar may be used in the recipe. If you don't have fresh dill use approximately one tablespoon dill seed or weed per head.**

# DILL PICKLES I

| | |
|---|---|
| 1 head fresh dill for each jar, or | 3 cups water |
| 1 tsp. dry dill | 1 cup apple cider vinegar |
| Cucumbers, sliced lengthwise | 1/4 cup salt |
| 1/4 tsp. alum | 1 shake garlic or onion salt |

Put dill in jars with cucumbers. Boil remaining ingredients and pour over cucumbers. Process in boiling water canner for 10 minutes.

*Nancy Kilmer, California, MO*

# DILL PICKLES II

*To make kosher dills, add 14 garlic cloves, split in half, to vinegar solution before boiling. Pour solution over cucumber filled jars, dividing clove halves evenly.*

4 lb. 4-inch cucumbers
6 T. salt, scant
3 cups vinegar

3 cups water
1 cup dill seed
21 peppercorns

Cut washed cucumbers in half lengthwise. Bring salt, vinegar, and water to a boil. Pack cucumbers into 7 hot pint jars. Add approximately 2 T. dill seed and 3 peppercorns to each jar. Fill with pickling syrup. Immediately adjust lids. Process in a boiling water canner for 15 minutes.

*Nora Fox, Novelty, MO*

**Canning or pickling salt is recommended for pickling. Regular table salt can be used but may make the brine cloudy.**

# KOSHER DILL PICKLES

30 to 36 3 to 4-inch cucumbers
3 cups water
3 cups vinegar
6 T. salt

Fresh or dried dill
Mustard seed
Minced garlic, opt.

Bring water, vinegar and salt to a boil. In each quart jar put 1 teaspoon dill seed, 1 teaspoon mustard seed and 1/4 teaspoon minced garlic. Pack jars with cucumbers and fill with brine. Process 10 minutes in boiling water canner.

*Mrs. Lloyd E. Troyer, Farmville, VA*

# SEMISWEET DILL PICKLES

Cucumbers
1 1/2 cups vinegar
1 1/2 cups sugar
1/2 cup water
1 tsp. salt

1/2 tsp. pickling spice
1 clove garlic
1/8 tsp. alum
1 head dill

Slice cucumbers lengthwise; place in quart jars. Mix vinegar, sugar and water; pour into jars; bring to a boil. (This liquid is enough for 2 jars – make as much as needed.) In *each jar* place the given amount of salt, pickling spice, garlic, alum and dill. Screw on lids and place in canner. Process in boiling water canner for 10 minutes.

*Grace Shirk, Goshen, IN*

## SWEET DILL STICKS

Cucumbers, sliced lengthwise
Dill seed
4 cups water
3 3/4 cups vinegar

6 cups sugar
3 T. salt
2 tsp. turmeric, scant
3/4 tsp. mustard

Fill 6 quart jars with cucumbers; add 1/2 teaspoon dill seed to each jar. Combine remaining ingredients. Bring to a boil and pour over cucumbers. Process in boiling water canner for 10 minutes.

*Mrs. Sam Newswanger, Goshen, IN*

It takes approximately 9 pounds of cucumbers to make 9 pints. It takes approximately 14 pounds of cucumbers to make 7 quarts. A bushel of cucumbers weighs approximately 48 pounds and yields 16 to 24 quarts. As a general rule it takes about 2 pounds of cucumbers per quart.

## SWEET GARLIC DILL PICKLES

2 cups vinegar
2 cups water
3 cups sugar
2 T. salt

Dill heads
Garlic cloves
Cucumbers sliced 1/3 to 1/2-inch
    thick

Bring first 4 ingredients to a boil. (This brine makes enough for 2 to 4 quarts- make as much as needed.) Put 1 head of dill and 1 clove of garlic in a quart canning jar. Fill with sliced cucumbers. Add more dill and garlic on top. Fill jars with hot liquid. Process in a boiling water canner for 10 minutes.

*Mrs. James Kulp, Unity, WI      Esther Martin, Decker, MI      Edna Miller, Snover, MI*

## PICKLE RELISH I

8 cups finely chopped cucumbers
1 cup finely chopped onion
1 T. salt
3/4 cup vinegar
3/4 cup water

3 cups sugar
1 tsp. celery seed
1 tsp. celery salt
1 tsp. turmeric

Mix cucumbers and onion. Let stand 1 hour. Drain. In a large kettle combine all ingredients and boil 20 minutes. Put in pint jars. Process in boiling water canner for 10 minutes.

*Esther Horst, East Earl, PA*

## PICKLE RELISH II

8 cups cucumbers, ground with
    peelings
4 cups chopped onion
3 red sweet peppers
3 ribs celery
1/2 cup salt

6 cups sugar
4 cups vinegar
1 T. mustard seed
1 T. celery seed
1 tsp. turmeric
1/2 cup Clearjel, opt.

Grind first 4 ingredients. Sprinkle with salt. Let stand 2 hours. Drain and add remaining ingredients. Boil 5 minutes. Put in pint jars. Process 10 minutes in a boiling water canner.

*Sarah Imhoff, Sheridan, MI*

## PICKLES

Small cucumbers
1 cup vinegar
1 cup sugar

2 cups water
1 tsp. salt

Fill jars with small cucumbers. Bring remaining ingredients to a boil and pour over cucumbers in jars. Process 10 minutes in boiling water canner.

*Vera Fox, Memphis, MO*

## 13 DAY SWEET PICKLES

2 gallons fresh firm 2 to 4-inch
    cucumbers
1 cup salt to 1 gallon boiling
    water
1 oz. alum to 1 gallon water
8 cups vinegar

8 cups sugar, divided
2 T. mixed pickling spices
1 T. celery seed
1 T. whole allspice
1/2 box stick cinnamon

**Day 1:** Wash cucumbers, Drain and cover with salt water. **Day 2 to Day 7:** Let pickles stand, removing scum every day. **Day 8:** Drain and cover with boiling water. **Day 9:** Drain and cover with the water and alum mixture. Let stand 24 hours. **Day 10:** Drain well. Prick with fork or slit pickles with tip of paring knife. Add hot syrup made with vinegar and spices (tied in a cheesecloth bag) and only 2 cups sugar. **Day 11:** Drain off syrup and add to it 2 cups sugar. Heat; pour over pickles and stir well. **Day 12:** Heat syrup adding 2 more cups sugar. Pour over pickles. **Day 13:** Heat syrup, adding last 2 cups sugar. Pack pickles in jars and cover with hot syrup. Process in boiling water canner- pints 5 minutes and quarts 10 minutes.

*Mrs. Vernon Kurtz, Ewing, IL*

# SWEET GHERKINS
*Four-inch cucumbers can be used and cut into chunks.*

7 lb. 1 1/2 to 2-inch long
  cucumbers
1/2 cup salt
8 cups sugar, divided
6 cups vinegar

3/4 tsp. turmeric
2 tsp. celery seed
2 tsp. mixed pickling spice
Cinnamon sticks, opt.

**Day 1:** Place cucumbers in a glass, ceramic or stainless steel container. Cover with boiling water in the morning. In the afternoon drain and recover with boiling water. **Day 2:** Drain and cover with boiling water. In the afternoon, drain then cover with brine formed by adding the salt to about 6 quarts boiling water. **Day 3:** Drain, rinse and prick cucumbers. Make syrup using 3 cups sugar, 3 cups vinegar and all spices. Bring to a boil and pour over cucumbers. In the afternoon drain syrup back into pan; add 2 cups sugar and 2 cups vinegar. Heat to boiling and pour over cucumbers. **Day 4:** Drain syrup back into pan; add 2 cups sugar and 1 cup vinegar. Heat to boiling and pour over pickles. In afternoon drain into pan, add remaining sugar and, if desired, either 2 teaspoons vanilla or 1 teaspoon chopped arrowroot and 1 teaspoon nutmeg. Heat to boiling. Pour over pickles that have been packed in pint jars; add 1/2 stick cinnamon to each. Process 10 minutes in boiling water canner.

*Vera Witmer, Goshen, IN*

**A bushel of tomatoes weighs approximately 53 pounds and will yield anywhere from 16 to 20 quarts of tomatoes. Because acidity in tomatoes varies, the U. S. D. A. recommends adding 2 tablespoons of lemon juice or 1/2 teaspoon of citric acid per quart of tomatoes, and 1 tablespoon lemon juice and 1/4 teaspoon citric acid per pint. If you think the lemon juice affects the taste add a teaspoon of sugar per quart of tomato juice.**

# PIZZA SAUCE I

6 quarts tomato juice
3 medium onions
2 T. dried parsley
4 to 5 cloves garlic
1/8 tsp. red pepper
1 cup cooking oil

1 T. salt
1/4 cup sugar
1 pkg. Chili-O-Mix
2 T. Italian seasoning
2 tsp. rosemary leaves

Cook onions and parsley with tomatoes. Put through food mill. Mix everything together. Simmer 1 1/2 to 2 hours. Pour into jars. Process in boiling water canner, 35 minutes for pints and 40 minutes for quarts; or in a pressure canner at 10 pounds of pressure – pints 20 minutes and quarts 25 minutes.

*Kathleen Ramer, New Paris, IN*

## PIZZA SAUCE II

1 rounded bushel tomatoes to
   make 7 to 9 quarts pulp
2 tsp. garlic salt
2 tsp. onion flakes
1 T. red pepper
1 1/2 tsp. black pepper

2 cups brown sugar
1 cup vegetable oil
2 1/2 T. salt
3 T. oregano
1/2 cup lemon juice

Cook and strain tomatoes, then strain juice through cheesecloth 10 to 15 minutes. Add remaining ingredients to pulp; stir well. Put into jars. Process in boiling water canner - 35 minutes for pints and 40 minutes for quarts. Or process in a pressure canner at 10 pounds of pressure - pints 20 minutes - quarts 25 minutes.

*Mrs. Marvin (Lydia) Sensenig, Penn Yan, NY*

**The measure of acidity or alkalinity is known as pH. The pH values range from 0 to 14. A pH of 7.0 is neutral. The lower the number the more acid food has; the higher the number the more alkaline it is. Foods that can be safely processed in a boiling water canner need to have a pH of 4.6 or lower. Most tomatoes have a pH of 4.5 or lower, however overripe tomatoes or tomatoes harvested from dead vines may be considerably lower in acid and higher in pH. Adding sufficient vinegar or lemon juice allows low-acid foods like to be safely processed in a boiling water canner. Vinegar should be added at the end of the cooking process, just before cooking.**

## PIZZA SAUCE III

3 quarts tomato juice
1 onion
1 cup brown sugar
1 tsp. salt
1 tsp. pepper
1 tsp. garlic

1 tsp. Italian seasoning
1 tsp. oregano
1 tsp. chili powder
1 tsp. basil
Clearjel

Bring to a boil and thicken with Clearjel. Put in jars and process in a boiling water canner – pints for 35 minutes and quarts for 40 minutes. Or process in a pressure canner at 10 pounds of pressure - pints 20 minutes and quarts 25 minutes.

*Mrs. Phillip Zimmerman, Versailles, MO*

***Where God guides He provides.***

## SALSA

*Roma-type paste tomatoes make less watery salsa. It helps to drain juice off chopped tomatoes, or to add more tomato paste. Use all sweet peppers for milder salsa.*

14 cups peeled, seeded and
   chopped tomatoes
3 cups chopped onions
2 cups chopped green or red
   peppers
1 cup chopped jalapeno peppers
4 cloves garlic, minced

1/4 cup sugar, opt.
1 T. dried cilantro, opt.
1 T. dried oregano
1/2 tsp. cumin
2 tsp. salt
1 1/2 cups vinegar or lemon juice
12 oz. tomato paste

Combine all ingredients in a large kettle. (Be sure to use rubber gloves when working with jalapeno peppers.) Bring to a boil; simmer 15 minutes. Carefully ladle hot salsa into pint jars. Process in a boiling water canner for 15 minutes.

*Mrs. Ray (Elsie) Hoover, Stratford, WI*

**To peel tomatoes, place in boiling water for 40 to 60 seconds, or until skins split. Put in cold water and slip off skins.**

## EASY SALSA

5 lb. tomatoes, peeled, seeded
   and chopped
2 lb. chile peppers, chopped
1 lb. onions, chopped

1 cup vinegar
1 T. salt
1/2 tsp. pepper

Combine all ingredients in a large kettle. Bring to a boil; simmer 10 minutes. Fill pint jars, leaving 1/2-inch headspace. Process 15 minutes in boiling water canner.

## SPAGHETTI SAUCE I

1 peck tomatoes or 4 1/2 qt. juice
1 clove garlic
2 green peppers, chopped
1 1/2 lb. onion, chopped
1 cup cooking oil

24 oz. tomato paste
1 cup sugar
2 to 4 T. salt
1/2 tsp. basil
1/2 tsp. oregano

Cook and strain tomatoes and garlic. Cook peppers and onions in oil for 30 minutes. Put through strainer. Add to juice along with remaining ingredients; cook until thick. Peppers and onions may be added to juice without cooking in oil if you like chunks in the sauce. Oil is then added to sauce also. Put in jars. Process in a pressure canner at 10 pounds of pressure – pints 20 minutes and quarts 25 minutes.

*Kathleen Ramer, New Paris, IN*

## SPAGHETTI SAUCE II

11 quarts thick tomato juice
6 garlic cloves
6 medium onions
1 cup fresh parsley, chopped
1/2 cup brown sugar
1/4 cup salt
3 T. oregano

Few bay leaves, opt.
2 T. basil
1 tsp. red pepper
2 tsp. chili powder
1 T. Tabasco sauce or to taste
1/4 cup cooking oil, opt.
1/2 cup Clearjel

Put juice in a big heavy saucepan. Save some to put in blender while chopping onions, garlic cloves and parsley. When chopped add to juice; add spices. Bring to a boil; simmer 4 hours or until thick. Put into jars. Process in a pressure canner at 10 pounds of pressure- pints 20 minutes and quarts 25 minutes.

*Rachel Ramer, Cazenovia, WI*

## TACO SAUCE

16 cups peeled chopped
    tomatoes, drained
2 cups chopped onion
2 cups chopped green pepper
1 cup chopped green chile
    peppers, seeded

8 small cloves garlic
2 tsp. salt
2 tsp. chili powder
1 tsp. cumin

Bring everything to a boil; reduce heat and simmer, uncovered, for 30 minutes. Put in jars. Process in a pressure canner at 10 pounds of pressure – pints 20 minutes and quarts 25 minutes.

*Rachel Ramer, Cazenovia, WI*

**Tomato vegetable juice blends with more than 3 cups of other vegetables to 7 quarts juice should be processed in a pressure cooker.**

## TOMATO JUICE

6 quarts tomato juice
1 1/2 cups sugar, scant
2 T. celery salt

2 T. onion salt
2 tsp. garlic salt

Combine ingredients and bring to a boil. Put in jars. Process in a boiling water canner 35 minutes for pints and 40 minutes for quarts.

*Ada Mae Miller, Nappanee, IN*

## VEGETABLE SOUP I

1 quart sliced celery
1 quart sliced carrots
1 quart cut green beans
1 quart lima beans
1 quart corn
1 quart peas
1 quart cubed potatoes

1 cup chopped onions
2 quarts cooked navy beans
1 peck tomatoes
5 lb. meat, cut fine and cooked, or
    browned ground beef
1 tsp. salt per quart

Mix vegetables and bring to a boil; boil 5 minutes. Put in jars, dividing liquid among jars. Add 1 teaspoon salt per jar. Process in a pressure canner at 10 pounds of pressure – pints 60 minutes and quarts 75 minutes.

*Hannah Kulp family, Mt. Herman, KY*

## VEGETABLE SOUP II

1 quart cut up green beans
1 quart peas
1 quart chopped cabbage
1 quart corn
1 quart diced celery
1 quart sliced carrots
1 quart diced potatoes

1 quart chopped onions
1 quart chopped tomatoes, opt.
2 lb. ground beef, browned
2 T. chili powder
Salt and pepper to taste
Approximately 4 quarts beef
    broth

Partially cook all vegetables. Drain and save water. Add browned beef and chili powder. Fill jars 1/3 full, then add 1 teaspoon salt to each quart. Mix remaining vegetables and reserved water with beef broth. Heat; pour over vegetables in jars. Process in a pressure canner at 10 pounds of pressure – pints 60 minutes and quarts 75 minutes. Tomato juice may be used instead of broth and water, if so, add 2 cups sugar. Spaghetti or noodles may be added after opening jars.

## ZUCCHINI RELISH

10 cups ground zucchini
4 onions, chopped
3 green peppers, chopped
3 red peppers, chopped
5 T. salt

6 cups sugar
2 1/2 cups vinegar
2 tsp. celery seed
1 tsp. mustard seed
1/2 tsp. alum

Cover first 5 ingredients with water and let stand overnight. Drain well. Combine remaining ingredients and stir into zucchini mixture. Simmer 1/2 hour. Put into pint jars. Process in a boiling water canner for 15 minutes.

*Naomi M. Zimmerman, Goshen, IN*

# MEAT

## CANNED BEEF OR PORK

Cut chilled meat into strips, cubes or chunks and remove excess fat. To raw pack put raw meat into jars leaving 1-inch headspace. Add 1 teaspoon salt per quart. Do not add liquid. To hot pack, roast, stew or brown meat until rare. Fill jars with precooked meat, add 1 teaspoon salt per quart, and then fill jars with broth, water or tomato juice. Process in a pressure cooker at 10 pounds of pressure – pints 75 minutes and quarts 90 minutes for hot or raw pack.

## CANNED CHICKEN

Cut chicken that has been chilled for at least six hours after butchering, into pieces. Larger chickens are more flavorful than frying chickens. Chicken can be canned with or without bones. To hot pack, cook or bake chicken until about 2/3 done. Add a teaspoon of salt to a quart jar then add chicken pieces and hot broth. Leave 1 1/4-inch headspace. To raw pack, put 1 teaspoon of salt into a quart jar then fill loosely with raw chicken pieces leaving 1 1/4-inch headspace. Do not add liquid. Process both hot and raw pack in a pressure canner at 10 pounds of pressure - pints for 75 minutes and quarts for 90 minutes.

## CANNED FISH

Eviscerate fish within 2 hours after they are caught and keep on ice until ready to can. Wash cleaned blue, mackerel, salmon, steelhead, trout, and other fatty fish (except tuna), removing all blood. Cut into 3 1/2 inch pieces. Fill pint jars, skin side next to glass, leaving 1-inch head space. Add 1/2 teaspoon of salt per pint. Do not add liquids. Process pint jars in a pressure canner at 10 pounds of pressure for 100 minutes.

## CANNED GROUND MEAT

Shape chilled meat into balls or patties, or cut sausage (made without sage) into 3 to 4 inch links. Cook until lightly browned, or sauté without shaping. Fill jars. Add boiling meat broth, tomato juice, or water, leaving 1-inch headspace. Add 1 teaspoon of salt per quart. Process in a pressure cooker at 10 pounds of pressure – pints 75 minutes and quarts 90 minutes.

411

# FRESH SAUSAGE

10 lb. trimmed pork
3 oz. salt
.7 oz. sugar

.5 oz. white pepper
.2 oz. ginger
.15 oz. rubbed sage, opt.

Mix spices with pork.  Grind once through a 3/8-inch plate then through a 3/16 plate.  Use in bulk or stuff in casings.  Freeze or can.

# FRESH ITALIAN SAUSAGE

10 lb. trimmed pork
2.4 oz. salt
.4 oz. fennel seed

.4 oz crushed red pepper
.4 oz. black pepper
.2 oz. paprika

Grind pork through a 1/4 or 3/8 inch plate.  Mix in remaining ingredients.  Refrigerate overnight for spices to marinate.

# BEST SUMMER SAUSAGE

2 lb. ground beef
2 T. Tender Quick
1 tsp. liquid smoke

1/2 tsp. garlic powder
1/2 tsp. black pepper
1/2 cup cold water

Mix ingredients thoroughly.  Cover pan and refrigerate for 12 to 24 hours.  Mix thoroughly again.  Make into 2 tightly packed rolls.  Tightly wrap each roll in foil with shiny side in toward meat, twisting ends of foil.  Poke several holes in foil with a fork.  Place on a broiler pan and bake at 325° for 1 1/2 hours.  Serve hot or cold.  Keeps in freezer several months if wrapped well.

*Irene Breneman, Elida, OH*

# TURKEY HAM

50 lb. meat
3 quarts salt
4 oz. soda

4 oz. saltpeter
2 lb. brown sugar
2 T. liquid smoke

Coat meat with salt.  Cover with water and let stand overnight at 40° or lower.  Make a brine of remaining ingredients, using enough water to cover meat well.  Keep at 40° or lower.  Ready in two weeks.  This can be frozen or canned.

*Mrs. Lloyd E. Troyer, Stella, MO*

**Some people pray for more than they are willing to work for.**

## BOLOGNA

50 lb. meat
1 1/2 lb. salt
1 T. saltpeter
2 T. cloves

1/2 cup pepper
2 quarts molasses
2 lb. brown sugar

Mix salt and saltpeter; salt meat with the mixture. Let meat stand 10 to 14 days at 40° or lower. Grind 3 times. Measure remaining ingredients into meat mixture; mix well. Stuff into cloth bags and smoke. Don't allow to freeze until thoroughly cured.

*Ella Horning, Penn Yan, NY*

## MINCEMEAT FOR PIES

2 lb. cooked meat, chopped fine
1 1/2 lbs. raisins
1/4 cup butter
2 quarts cherries
10 lb. apples, chopped fine
3 lb. sugar

1 T. cinnamon
2 tsp. cloves
1 tsp. ginger
1 tsp. nutmeg
1 quart cider

Mix all ingredients well. Put in freezer boxes and freeze until ready to make pies.

*Pauline Kulp, Stratford, WI*

# PIE FILLING AND FRUIT

## APPLE PIE FILLING

6 quarts blanched fresh apples
5 1/2 cups sugar
1 1/2 cups Clearjel
1 T. cinnamon

1 tsp. nutmeg, opt
2 1/2 cups cold water
5 cups apple juice
3/4 cup lemon juice

Slice peeled washed apples. Blanch one minute in boiling water; drain. Combine sugar, Clearjel, and spices in a large kettle with water and apple juice. Stir and cook over medium heat until mixture thickens and begins to bubble. Add lemon juice; boil 1 minute, stirring constantly. Fold in apple slices; immediately fill jars, leaving 1/2 inch headspace. Process both pints and quarts in a boiling water canner for 25 minutes.

413

# BLUEBERRY PIE FILLING

6 quarts fresh blueberries
6 cups sugar
2 1/4 cups Clearjel

7 cups cold water
20 drops blue food coloring, opt.
1/2 cup lemon juice

Wash and drain blueberries. Combine sugar and Clearjel in a large kettle. Add water and food coloring. Cook on medium high heat until mixture thickens and begins to bubble. Add lemon juice and boil 1 minute, stirring constantly. Fold in blueberries; immediately fill jars leaving 1/2 inch headspace. Process both pints and quarts in a boiling water canner for 30 minutes. Unsweetened thawed blue berries can also be used.

# CHERRY PIE FILLING

6 quarts fresh tart cherries
7 cups sugar
1 3/4 cups Clearjel

9 1/3 cups cold water
2 tsp. almond extract, opt.
1/2 cup lemon juice

Rinse and pit fresh cherries. Combine sugar and Clearjel in a large saucepan; add water and extract. Stir mixture and cook over medium high heat until mixture thickens and begins to bubble. Add lemon juice and boil 1 minute, stirring constantly. Fold in cherries; immediately fill jars, leaving 1/2 inch headspace. Process both pints and quarts in a boiling water canner for 30 minutes. Unsweetened thawed cherries can be used. Save juice and use to replace some of the water.

**Submerge fruit in a mixture of 1/2 teaspoon ascorbic acid or citric acid per quart of water, for one minute, to keep from darkening. Dissolving six 500-milligram vitamin C tablets in a gallon of water also works, as do various commercial products.**

# PEACH PIE FILLING

6 quarts sliced fresh peaches
7 cups sugar
2 cups plus 3 T. Clearjel

1 tsp. cinnamon
5 1/4 cups cold water
1 3/4 cups lemon juice

In a large kettle combine sugar, Clearjel and cinnamon. Add water. Stir and cook over medium high heat until mixture thickens and begins to bubble. Add lemon juice and boil 1 minute, stirring constantly. Fold in peach slices and heat another 3 minutes. Immediately fill and process both pint and quart jars in a boiling water canner for 30 minutes.

# PICKLED CRAB APPLES

| | |
|---|---|
| 8 lb. crab apples | 4 sticks cinnamon |
| 9 cups sugar | 1 T. whole cloves |
| 6 cups vinegar | Red food coloring |
| 2 cups water | |

Use firm, ripe crab apples. Do not pare. Leave stems on. Combine sugar, vinegar, water and spices. Boil 5 minutes. Add food coloring. Add fruit and cook slowly until tender. Let stand overnight. In the morning drain off syrup. Cook until it is the consistency of honey. Pack fruit into hot jars and cover with boiling syrup. Process in a boiling water canner–pints 5 minutes and quarts 10 minutes.

*Connie Rodes, Milford, IN*

# GRAPE JUICE I

| | |
|---|---|
| 7 lb. Concord grapes | 2 1/2 lb. sugar |
| 3 1/2 quarts water | |

Cook grapes and water a little. Put through a strainer or cheesecloth. Add sugar to juice. Process in a boiling water canner for 10 minutes. To serve, add an equal amount of water. This makes about 5 1/2 quarts. A bushel of grapes makes approximately 28 quarts.

*Mrs. Isaac Newswanger, Jr., Carson City, MI*

# GRAPE JUICE II

| | |
|---|---|
| 3 cups grapes | 3/4 to 1 cup sugar |

Put grapes into a quart jar. Put sugar into a 2 cup measure and fill with very hot water; stir to dissolve sugar. Pour over grapes. Process in a boiling water canner for 15 minutes. When ready to serve drain juice and discard grapes. Add water to make 2 quarts.

*Mrs. LaVerne (Virginia) Hoover, Goshen, IN*

*Before giving someone a piece of your mind, make sure you can spare it.*

# APPLE BUTTER, JAM AND JELLY

## APPLE BUTTER I

2 dozen medium apples
2 quarts sweet cider
3 cups sugar

1 1/2 tsp. cinnamon
1/2 tsp. ground cloves

Quarter apples; core but do not peel. Cook apples in cider until tender. Press through sieve or food mill. Measure 3 quarts apple pulp; add sugar and spices. Cook slowly until thick, about 1 hour; stir frequently to prevent sticking. Fill jars. Process 5 minutes in a boiling water canner.

## APPLE BUTTER II

6 gallons apple cider
10 gallons pared or 5 gallons
    ground apples

1/4 cup cinnamon or 1 T.
    cinnamon oil

Boil cider in two 18x12x5 roasters until it's reduced to 3 gallons, approximately 3 hours. Add 1 gallon ground apples at a time in each pan. Keep cooking slowly while adding apples, approximately 6 hours. Stir frequently and watch carefully to keep from burning. Move to a slow oven (under 200°) after all apples are added. This is done when it's thick and buttery, approximately 48 hours. Stir 3 times a day and once at night; watch carefully to keep from burning. Remove from oven; add cinnamon and cool completely. Fill containers and freeze. Makes approximately 25 pints.

*Mrs. William (Lena) & Nancy Kilmer, California, MO*

## APPLE BUTTER III

6 quarts applesauce
4 cups sugar
1 T. salt

2 tsp. cinnamon
1 tsp. allspice
3/4 tsp. cloves

Combine everything and put in a covered baking dish. Bake at 225° until it reaches the desired thickness, about 3 hours. Put into jars. Process in a boiling water canner for 5 minutes.

*Mrs. Lloyd E. Troyer, Stella, MO*

# BLUEBERRY JAM

**4 cups crushed blueberries**    **4 cups sugar**
**2 T. lemon juice**    **1 box fruit pectin**

Combine blueberries and lemon juice. Measure out sugar but don't add. Stir pectin into berries; bring to a full boil, stirring constantly. Quickly stir in sugar and return to a full rolling boil, stirring constantly. Remove from heat; skim off foam. Fill jars, leaving a 1/4 inch headspace. Process in a boiling water canner for 5 minutes.

# NO-COOK FREEZER BLUEBERRY JAM

**3 cups crushed blueberries**    **1 box fruit pectin**
**1 T. lemon juice**    **3/4 cup water**
**5 1/4 cups sugar**

Combine blueberries and lemon juice. Stir in sugar. Set aside for 10 minutes, stirring occasionally. Mix water and pectin; bring to a boil over high heat, stirring constantly. Boil and stir 1 minute. Stir pectin into fruit mixture. Stir constantly for 3 minutes. Fill freezer containers to within 1/2-inch of tops. Quickly cover with lids. Let stand at room temperature for 24 hours. Freeze.

# CHERRY JAM

**5 cups sugar**    **1 box fruit pectin**
**4 cups chopped cherries**

Measure sugar and set aside. Combine cherries and pectin; bring to a full rolling boil, stirring constantly. Quickly add sugar; bring to a full rolling boil again; boil 1 minute, stirring constantly. Remove from heat; skim off any foam. Fill jars. Process in boiling water canner for 5 minutes. If using frozen presweetened cherries use 4 3/4 cups thawed sweetened cherries and 4 1/2 cups sugar.

# NO-COOK FREEZER CHERRY JAM

**2 cups chopped cherries**    **3/4 cup water**
**4 cups sugar**    **1 box fruit pectin**

Stir sugar into cherries. Mix water and pectin; bring to a boil over high heat, stirring constantly. Boil and stir for 1 minute. Stir hot pectin mixture into cherries. Stir constantly for 3 minutes. Fill containers; let stand at room temperature for 24 hours. Freeze.

# GRAPE JELLY

7 cups sugar
5 cups grape juice

1 box fruit pectin
3/4 cup water

Measure sugar; set aside. Combine juice and pectin and bring to a full rolling boil over high heat, stirring constantly. Add sugar all at once; return to a full rolling boil; boil 1 minute. Remove from heat; skim any foam. Fill jars quickly. Process in a boiling water canner for 5 minutes.

# NO-COOK FREEZER GRAPE JELLY

3 cups grape juice
5 1/4 cups sugar

1 box fruit pectin
3/4 cup water

Stir sugar into juice; set aside for 10 minutes, stirring occasionally. Mix pectin and water; bring to a boil over high heat, stirring constantly. Continue boiling and stirring for 1 minute. Stir pectin mixture into juice. Stir constantly for 3 minutes. Fill containers; let stand at room temperature for 24 hours. Freeze.

# GREEN TOMATO JAM

4 cups blended green tomatoes
4 cups sugar

2 T. lemon juice
6 oz. raspberry gelatin

Bring first 3 ingredients to a rolling boil, stirring a couple times. Turn to slow boil for 20 minutes. Stir a few times. Remove from heat. Add gelatin very slowly, stirring all the while. Put in jars. Process in a boiling water canner for 5 minutes.

*Mrs. Cyrus Kulp, Auburn, NY*

Adding 1/4 teaspoon of butter or margarine to jam during cooking cuts back on the amount of foam.

# PEACH JAM

4 cups crushed peaches
2 T. lemon juice

5 1/2 cups sugar
1 box fruit pectin

Combine peaches and juice. Measure sugar and set aside. Stir pectin into peaches and bring to a full rolling boil; quickly add sugar. Return to a full rolling boil and boil 1 minute. Remove from heat; skim any foam. Fill jars quickly. Process in a boiling water canner for 5 minutes to ensure seal.

# NO-COOK FREEZER PEACH JAM

**2 1/4 cups crushed peaches**          **3/4 cup water**
**2 T. lemon juice**                    **1 box fruit pectin**
**5 cups sugar**

Combine peaches and juice; stir in sugar. Let stand 10 minutes, stirring occasionally. Mix water and pectin; bring to a boil over high heat, stirring constantly. Boil one minute. Stir hot pectin into peach mixture. Stir constantly for 3 minutes. Fill containers to within 1/2-inch of the top. Cover quickly. Let stand at room temperature for 24 hours. Freeze.

# PEACH PINEAPPLE JAM

**5 cups crushed fresh peaches**        **1 cup crushed pineapple**
**7 cups sugar**                        **6 oz. orange or peach gelatin**

Boil peaches, sugar and pineapple 10 to 15 minutes. Add dry gelatin; stir until dissolved. Can or freeze.

*Mrs. Aaron Weaver, Penn Yan, NY*

# RASPBERRY OR BLACKBERRY JAM

**7 cups sugar**                        **1 box fruit pectin**
**5 cups crushed raspberries**

Measure sugar; set aside. Add pectin to raspberries and bring to a full rolling boil, stirring constantly. Quickly add sugar. Return to a rolling boil and boil 1 minute, stirring constantly. Remove from heat; skim off any foam. Fill jars quickly, leaving 1/4-inch headspace. Process in boiling water canner 5 minutes.

# NO-COOK FREEZER RASPBERRY JAM

**3 cups crushed raspberries**          **3/4 cup water**
**5 1/4 cups sugar**                    **1 box fruit pectin**

Stir sugar into raspberries; set aside for 10 minutes, stirring occasionally. Bring water and pectin to a boil over high heat, stirring constantly. Boil and stir 1 minute. Stir hot pectin into raspberry mixture; stir constantly for three minutes. Fill freezer containers. Let stand at room temperature for 24 hours. Freeze.

*Never start the day with the face of your soul unwashed.*

# RHUBARB PRESERVES

5 cups finely chopped rhubarb
3 to 4 cups sugar

3 oz. box cherry, strawberry, or
    raspberry gelatin

Mix rhubarb and sugar; let stand until juice forms. Bring to a boil; boil until rhubarb falls apart, approximately 10 minutes. Remove from heat; add gelatin, stirring until it dissolves. Freeze or can.

*Mrs. Allen Garmen, Roaring Spring, PA*    *Laura Kulp, Stratford, WI*    *Mary Beth Shaum, Goshen, IN*

# RHUBARB AND PINEAPPLE JAM

5 cups chopped rhubarb
5 cups sugar

20 oz. can crushed pineapple
6 oz. strawberry gelatin

Combine rhubarb, sugar and undrained pineapple in a large heavy saucepan. Cook over low heat, stirring frequently. Cook at gentle boil 20 minutes. Remove from heat; add gelatin, stirring until dissolved. Process 5 minutes.

*Mrs. Cyrus Kulp, Auburn, NY*

# STRAWBERRY JAM

7 cups sugar
5 cups crushed strawberries

1 box fruit pectin

Measure sugar; set aside. Add pectin to strawberries; bring to a full rolling boil, stirring constantly. Quickly add sugar. Return to a full rolling boil and boil 1 minute, stirring constantly. Remove from heat; skim off any foam. Fill jars quickly to 1/8 inch of tops. Process 5 minutes in a boiling water canner.


**Not using the right amount of sugar is the most common cause of failure in jam-making. Sugar, pectin and acid need to be in proper proportions to make a good gel. Jams and jellies may not set if you double the recipe.**

# NO-COOK FREEZER STRAWBERRY JAM

2 cups crushed strawberries
4 cups sugar

3/4 cup water
1 box fruit pectin

Combine strawberries and sugar. Set aside for 10 minutes, stirring occasionally. Bring water and pectin to a boil over high heat, stirring constantly. Boil 1 minute. Stir hot pectin into strawberry mixture. Stir constantly for 3 minutes. Fill freezer containers to within 1/2 inch of tops. Quickly cover with lids. Let stand at room temperature for 24 hours. Freeze.

# CHEESE, YOGURT and MISC.

# CHEESE

## COTTAGE CHEESE

4 quarts milk
1 quart cultured buttermilk

Salt
Cream

Mix milk and buttermilk in a large pan. Set pan in a sink full of hot water; stir a few times. Let set overnight or until thick. Cut through both ways. Heat slowly on top of stove, stirring often. Heat till too hot to hold finger in it, approximately 115°, or put in oven at 250° for 1 hour. Drain in strainer; let cold water run through it. Drain overnight. Add salt and cream as desired. If you want to make more cottage cheese, no need to buy more buttermilk. Just save 1 quart of the mixture before heating and keep refrigerated until used.

*Mrs. Elvin (Mary) Hoover, Goshen, IN*

## CROCK CHEESE

1 gallon thick sour milk
1 1/2 tsp. salt
1/2 tsp. soda

1 1/2 T. margarine
2/3 cup cream

Scald sour milk till it's too hot to keep your hand in it. Drain through a cloth sack. Squeeze out ALL whey. Place in a stainless steel bowl; crumble until fine. Add salt and mix well. Cover with cloth and set to ripen 3 days at room temperature. Mix soda in on third day. Let stand 3 hours. Melt margarine in a heavy 4 quart kettle; add cheese. Stir over low heat till dissolved; add cream. Continue stirring until mixture comes to a boil. Pour into a glass casserole dish. Can be frozen.

*Nancy Kilmer, California, MO*

## MUENSTER CHEESE

4 gallons milk
2 cups thick buttermilk
1/2 cheese rennet tablet

1/4 cup cold water
3 T. salt

Heat milk and buttermilk to lukewarm (86°). Dissolve tablet half in water. Add to milk. Let set 1 hour. Cut into 1/2-inch squares. Pour off whey. Add salt; put in a press overnight. Use when needed or refrigerate 2 weeks before using.

*Mrs. Ernest Newswanger, Kutztown, PA*

## SODA CHEESE

1 gallon sour milk
1/2 tsp. soda
3 T. butter

1 cup cream
1 tsp. salt
1 egg, beaten

Heat sour milk to 115°. Cut through both ways with a knife to aid heating. Pour into a cloth bag and hang overnight to drain thoroughly. When dry, crumble and stir in soda and butter. Let stand 5 hours. Place in double boiler and allow to melt. Add cream; stir until smooth. Add salt and egg. Boil 3 minutes or until egg is cooked. Pour into a dish. Less cream will make a firmer cheese.

*Mrs. Elvin (Mary) Hoover, Goshen, IN      Mrs. Phares Shirk, Liberty, KY*


# YOGURT

## YOGURT

3 cups powdered milk
6 cups warm water
2 pkg. unflavored gelatin

1 1/2 cups cold water
1/4 cup live-culture yogurt or 2
    pkg. yogurt starter

STEP ONE: Mix milk and warm water in a 3-quart glass bowl. STEP TWO: Soak gelatin in cold water, 5 to 10 minutes. STEP THREE: Mix 1/4 cup of step one with yogurt. STEP FOUR: Mix everything together. STEP FIVE: Put in yogurt maker for 5 hours. This can also be made in your gas oven if you have a continuously burning pilot light. Turn oven to warm, then turn OFF before putting yogurt in. Pilot light supplies needed heat. Takes 5 hours or more.

*Mary Ann Martin, Sauk Centre, MN*

## SLOW COOKER YOGURT

1 T. unflavored gelatin
1 quart milk

1 rounded T. live-culture yogurt

Sprinkle gelatin over milk. Heat to almost boiling (180°). Cool to a little warmer than lukewarm (110°). Mix in room temperature yogurt. Pour into wide-mouth quart jar. Preheat slow cooker. Set jar in and fill cooker with warm water. Cover. Unplug! Let set till yogurt is thickened, approximately 5 hours. Save a little yogurt for starter for your next batch of yogurt. To make flavored yogurt, make plain yogurt, but omit unflavored gelatin. Mix 3 ounces of flavored gelatin with a half cup of boiling water; stir into warm yogurt. Add 1/2 to 3/4 cup crushed fruit too, if desired. Stir only enough to mix. Refrigerate.

*Vera Fox, Memphis, MO*

# MISCELLANEOUS

## NOODLES I

**12 egg yolks**
**3 egg whites**

**3/4 cup water**
**Robin Hood flour**

Mix eggs and water; add flour until you have real stiff dough. Let set 1/2 hour. If you have a noodle machine take a piece of dough; roll in flour and put through thickest roller. Sprinkle with flour and put through again to desired thickness. Dry just enough so it won't break to put through a cutter. Without a cutter dough can be rolled out 1/16th of an inch thick on a floured surface and cut into desired widths. Dry thoroughly after cutting.

*Edna Miller, Snover, MI*

## NOODLES II

**5 dozen eggs**
**2 cups water**

**Approx. 25 lb. flour**

Mix everything together. Use enough flour to make very stiff dough. Knead thoroughly. Let set awhile. Use a noodle maker or roll out to desired thickness on a floured surface and cut into desired widths. Dry thoroughly after cutting.

*Mrs. William (Lena) Kilmer, California, MO*

## FLAVORED GELATIN MIX
*No flavored gelatin on hand? Try this!*

**2 T. unflavored gelatin**
**1 cup cold water**

**2/3 cup sugar**
**1 pkg. unsweetened Kool-Aid**

Sprinkle gelatin on water; add sugar and Kool-Aid. Add 1 1/2 cups boiling water and stir to dissolve. Add 1 1/2 cups cold water or ice. This is equivalent to 6 ounce box of gelatin.

*Edna Miller, Snover, MI*

## DANISH DESSERT MIX

**1 cup Clearjel**
**2 cups sugar**

**2 pkg. Kool-Aid**

Combine and mix well. Store until ready to use. To each 3/4 cup of mix use 2 cups water. Cook until thickened. When cooled, add fresh, canned or frozen fruit.

*Mrs. Clay Zimmerman, Paltinis, Romania*

# TACO SEASONING MIX

1/4 cup instant minced onion
3 T. chili powder
2 T. cumin
2 T. salt

1 T. crushed red pepper flakes
1 T. minced garlic
1 T. cornstarch
2 tsp. oregano, crushed fine

Mix everything together.  Divide into 6 equal parts; place in small envelopes or bags.  To use, mix 1 pound browned ground beef, 1 T. ketchup, 1/2 cup water and 1 envelope of taco seasoning mix.  Simmer and stir, uncovered, till water evaporates.

*Rhoda Martin, Nappanee, IN*

# SEASONED SALT

1 cup salt
2 T. onion powder
1 tsp. garlic powder
1 T. celery salt

2 tsp. paprika
1 tsp. chili powder
1 tsp. dried parsley, ground

Mix everything together.  Store in a jar or shaker with lid.

*Edna Miller, Snover, MI*

# SWEETENED CONDENSED MILK

1/2 cup boiling water
3 T. butter or margarine

1/2 cup sugar
1 1/3 cups powdered milk

Measure boiling water into blender.  Add butter, sugar and dry milk.  Blend 30 seconds.  Pour out and let stand till thick and cool.  Makes 14 ounces.  This can also be made using 1/3 cup boiling water, 2/3 cup sugar and 1 cup dry milk.

*Edna Miller, Snover, MI     Mrs. Marvin (Lydia) Sensenig, Penn Yan, NY*

# BABY FORMULA

12 oz. evaporated milk
2 1/4 cups water

2 T. dark corn syrup OR 2 T.
sugar or brown sugar

Mix, then it is ready to use.  Refrigerate.  Keeps for several days.  Because this doesn't have vitamins and iron I usually mix this with an equal amount of commercial formula.  This formula is from Dr. Spock's *Baby and Child Care.*

*Laura Kulp, Stratford, WI*

# SOURDOUGH CULTURE

**1 cup milk**                                    **1 cup flour**

Allow milk to stand in a warm place for 24 hours.  Use a wooden spoon to stir in flour.  Allow to stand in a warm place until it bubbles and becomes very sour.  Place in a large loosely covered container and refrigerate.  Replace or feed every 4 days by adding 1 cup milk, 1 cup flour and 1/4 cup sugar.  Do not use for at least 24 hours after feeding.  If it doesn't increase fast enough, divide into 2 bowls.  When you use your culture always allow 1 1/2 cups to remain in the container.  If you can't use for awhile, freeze it.  Thaw 24 hours or until it is bubbly again.  The longer a culture is kept the better it gets.  If it is well cared for it can be kept for years.  This can be used instead of sour cream, sour milk and buttermilk in recipes.  Share a cup of sourdough starter with a friend.

*Arlene Hoover, Fortuna, MO*

# SAUERKRAUT

**Shredded cabbage**                              **Salt**

Shred cabbage into a large crock.  For every 5 pounds cabbage sprinkle 3 to 4 tablespoons of salt over cabbage.  Using a potato masher, stomp cabbage very thoroughly to form juice.  Continue adding cabbage and salt.  Stomp down after each addition.  Fill a strong plastic bag with water and tie shut securely.  Place on top of the cabbage.  This forms a seal over cabbage as it ferments.  Be sure to work the air out from under the bag so the bag fits down against the cabbage and all around the crock edges.  Let sit at 65° to 70° for 3 to 6 weeks.  Ready to can when it tastes like sauerkraut.  Heat sauerkraut and juice to almost boiling.  Put into jars and cover with liquid. Process in a boiling water canner - pints 15 minutes and quarts 20 minutes.

*Vera Witmer, Goshen, IN*

# NON-EDIBLE MISCELLANEOUS

## PLANT FOOD

**1 tsp. cream of tartar**                        **1 tsp. Epsom salt**
**1 tsp. saltpeter**                              **1 gallon warm water**
**1 tsp. ammonia**

Mix everything together.  Give to plants once a month.

*Mrs. James (Arlene) Martin, New Paris, IN*

# DOUGH FOR PLAY I

2 cups flour
1 cup salt
1/2 cup cornstarch
1 T. alum

2 cups water
1 T. cooking oil
Food coloring, opt.

Mix all ingredients in a saucepan. Stir constantly over low heat until mixture is the consistency of dough. Remove from heat and let set until cool enough to handle. Place on foil, wax paper or formica top and knead until smooth. Store in an airtight container. Keeps for months and offers many hours of entertainment.

*Arlene Hoover, Fortuna, MO*

# DOUGH FOR PLAY II

2 cups flour
1/2 cup salt
1 T. cream of tartar

1 3/4 cups boiling water
2 T. oil
Food coloring

Combine dry ingredients. Stir in boiling water, oil and food coloring. Let cool 10 minutes. Knead until smooth, adding more flour if necessary. Store in an airtight container.

# GOOEY DOUGH FOR PLAY

1 cup cornstarch
1/2 cup water

Food coloring

Mix well. Divide into several dishes if you want more than one color.

# FINGER PAINT

1/2 cup cornstarch
3/4 cup cold water
1 T. unflavored gelatin
1/4 cup cold water

2 cups hot water
1/2 cup powdered detergent
Food coloring

Combine cornstarch and 3/4 cup cold water. Combine gelatin and 1/4 cup cold water. Stir hot water into cornstarch and bring to a boil. Remove from heat; stir in gelatin. Add detergent and stir until dissolved. Divide and color as desired.

# Index

441

**MAIN DISH PIES**

**MAIN DISHES, MEAT/VEGETABLE**

**MAIN DISHES, MEXICAN/ITALIAN**

# Index

447

# Index

# Index

# Order Form

Shipping Address:

name _____

street address _____

city, state zip code _____

| TITLE | AMOUNT | QUANTITY | TOTAL |
|---|---|---|---|
| The Basics and More Cookbook | $13.95 | | |
| The Practical Produce Cookbook | $12.95 | | |
| Grandma's Recipes | $11.95 | | |
| | | | |
| | | Subtotal | |
| Shipping and Handling $3.00 per book | | | |
| | | Subtotal | |
| Wisconsin Residents add 5.5% tax | | | |
| | | order total | |

Payment Options: (check one)  ☐ check

☐ Visa  ☐ Mastercard  ☐ Discover

Credit Card Number _____

Expiration Date _____


Send order to:  Ray and Elsie Hoover
EP 4230 March Rapids Ave.
Stratford, WI  54484

Phone  715-687-4558